The Roman
Barbarian Wars

For my grandfather, Heinrich Leng, who survived seven years of battle and captivity in one of history's most terrible wars.

And to the memory of all the men, women and children, who suffered through the wars that sadly mark the history of humanity.

The Roman Barbarian Wars

The Era of Roman Conquest

Ludwig Heinrich Dyck

Pen & Sword
MILITARY

First published in Great Britain in 2015 by
Pen & Sword Military
an imprint of
Pen & Sword Books Ltd
47 Church Street
Barnsley
South Yorkshire
S70 2AS

ISBN 978 1 47382 388 4

A CIP catalogue record for this book is available from the British
Library

Typeset in Ehrhardt by
Mac Style Ltd, Bridlington, East Yorkshire
Printed and bound in the UK by CPI Group (UK) Ltd,
Croydon, CRO 4YY

Pen & Sword Books Ltd incorporates the imprints of Pen & Sword
Archaeology, Atlas, Aviation, Battleground, Discovery, Family
History, History, Maritime, Military, Naval, Politics, Railways, Select,
Transport, True Crime, and Fiction, Frontline Books, Leo Cooper,
Praetorian Press, Seaforth Publishing and Wharncliffe.

For a complete list of Pen & Sword titles please contact
PEN & SWORD BOOKS LIMITED
47 Church Street, Barnsley, South Yorkshire, S70 2AS, England
E-mail: enquiries@pen-and-sword.co.uk
Website: www.pen-and-sword.co.uk

Contents

Maps		vii
Acknowledgements		xii
Preface		xiii
Introduction		xv
Chapter 1	The Dawn of Rome	1
Chapter 2	"Woe to the Vanquished" – the Battle on the Allia River and the Gallic Sack of Rome	6
Chapter 3	Telamon, the Battle for Northern Italy	18
Chapter 4	Viriathus, Hero of Spain	28
Chapter 5	Numantia, Bastion of Spanish Resistance	39
Chapter 6	Liguria and the Foundation of Gallia Narbonensis	47
Chapter 7	"Wolves at the Border" – the Migrations of the Cimbri and Teutones and their War with Rome	52
Chapter 8	The Helvetii Invasion of Gaul, Caesar's First Great Battle	67
Chapter 9	Ariovistus, King of the Suebi	77
Chapter 10	Caesar Against the Belgae, the "Bravest of the Gauls"	88
Chapter 11	Caesar's Grip Tightens	100
Chapter 12	Caesar in Britannia	108
Chapter 13	The Belgic Tribes Revolt	118
Chapter 14	Vercingetorix, the Last Hope of the Gauls	134

Chapter 15   Decision at Alesia   144

Chapter 16   Onward to the River Elbe   155

Chapter 17   "Death March of the Legions" – the Battle of the
Teutoburg Forest   167

Chapter 18   Germanicus and Arminius   185

Notes   207
Sources   221
Bibliography   230
Index   234

Alps Mountains

Gallia Cisalpina

Insubres

Lake
Como
196 BC

Mediolanum

Liguria

Cenomani

Veneti

Taurisci

Cremona

Mincio 197 BC

Placentia
Clastidium 222 BC

Po River

Boii

Illyricum

Marzabotto

Pisae

Mt. Fumaiolo

Senones

Sena Gallica

Arno R.

Arretium 284 BC

Sentinum 295 BC

Camerinum 295 BC

Etruria

Tiber R.

Clusium

Adriatic Sea

Corsica

Telamon
225 BC

Lake Vadimo
283 BC

Sabines

Tarquinia

Veii

Allia 391 BC

Fidenae

Aequi

Rome

Volsci

Saminites

Latini

Circeian
Promontory

Cumae

Sardinia

Tyrrhenian
Sea

Campania

Sicily

ROMAN GALLIC WARS FOR ITALY
391 - 191 BC

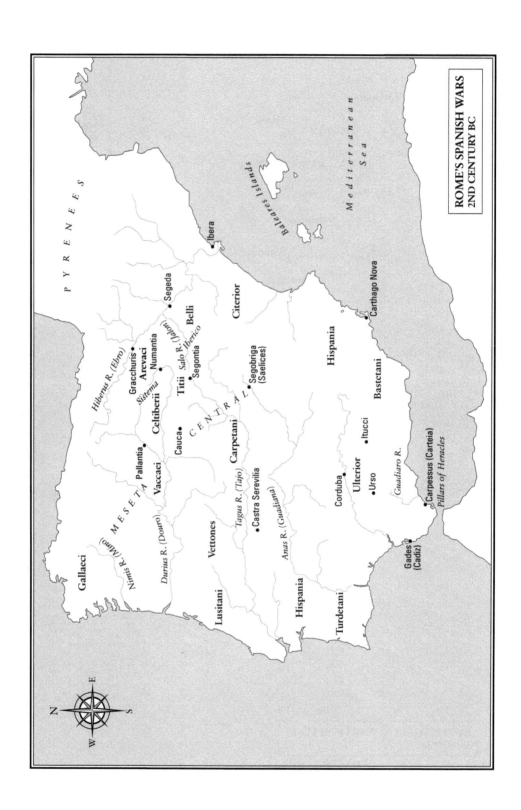

ROME'S SPANISH WARS
2ND CENTURY BC

Mediterranean Sea

PYRENEES

Baleares Islands

Ibera

Segeda

Citerior

Belli

Carthago Nova

Hiberus R. (Ebro)

Gracchuris

Arevaci

Numantia

Salo R. (Jalon)

Iberico

Titii

Segontia

Celtiberri

Sistema

Hispania

Bastetani

CENTRAL

Segobriga
(Saelices)

Cauca

Carpetani

Itucci

Ulterior

Pallantia

Vaccaei

MESETA

Corduba

Urso

Durius R. (Douro)

Tagus R. (Tajo)

Castra Serevilia

Guadiaro R.

Nimis R. (Mino)

Vettones

Anas R. (Guadiana)

Carpessus (Carteia)
Pillars of Heracles

Gallaeci

Lusitani

Hispania

Gades
(Cadiz)

Turdetani

N E
W S

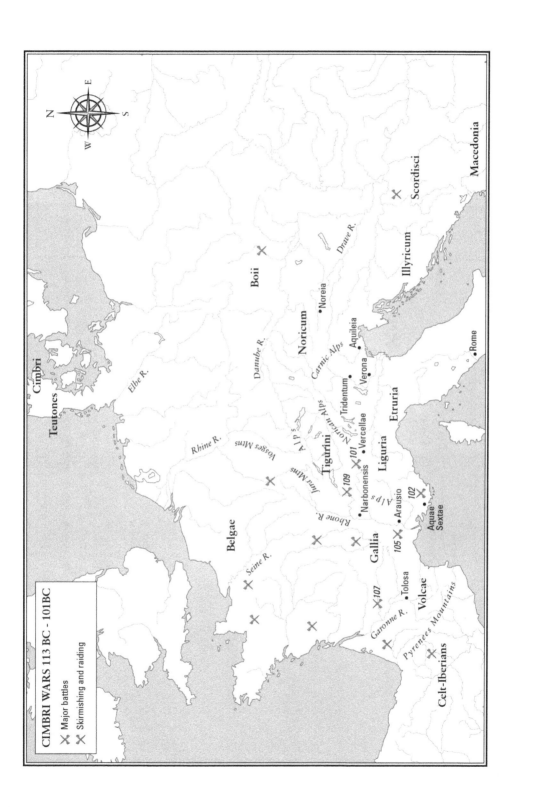

CIMBRI WARS 113 BC - 101BC

Major battles

Skirmishing and raiding

Cimbri

Teutones

Belgae

Gallia

Volcae

Tolosa

Celt-Iberians

Pyrenees Mountains

Garonne R.

Seine R.

Elbe R.

Rhine R.

Danube R.

Jura Mtns

Vosges Mtns

Rhone R.

Narbonensis

Tigurini

Noric Alps

Alps

Arausio

Aquae Sextae

Liguria

Vercellae

Tridentum

Verona

Etruria

Aquileia

Carnic Alps

Noricum

Noreia

Boii

Drave R.

Illyricum

Scordisci

Macedonia

Rome

107

105

102

109

101

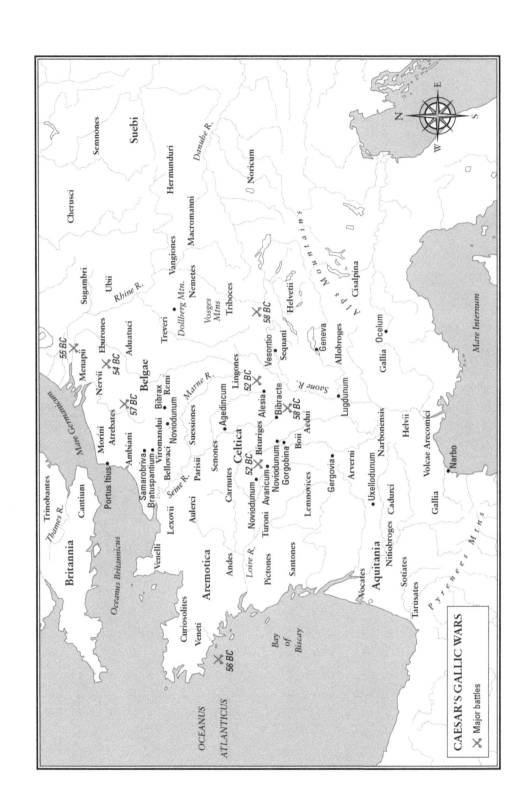

CAESAR'S GALLIC WARS

✗ Major battles

Britannia

Trinobantes
Cantium
Thames R.

Mare Germanicum

Menapii
55 BC
Morini
Portus Itius
Atrebates
Ambiani
57 BC

Eburones
54 BC
Nervii
Belgae
Aduatuci

Suebi
Semnones

Cherusci

Hermunduri
Danube R.
Macromanni

Sugambri
Ubii
Rhine R.

Vangiones
Nemetes
Triboces

Noricum

Treveri
Dollberg Mtn.
Vosges Mtns

Vesontio
58 BC
Sequani
Helvetii

Alps Mountains

Cisalpina

Geneva
Allobroges
Ocelum
Gallia

Lugdunum
Saône R.

Samarobriva
Bratuspantium
Viromandui
Bellovaci
Noviodunum
Bibrax
Remi
Suessiones
Marne R.

Lingones
52 BC
Agedincum
Bibracte
58 BC
Aedui

Mare Internum

Curiosolites
Veneti

Aremotica
Venelli

Lexovii
Aulerci
Parisii
Senones
Carnutes
Celtica
Turoni
Noviodunum
52 BC
Avaricum
Bituriges
Alesia
Noviodunum
Gorgobina
Boii

Seine R.

Lemonices
Gergovia
Arverni

Narbonensis
Helvii

Volcae Arecomici
Narbo

Andes
Loire R.
Pictones
Santones

Ukellodunum
Cadurci
Gallia

Nocates
Aquitania
Nitiobroges
Sotiates
Tarusates

Pyrenees Mtns

OCEANUS
ATLANTICUS

56 BC

Bay
of
Biscay

Oceanus Britannicus

N
E
W
S

EARLY ROMAN EMPIRE - GERMANIA
13 BC - AD 17

Cimbri

Charudes

M a r e

G e r m a n i c u m

Frisii

Chauci

Albis R.

Langobardi

(Elbe)

Suebi

Gotones

Angrivarii

Ampsivarii

Amsia R. (Ems)

Wiehen Hills

Visurgis R. (Weser)

Semnones

Tubantes

Batavi

Usipetes

Bructeri

Teutoburg Forest

Cherusci

G E R M A N I A

Vetera
(Xanten)

Aliso (Haltem)

Lupia R.

Ameppon

Hedemünden

GERMANIA

Novaesium
(Neuss)

Oberaden

Sugambri

Marsi

M A G N A

INFERIOR

Oppidum
Ubiorum
(Cologne)

Chatti

Eder R.

Mosa (Meuse)

Lahn R.

Waldgermis

Moenus (Main) R.

G A L L I A

Bingium
(Bingen)

Moguntiacum
(Mainz)

Macromanni

G E R M A N I A

Civitas
Vangionum
(Worms)

Hermunduri

S U P E R I O R

Noviomagus
Nemerum
(Speyer)

Suebi

B E L G I C A

Danuvius (Danube)

Argentorate
(Strassburg)

Rhenus (Rhine)

Rhaetia

N

W E

S

Acknowledgements

I would like to give thanks to my girlfriend, friends and family, who have encouraged me to write articles and to write this book. Special thanks to retired college dean Lawrence Fast, who checked the edits for spelling and for grammatical errors. Thanks as well to my editor Barnaby Blacker and the helpful and friendly staff at Pen & Sword.

Preface

The initial concept of *The Roman Barbarian Wars* grew out of my fondness for J.F.C. Fuller's classic *Decisive Battles of the Western World* and out of my fascination with the Roman barbarian age. Fuller's book retold western history from the viewpoint of its greatest battles. His expressive writing wove together the prominent events and personalities of history, whose influences and fates, respectively, cumulated in decisive, history changing, battles. Inspired by Fuller's book and by his style of writing, I set upon the task of writing a book that treated Roman barbarian history in a similar fashion.

My fondness for the Roman barbarian age (and of reading and writing) heralds back to my teens. In those days, I spent many an entrancing hour delving into the works of J.R.R. Tolkien, Michael Moorcock and especially Robert E. Howard. I resolved to find out more about the real history and cultures on which the fantasy worlds of the aforementioned authors were based. As the years passed by I became more interested in the reading of history and less in fantasy and fiction.

Turning the concept into an actual book was immensely facilitated by my part time career as a magazine writer. Before I conceived of the idea of the *Roman Barbarian Wars*, I wrote a short article about pirates for the now defunct *Command* Magazine. Encouraged by its publication, I wrote a feature piece about the Gallic sack of Rome in 390 BC. It was published in *Military Heritage* magazine and became the basis for the second chapter of this book. I continued to write many more articles both for Sovereign Media, which published *Military Heritage*, and for the Primedia (now Weider) History Magazine group. To my good fortune, every article I wrote eventually saw publication. I wrote not just on the Roman barbarian age, but also about the Second World War, the Habsburg-Ottoman Wars, and on diverse subjects like the First Chinese Emperor or Brian Boru, the Irish Warrior King.

Many of my magazine articles, however, continued to concern the battles of the Roman barbarian age. These articles formed the chapters of my slowly evolving book which first saw publication by Trafford Publishing in 2011 before being released, as a revised edition, by Pen & Sword Books. Since most of the chapters in *The Roman Barbarian Wars* are thus based on magazine articles, for the most part, each can be read independently of the others. On the other hand, reading the chapters in proper sequence will allow for greater appreciation of the background of the different cultures and personalities involved. The histories of those cultures, of the tribal peoples of Europe – the Celts, the Iberians and the Germans – and of the Roman Empire, turned out to be every bit as fascinating as any of the fictional literature which first inspired me to read and write.

L.H. Dyck

Introduction

It has been my privilege to re-tell the battles and wars of the Roman barbarian age so that the prominent individuals, the people they led and the cultures they hailed from, will not be forgotten. The time frame of the Roman barbarian wars spans over 800 years. This book provides a background of the founding of Rome and chronicles the first four centuries of the Roman barbarian wars. Those wars began in 390 BC, when the Gauls laid waste to Rome. Thereafter followed an era of nearly unrelenting Roman conquest. Only deep within the forests of Germania, four centuries later, was Roman expansion against the barbarians brought to a decisive halt.

The growth of her civilization put Rome at odds with other simultaneously expanding or migrating cultures. Around the Mediterranean, Rome clashed with the civilizations of Greece, Parthia and Carthage. In the Alps and the Balkans, amidst the plains, swamps and forests of Gaul, Britannia and Germania, and in the hills of Spain, the Romans faced a different sort of enemy. Here dwelt the Celts and Germans, Ligurians and Iberians, tribal peoples who are commonly referred to as barbarians.

The term *barbarian* requires some clarification. The word was coined by the Attican Greeks, who derided anyone else's tongue as unintelligible chatter, i.e. "bar, bar, bar" or "barbarian". Both Greek and Roman writers came to use it in reference to any culture outside the Greco-Roman world that they considered uncultured, backward and brutish. Thus the Romans denounced their Carthaginian arch-enemies as barbarians even though the Carthaginians were no less civilized than the Romans. More frequently, the term barbarian was used in reference to the Celts and Germans. Although the Celts reached a state of semi-civilization within their fortified towns, neither they nor the Germans were a literate people. They certainly had nothing to compare to the sprawling cities and the volumes of literature of the civilized Mediterranean world. What they did have, were unique cultures whose histories were as dramatic and enthralling as those of the classical world.

In order to bring the period to life and to avoid reducing the tribes and legions to names and numbers, I have included lively descriptions of the barbarian peoples and their Roman adversaries. *The Roman Barbarian Wars* reveals how the combatants fought, what they looked like and what the world was like that they lived in. To this end, sections of the text include recreated historical scenarios. The scenarios are based on a montage of information from archaeology and from primary and secondary written sources. For example, a source text written by a Roman or Greek historian may tell us of a battle but omit the weapons used by the combatants. To recreate a fight scene in that battle, I relied on weapons found in archaeological finds, weapons depicted in sculpture, and on weapon descriptions of relevant modern written sources.

Archaeology has revealed a picture of barbarian cultures more closely attuned to the natural world than the civilizations of the Mediterranean; of peaceful traders, farmers, hunters and craftsmen, but also of warriors who became even more warlike as their contact with the Roman world increased. Unfortunately, by its very nature, archaeology is limited in what it can tell us about a people's history. Since the barbarian peoples had no written word of their own, the major source for their history comes from the reed-pens[1] of classical historians. At times classical writers, most notably Cornelius Tacitus (AD 56–117), idolized the primitive innocence of the barbarians, when compared to the corruption and decadence of Rome. "Good morality is more effective in Germany than good laws are elsewhere," and " no one in Germany finds vice amusing, or calls it 'up-to-date' to seduce and be seduced,"[2] wrote Tacitus. Even Tacitus, however, stressed the warlike nature and inherent danger of the barbarian tribes, most notably the Germans. Although barbarian tribes were often allies of Rome, for the most part they were portrayed as savage hordes who presented a continual danger to the noble, civilized Romans.

From the Roman viewpoint the image of the warlike barbarians certainly had merit. Barbarians raided the provinces of the Empire and ravaged the countryside. To many tribes, banditry and looting were an honorable way of life. Entire peoples sought entrance into the Empire and if they were denied they readily turned to warfare. Roman soldiers taken prisoner were slaughtered, sacrificed, enslaved or tortured. However, the negative, warlike, Roman portrayal of the barbarians was hypocritical. After all, Roman civilization was based on aggression, conquest and slavery. Rape and massacres of the conquered peoples were the rule rather than the exception for Roman armies. The Romans reveled in violence on an unprecedented scale, even in their favorite social pastimes. Throughout the arenas of the empire, untold thousands of gladiators, war captives and wild animals were regularly killed, executed and tortured for the entertainment of the masses. "Thus love of violence was not simply an unsavory excrescence of the Roman social system; it was the gel which held it together."[3]

On the other hand, political reasons often compelled Rome to spare those whom she defeated in battle. Utterly ruthless against her enemies, those that accepted her will were honored with loyalty and favor. If Rome brought oppression to the conquered, in the long term she also brought peace, *Pax Romana*, to regions once scourged by tribal wars and conflicts. By the same token, the barbarian tribes too could be capable of chivalrous deeds and often sought peaceful relations with Rome.

Not only did the Classical historians create a rather one-sided image of the tribal peoples of Europe, but because modern western civilization inherited so much from the classical world, the barbarians, both in popular culture and even in the academic world, are often not given their due. Even people untutored in classical history may have heard of the Carthaginian general Hannibal and of his crossing of the Alps with elephants to make war on Rome. But how many have heard of the battle of Arausio? Yet at Arausio more Roman soldiers were lost to a Germanic-Celtic army than at Hannibal's celebrated victory of Cannae.[4] "Julius Caesar" is a household name, but relatively few know of Arminius, whose victory over Rome's legions in the depths of the Teutoburg forest can be considered among the most important battles in the history of the western world. Historians, too, have traditionally slighted the barbarians, being only too ready to accept as factual the impossibly huge barbarian armies presented in the classical sources.[5] After all, if not by sheer numbers, how could poorly armed savages in furs defeat the disciplined legions of brilliant civilized Rome? In reality it was Rome, with her much larger population base and superior organization, who could field the larger armies. That being said, for sheer ingenuity, siege craft and tenacity, few armies in history can match the Roman legion in its prime.

The classical sources are usually not only patriotic and moralistic, and anything but unbiased, but they are often highly unclear and contradictory. Different sources can relate contradictory events and even within the same source there are often glaring contradictions. The authors often wrote about events that happened decades, if not centuries, before their own lifetimes so that they themselves may have been unclear on what really happened. Furthermore, the style of classical historians follows the oratory tradition of Greek epic poetry, which embellishes historical events. For example, the authors are fond of partially or wholly fictionalized dramatic speeches. "I have put into each speaker's mouth," wrote the 5th century historian Thucydides, "sentiments proper to the occasion, expressed as I thought he would be likely to express them."[6] I have included many such speeches to flesh out the historical narrative, but the reader should bear in mind to take these with a grain of salt. Besides the written inconsistencies and the fictionalized aspects, what the classical historians wrote is not always corroborated by archaeological finds. All these uncertainties necessarily lead to different speculations by modern historians on what really occurred. In order to keep the flow of the narrative, I've avoided crowding the text with justifications and alternative explanations and for the most part relegated these to a note section for each chapter.

The history of the barbarian peoples is filled with dramatic wars and migrations, and with charismatic and often farsighted leaders. Inevitably, their greatest challenge was their struggle with the renowned military might of Rome. Although often outnumbered and faced by better equipped and trained Roman legions, the barbarians could inflict devastating defeats upon Rome. Fickle in battle, the barbarian warrior was capable of reckless bravery. The Romans themselves admired the size and strength of the barbarians which, combined with a life of hardship and intertribal warfare, made them dangerous opponents. The barbarian cavalry was especially effective, so much so that Gallic, German, Spanish and Numidian mercenaries often provided the most formidable horsemen fighting under the Roman banner.

This book, however, is as much about Rome as it is about the barbarians. The text begins with the foundation of the city of Rome and follows her growth into a martial empire, complete with its pageantry and glory, its genius, its brutality and its arrogance. References to Rome's wars with the civilizations of the Mediterranean world allow the reader to appreciate the Roman army's commitment in multiple theatres of war and to understand Roman history in a larger context.

In the end, it is hoped that this book takes the reader to another time, to be immersed in the world and the battles of a tumultuous age, and to inspire him or her to learn more about the Roman barbarian wars.

L.H. Dyck

Chapter One

The Dawn of Rome

"Pythian Apollo, guided and inspired by thy will I go forth to destroy the city of Veii, and a tenth part of its spoils I devote to thee."[1]

Prayer of M. Furius Camillus

The River Tiber arose from springs that poured forth from Mount Fumaiolo. Joined by creeks and brooks that trickled from limestone caverns and gullies, the Tiber twisted its way through the deep valleys of the Apennine Mountains. On the river banks and up the slopes, there grew highland woods of oak, beech and chestnut. Volcanic summits towered far above the river and the woods. Lakes nestled in the craters, whose clear waters would ripple now and then from minor tremors. The volcanoes lay dormant though, like the snoring of sleeping giants; the tremors served as a reminder that they could waken again. The Tiber flowed on, leaving the mountainsides to meander through hillsides of scattered evergreen shrubs. From out of the hills, the river's swollen waters inundated the coastal plains before emptying into the turquoise Tyrrhenian Sea.

The land of the Tiber was blessed with short, mild winters and, for most of the year, basked below crystal blue skies. Upon its sylvan landscape, at the beginning of the Italian Iron Age, c. 800 BC, were sown the seeds of Rome. At that time, Rome, the city, the republic and the empire, was not even a dream of the people who made the land their home.

The Tiber was deep and difficult to ford even in the arid summers. It was thus only natural that the river came to form the boundary of the two cultures that dwelt north and south of the river. Both cultures proved instrumental in the genesis of Roman civilization. South of the Tiber estuary to the Circeian promontory, and inland to the Apennines, lay the land of Latium. It was home to the Latini and a number of lesser clans. They were among the youngest of the great mosaic of peoples that called Italy their home. The Latini built their villages on the hillsides and protected them with wooden palisades to keep out invaders. In times of peace, the inhabitants came out to tend their flocks of sheep and to till the lowland soils. Although illiterate, the Latini and their neighboring clans shared a common language and the worship of Jupiter (the sky god), Diana (a fertility and nature goddess) and Venus (originally a garden goddess). The volcanic base of Latium's soil made it unusually fertile and allowed for the human population to blossom. Life was simple and idyllic. At the time no one could have imagined that one day, the world's mightiest empire would evolve here. Such a fate would have seemed much more appropriate for Latium's northern neighbor, the Etruscans.

As shall later be seen, the Etruscans played a major role not only in the early history of Rome but, more specifically, in Rome's first war with the "barbarian" Celts. The origin of the Etruscans remains somewhat of a mystery. Their exotic language is unrelated to the other Indo-Aryan tongues of Europe, indicating perhaps a West Asian background, but against this the archaeological records indicate that their society evolved from a local people.[2]

The heartland of the Etruscans, Etruria, reached north along the coast and the Apennines to the River Arno. The Etruscans carried out much land clearing, drainage and road building in the surrounding wilderness. The hilly country favored the emergence of individual city-states, whose agricultural base was supplemented by hunting and fishing. Unlike Latium, Etruria was rich in minerals, especially in copper and in iron but also in tin, lead and silver. By the 8th century BC, this mineral wealth was in high demand by Greek and Phoenician merchants. Exporting her wealth, Etruria grew into an affluent civilization of a league of twelve cities. With such power and influence, Etruscan dominion did not remain limited to Etruria and from the seventh century onwards spread southward into Latium.

The Etruscan conquests in Latium included the settlement of Rome, right on the southern Etrurian border. Rome was founded sometime during the eighth century on the Palatine Hill (Palace hill). The Palatine rose amidst a group of low hills on the eastern bank of the Tiber. Perched on the hill, Rome lay above the seasonal inundation of the river and allowed her to reap the bounty of the fertile Latin plain. With its location in the middle of Italy and with the Tiber's estuary and the sea being only 15 miles away, Rome was perfectly positioned to become Italy's future capital.

Native legend identified the hero Romulus with the founding of Rome. Born out of wedlock, the babe Romulus was thrown into the Tiber. He was saved by fate when the current cast him back on shore and a she-wolf found and suckled him. The shepherd Faustulus discovered Romulus in the wolf's lair, adopted the child and raised Romulus on the Palatine Hill. When Romulus grew to manhood, he founded the city of Rome and named it after himself on the traditional date of 753 BC.

The basic tale of Rome's founding originated in the fourth century and was later embellished to make it more heroic, as was befitting to the powerful city that Rome was to become. Greek and Etruscan influences provided the hero Aeneas, a Trojan fugitive from the legendary Trojan War, as the brothers' ancestor. Romulus gained the twin brother Remus and both of them were born to a virgin priestess seduced by Mars, the protector god of Rome. The two brothers became part of a dynastic struggle. After having been saved by the she-wolf and shepherd, Romulus and Remus slew a tyrant and returned their deposed grandfather to the throne of the nearby settlement of Alba Longa. When the two brothers decided to build a new city on the Palatine Hill, Remus mockingly jumped over the walls his brother had constructed. Romulus became enraged and murdered his brother. Other additions to the tale include Romulus' rape of the neighboring Sabine women to provide wives for the settlers. Romulus is credited with giving Rome her military and political institutions, including the Senate. The more popular version of Romulus' death was that he was carried to the heavens by storm clouds to become a god. There, however, remained a rumor that the senators had murdered Romulus, literally tearing him to pieces. Romulus the warrior king was followed by a priest king who set up the religious establishments of Rome. The next two kings expanded local Roman influence but thereafter Rome fell under Etruscan sway.

Of the last three kings of Rome, the first and last were Etruscan while the second was a Latin son-in-law of the first. It was during the reign of these kings, from 616 to 510 BC, that the villages around the Palatine Hill were merged into the city-state of Rome. From the Etruscans the Romans absorbed many customs and traditions that became representative of Roman culture: the sacred arts of divination, chariot racing and a strong admiration of Hellenism. During this period the Romans also learned the alphabet, either from the Etruscans, who themselves had learned it from the Greeks, or from the Greeks themselves, whose colonies spread over southern Italy. Rome prospered, lands were drained and Etruscan architectural and engineering skills gave birth to monumental buildings like the Forum with its temple precinct. Nevertheless, the Latins continued to resent being ruled by foreigners and around 510 the Romans cast out the last Etruscan king in an allegedly bloodless revolution. According to the historian

Hans Delbrück, Rome's dominion at the time covered a mere 370 square miles and some 60,000 inhabitants.[3] Not much, but it was soon to become larger.

The Roman monarchy had become so unpopular that the Romans forever resented being ruled by any Rex. A republic gradually became the new form of government. Other Latin cities followed Rome's example and found a new ally in Rome against their Etruscan overlords. A like-minded ally was also found in the Greek colony of Cumae. Located to the south of Latium, in Campania, Cumae already had its own history of clashing with the local Etruscan colonies. Around 506 BC, the destiny of Latium was decided at Aricia when the Etruscans met defeat at the hands of Romans, other Latin tribes and Greeks. The issue of who would rule Campania remained undecided for some time. In the end it was neither the Greeks nor the Etruscans who would lay undisputed claim to the land. By 420 a mountain tribe known as the Sabellians descended from the high country and overran the whole area.

For the next century Rome was busy asserting its dominance among the Latin tribes, subduing its own local hill peoples, the Sabines, Aequi and Volsci, and eliminating the city of Fidenae, the last Etruscan bridgehead into Latium. In 405 BC, after having secured her home ground, Rome set foot on the road of the conqueror. Mars was transformed from an agricultural deity into a war god. "Mars Vigila" (Mars awake!) Rome's warriors shouted out, as they struck north across the Tiber and into Etruria herself. There, a mere twelve miles from Rome stood the Etruscan City of Veii.

The war of Rome with the city of Veii lasted ten years. Rome and her Latin allies were greatly helped by lack of military cooperation among Etruscan cities. The powerful city of Tarquinia, two minor southern Etruscan states and an assortment of volunteers from other Etruscan towns came to Veii's aid but as a whole the twelve-city Etruscan league abstained from the war. In 396 BC, the war came to an end. The Roman commander Marcus Furius Camillus finally captured Veii. The city had endured a lengthy and grueling siege and was finally carried by assault, its people massacred or sold into slavery by the Romans. The siege itself became part of Roman legend, the equivalent of the equally lengthy and mythical Greek Trojan War.[4]

Expelled from Latium and Campania, the Etruscans looked for new conquests to the north of their homeland and from 500 BC onward spread into the Po River valley. Here their colonies at Felsina, Spina and Marzabotto flourished for another century. However, during these years, the Etruscans had not been the only civilization to extend its dominion over Italy and her adjacent seas. In addition to Greek colonies in southern Italy, Phocaeans from the Middle East and Carthaginians from Africa vied for control of the western sea and the islands. But Etruria's newest threat, one equal to that of Rome, came from a people that marched out of the north and would shake the foundations of the Mediterranean civilizations: the Celts.

Chapter Two

"Woe to the Vanquished"
The Battle on the Allia River
and the Gallic Sack of Rome

"When the tribune protested, the insolent Gaul threw his sword into the scale,
with an exclamation intolerable to Roman ears, "Woe to the vanquished!"[1]
Titus Livius "Livy," Roman historian (59 BC–AD 17)

Around 2000 BC the Indo-European peoples wandered the great steppe lands north of the Black Sea, between the Danube and Volga rivers. Their language branch included many of the cultures that would so prominently come to shape the future history of mankind. It included the dialect spoken on the Latium plain, which probably originated somewhere in the Danube area. It also included the language of the Celts, who drifted into central Europe.

Celtic culture in central Europe thrived during the first half of the first millennium. From the east, the Celts learned the use of the war chariot and the mystical secret of iron to supplant the weaker bronze. The Celtic warriors became more formidable. They were proud and fierce men, particularly those who served as the personal retainers of chiefs and warlords. The nobility lorded over an agricultural people, who cultivated and harvested wheat and oats, lentils, peas and common vetch. In the fields, the people tended herds of pigs and cattle. No doubt there were woodsmen who spent much time in the forest, but for the most part hunting only provided a minor portion of the Celtic diet. The Celts were also merchants and trade flourished with the Greeks and the Etruscans. Raw minerals, crops and slaves, flowed south in exchange for oil, exquisite pottery, jewelry and above all wine.

Large hilltop fortresses appeared among villages of farmers and herdsmen that lay scattered among vast primordial forests. One such fort was first built somewhere between the 5th and 4th Centuries BC, on the 2000-foot-high Dollberg, in the Saarland of Germany. Due to the impenetrable rock base of Taunus quartzite, the fortress springs provided water all year round. For early

Celtic tribes who settled in the area to mine local iron-ore deposits, the Dollberg fortress provided a handy refuge or a seat of rulership.

The wealth of trade flowed into the hands of the powerful Celtic warrior chiefs. When they died, the chiefs were buried under huge mounds alongside their treasures, weapons, wagons and horse gear. Social stratification gave rise to kings, nobles, free commoners and small states, the *tuath*. The tribes, however, never formed a unified Celtic empire. The walls of fortresses, like the one that towered on the Dollberg, protected the tribes not only against the savage Germanic tribes to the east, but also against other Celtic tribes.

The 1st century AD Greek geographer Strabo wrote of the Celtic nature:

"The whole race, which is now called Celtic or Galatic, is madly fond of war, high spirited and quick to battle, but otherwise straightforward and not of evil character … At any time you will have them ready to face danger, even if they have nothing on their side but their own strength and courage … To the frankness and high-spiritedness of their temperament must be added the traits of childish boastfulness and love of decoration."[2]

Successive waves of Celts spread west and northwest. The natives they encountered were themselves proto-Celtic cultures, who more than a thousand years earlier had settled among Stone Age farmers and hunters. They proved unable to withstand the long slashing swords, cavalry and war chariots of the Bronze Age and Iron Age Celts. From the Alps to Spain and northward to the British Isles, most of Western Europe was transformed into a Celtic world.

To the literate civilized cultures of Greece and Italy, the Celts were barbarians. The Greeks called them the *keltoi*, a loose reference applied to the people north of the Alps. Those Celtic tribes who settled in today's France were generally known to the Romans as the Galli, or Gauls. The Greeks and the Romans paid the Celts scant attention and neither considered them a serious threat. Their perception was put to the test when the wealth of the Mediterranean countries induced the Gauls, led by the Senones tribe, to drift southward into the northern Italian plain. According to the Roman historian Livy, the Celts "attracted by the report of the delicious fruits and especially the wine – a novel pleasure to them – crossed the Alps."[3] A contemporary of Livy, Pompeius Trogus, further adds that the Gauls outgrew their land, which is reflected in the growth of the number of cemeteries found in the archaeological record.

The initial Celtic inroads into northern Italy may have been peaceful but after 400 BC they turned violent. Calls for war and raids were proclaimed during banquets like the one described in the writings of Athenaeus.

> "When several dine together, they sit in a circle; but the mightiest among them, distinguished above the others for skill in war or family connections, or wealth, sits in the middle like a chorus leader. Beside him is the host and next on either side the others according to their respective ranks. Men-at-arms, carrying oblong shields stand close behind them while their bodyguards seated in a circle directly opposite, share in the feast like their master."[4]

Probably present too at these Celtic councils, were their priests, the druids, whose creed even at this time was considered ancient and whose origin may have dated to proto-Celtic times.

The lands and cities north of Etruria, belonging to a mosaic of peoples, were steadily looted and annexed by waves of Gallic tribes. Circa 396 BC Melpum fell to the Insubres and five years later, the Boii sacked the Etruscan colony at Marzabotto. In 391 the Senonian chief Brennus[5] led large bands of Gauls into Etruria proper and threatened the town of Clusium. With no help forthcoming from the other members of the politically divided Etruscan cities, Clusium appealed to Rome for help.

In response to Clusium's pleas, the Roman Senate sent envoys, the sons of the influential patrician (aristocrat) Fabius Ambustus, to forewarn the invading Gauls. The envoys came in peace but tempers soon flared. The Gauls stated that they had no quarrels with the Romans but when asked as to what right they had to the lands of the Etruscans, the Gauls replied "that they carried their right in their weapons ... and that everything belonged to the brave."[6] The Fabii, the sons of Fabius, saw that the proud Gauls had no intention of leaving the Clusians in peace. Eager to test the haughty barbarians' mettle, the Fabii incited the Clusians to sally out against their besiegers. In the engagement one of the Fabii ran his spear through a Gallic chieftain. Whilst the Fabii despoiled his slain foe of his armor, Brennus saw him and swore upon the gods that, contrary to holy practice, an ambassador who allegedly came in peace had taken up arms with the enemy!

Flabbergasted by the actions of the Fabii, the Gauls retreated from Clusium in order to debate on the Roman intervention. Boiling with anger, some called for an instant advance on Rome but the cooler heads of the elders counseled that ambassadors should be sent first. The elders had their way and the Gallic envoys stated their case in front of the Roman Senate: war could be avoided if Rome surrendered the Fabii ambassadors.

The Senate appreciated the validity of the Gallic demands as did the Fatiales, the priestly guardians of peace. The father of the Fabii brothers, however, had more pull among the masses than either the Senate or the Fatiales. More popular than ever, the warmongering Fabii brothers were even elected as consular tribunes. The consular tribunes in essence shared the power of the former Roman King and the command of the army. To the Gauls this was a slap in the face. The envoys threatened war and returned to their people.

Soon messages from Clusium arrived at Rome: the Gauls had arisen in rage and with celerity stormed southward against Rome. In fear of the Gallic hordes, cities shut their gates while the rural folk took to flight. But for the most part, the Gauls spared the countryside of Rome's neighbors. Their quarrel was with Rome. Everywhere they went, the Gauls shouted that they were going to Rome. Despite all this the Romans remained complacent. Although alarmed by the speed of the Gallic advance, the Roman commanders were sure that they could handle the barbarian rabble. An army was hastily raised by a levy. Less than eleven miles from Rome, the Romans intercepted the Gauls on 18 July 390 BC on the left bank of the Tiber near its confluence with the River Allia.

Whatever their preconceptions, the Romans were shocked at the sight of the Gallic army. Here was no orderly phalanx confronting them, but a well over 30,000-strong mob, of tall, big-boned men.[7] The Gauls smeared their long curly hair with thick lime wash, and swept it back from their forehead like a flying horse's mane. Their faces sported full mustaches which drooped down the sides of their chins. Torcs of gold, electrum, silver and bronze, akin to magical talismans, adorned their necks. Some warriors may have stripped completely naked, in accordance with religious and social customs. Others bared only their upper body or wore a tunic alongside their trousers, both of colorful checkered or striped patterns.

The bulk of the Gallic warriors fought as light infantry swordsmen. The early Gallic iron long-sword measured 25 to 30 inches overall. The double-edged blade ended in a pointed tip and judging by archaeological finds was of superb quality. On the other hand, the Greek historian Polybius described Celtic swords as "effective only on the first blow; thereafter they are blunt, and bend so that if the warrior has no time to wedge it against the ground and straighten it with his foot, the second blow is quite ineffective."[8] Other weapons were spears, at times over 2 yards long, javelins, battle-axes and slings.

For most warriors their sole protection was their shield. Those of the infantry were shaped as yard-long, oblong hexagons or truncated ovals. Cavalry shields were commonly rounded. Bronze, or rarely iron, helmets resembled jockey caps and were festooned with horns, crests of animal designs or the Celtic symbol of war, the wheel. Rarest of all was body armor, reserved for a few of the chiefs and noble warriors who boasted mail shirts or round breastplates and even the occasional piece of armor for their horses.

In pompous displays, nobles arrived at the battle site in chariots but chose to fight the actual battle on foot or mounted steeds to lead the cavalry. Howls and wild cries, accompanied by the blaring of horns and trumpets, resounded over the battlefield as the Gauls worked themselves into a battle frenzy.

Upwards of 15,000 Romans and allies from neighboring Latin cities faced the Gallic horde. The Roman units were concentrated into the "Legio", a levy "gathered from the clans", of 6,000 warriors blessed by Mars, the Roman god of war. Tactically the Legio relied on the shock value of a phalanx of hoplites (heavy infantry). The hoplites were ideally armored with helmet, breastplate, greaves and a round shield, the *clipeus*, affixed to the forearm. They were armed with a thrusting spear and a sword. The legionaries were drawn from Rome's citizens. Hoplite tactics were widespread throughout Greece and Etruria and were introduced from Etruria into Rome during the mid-sixth century. In addition to the heavily armed hoplites, the legion also included light troops and was further supplemented by some 600 Roman cavalry.

Despite the superior numbers of the enemy, the Romans made no attempt to fortify their position. To prevent being outflanked by the Gauls, who had formed a broad front, the Romans greatly extended their wings. The extra men required for this were apparently taken from the Roman center, which was thus weakened. Even so there were insufficient men to make the Roman front equal to that of the Gauls. As a result the Gallic army not only extended beyond the wings of the Romans but, on the average, was twice as deep and even more so opposite the Roman center. To the right of the Romans there was a small hill and here the Romans stationed their reserves. They were the weakest troops in the Roman force, poorly armed and inexperienced.

Brennus, the Gallic chieftain, suspected that behind the scanty numbers of the enemy lurked some Roman ruse. He feared that the Roman reserves on the hillock would outflank his left wing and strike at his army from the rear while his men were engaged with the legion. As a result Brennus opened the battle by attacking the reserves with elite detachments, possibly cavalry, from his left wing.

The drone of trumpets blared across both sides. From the higher ground on the hillock, the Roman reserves managed to hold out for a while. But then the brute power of the barbarians proved too much. Some of the reserves were driven back into the hills while others were pushed onto the main Roman battle lines.

Upon the rest of the Roman army the shouts and clamor of battle on the hill had a disastrous affect. Not only was the Roman right wing and center thrown into confusion but panic spread from those nearest to the reserves, like a domino affect, all the way across the lines. At this moment the whole Gallic army charged. The ferocity and momentum of the barbarians completely shattered the Roman phalanx. The Gauls could scarcely believe their good fortune. "None [the Romans] were slain while actually fighting; they were cut down from behind whilst hindering one another's flight in a confused, struggling mass," wrote Livy.[9]

The Roman left wing and possibly the entire center were swept into the Tiber. Along the banks of the river, there was a great slaughter. The Gallic longswords hewed down upon the Romans like butcher's cleavers. Many legionaries tried to swim across the river, but the current sucked down those too wounded or unable to swim or those too hampered by the weight of their cuirasses. From along the banks, the Gauls peppered the swimmers with missiles. The Romans who reached the other side fled to entrench themselves at the deserted site of Veii. On the Roman right wing the situation was much better. Instead of fleeing toward the river, the majority of the legionaries retreated into the hills and then to Rome. In Rome they fled up to the Citadel on the Capitol Hill but were in such haste that they neglected to close the city gates.

The Gauls were astonished by their easy victory. They piled up the enemy weapons in great heaps as an offering to their gods and decapitated their fallen foes. Grizzly trophies dangled from bloodied hair, tied to Gallic spears, chariots and horse harnesses.[10] The time of the battle was just after the summer solstice. At night, like some baleful eye, a nearly full moon shone upon the grim field of slaughter.

The next day the Gauls set off towards Rome. The sunset painted the horizon red as the Gauls tramped up to the city gates. Ahead of the main Gallic host the cavalry had carried out reconnaissance. To what must have been an astonished Brennus, the cavalry reported that they had encountered no enemy pickets, that the gates to the city were not shut and that no troops manned the walls. Suspicious of the virtually effortless way they had defeated the reputable might of Rome, the Gauls suspected a trap. Instead of marching right into the undefended city, they bivouacked between Rome and the nearby River Anio and sent further patrols to reconnoiter the walls.

Within the walls of Rome, the wailing and lamentations for the fallen at the River Allia were replaced by a silent terror of the enemy. Throughout the night, the yells and galloping of enemy cavalry could be heard outside the city walls. For those inside the city the tension was nearly unbearable. But due to Gallic indecision, no attack came during the night.

The citizens decided that the city itself was doomed. There was a lack of fighting men and the walls, which consisted of little more than an *agger* (earth rampart) and a ditch, were wholly inadequate. The only defendable spot was the Citadel on the steep Capitol Hill, where the Senate and the men of military age, along with their families, sought refuge. The priesthood fled from the city, taking with them the most sacred religious relics. As to the common folk, the plebs, many followed the priests' example and streamed out of the city in unorganized mobs to seek safety in the countryside or within neighboring cities.

About three days after the battle at the River Allia, the Gauls entered the city unopposed. Although they had carried out nightly cavalry reconnaissance, they could not have been very thorough. The Gauls were surprised at the large number of people who, along with their possessions, had already slipped through their grasp. The Gauls stationed a squad of troops around the Capitol Hill, and then, like frenzied wolves, let loose their wrath on those that remained behind or on those who were still in the process of fleeing. For the next few maddening days and nights, the Romans on the Capitol watched helplessly as below them their cherished city was torched. From out of the roaring inferno, as from the fiends of hell, resounded the bellow of the barbarians and the pitiful cries of citizens put to the sword.

After nothing survived amidst the ashes and ruins, the Gauls stormed the Citadel. In stark contrast to the battle of Allia, the Romans now put up a stout defense. The Gauls came on with a battle-shout and locked their shields above their heads to protect themselves against missile fire. The Romans let the enemy advance about halfway up the hill to where the ground was steepest, and then charged. Because of the steep gradient the Romans proved unstoppable and completely scattered their foes.

Wisely deducing that any further attempts to take the Capitol would be fruitless and only result in more Gallic casualties and that in any event time was on their side, the Gauls surrounded the Capitol in a blockade. The problem was how to feed their own troops since the fire had burnt the grain supplies in the city and the surrounding fields had been stripped bare by fleeing citizens. The Gauls decided that half of their numbers would scour the countryside for provisions while the other half continued the siege.

At Rome, a period of relative calm set in. The Romans remained secure within their hilltop fortification while the besiegers continued their investment. Elsewhere there was more activity. At the city of Ardea the Roman general Marcus Furius Camillus, the renowned conqueror of Veii, rallied the citizens against Gallic raiding parties. Not far from Ardea, they surprised and slaughtered a large throng of Gauls. Meanwhile, the Roman troops still encamped at the ruins of Veii fought against various Etruscan bands. Sensing easy spoils, the Etruscans made forays into Roman territory. Volunteers from the rest of Latium steadily swelled the Roman army at Veii. All that was needed was a capable leader. It turned out to be Camillus. With the consent of the Roman Senate, notified by a secret messenger, Camillus was nominated Dictator by order of the people.

According to Roman tradition, the Gauls attempted to infiltrate the Capitol by stealth. At night, a small party scaled the hill near the Temple of Carmentis, a goddess of birth. The climb was precarious but the party gained the summit and completely eluded the Roman sentinels. The Gauls did not even wake the guard dogs. Fortunately for the Romans, the Gauls next passed by the temple of Juno, the goddess of marriage and the wife of Jupiter. Here were kept a flock of sacred geese which put up such a racket that the Roman guard was finally roused. Led by Marcus Manilus, a veteran soldier, the guards confronted the infiltrating Gauls. Manilus faced two of the enemy, one of which wielded an axe. Manilus' sword flashed and sliced through the axe-man's right wrist. Blood spurted from the stump as the severed hand and axe hurled through the air. Manilus instantly confronted the second Gaul and smashed his shield into his adversary's face. The Gaul tumbled backward, right over the parapet and down the cliff. The rest of the Gauls who had gained the parapet were dealt with likewise while a volley of javelins and stones dislodged the Gauls who still clung to the rocks. For his bravery, the surname Capitolinus was bestowed upon Manilus. The result of the fiasco was that the Romans kept stricter watch. The Gauls too tightened their security around the hill, for they had come to realize that messages were passing between Veii and Rome.

Despite their valiant defense of the Capitol, the Roman condition was far from desirable. The blockade continued for seven months and reduced them to famine. The Gauls equally suffered from malnutrition, along with severe outbreaks of malaria. Their dead piled up in such great numbers that efforts were no longer made to bury them. The corpses were simply piled into heaps and burnt.

Hunger so gnawed at the defenders of the Capitol that they gave up any hope of being relieved by Camillus. All that was left was to sue for a peace. A conference between the consular tribune Q. Sulpicious Longus and Brennus ended with the Romans agreeing to pay 1000 lbs of gold for the peaceful withdrawal of the Gauls. When it was time to weigh the gold, the Gauls produced heavier, false counter-weights. The Romans complained but to no avail, for Brennus threw his own sword on the scales and haughtily proclaimed "Woe to the vanquished!"[11]

What happened next is shrouded in legend. Livy wrote that Camillus and his army now appeared on the scene. He at once ordered the Gauls to leave the gold and to march away from the city. When they refused to do so, a chaotic battle erupted as Romans and Gauls fought each other within the streets and alleys of the ruined city. The end was that the famished and disease-stricken Gauls were easily routed and driven out of the city. At the eighth milestone on the road to Gabii, the Gauls rallied but were again defeated by Camillus' pursuing force. Plutarch mirrors Livy's tale, except that he maintains that the skirmish in the city resulted in few Gallic casualties and that the Gauls retreated in good order until their defeat on the road to Gabii. In contrast to Livy and Plutarch, Polybius makes no mention of Roman heroics and tells us that the Gauls raised the siege because their own lands were threatened by an invasion of the Veneti,[12] a pre-Celtic people of north-eastern Italy. Diodorus gives us yet another account in which the Gauls left Rome of their own free will after receiving the gold. Later they were defeated on two separate occasions, by Camillus at the town of Veascium and by the Caeretans in Sabine territory.

Most modern historians consider Camillus' defeat of the Gauls to be little more than a fanciful revision by classical historians who were loath to admit Rome's defeat at the hands of mere barbarians. But there is probably a bit of truth in the classical accounts. Perhaps the Gauls accepted the ransom because

of pestilence and malnutrition within their own ranks and because of rumors
of the Veneti invasion and a possible large gathering of fresh Roman forces in
the countryside. On their way home the Gauls no doubt spread into smaller
bands to ease their living off the land. Romans and other tribes might well have
ambushed many of these bands and recovered part of the ransom gold.

Whatever the truth of the Gallic departure, the Romans ever after called their
defeat at the Allia the *dies ater* ("black day"). The sack of their city left a deep
impression on the Romans. Clearly the army needed improvement and the city
defenses strengthening, to prevent future disasters at the hands of the Gauls.
The first of these problems was addressed by Camillus. He began a series of
army reforms that were further enhanced during the late fourth century wars
against the Samnites, the tough mountain tribes of the south-central Apennines.
The easily disordered phalanx was abandoned in favor of the tight, independent
unit of the maniple. The maniple averaged 60 to 120-men strong, placed at
intervals in a line.[13] The maniples were much more elastic, both in attack and
defense, than the old phalanx. Each maniple could independently fall back or
advance, as the situation required, without messing up the whole battle line.

Volleys of javelins were used to prepare the way for combat with the short
sword. The round shield was replaced by the more familiar Samnite *scutum*, a
large semi-cylindrical four-cornered shield. Alongside the new army, Rome's
agger was raised and backed by a 12-foot thick and 24-foot high solid stone wall,
circling the whole city for a distance of over five miles. Greek contractors may
have built the wall, the labor being done by the Roman army and by Veientine
captives.

The defeat at the River Allia discredited Rome in the eyes of her neighbors.
The loyalty of Rome's Latin allies began to waver while erstwhile enemies,
the Aequi, Volsci and Etruscans, reopened old wars. What was won in over a
hundred years was lost in a single battle. Fortunately for the Romans, for a long
time after the battle on the Allia, the Gauls only raided into peninsular Italy
sporadically. Instead, the Gauls concentrated on consolidating their hold on
the north Italian plain, which, until the end of the Republican period, became
known as Gallia Cisalpina.

To the east of Italy, other Celtic tribes pushed into Greece, Russia and Asia
Minor. "We will keep faith unless the sky fall and crush us or the earth open and
swallow us or the sea rise and overwhelm us."[14] So spoke the ambassadors from
the Dalmatian mountain Celts who, impressed by Alexander the Great's deeds,
sought to befriend him in 335 BC. This famous Gaelic oath of allegiance was still

used by the Irish a thousand years later but it did not impress Alexander the Great who afterwards called them "Braggarts!" Perhaps Alexander would have thought otherwise had he known that for the next century the Celts wandered far and wide, to bring terror and woe to the civilizations of the south.

Less than fifty years after Alexander's death, the Celts invaded and pillaged Macedonia, killing King Ptolemy Ceraunus in 279 BC and defeating his army. Lured by tales of the gold and silver that abounded in the temples of Greece, Celtic warriors pushed into the Greek heartland. At the fateful pass of Thermopylae they routed a Greek army of Athenians, Phocians and Boeotians and went on to rob the treasures of the sacred city of Delphi.

The oncoming of winter forced the Celtic army to turn back north to Macedonia. Greek writers fancifully added that the Celtic retreat came at the hands of the gods. Earthquakes erupted beneath the invaders, thunderbolts smote them and the ghosts of Greek heroes arose around the fleeing Celts.

From Macedonia many of the Celts wandered north to the Danube valley where they mixed with other Celtic tribes to give birth to the Scordisci. The remainder crossed the Hellespont into Asia Minor to plunder yet more Greek city states. Similarly, along the Thracian coast, Greek cities were so browbeaten by the Celts that they were forced to pay tribute to the barbarians. Other Celtic tribes wandered farther northeast, crossing the Prute and Dnester Rivers into Scythia (Ukraine/Southern Russia).

The Celtic crisis proved short-lived, the barbarians being defeated by Antigonus Gonatus, the pretender to the Macedonian throne, at Lysimacheia in 277 BC. Antigonus' Greek victory was paralleled by Antiochus I's triumph over the Asia Minor Celts in 275. The barbarian survivors were settled in northern Phrygia where they gave their name to Galatia. The Galatians refused to settle down peacefully, however, and continued to harry the western coastlines and raid all the way into Syria.

After a period of relative quiet, the Roman Republic was likewise beset with further Gallic invasions. Twice, in Gallic forays of 360 BC and again in 349, battle was avoided when the combatants lost their nerve. On the former occasion the Romans sought safety behind their walls, while on the latter it was the Gauls who withdrew before a force of Romans and Latins. In 331, the Senones concluded a peace with Rome that for a time gave Rome a respite.

The peace between Senones and Romans came to an end in 295 BC. That year the Senones made common cause with the Samnites. Senones and Samnites destroyed a Roman army at Camerinum but then both met defeats by Roman arms at the battle of Sentinum. Sentinum saw the Romans marshal an army of up to 40,000 men, at the time probably the largest concentration of troops ever seen in Italy.

In 284 BC another foray by the Senones put Etruscan Arretium under siege and wiped out a Roman relief force, killing its *praetor* (army commander), Lucius Caecilius. In reprisal the Romans struck into the invader's homeland. The Senones were expelled from their land, which was so thoroughly scorched that it remained a wasteland for fifty years.

The neighboring Boii feared that unless Roman power was crushed, they would share the fate of the Senones. Joined by Etruscans in 283 BC, who abandoned the Roman cause, the combined army reached within fifty miles of Rome. At Lake Vadimo the Boii–Etruscan alliance went down in defeat, with most of the Etruscans cut to pieces. A second Boii–Etruscan invasion the next year proved no more fruitful and resulted in a peace treaty.

Caught between Gauls and Romans, the future of the Etruscan cities looked increasingly dim. Even when the Etruscan league finally united against Rome in 359 BC, and even when aided by the Gauls in 283, they could not overcome the sons of Mars. In the Etruscan city of Tarquinia, scenes of demons and monsters of the underworld replaced tomb frescos once radiant with depictions of joyous banquets, dancers and musicians. All over Etruria, the writing was literally on the wall. The Etrurian sun was setting, just as that of the Gauls and the Romans was on the rise. But Italy would know only one master. The final battle had yet to be fought.

Chapter Three

Telamon, the Battle for Northern Italy

"The Gaesatae had discarded these garments owing to their proud confidence in themselves, and stood naked, with nothing but their arms, in front of the whole army."[1]

Polybius, Greek historian (ca. 203–120 BC)

Nearly fifty years after the Boii's peace treaty with Rome in 282 BC, trouble stirred again among the Boii. A new generation of Gallic warriors had grown up, "full of unreflecting passion and absolutely without experience of suffering and peril"[2] as Polybius put it. The Boii chiefs invited Gauls from Transalpina, meaning the region beyond the Alps, to aid in a new assault on Rome. A Roman army was hastily sent to intercept the invaders but the matter proved a false alarm. Quarrels between the suspicious Boii and the newcomers boiled over into a pitched battle in which the Transalpina Kings Atis and Galatus were killed.

Nevertheless, the Boii refused to let the matter rest. At the core of the problem was Roman expansion into the former territory of the Senones. To begin with the Roman colony of Sena Gallica had been founded along the coastal strip. And now the hinterland, which had finally recovered from the Roman ravages, was given to Roman citizens. The settling of such colonies was done in a military manner. Enlisted in Rome, the colonists marched beneath a *vexillum* (a standard) to their new home. A ritual bronze plow was used to delineate the colony borders: yet another custom adopted from the Etruscans.

Justly anxious that Rome would not stop until all of Gallia Cisalpina was hers, the Boii once more looked for allies against the Romans. The equally powerful Insubres shared the Boii's concerns. To recruit yet more allies, the two tribes again sent messengers across the Alps, this time to the Gaesatae, a renowned mercenary tribe, who dwelt near the Rhône and Alps.

We can imagine how the Boii and Insubres ambassadors stood in the midst of the seated circle of the Gaesatae Kings, Concolitanus and Aneroestes, by whose sides sat their warrior champions and their druid advisors. With eloquent tongue, the ambassadors offered a large sum of gleaming gold, which was but a paltry amount compared to what could be looted from the rich and prosperous lands of the Romans. The Boii, Insubres and Gaesatae, proud allies, would honor the deeds of the Gauls who long ago crushed the legions at the River Allia and made themselves masters of Rome for seven months! The heroic tales roused the Gaesatae's lust for war. "On no occasion has that district of Gaul sent out so large a force or one composed of men so distinguished or so warlike," wrote Polybius.[3]

In 225 BC, the Gaesatae descended into the plain of the River Po to be welcomed by their Boii and Insubres allies. No doubt more feasts were held, alongside prayers and sacrifices to the gods, when a fourth tribe, the Taurisci, declared their alliance to the Boii, Insubres and Gaesatae coalition. The Taurisci were a tough mountain people from Slovenia's Julian Alps.[4] Not all Cisalpina tribes, however, declared themselves against Rome. The Veneti and the Gallic Cenomani wanted nothing to do with the coming war and even sent embassies of friendship to Rome. With these pro-Roman tribes on their borders, the Boii and Insubres were obliged to leave a sizeable part of their army at home. Even then the Gallic horde that poured into peninsular Italy was the largest Gallic invasion to date, boasting some 20,000 cavalry and chariots, and 50,000 foot men.[5]

Unlike nearly two centuries ago, when she was sacked by the Gauls, Rome was no longer merely a powerful city-state. Victorious in numerous wars, the Roman Republic had laid the foundation of an empire. After the *dies ater*, Rome consolidated its hold over Etruria, re-subdued the neighboring Latin tribes of central Italy and conquered the tribes of southern Italy, most notably the Samnites with whom there were no less than three wars. The Roman expansion unnerved the Greek cities of south Italy who called for the aid of King Pyrrhus of Epirus, the leading Greek soldier of his day. Pyrrhus twice defeated the Romans, but at Beneventum in 276 BC he suffered a devastating loss and withdrew to Epirus. By 264, through a complex process of alliances, conquest, colonization and the granting of citizenship, Rome had expanded her sway over all of peninsular Italy. Rome next turned her interest to Sicily and found herself dragged into the First Punic War (264–241), against the burgeoning Carthaginian Empire of North Africa and Southern Spain. Rome again was victorious and Sicily and the Carthaginian domains of Sardinia and Corsica passed under her control. Rome further extended her maritime presence when a military expedition was sent against the Illyrian pirate-queen Teuta.

The Roman army reforms initiated by Camillus after the Gallic sack of Rome were further tempered in battle with a myriad of nations. On land and on sea, in sieges and on the open field, through defeats and through victories, the Roman army grew bigger and better. At the end of the fourth century it had grown from a single legion to four legions, their symbols the wolf, the boar, the horse and the Minotaur. By the time of the great Gallic invasion of 225 BC, there were at least ten legions.

Having just secured her volatile relations with Carthage in a treaty, Rome was free to direct her whole martial might and that of her allies against the Gallic menace. Terrified of the Gallic invaders, all of peninsular Italy heeded Rome's call to arms. Legions and allies were mustered, and huge supplies of grain were collected. Joining Rome's legions were tens of thousands of Sabines, Samnites, Lucanians and Marsi[6] and a host of other peoples until more than 150,000 infantry and cavalry stood ready to fight for Rome. This armed might was stationed in three armies: one in Etruria; another to the east on the coast of the Adriatic Sea (Mare Hadriaticum); and the third on Sardinia. In addition, an army of Cenomani and Veneti assembled to invade the territory of the Boii.

Seemingly oblivious of what awaited them, the Gauls crossed unopposed into Etruria by means of an unguarded pass in the western Apennines. They plundered at will and struck straight for the heart of their enemy, at Rome. To the Gauls, it looked as if history would repeat itself, and soon Rome would once again fall to the barbarians. They advanced all the way to Clusium, the Etruscan city over which Romans and Gauls first went to war nearly two hundred years before. The invaders were only three days march from Rome when their scouts reported that a large Roman force was at their heels. It was the Roman army stationed in Etruria, which the Gauls had managed to bypass earlier but which had now caught up with them. The Gauls had little choice but to confront their foe or risk being caught between the legions and the walls of Rome. At sunset both armies laagered for the night, within sight of each other's campfires.

The Roman army must have been of fair size, for the Gauls decided to avoid an open battle, and came up with a clever ploy. The cavalry remained beside their campfires while, under cover of darkness, the infantry secretly retreated down the road to a town called Faesulae. In the wood and shrub-covered hillside near Faesulae, the Gallic infantry hid themselves in ambush.

At daybreak the Romans thought that the Gallic infantry had taken to flight. The Roman army advanced towards the remaining Gallic cavalry and, in a feint retreat, the Gallic horsemen took off towards Faesulae. The Romans came in hot pursuit. Polybius' account is unclear, but it seems that the Gallic infantry unexpectedly set upon the Roman columns marching past them. At this point the Gallic cavalry would have turned and fallen on their pursuers.

Caught between the Gallic cavalry and infantry, the situation was desperate. Had the Romans still relied on the unwieldy phalanx system of the *dies ater* days, they probably would have met their doom there and then. However, by now the internal cohesion of their maniples was ingrained into the legions. The legionaries gathered around their straw bundle field ensign, the *manipulis*, and were able to retain some sort of order. Although the battle went against them, and more than 6,000 Romans were slain, the remainder retreated to an easily defendable nearby hill. Onward came the Gauls, but the exertion of their night's march, compounded by the battle and now a fight up the slope, was beginning to show. The Romans stood their ground and inflicted heavy casualties before the Gauls wisely decided to retire and get some rest, stationing some cavalry around the hill to keep guard.

Unfortunately for the Gauls, time was not on their side. Consul Lucius Aemilius Papus, commander of the Roman Army on the Adriatic, had gotten word of the Gallic inroads and their proximity to Rome. Force-marching his men, he forthwith arrived on the scene and camped near the Gallic army. His campfires sparkled in the night, a welcome beacon to the besieged Romans on the hill. Under the cover of darkness and a nearby wood, one of the Romans on the hill sneaked through the Gallic lines and informed Papus of the plight of his countrymen on the hill.

The fires of the new Roman arrivals did not go unnoticed by the Gauls, who held council on what to do next. Aneroestes, one of the Gaesatae Kings, argued that they should retreat with their considerable booty, including an enormous number of slaves, cattle and other spoils, and avoid battle for now. Once the loot was safely brought back to their homelands, they could always return to deal with the Romans later. Aneroestes' prudent idea was accepted and that very night the Gauls again gave the Romans the slip.

At dawn Papus' military tribunes (legion officers) marshaled the infantry, while he himself rode with the cavalry to the hill. Although the Gauls were gone, the tracks of thousands of soldiers and horses could obviously not be concealed. The combined Roman armies followed in the Gauls' wake. With the Romans blocking their way north, and impassable wooded hills to their east and west, the Gauls at first back-tracked south. When the terrain opened up at

Lake Bolsena, the Gallic army struck west for the Etrurian coast and from there turned north.

Near Cape Telamon, foraging Gauls ahead of the main army suddenly stumbled upon Roman soldiers coming the other way. Both sides were almost certainly mounted, but it was the Gauls who yielded in the encounter and were taken prisoner. Together they rode back to the Romans' camp. The captured Gauls were alarmed to behold that their captor's camp lay not behind them but ahead of them! It could only mean even more Roman reinforcements. The Gallic foragers had been captured by the third Roman army from Sardinia. The latter had landed at Pisae (Pisa) to the north and was on its way to Rome.

The prisoners were brought before consul Gaius Atilius Regulus and described all that occurred, including the position of their army. Regulus hailed from a distinguished family, whose members had served as consuls for four generations. His warmongering father, Marcus A. Regulus, had become a Roman hero after he was captured and allegedly brutally executed by the Carthaginians during the First Punic War. Ready to win renown for himself, Gaius A. Regulus gloated; the Gauls would be squeezed and annihilated between his and Papus' army. He ordered his tribunes to march in fighting order as far as the terrain permitted.

Ahead of his army, Regulus noticed that the Aquilone hill was right beside the road on which the Gauls were coming to meet his forces. Regulus was eager to gain the hill before the Gauls and to initiate a battle that would surely be a Roman victory. He bolted towards the hill with his cavalry. When the Gauls saw some Roman cavalry gallop up to a hill in front of them, they naturally assumed that it was Papus' cavalry, which had somehow outflanked them at night. The Gallic cavalry and light skirmishers rode out to contest the hill. In the process the Gauls took some prisoners who told them that the Roman cavalry belonged to yet another Roman army.

For the Gauls the situation looked grim. This time there was no escape from the Roman vice. They were in for the fight of their lives. The Boii and the Taurisci formed up to meet the army of Regulus. Behind them, the Gaesatae and Insubres faced in the opposite direction to engage Papus' approaching army. The Gauls stationed their chariots and wagons on their flanks while a body of guards stood guard over the booty in the neighboring hills.

The cavalry melee on the hill went on with wild abandon and was gazed upon by both the Roman and Gallic infantry. Regulus fought alongside his men until he succumbed to a Gallic blade. His body was beheaded and the grim trophy of his head was carried back to the Gallic kings. The fight for the hill continued nonetheless and was still in progress when Papus' army arrived on the scene. Although he already knew of Regulus' landing at Pisae, Papus had not imagined that Regulus was in such close proximity. Drawing up his legions to advance on the Gauls, Papus sent forth his cavalry to aid in the hill battle. The Gallic horse was at last bested and the hill in Roman possession.

Now it was the time for the infantry. Although encouraged by having trapped their foe, the Romans were intimidated by the barbarian horde as Polybius relates:

> "They were terrified by the fine order of the Celtic host and the dreadful din, for there were innumerable horn-blowers and trumpeters, and, as the whole army were shouting their war-cries at the same time, there was such a tumult of sound that it seemed that not only the trumpets and the soldiers but all the country round had got a voice and caught up the cry."[7]

The tall Gallic warriors, outnumbered and surrounded, built up their confidence with cries and gestures of valor. From beneath bronze helmets swept tawny and fiery red manes and flickered savage eyes. Horns, plumes, or small stylized wheels, the Celtic symbols of war, adorned their helmets and fantastic curvilinear patterns graced their oval or hexagonal shields. Most of the Gauls wore their typical multi-colored checkered trousers and cloaks. Not so the Gaesatae who, in what was perhaps a deep spiritual reverence to nature, went into battle stark naked. The Gauls wielded large thrusting spears, javelins, slings and great swords. Since the days of the Allia, the Gallic sword had become a pure slashing weapon, a yard long and rounded at the end as opposed to pointed. Overall sword quality remained high, a few being more akin to steel than iron. Armored in corselets of mail and bedecked in torcs, armlets and bracelets of precious metals, the chiefs and their champions inspirationally formed the front ranks.

The Roman consuls opened the infantry clash by sending forth their light troops, who by the thousand streamed through the gaps between the maniples. Skins of wolfs, badgers and other beasts adorned their helmets. Inside their round shields they carried handfuls of javelins which they hurled, volley after volley, down upon the Gallic front ranks. Although the Gauls' large body shields offered some protection, all too many of the Roman javelins found their mark. The Gauls lacked sufficient missile weapons of equal range to harm their foes.

The naked Gaesatae, who formed the front ranks of the Gauls facing Papus, suffered most of all. In rage at their impotence, the bravest Gaesatae stormed forward only to be impaled by javelin shafts before they had a chance to exchange blows with the Romans. Other Gauls of fainter hearts pressed backward, throwing their own ranks into disorder.

Trumpets blared and the ground shook beneath the tramp of tens of thousands of legionaries. With standards raised, the maniples advanced upon the Gallic horde. From the first maniple line, the *hastati*, another barrage of heavy javelins (*pila*) rained upon the Gallic shield wall. The iron javelin heads were barbed and remained embedded when penetrating a shield, making it cumbersome to use. Roman short swords slid from thousands of scabbards, as the hastati charged.

In close combat the Romans again held the tactical advantage. Swinging his longsword in great arcs, the Gallic warrior found it vexingly difficult to avoid the short Roman thrusting blades, to bypass the Roman guard and to inflict a decisive blow. Unlike the Gauls' own shield, the oblong Roman *scutum* bent backward to enclose part of the bearer's body. Above the upper shield rim, all the Gaul could see was a slit of his foe's eyes beneath a bronze helmet. Even below the shield, the forward legionary's leg was protected by a bronze greave. When the legionary let down his shield he was further protected by body armor. The *hastati* wore a pectoral shield, while the legionaries of the second and third Roman lines, the *principes* and *triarii*, wore mail hauberks. The Gallic warrior made up for his disadvantages with skill, brute force and raw courage. His mighty sword splintered Roman shields and a direct hit bit through the bronze of the Roman helmet, and split the skull beneath!

The Gauls fought on and for a time it looked like the battle could go either way. On the Aquilone hill, the victorious Roman horsemen reined in their steeds. Now was not the time to pursue the fleeing Gallic horsemen. It was time to come to the aid of the legions. Down the hill the Roman cavalry thundered, into the flank of the Gallic infantry. Roman cavalry spears struck wildly into the panicked mob. The unexpected cavalry charge broke the spirit of the Gauls who were cut to pieces. When it all was over, 40,000 Gauls lay dead and another 10,000 marched into captivity and slavery, among them King Concolitanus. King Aneroestes escaped the slaughter with a few of his followers but overcome by grief over the disaster, took his own life.

Papus collected the Gallic booty and sent it to Rome, from where it was returned to its owners. Vengeance in his heart, Papus pushed onward with his legions toward the lands of the Boii. His legions brought flame, murder and rape. Lucius Aemilius Papus returned to Rome in a triumphal march, with his loot and captives, through streets adorned with Gallic standards and precious torcs.

The battle of Telamon marked the rapid decline of Gallic fortunes in northern Italy. In the following three years, a series of Roman campaigns broke the back of Gallic independence in the Po valley of northern Italy. The last of these in 222 BC, at Clastidium, saw the personal duel between the Roman general M. Claudius Marcellus and Virdomarus, the Insubres chieftain, in front of the assembled Gaul and Roman armies. Virdomarus bellowed that he had been born from the waters of the Rhine and would make quick work of the Roman invader. Both leaders hurled their spears and both missed. Blades in hand, they fell at each other to the exuberant cheers of their countrymen but it was Marcellus' sword which slit Virdomarus' throat. Without their leader the Gauls crumbled before the advance of the legions.

Among the Insubres fought a group of Germanic tribesmen.[8] Their presence was indicative of the poorly understood tribal interactions that occurred beyond the Roman-Celtic frontiers during the 3rd century BC. While Rome fought the Gauls in Gallia Cisalpina, Germanic and Celtic tribes continued to absorb or replace each other north of the Alps. In the Saarland, for example, the earlier Celtic culture that had thrived in and around the imposing fortress on the Dollberg Mountain for over 300 years came to end around 250 BC. It was replaced by the Celtic Treveri, a tribe which prided itself on its Germanic origin.

Another event of future consequence for Clastidium was the Roman capture of the Insubres town of Mediolanum, the future Milan, which would come to replace Rome as the seat of the Emperor. Such events, however, were many centuries away. For now, Rome was on a meteoric rise. Only two years after Clastidium, most of the Gallic tribes of the Po valley submitted to the Romans who further solidified their gains with the establishment of Latin colonies at Placentia and Cremona. But the final conquest of Gallia Cisalpina would have to wait as Rome was faced with the rebirth of a bitter enemy, Carthage.

In 219 BC the Carthaginian general Hannibal Barca besieged Saguntum, one of the Greek towns along Spain's Mediterranean shore, which enjoyed the protection of Rome. The incident escalated into the Second Punic War (218–201). The advent of Hannibal was a godsend for the Cisalpina Gauls but in typical Gallic character, their support for Hannibal was erratic at best. During the entire war a force of two legions sufficed to hold all of Gallia Cisalpina in check. According to Livy, Hannibal thought "that there was more smoke than fire to Gallic resistance."[9]

Even before Hannibal and his elephants crossed the Pyrenees on his way to Italy, 10,000 of his Celtiberians (a mixture of Spanish Celts and Iberians) deserted his cause and some even became scouts for the Romans. On his march from Saguntum to Italy some tribes became allies, others proved indifferent or even hostile. The Boii flocked to his cause but the Ceutrones, who at first supplied Hannibal with provisions, later ambushed the Punic army in a narrow mountain pass. At the battle of the Trebia in 218 BC, the Gauls holding Hannibal's center deserted their lines while a snowstorm blew over the area. In contrast, at Cannae in 216, his 8,000 Spanish and Gallic heavy cavalry drove the Roman cavalry from the field and smashed into the rear of the legions, clinching Hannibal's resounding victory in what, in terms of casualties, was the greatest Roman defeat to date.

Although a master of maneuver, Hannibal was increasingly outnumbered and was unable to obtain a decisive victory in Italy. When the brilliant Roman general Scipio Africanus took the war to Africa, Hannibal was forced to come to the rescue of his threatened homeland. Only a smattering of Hannibal's Gaul and Celtiberian cavalry accompanied him back to Africa. Their absence contributed to his final defeat at Zama in 202 BC, where Hannibal was confronted by a Roman army reinforced by mounted troops from Numidia.

Only after Hannibal's defeat, when it was too late, did the Gauls wholeheartedly stir into action. United by a Carthaginian general named Hamilcar, who had remained in Italy after the close of the Second Punic War, in 200 BC, the Insubres, the Cenomani, the Boii and Ligurian tribes (see chapter VI) assaulted the river fortresses of Placentia and Cremona and destroyed the former. Thereafter the Gauls held at bay inadequate Roman forces for two years. That they did so was largely due to continuing Roman commitments against yet another foe, Philip of Macedon. Awestruck by Cannae, Philip of Macedon entered into an alliance with Hannibal and drew Rome into the First (214–205) and Second (200–197) Macedonian Wars during which Rome played on the political divisions within the Greek world and ostensibly acted as the savior of Greece against Macedonian expansionism. The war reached its turning point with Philip's defeat at Cynoscephalae in 197.

Freed from its commitments in Greece, Rome was able to press the war against the Gauls. In 197 BC two Roman armies were sent against the Cenomani and Insubres who were defeated on the banks of the Mincio River near Mantua. This was followed by another victory in 196 near Lake Como. Both Gallic tribes sued for peace. The stalwart Boii did not stop fighting until 191 when they were defeated by consul Publius Cornelius Scipio Nasica. Forced to surrender half their lands, the dispossessed Boii refused to live under the Roman yoke. They drifted away to the east, where in the Danube regions they met with others of their tribe who had settled there earlier and gave their name to the region of Bohemia. Roman roads and Roman colonies spread across northern Italy, an area nearly as large as peninsular Italy. When Polybius wandered across the land nearly half a century later, he remarked that the roadside lands were already Italianized. Like the ancient Etruscans, the Gallic realms of Northern Italy were absorbed into the Roman world.

Chapter Four

Viriathus, Hero of Spain

"The war between the Romans and the Celtiberians was called the 'fiery war,'
so remarkable was the uninterrupted character of the engagements."[1]

Polybius

In 150 BC a young shepherd wandered down from the hills to surrender with others of his kind to the Romans. His name was Viriathus and his people were the Lusitani, one of the large Spanish tribal groups. Their home bordered the Atlantic coast, roughly central Portugal, between the mouths of the rivers Durius (the Duro) and Tagus (the Tajo). They were part of the Celt-Iberian peoples that had come into being after 900 BC, when the Celts drifted into the northern two thirds of Spain and mixed with the local pre-Indo European Iberians.

The Lusitani began fighting the Romans in the aftermath of Carthage's defeat in the Second Punic war (218–201 BC). Straddling the Mediterranean Sea, Punic Spain became Roman Spain. Two new Roman provinces, Hispania Citerior ("Nearer" Spain) and Hispania Ulterior ("Farther" Spain) set out to drain the country of its vast riches. Spanish gold and silver that once funded the Punic war machine now did the same for Rome. Soon 40,000 slaves toiled under the Roman whip at the silver mines of Carthago Nova (Cartagena). Only ten years after the Roman occupation, 59,000 kilograms of silver and 1,800 kilograms of gold were shipped to Rome. Spain, as Edward Gibbon put it, "was to Rome as Peru and Mexico would become to the Old World."[2]

Roman Spain was the home of pure Iberian tribes who avoided the Celtic assimilation of their northern kin. More "civilized" than the Celt-Iberians, the Iberians tolerated the colonies of Phoenician and Greek traders along their Mediterranean shore. The locals, however, were less inclined to cringe before their new Roman masters. Already in 206 BC, when the Carthaginians abandoned their Spanish territories, the tribes rose in rebellion. They were squashed in the following year but in 197, Iberian and Phoenician uprisings again flared up all over the provinces. By 194 the rebels were once more subdued but in the process Rome had gone to war with mercenary Celt-Iberian tribes who had helped the rebels. That year the Lusitani raided into Hispania Ulterior. The Celt-Iberians doggedly defied the Romans, avoiding set piece battles and excelling in guerrilla raids. When in 179 they were finally subdued it had as much to do with Roman martial triumphs as with the trust and respect the Spaniards had come to hold for the Roman commander Tiberius Sempronius Gracchus.[3]

Gracchus was an honorable man of his word. Unfortunately the successive Roman governors were not. The Spanish complained of Roman corruption but the Senate was deaf to their sufferings or retorted with empty promises. The blood of young Celt-Iberian warriors boiled in anger. They were ready to fight their oppressors, just as their fathers and grandfathers had done. In 154 BC the Lusitanians invaded Hispania Ulterior. The next year the Celtiberii tribal confederation of central Spain rose in revolt. A 153–152 Roman expedition into the heartland of the central Spanish tribes ended in the first Roman defeat in front of the stronghold of Numantia. Nevertheless, the Roman intrusion convinced the Celtiberii to agree to a peace that lasted for eight years.

The Lusitani, however, fought on. In 153 BC some of them even crossed the Pillars of Hercules and struck into Africa. Two years later, they humbled the army of Hispania Ulterior's Governor, Servius Sulpicius Galba. The same year, Lucullus, Governor of Hispania Citerior, hungry for loot, massacred the inhabitants of the Vaccaei town of Cauca, even though this Celt-Iberian tribe thus far had stayed out of the war. Lucullus was Galba's kind of man. Together, the two came up with a plan to deal with the elusive Lusitani.

Tired of the constant war, the burning of their homes, the slaughter and enslavement of their people, the Lusitani desired peace. Word came to the villages that Lusitani envoys had gone to Galba and asked him to renew an earlier peace treaty. Sympathetically Galba answered that he understood why the Lusitani had made war. "Poorness of the soil and penury force you to do these things. But I will give my poor friends good land, and settle them in a fertile country, in three divisions."[4] No doubt the older remembered and the younger had heard tales of the great Gracchus and his long lasting peace settlement. Likewise, Galba seemed a man of honor who understood the Lusitani's plight … or so many villagers hoped.

Alongside Viriathus, 30,000 Lusitanian men, women and children came down from their villages in the hills to gather at the place appointed by Galba. The

Romans divided them into three parts, telling them they would thus be settled on their new lands. Each group was then led out of sight of the other two.

Galba came to the first group and asked them to lay down their arms in a gesture of good faith. The naïve Lusitanians did as they were told. Women with babes in their arms, old couples supporting each other and young warriors who clenched their fists, watched in helpless apprehension, as Roman soldiers with spades moved around them. The Romans dug as only Romans could until a vast trench surrounded the Lusitani. Swords slid out of scabbards as the legionaries moved in. Children cried, frantic women screamed and clung to their men who cursed in anger. Roman soldiers pushed their way through the panicked mob to single out the able bodied men and cut them down like sheep. The others were "saved" for the slave markets. The slaughter was repeated with the other two Lusitani groups. Of the plunder, the greedy Galba kept most of it for himself and only gave a little to his soldiers, even though he was already a man of great wealth.

During the butchery the Romans likely came upon the odd Lusitani warrior who had mysteriously died by his own hand. To give them a quick death in a hopeless situation, Spanish warriors commonly carried a fast acting poison derived from the Sardonia plant *(Ranunculus sceleratus)*. It contracted their lower jaw into a sinister smile. To the Romans it must have seemed as if the corpses mockingly cursed them with ill luck. If so, the corpses were right, for some Lusitani escaped that day. Among them was the shepherd Viriathus. From that day on, his heart pounded with black hatred against the Romans.

Galba's silver-tongued promises had fooled and lured many Lusitani to death and into slavery. But others remained in the hills, ready to take up the sword once more. Even back in Rome, Galba's conduct caused an outrage in the Senate. But money could prove more powerful than justice, and Galba had plenty of the former.

Lust for vengeance and for loot brought the tribes together. In 147 BC, 10,000 Lusitani gathered to raid into Roman pacified Turdetania. Viriathus, now a young chieftain, was among them. The Spanish attack came at a bad time for the Romans who since 149 had been preoccupied with the Third Punic War. Still, legate Gaius Vetilius was reinforced from Rome and with some 10,000 troops moved against the Spanish raiders. He killed their foragers and managed to outmaneuver the Lusitani army, trapping it against a watercourse.

The Lusitani could hold out and face starvation or face the Romans in battle. Downcast, the Lusitani sent envoys with olive branches to Vetilius. They begged him to give them lands to settle on. Vetilius agreed to their requests if they would first surrender their weapons.

Viriathus had had enough; he had heard all these words before. Wary like a wolf that escaped a man's trap, to Viriathus the Roman words stank of deceit. He called upon his comrades to remember the treachery of Galba and the value of a "Roman" oath! His speech stirred their hearts and raised their confidence and they made him their war leader.

Vetilius watched as the Lusitani drew up their lines in front of his army. So the Spanish rabble decided to fight after all!

Yet as soon as Viriathus mounted his horse the entire Spanish infantry fled in all sorts of different directions. Vetilius was dumbstruck, what was going on? The Spanish cavalry, however, stayed on the field and on Viriathus' signal charged straight at the Romans.

But then, as soon as the Spanish horsemen engaged, they immediately disengaged!

In such a fashion, Viriathus' cavalry skirmished all day long to keep the Romans busy and allow for his foot men to make good their escape. That he was able to do so was because of the inherent superiority of his cavalry. Not only did Spanish cavalry make up twice the proportional number as it did in Roman armies, but to the Spanish, the horse itself was of special significance.

Spain was home to herds of horses that roamed wild and free. The Spanish admired the great beauty, speed and stamina of the horse and worshipped its spirit as a divinity. In show of their affection, the riders bedecked their steeds in colored wool trappings and hung tiny bells from their necks. Spanish horses could kneel and be quiet at command. The bond between rider and horse was so strong that the riders were known to dismount and form protective circles around their horses in battle. Celt-Iberians may have even invented the horseshoe in the 4th century BC.

Vetilius must have been furious that his cavalry was unable to come to grips with the superb Spanish horsemen. Finally at night, Viriathus left the field for good to rejoin his infantry at Tribola. After him came Vetilius but due to the heavy weight of his legionaries' armor and ignorance of the roads, the Romans soon lost sight of Viriathus' raiders.

Boiling with anger, Vetilius continued his pursuit of the rebels. But whenever he drew close to his irksome quarry, the fleet Spanish horsemen again spurted out of his reach. Somewhere near Tribola, possibly in the Guadiaro River valley, the Romans entered a narrow pass with a slope covered in dense thickets on one side and a cliff edge on the other. Once again, Vetilius beheld Viriathus' cavalry ahead on the path. But now, instead of bolting in flight, the Spanish cavalry suddenly reined their horses about and charged at the Romans! At the same time thousands of Lusitani infantry burst out of the thickets and stormed down to the Roman lines.

Viriathus had lured Vetilius into a death trap! When fighting behind a wall of their oblong body shields, armored in bronze helmets and mail tunics, the legionaries were nearly invincible. But on the narrow pass, the Romans lacked sufficient space to properly deploy their heavy infantry. Spanish javelins, the *soliferrum*, made completely of iron, whistled into the Roman ranks. The small, barbed, javelin heads transfixed shields and cuirasses at short range.

The Lusitani struck the Roman column from the front, rear and side. Here and there the Romans faced the Lusitani heavy infantry, the *scutati*, warriors sporting scale mail corselets or bronze pectoral plates and plumed helmets. The *scutati* blocked with large rectangular shields of the Celtic pattern and thrust with heavy spears mounted with murderous 23–inch long heads.

By and large, however, like their Celtic kin, the Lusitani's equipment was rarely uniform and most were lightly armed. Many wore no headgear at all, or perhaps a leather cap. Their preferred close combat weapons were a small round buckler and a short straight or a curved sword. The straight sword was the inspiration for the famous Roman *gladius hispanienses* adopted during the second Punic war or earlier. The Spanish curved sword, the *falcata*, widened toward the tip and only the inside edge was sharpened. The quality of these blades was unsurpassed. According to Diodorus, the falcata could hack through virtually anything.

Fending off the array of the Spanish arsenal hurling and slashing at them, the disciplined legionaries did their best to form up around their standards. Of the 10,000 Romans, 6,000 managed to fight their way back to the city of Carpessus (Carteia), on the seashore near the Pillars of Hercules. The remainder were killed, driven over the cliff or taken prisoner.

A Spanish warrior captured Vetilius but it seemed inconceivable to the warrior that an old fat man such as this could be the Roman leader. The Spanish put great value on a warrior's trim physique, even wearing a broad belt to slim down their waistline. Thinking Vetilius to be no one of importance, the warrior skewered him on his spear.

The Romans next raised 5,000 allies from the Celtiberii Belli and Titii and sent these against Viriathus. They marched off into the hills of the Lusitani. All of them were presumably killed, or perhaps some deserted to Viriathus, as none returned to tell the tale.

Viriathus' fame among the hill tribes grew and many flocked to his side. Around the campfire men told of a leader, who always was first to face danger, one whom others followed through great adventures, who even the Romans could not beat. When it came to dividing the loot, Viriathus was known to deal fairly. He never took the lion's share for himself and distributed even his own allotment among his bravest warriors. He was satisfied with whatever food and drink stilled his hunger and was content to sleep under the stars.

Diodorus left us with a tale of the wedding of Viriathus. Unimpressed by the opulent wealth, the gold, the silver and the colorful fabrics, of his father-in-law, who had accepted Roman ways, Viriathus refused to take a seat of honor. Instead he leaned on his spear and ate the barest of meat and bread with his personal companions. To his bride he offered sacrifice in the Lusitanian way, sat her on his horse and rode away into the hills.

Nevertheless, many tribes whom the Romans had cowed earlier remained loyal to their new masters. In addition, the resources of the Roman Empire were such that despite heavy commitments in Africa, in 146 BC Gaius Plautius brought another 10,000 Roman foot and 1,300 horse to Spain. Plautius led his army against Viriathus who was raiding the fruitful Carpetani lands. When Viriathus fled before the superior Roman forces, Plautius sent 4,000 men in pursuit. At the signal of rounded ceramic horns, Viriathus' warriors once again snapped back at their pursuers. Strung out in disorder, the heavily armored legionaries were at a disadvantage to the agile, lightly armed Spaniards; 4,000 Romans were killed. Plautius nevertheless kept after Viriathus, who crossed the Tagus, and at an olive covered mountain, known as Mt. Veneris ("Venus" mountain), decisively routed Plautius' army. Defying the odds, Viriathus had outfoxed the Romans again and again. The Romans subsequently coined a name for this Spanish feint and counterstrike method of fighting, the *concursare*.

The initiative back in his own hands, Viriathus harassed Roman garrisons in central Spain, captured Segobriga (Saelices), and took what crops he liked with impunity. After defeating another Roman army commanded by Claudius Unimanus, Viriathus ordered the captured Roman standards and paraphernalia displayed throughout the mountain countryside. Unimanus left us with a rousing account of the fighting:

"In a narrow pass 300 Lusitani faced 1000 Romans; as a result of the action 70 of the former and 320 of the latter died. When the victorious Lusitani retired and dispersed confidently, one of them on foot became separated, and was surrounded by a detachment of pursuing cavalry. The lone warrior pierced the horse of one of the riders with his spear, and with a blow of his sword cut off the Roman's head, producing such terror among the others that they prudently retired under his arrogant and contemptuous gaze."[5]

Viriathus' winning streak appeared unbreakable, but there were ominous signs of woeful days to come. With the Third Punic (149–146 BC) and the Fourth Macedonian (149–148) wars victoriously concluded the axis of Roman martial might tilted toward Spain. In 145 consul Fabius Maximus Aemilianus, of the prestigious Scipio family, arrived in Urso, Hispania Ulterior. He brought with him two green legions and allies totaling 15,000 foot and 2,000 horse.

Instead of flinging his untrained men directly at Viriathus' hard-bitten veterans, Fabius restricted his engagements to skirmishes and concentrated on training his forces. He also took time off to endear himself to the locals, even sailing to Gades (Cadíz) to partake in religious rituals of the Phoenician Melqart, whom the Romans equated with Heracles.[6]

In 144 BC, Fabius finally confronted Viriathus and gave him a bloody nose, capturing two cities one of which he burnt to the ground. Viriathus survived, but in the course of the campaign his respect for the Romans grew even as his hate diminished.

When Quintus Pompeius replaced Fabius in 143 BC, Viriathus quickly regained the initiative. Although Quintus at first routed Viriathus the latter withdrew to Venus Mountain and in a repeat of three years earlier suddenly turned on his pursuer and slew 1000 of Quintus' men. In lieu of his success, Viriathus won over the Celtiberii Arevaci, Belli and Titii of central Spain. They began the Numantine war that was named after the defiant fortress Numantia. With the timid Quintus hiding in Corduba (Córdoba), Viriathus ran rampant in the rich Bastetani region of Hispania Ulterior where he drove out the garrison of the city of Itucci.

The next year saw the arrival of consul Fabius Maximus Servilianus in Hispania Ulterior. He was the adoptive brother of Fabius Maximus Aemilianus and like him gave Viriathus trouble. Servilianus commanded two new legions and allies amounting to 18,000 foot and 1,900 horse, among them 300 cavalry and a handful of war elephants from Africa. On the way to Itucci in 142 BC, 6,000 of Viriathus' Spaniards attacked part of Servilianus' column with much clamor and noise, shaking their long hair to terrify their enemies. Such wild displays were part of Spanish tactics designed to intimidate their enemy and boost their own courage. If time permitted, they would even carry out ritual chants and dances. Servilianus, however, remained unmoved and in control, driving off the enemy who accomplished nothing.

After Servilianus assembled his entire army, he advanced against Viriathus and defeated him. But the Roman pursuit of the fleeing Spaniards became disorderly. Viriathus rallied and in one of his textbook counterstrikes annihilated 3,000 Romans. The tables were suddenly turned. The hunter became the prey and the Romans were driven back to their camp. There the coming of darkness saved them, for the Lusitani did not like to fight at night due to religious customs. In the days that followed, Viriathus' harrying attacks forced Servilianus back to Itucci.

Viriathus emerged victorious once more, but he lacked the numbers to finish off Servilianus' army. His army was worn down by attrition and so was Viriathus. He could shrug off heat and cold, hunger, and any other physical hardships, but it seemed that Viriathus was becoming mentally weary of the ceaseless war and bloodshed. Viriathus burned his camp and fell back from central Spain to Lusitania. By doing so he abandoned the towns he had won over, to the Romans.

Of the towns allied to Viriathus, Servilianus spared some and sacked others and then pushed on towards Lusitanian territory. On the way he fought local Spanish bandits and a huge raiding army under two Roman renegades. Although at one point Servilianus lost his baggage train, he captured 10,000 prisoners, 500 of which were beheaded, the rest sold into slavery.

The existence of such large bandit armies showed that Viriathus was losing influence among the Spanish. He pulled out of central Spain partially due to a lack of manpower. There were clearly thousands of warriors still available, but the problem was that in trying to form a united front against the Romans, Viriathus was going against the grain of Spanish heritage. Banditry was considered an honored way for young men to prove their valor. These bandits did not raid their own tribes, but anyone else was fair game. There was disunity, and it played right into the Roman hands.

In Lusitania, Servilianus laid siege to the town of Erisana. Coming to the city's rescue, Viriathus trapped the Romans in a defile and then suddenly offered them peace terms! Viriathus wanted the war to end. His only demand was that the Romans should respect the Lusitani borders and that his people be granted the status of *amici populi Romani* – "Friends of the Roman People".

Servilianus accepted and the Senate ratified the terms. But the Spanish guerrilla leader had humiliated Rome and that was something Roman pride could not swallow. There would be no rest for Viriathus. Before the end of the year another of Servilianus' brothers, consul Q. Servilius Caepio, arrived in Hispania Ulterior. Caepio complained that the treaty "was most unworthy of the dignity of the Roman people."[7]

After incessant provocations authorized by the Senate and carried out by Caepio, warfare with the Lusitani erupted anew in 140 BC. Caepio finally captured Erisana. With his much greater army he chased Viriathus through Carpentania, Lusitania and the land of their allies, the Vettones. Caepio was the first Roman to push into the mountains of the Gallaeci. He built a road from the River Guadiana (the Anas) to the Tajo and a great camp, the Castra Serevilia, near Caceres. Wherever the Romans went, they left behind a wasted countryside. As if the Romans were not enough of a scourge, large bands of robbers increasingly terrified the locals.

Not only the enemy but also Caepio's own troops, especially the cavalry, suffered from his ill character. He treated his men so harshly and cruelly that they slandered him in jeers and jokes around their campfires. His petty ego bruised, Caepio ordered 600 of his cavalry to collect wood on a slope in the vicinity of Viriathus' camp, a veritable death mission. When the horsemen managed to return alive with wood, they piled it around Caepio's quarters and "accidentally" set it alight. Caepio barely escaped with his life!

It was not until a further Roman army from Hispania Citerior, under Caepio's superior, Popillius Laenas, joined Caepio, that the exhausted Lusitani implored Viriathus to make another peace attempt. To Viriathus it must have seemed like there was no end to the numbers of soldiers Rome could muster while the Spanish tribes seemed more interested in looting each other, rather than fighting the Romans. In fact, the Spanish and Punic Wars had severely depleted Roman manpower. During the years of 153–133 BC, the Roman population actually declined with Roman and Italian casualties estimated at over 150,000.

Nevertheless, the Romans had weathered the war of attrition better than Viriathus. If Viriathus wanted peace, Laenas in turn demanded the surrender of Roman deserters and the handing over of all weapons. The hapless turncoats were given to the Romans who, following a tradition that the Romans had adopted from the Spanish, chopped off their right hands as punishment. Viriathus was naturally more loathe surrendering his weapons and sent three of his most trusted friends to the Romans for further negotiations. The three men were Audax, Ditalco and Minuros, whose loyalty Viriathus badly misjudged.

Through years of guerrilla warfare, always one step ahead of his foes, Viriathus had learned to do with little sleep and to take his rests in full armor. But such precautions did not protect him against the treachery of his own men. At night, while Viriathus lay soundly asleep, his three "friends" came to his tent, telling the guards that despite the late hour they had pressing business with Viriathus. Once inside, two of them held him down, their hands holding his mouth shut, while the third slit a slim knife into Viriathus' unprotected neck. The murder was so quickly carried out that the guards outside remained unaware. Even when daylight came, his attendants thought Viriathus was still resting. Curious about his unusual long sleep, someone entered the tent and discovered the grim truth.

Instantly the whole camp broke out in wailing and lamentation. What pained them most is that they could not take vengeance, for they remained clueless about who had committed the crime. The three traitors had meanwhile slipped back to the Roman lines. Having been paid an advance for their foul deed, they now requested the remainder of their reward. But Rome declared that she did not pay traitors and they were given nothing more. Treachery was repaid by treachery.

Viriathus' body was arrayed in rich garments and numerous sacrifices were offered for him. As he burnt atop a funeral pyre, his warriors ran and rode around the pyre, singing their praises and then sitting down to wait until the fire burnt out. Then there were gladiatorial contests in their former leader's honor.

Viriathus' death marked the beginning of the end of Lusitani resistance. Although a warrior named Tantalus led an attack on Carthago Nova he was unsuccessful and unable to revive Lusitani morale. In 139 BC the tribesmen surrendered in droves to Laenas. Fortunately, Laenas proved true to his earlier promises. He distributed farmland to the defeated, deported some to new regions and gave the best lands to those Spaniards that accepted Roman dominion the earliest.

The submission of the Lusitani did not, however, mean the end of the Roman war in Spain. Bands of robbers devastated the countryside, raiding into Lusitania. In 138 BC the Roman commander Sextus Junius Brutus struck out to subdue the rabble, eventually striking all the way to the River Nimis (the

Mino) into the northernmost parts of Spain. Lenient to some, at other times he plundered all he could carry and destroyed all who opposed him. Towns and their inhabitants, women who bore arms and fought alongside the men, none were spared by Brutus. "Of the women who were captured some killed themselves, others slew their children also with their own hands, considering death preferable to captivity,"[8] wrote Appian. In spite of these Roman advances, Lusitania was for the time being not incorporated into Hispania Ulterior and the River Tagus remained the northern frontier of that province. In central Spain, meanwhile, the stronghold Numantia continued to defy Rome in an epic stand that became as legendary as the deeds of Viriathus.

Chapter Five

Numantia, Bastion of Spanish Resistance

"Swift and terrible was the appearance of the defenders, the signals being everywhere hoisted ... the trumpets sounding on every tower, so that the whole circuit of fifty stades at once presented to all beholders a most formidable aspect."[1]

Appian

In 195 BC, the Roman consul Porcius Cato marched eight cohorts into the Celt-Iberian lands of the River Salo (the Jalon). The Romans had followed the Salo up from its confluence with the mighty River Ebro. The tributary led the Romans through the Sistema Iberico mountain range and into the *Meseta*, the central plateau of Hispania.

Great and ancient stands of Holm oak grew amidst the massifs, cliffs and crags that rose above the Roman columns. In those days most of Spain remained covered in woodlands, the deforestation initiated by the Roman axe having barely begun. In the valleys the agricultural Celt-Iberian Belli and Titii plowed the soil, while fierce nomadic shepherds, the Arevaci, grazed their flocks up mountain meadows. The Belli, Titii and Arevaci formed a Celtiberii tribal confederation. Their walled villages provided safe havens from local bandits but could offer little resistance to Cato's cohorts. The fortified towns of the Celtiberii, however, proved a more daunting task.

When Cato was unable to seize the stronghold of Segontia, he set up a base some four miles from another fortress town, Numantia. Numantia appears to have served as a Celtiberii tribal capital. As it happened, Cato's base would be used by all subsequent Roman operations against Numantia. The war with the Celt-Iberians raged on but for a long time no other Romans came anywhere as close to Numantia's walls as had Cato. Nevertheless, after a series of massive Roman campaigns, in 179 BC the Celt-Iberians accepted Tiberius Sempronius Gracchus' peace agreement. Like the Lusitani, the Celt-Iberians of central Hispania held Gracchus in high regard and put their faith in a Roman-led alliance. Gracchus' peace settlement gave Rome control of most of Spain with the exception of the Atlantic coast.[2]

The Spaniards stayed true to the terms of the settlement but the Romans misused it as they saw fit.[3] In 153 BC the Celt-Iberians rose in revolt, inspired by a Lusitani invasion of Hispania Ulterior in the previous year. With 30,000 soldiers, consul Fulvius Nobilior drove the Belli and Titii out of their valley and burnt the abandoned Belli capital of Segeda in 153. The homeless tribes allied themselves with other tribes in the Numantia region. Led by their warlord, Caros, some 25,000 Celt-Iberians ambushed the Roman column in a dry wooded valley on August 23, the day of the Roman feast of Vulcan. Roman discipline allowed Nobilior to fight his way out of the trap but not before losing 10,000 of his men. The Celt-Iberians too suffered heavily and Caros was counted among the dead.

Undaunted Nobilior pushed on, reinforced with Numidian war elephants and cavalry. Outside Numantia, Nobilior's elephants threw the assembled Spaniards and their horses into a panic. The Spanish horses especially were completely startled by the gray titans. But during the ensuing siege, a large stone tumbled down from the battlements and struck one of the elephants on the head. The wounded beast went berserk. Its cries convinced the other elephants that danger was all around them. No longer distinguishing between friend and foe the elephants steam-rolled through the Roman ranks, squashing men into pulp and tossing them left and right like rag-dolls!

At this opportune moment the Numantians sallied out of the gates, killing 4,000 Romans and 3 elephants for a loss of 2,000 of their own warriors. The Romans suffered from further engagements with no concrete gains. Nobilior sat out the winter at Cato's old site, his men hungry and shivering in the cold and wet weather. Nobilior's army was reduced to 5,000 men. When Nobilior returned to Rome, he and members of his force unabashedly admitted to the "great losses suffered by the Romans and the valor of the Celtiberians."[4] Cary and Scullard aptly described the fiasco as "the first grave in the cemetery of Roman reputations at Numantia."[5]

The following year, Nobilior's successor, Metellus Claudius Marcellus barely avoided another enemy ambush. Marcellus proceeded to pillage the country and induced the Celt-Iberians to parlay for peace based on Gracchus' settlement. When the warmongering Roman Senate scoffed at the Celt-Iberian's pleas for peace, Marcellus defied his own government. He deftly negotiated a peace with the Belli, Titii and Arevaci that gave Hispania Citerior eight years of peace from central Spain.

Marcellus' peace agreement came in the nick of time because a second Roman army under his replacement, Licinius Lucullus, was already on the way. As was previously mentioned, the avaricious Lucullus went on to commit atrocities in the neutral lands of the Vaccaei. Despite such acts by their new Roman allies, the Celtiberii remained loyal to Rome. For a while, the Belli and Titii even supplied warriors to fight against the indomitable Lusitani guerrilla chieftain Viriathus. By 143 BC, however, Viriathus' successes inspired the Celtiberii to switch sides once again.

Roman retribution was swift and ruthless as consul Q. Caecilius Metellus swept up central Spain in a campaign of conquest that left only a handful of fortresses in Celtiberii hands. Although at this point the Belli and Titii were again subdued, Numantia remained defiant and turned the tables on besieging Romans in 141–140 BC and in 137. Incredibly, each time the Roman commander was able to worm his way out of the situation through lies and empty promises. In 140, Q. Pompeius even duped the Numantians into paying an indemnity. In 137, Hostilius Mancinus' army was saved by Gracchus' son, Tiberius, whose father's name was still held in respect by the Numantians. Tiberius, who was a quaestor in Mancinus' beleaguered army, reached an agreement with the Numantians. The Senate, however, was of other mind and called Mancinus back to Rome to stand trial.

During the ensuing two years no Roman army dared to challenge Numantia. Instead, Hispania Citerior's commanders falsely accused the hapless Vaccaei of supplying Numantia with provisions. The Romans laid siege to the Vaccaei city of Pallantia but achieved only more bloodshed and a humiliating retreat in which many Roman soldiers succumbed to starvation. Although the Roman commander was chastised, his replacement was back raiding the Vaccaei lands in 135 BC. Meanwhile, the Senate rejected Mancinus' peace agreement after a lengthy dispute with Numantian envoys. Mancinus was made the scapegoat and delivered naked to the Numantians, who, however, refused to receive him.

Just as Rome had no intention of coming to any sort of peaceable agreement with Viriathus, so she would not be satisfied with anything but the total destruction of Numantia. Unfortunately Rome's commanders in Hispania Citerior seemed more eager to pillage the Vaccaei lands than risk themselves in a confrontation with Numantia.

Ever since Nobilior's defeat, fear of the Celt-Iberians pervaded the Roman army. Young men avoided enrollment with whatever excuses they could find and even the posts of legates, tribunes and lesser officers remained unfilled. Veteran legionaries had never seen such fear of the enemy as filled the new recruits. The man that Rome hoped would change all this was consul P. Cornelius Scipio Aemilianus. He hailed from the renowned Scipio family that gave Viriathus such trouble. Scipio Aemilianus had already shown his qualities in 146 BC, when, through sheer tenacity and will power, he burst asunder the stout defenses of Carthage and razed the city to the ground. In 134, Scipio Aemilianus took command of Rome's legions in Spain.

With Scipio Aemilianus' arrival a new wind blew through the Roman army in Spain, which had lost its zeal due to idleness, discord and luxury. Prostitutes, traders, soothsayers and diviners were booted out of the camps along with all unnecessary items. Scipio Aemilianus got rid of animal sacrifices used for divination purposes because the soldiers, demoralized by defeats, had become used to relying on omens. The soldiers' food was limited. Each one was ordered to carry a month's rations and they were forbidden to have beds. As an example to his men, Scipio Aemilianus was the first to sleep on straw. While on the march the soldiers were no longer allowed to ride on mules. "For what can you expect in a war," said Scipio Aemilianus, "from a man who is not even able to walk?"[6] Any offences were punished with the vine stick.

Along with the new restrictions came severe training. Scipio Aemilianus marched his men all over the nearby plains, building, fortifying and then demolishing one camp after another. Trenches were dug and then filled in, walls erected and then torn down. Scipio Aemilianus was always there to oversee everything. A guard was always deployed and cavalry sent to scour the countryside.

Scipio Aemilianus was harsh but this does not mean he was a man without a heart. When he saw sick soldiers on the march, he mounted them on the horses of his cavalry and told the latter to walk on foot. He even lightened the load of overburdened mules and made his foot soldiers carry the extra load. Scipio Aemilianus commented on his strict discipline: "Those generals who were severe and strict in the observance of law were serviceable to their own men, while those who were easy going and bountiful were useful only to the enemy."[7]

One soldier who appreciated Scipio Aemilianus' reforms was Gaius Marius. The young Marius had grown up in a village near Arpinum, in central Italy. Scipio's campaign against the Celtiberii was Marius' first assignment as a soldier. Marius detested the corruption that had beset his fellow soldiers and cheerfully complied with the hard but effective new training. Marius' keenness was noted by Scipio Aemilianus but even he could not have guessed just what an exceptional soldier Marius was to become.

In May of 134 BC, when Scipio Aemilianus deemed his men ready, he marched toward Cato's old camp near Numantia. Numantia covered some 54 acres, with around 2,000 houses and a population of 10,000 men, women and children. Including warriors who would have drifted in from nearby villages, its defensive strength was therefore no more than 4,000–6,000 men.[8] However, the Numantians could feel secure behind practically unconquerable natural defenses, boosted by three concentric rings of formidable walls strengthened by towers. Although the walls were damaged on the south and western sides, the Numantians had thrown up stakes, stones and ditches. The walls and city towered on a hill top, today's Muela de Garray, some 3,540 feet above sea level. Two rivers, the Duero and the Merdancho, flanked the fortress-city from the southwest and the west, while to the north small lakes were fed by a tributary of the Duero. A slope to the northeast provided the only means of attacking the city.

Scipio Aemilianus had no intention of letting his army bleed itself to death by futile assaults. For the time being he remained on the defensive, studying the lie of the land and the intentions of his enemy. His foraging units cut down the unripe grain in the fields. Instead of tackling Numantia, Scipio Aemilianus decided to pillage the Vaccaei. Not surprisingly, the latter were now hostile to Rome and were selling food supplies to Numantia. Scipio Aemilianus took what food he needed from the Vaccaei lands and burnt everything else. The Vaccaei retorted by ambushing a Roman foraging party and came close to trapping a number of retaliatory Roman cavalry squadrons. Scipio Aemilianus barely avoided another ambush at a river crossing, but the alternate route he took caused him to lose some of his horses and pack animals which perished from thirst.

When Scipio Aemilianus arrived back in Numantian territory in late summer he was joined by Jugurtha, grandson of the Numidian King and Roman vassal, Masinissa. Jugurtha brought with him twelve elephants and accompanying archers and slingers. Scipio Aemilianus now commanded around 60,000 men, including a personal guard of 4,000 under Bueto his nephew, which he brought with him from Italy and which, alongside 10,000 Roman and Italian troops, made up the core fighting strength of his army. Then there were 10,000 auxiliaries, 5,000 warriors rallied from the conquered Belli and Titii and thousands of other unspecified and less than reliable troops. Still, Scipio Aemilianus avoided an assault on Numantia. Instead he continued to loot the countryside, fighting off an ambush in the Guadarrama valley without serious casualties.

Scipio Aemilianus established two camps very close to Numantia, one to the north, under his direct command, the other to the southeast, under his brother Maximus. When the Numantians sallied forth he refused to be taunted into battle. In light of the previous failed Roman assaults, Scipio Aemilianus was determined to reduce the Numantians by starvation. Within a single day, the Romans erected a 2.5-mile long palisade, reinforced with stones and with a half-yard deep ditch lined with stakes, across the city's approachable northeastern slope. A strong Roman guard was always present and prevented the Numantians from seriously disrupting the work.

Behind the palisade Scipio Aemilianus built another stone wall, 13 feet thick at the base, 8 feet thick at the 10-foot high top and protected by a further "V" shaped ditch. The second wall spanned 5.6 miles, virtually enclosing the whole city. The wall linked together 300 separate towers, one every *plethron* (103 feet), plus a total of seven roughly equally spaced forts. The forts were located on naturally defensive positions.[9]

Within the forts and mounted on the towers were catapults and *ballistae*, hurling 1 to 2-lb balls or shooting bolts to a range of a 1,000 feet. Furthermore within the forts there were 50 heavy ballistae with 10lb shot, although some super-heavy siege engines may have thrown 27lb, 76lb or even 156lb stones.

The potential weak points in Scipio Aemilianus' wall were a lake or marsh to the north and the river systems that flanked Numantia to the west. The marsh was breached with a dike which was surmounted by the wall. Bridges were thrown across most of the rivers, except the Duero whose deep sloping banks and 270-foot width thwarted even the Roman engineers. When the Numantians used boats to bring in supplies, the Romans threw booms of iron-spiked wooden beams moored into the water and erected another two forts to cover the waterway.

Thirty thousand troops were held in the forts and camps as support while the other 30,000 manned the walls. A red flag was used to signal any point that was threatened in the daytime while lanterns and torches were used at night. The Roman soldiers lived in houses built in the Celt-Iberian manner. Each house had two floors, one on ground level and a cellar room below to give shelter from extreme heat or cold.

Scipio Aemilianus' fortifications, completed by November 134 BC, were a deadly marvel of Roman engineering skills. In effect they enclosed the fortress-town of Numantia within an even greater fortress. The Numantians lacked archers and since their spears and slings had a maximum range of 150 and 300 feet respectively, they could not fire upon the Romans from the safety of

Numantia's walls. The range of the Roman siege engines, however, reached well within the city walls. The terrifying racket of catapult balls and spears, as they fired and hurled through the air, and the impending boom of their impact, further tore away at the morale of the defenders. Attempts to sally forth and stop the constructions floundered in face of superior Roman numbers. One can imagine how disheartening the awesome display of Roman military power must have seemed to the trapped Numantians.

Yet the brave Spaniards did not sit idly by to await their doom. Diversionary sorties were launched against the Roman walls and attempts were made to lure the Romans out into open battle. But they were like gnats biting a giant. Scipio Aemilianus refused to budge. The Romans even had orders not to stop Numantians from gathering firewood and water in the enclosed area. The quicker they used up their last meager resources, the sooner starvation would set in.

Often at the forefront of the fighting was the aforementioned young Roman soldier Gaius Marius. His courage was far above that of his comrades and once, in front of Scipio's eyes, Marius defeated an enemy in single combat. As a reward Marius earned several honors.

With the future of the city looking grim, a Numantian named Retogenes Caraunios made a last ditch attempt to summon help. At night, he and five friends and their five servants scaled the Roman walls with a rope ladder and killed the sentries. They stole some horses and rode to the Vaccaei, seeking help. The Vaccaei, however, had suffered so much under Roman brutality that the fear of Rome was instilled into them. Town after town refused to aid Retogenes until he came to Lutia. Against the wishes of the town elders, 400 bold young warriors volunteered to come to Numantia's aid. The town elders sought to avoid Roman reprisal by sending word to Scipio Aemilianus. At dusk the next day, Roman light troops led by Scipio Aemilianus himself surrounded the town. Scipio Aemilianus threatened to sack the town if the rebels were not immediately surrendered. The citizens told him that the rebels had already fled with Retogenes. Scipio Aemilianus refused to believe their words and did not leave until the town surrendered 400 innocent youths. Their right hands were struck off as punishment.

With Retogenes' relief attempt having come to naught, the Numantians sent an envoy to Scipio Aemilianus to reach some sort of peace agreement. It was the spring of 133 BC and Scipio, aware of the desperate condition of his trapped foe, demanded nothing less than unconditional surrender and the handing over of all weapons. The envoys returned to Numantia and presented Scipio Aemilianus' terms. The Numantians became enraged over Scipio's demands. After all the hardship Numantia had endured, her people were to surrender like helpless sheep? Frustration, desperation and fear fed the Numantians' anger and clouded their judgment so that they falsely accused the envoys of double-dealing with the Romans. The envoys were murdered as punishment.

Severe starvation nagged at the Numantians' bodies and minds like an evil specter. Their plight took on an increasingly morbid countenance. When all the meat, bread and animal forage were exhausted, the Numantians ate the boiled hides of animals. After the hides, there was nothing left to eat but themselves. First the dead, then the ill and the weak, became victims of cannibalism. Others chose a more heroic end, fighting each other to the death. One Numantine of wealthy standing set all his beautiful houses aflame and then threw himself into the fire.

By flame, by iron or by poison, many took their own lives. Those that were left surrendered to Scipio Aemilianus at the end of July or early August 133. After enduring nine months of siege, the emaciated Numantians that shuffled out of the city gates and surrendered their weapons were more akin to walking skeletons than human beings. Eyes within sunken sockets reflected the mental horrors of hunger, and of the eating of human flesh. For those that survived, a life of slavery awaited. Fifty of them, presumably the handful that remained in presentable shape, were selected for Scipio Aemilianus' coming triumphal march in Rome. Scipio Aemilianus, the destroyer of Carthage, did the same to Numantia. The city was razed to the ground, its rebuilding was forbidden and Roman soldiers were stationed to prevent anyone from living in the ruins.

Scipio Aemilianus was honored with the title of "Numantinus". While attending an entertainment, someone asked Scipio Aemilianus where the Romans, after Scipio, could find another great general? Scipio turned to Gaius Marius, who sat next to him, gently clapped the young soldier's shoulder, and replied "Here perhaps."[10]

The siege of Numantia and the war against Viriathus marked the most dramatic events in the Roman conquest of Spain. But even after both city and man yielded to the might of Rome, resistance in Spain continued for many years. Not until the age of Emperor Augustus in 19 BC, was all of Spain truly subdued.

Chapter Six

Liguria and the Foundation of Gallia Narbonensis

"Wars with the Ligures ... had always been associated with wars against the Gauls."[1]

Tribune Blaseus quoted in Livy

Before the coming of the Celts into central Europe and the founding of Rome during the 1st millennium BC, the Neolithic Ligures dwelt in the mountainous regions that stretch from Austria to southeastern France. Like the Celts and Italians, the Ligures spoke an Indo-European tongue but, as Cary and Scullard suggest, this was probably imposed upon them by invading tribes.[2] Little is known about the true origins of the Ligurians except that their tribes were gradually pushed into the heartland of Liguria, the coastal strip and hinterland of north-western Italy, bordering Mediterranean Gaul.

During Rome's wars with the Gauls of northern Italy, the barren Ligurian heartland was of little interest to the Romans other than the military assistance its savage tribes continued to give to Rome's enemies. As the plebian tribune P. Sempronius Blaseus observed: "wars with the Ligures ... had always been associated with wars against the Gauls."[3] Ligurian mercenaries also aided Hannibal during the Second Punic War (218–201 BC). When Punic Spain became Roman Spain, Rome was given further reason to pacify the Ligurian tribes, whose banditry and piratical activities made the land and sea routes from Rome to Spain an increasing liability for Roman merchants.

After Hannibal's defeat in Africa, the Ligurians flocked to the aid of the Carthaginian general Hamilcar who had remained in Italy. In 200 BC, Hamilcar rallied the Boii and other Gallic tribes to sack the Latin colony of Placentia and to besiege Cremona, but his Gallic-Ligurian army was crushed, and he himself killed, by two legions and by allied troops under the command of praetor Furius Purpureo. In 197 while Rome was carrying out successful counter operations against the Gauls, the Ligurian towns of Clastidium and Cerdiciates submitted to Roman arms. Clastidium was put to the torch. With fortunes turning against their allies, the last free Ligurian tribe, the Ilvates, surrendered.

Nevertheless, although its tribes had surrendered, in 194 BC Liguria suffered yet another Roman raid. Consul Scipio Africanus plundered all but the most remote villages, which, hidden in deep forests and expansive marshlands made access for the Romans difficult or dangerous. The next year the Ligurian tribes assembled en masse and stormed south toward the coastal city of Pisae in the Arnus estuary. According to Livy 40,000 tribesmen beleaguered the city, joined daily by more and more warriors hungry for loot. Consul Quintus Minucius arrived southeast of Pisae, at Arretium, to muster his troops and from there marched forth to Pisae. His arrival no doubt saved the city. Crossing the river, he camped half a mile from the enemy. Unsure of his newly levied "green" troops, Minucius limited his actions to skirmishes; effectively blocking the larger Ligurian army at Pisae. Simultaneously, however, Minucius found that he was held at bay by the Ligurian army. He was powerless to prevent Ligurian raiders from scouring the countryside and returning with convoys of booty and livestock to their villages.

Satiated with loot, the Ligurians at Pisae dispersed back to their homeland and until the end of 193 BC peace reigned. At this time a consul's camp was attacked. Not long after the incident, a Roman army found itself marching through a defile when its way ahead was blocked by Ligurians. The commanding consul ordered a halt and then turned his column about, determined to avoid battle within the narrow area, and marched his men back the way they came. To their horror the Romans beheld Ligurians at the other end of the exit as well. The Romans were trapped. In their minds rose the terrible specter of the Caudine disaster, when in 321 BC Samnites caught the Roman forces in similar circumstances. At that moment the commander of the consul's auxiliary Numidian cavalry stepped forth. He swore that his 800 Numidians would break out of the Ligurian blockade, be it the one behind or the one in front. He would then seek out the Ligurian villages, set fire to their buildings and by doing so force the Ligurians to break their blockade of the pass. Heartened by the Numidian's daring plan, the consul agreed and promised him rewards.

The Numidians mounted their steeds and in a deceptive ploy approached the enemy outposts like a bunch of buffoons. Apart from their javelins, the Numidians were unarmed. They fell off their horses to exaggerate their incompetence. In this way they edged their way closer to the enemy pickets. The latter gradually let down their guard, fascinated by the ridiculous spectacle. Suddenly the Numidians put the spurs to their horses and burst through the startled enemy. From there on, wherever the African cavalry rode it left behind flaming buildings.

The Ligurians watched as smoke clouds billowed from the countryside. Cries of terror erupted from the villages. Panicked women, children and the old, refugees from the Numidian raids, trickled into the Ligurian blockade camp. As the Numidians had hoped, the Ligurians abandoned their position to rush to the aid of their families and homes. The blockade was broken, the Roman army saved.

The war, however, continued. In 191 BC, a Ligurian army made a night attack on the camp of proconsul Quintus Minucius. From their ramparts, Minucius' legionaries kept the wild attackers at bay. At daylight the Romans sallied forth from two gates at once but their charge failed to scatter the Ligurians. For two hours the Romans fed column after column at the Ligurians who, worn out by lack of sleep, finally abandoned the field. They had left behind 4,000 dead; inflicting an alleged mere 300 casualties on the Romans and their allies. With reinforcements Minucius might have brought the current Ligurian war to an end. That same year, another Roman army under consul Publius Cornelius Scipio Nasica was busy dealing the final blow to the Boii. The victorious Nasica was more interested in receiving his triumph than in hurrying to Minucius' aid.

For now, Liguria remained unsafe. A Roman governor was ambushed while on his way to Spain in 189 BC. Fifteen years later another governor was killed. Between 186 and 180 two consular armies struck to subdue the troublesome tribes. But as in Spain, the heavy legionary infantry found it difficult to come to grips with the local light-armed skirmishers. Most of the fighting occurred in hills inland from the two Roman naval outposts of Genua and Luna.

Nevertheless, despite initial Roman reverses and fruitless victories, in 181 BC Aemilius Paullus subdued the Ingauni tribe to the west of Genua. The next year, two proconsuls conquered the Apuani, who dwelt between Genua and Luna, and deported 40,000 of them to Samnium. Punitive expeditions were also carried out against the Ligurian piratical allies on Corsica and Sardinia. After these campaigns Liguria was essentially pacified, at least for the moment. Roman commanders eager for glory continued to raid the region. Whether the tribes were guilty of infractions against Rome or not was of less importance than getting loot and slaves, as in consul M. Popillius' raid of 173.

Naturally, raids such as Popillius' did nothing to sooth Liguria's mistrust of Rome. In 154 BC Ligurian raiders made a nuisance of themselves to the Greek cities of Nicaea and Antipolis along the Mediterranean coastal strip of Gallia Transalpina. Rome's stout ally, the ancient Greek colony of Massilia asked for

Roman help. Although Massilia safeguarded Rome's route to Spain, Rome tried to stay out of Massilian-Greek affairs until one of her envoys was insulted by the Ligurians. A Roman army led by consul Opimius drove the Ligurians back into their hills, but thirty years later in 125 they were back. When the Massilians again appealed to Rome for help, consul M. Fulvius Flaccus struck at the Ligurians from the rear by marching his army across the Genevre pass of the western Alps. His campaigns in 125 and 124 conquered first the coastal pirates and then an inland tribe between the Durance and the Isère. C. Sextius Calvinus successfully followed up Flaccus' gains with a further two years of campaigns. He founded a settlement of Roman veterans at Aquae Sextiae (Aix) to guard the Massilian backcountry.

Liguria was finally subdued but for a Ligurian chieftain, who fled to the Gallic Allobroges farther inland in the Alp foothills. The Allobroges refused to hand over the fugitive to the Romans, who forthwith became ensnared in Gallia Transalpina's politics. Roman relations with the Allobroges soured further when another tribe, the Aedui, who were Massilia's trade partners, called the Allobroges breakers of the peace. Matters escalated until proconsul Gnaeus Domitius Ahenobarbus' unstoppable Elephant corps crushed the Allobroges' army in 121 BC, in the vicinity of Avignon. The Rhône's entire left bank was now under Roman sway.

But the Allobroges cried for delivery and the Arverni heard their cries. King Bituitus led his rambling Gallic horde to the confluence of the Rhône and the Isère to meet the Romans in a battle on which hinged the destiny of Mediterranean Gaul. But the scale of victory tilted towards consul Q. Fabius Maximus' outnumbered legions. The panicked Gauls collapsed a number of bridges they had earlier thrown across the Rhône. The trapped Gauls were decimated, the Romans claiming a highly suspect 120,000 slain against a loss of fifteen of their own.

Maximus returned to Italy after his great victory, handing over command to his subordinate G. Domitius Ahenobarbus. King Bituitus who had escaped the disaster at the Isère was now ready for peace negotiations. Domitius promised him safe conduct but when Bituitus arrived, Domitius promptly had him shipped off to Rome as a prisoner in 121 BC. Despite the Roman treachery, the Arverni accepted peace and ceded part of their lands on the Rhône's right bank to Rome.

Domitius built a high road from the Rhône to the Pyrenees. Named after himself, the "Via Domitia" crossed Mediterranean Gaul and linked Italy with

Spain. Along the road, in the Gulf of Lions, Domitius founded the colony port city of Narbo with Roman veterans. Narbo lay close to the mouth of the navigable River Aude. Here was the end of the tin route from Britannia, which followed the river through the Carcassonne Gap between the Pyrenees and the Massif Central of France. On the other side of the Gap, the tin route led to the town of Tolosa (Toulouse), on the banks of the River Garonne, and from there to the Atlantic. The hills around Tolosa were rich in silver and gold. The importance of the Tolosa was not lost on the Romans who annexed the Gallic town in 118 BC.

The whole area of today's French Riviera was eventually incorporated into the new province of Gallia Narbonensis. Within it, Greek Massilia retained her independence until, over half a century later, she disastrously chose the wrong side in the civil wars that marked the end of the Roman Republic. From Gallia Narbonensis, Rome concluded what would become a long lasting alliance with the Aedui who dwelt northeast of the Arverni. The stage was thus set for Rome to meddle in the affairs of Gaul, which would soon feel the brunt of a new invader who would shake the foundation of the Roman Republic.

Chapter Seven

"Wolves at the Border"
The Migrations of the Cimbri
and Teutones and their
War with Rome

"The Cimbri and Teutones' courage and daring made them irresistible, and when they engaged in battle they came on with the swiftness and force of fire, so that none could withstand their onset but all who came their way became their prey and booty."

Plutarch[1]

In 113 BC the Cimbri and Teutones marched into the limelight of recorded history when they appeared on the Roman Balkan frontier. Clad in primitive hides and furs and rumored to be eaters of raw flesh, the tall, flaxen and rusty haired, blue-eyed people appeared to the Romans as a race of savage giants. In lumbering wagons, literally huts on wheels, they traveled with their entire families alongside herds of livestock.[2]

The Cimbri and Teutones' origin mystified the Romans for in those days the Romans knew little of the realms and peoples of northern Gaul and Germania. Most claimed that they were Germans; some thought they were Celts. Others pondered if they were Galloscythians, a mix of the Gauls and the Scythian peoples of the eastern steppes, or the Cimmerians of Greek legend who lived in eternal darkness at the world's edge.

Many modern scholars believe that the Cimbri and Teutones were Germans. This Germanic argument is based on the homelands of the Cimbri and Teutones in northern Denmark, which was within the Germanic, and outside of the Celtic domains. Nevertheless, the names of their chieftains are Celtic, which leads some historians to maintain that the Cimbri and Teutones were Celts. However, classical authors might have transmitted German names to us in Celticized form because they were more familiar with the Celtic language.[3]

Whether they were Germans or Celts, the incredible saga of the Cimbri and Teutones began during the late 2nd century BC when a rise in the ocean level inundated large tracts of the Danish coast. A scattering of tribes were forced to seek homelands elsewhere; they were led by the Teutones and Cimbri. Classical historians hopelessly exaggerated their numbers, either to justify Roman defeats at the barbarians' hands or to magnify the scale of the final Roman victories. Plutarch claimed that there were 300,000 warriors! The precise number of Cimbri and Teutones will never be known but it is likely that together the two tribes numbered less than 150,000 men, women and children, a figure on a par with the larger German tribes of the 5th to 7th centuries AD.[4]

From northern Denmark the two tribes wandered south along the Elbe, then east along the Danube. In Bohemia they met the Celtic Boii whose resistance persuaded the Cimbri and Teutones to trek further south into the Balkans. There they clashed with the Celtic Scordisci. As a result of this encounter the Scordisci were pushed south into Macedonia while the Cimbri and Teutones were deflected westward towards Italy via the valley of the Drave and the passes of the Carnic Alps. They now threatened the Celtic Kingdom of Noricum and the iron mines of Noreia, a close trading partner of Rome. This placed them dangerously close to borders of the Roman Republic.

To meet this new barbarian incursion, consul Papirus Carbo was sent to bar their way in the heights north of Aquileia. Although outnumbered, Carbo felt that his disciplined legions could deal with the crudely armed barbarian rabble. Having had little contact with the civilized world, the half-naked Cimbri and Teutones warrior probably had little more than a wooden shield for protection, his main weapon a wooden, bone or an iron-tipped spear. Cavalry was uncommon and the bulk of the warriors fought as infantry. A few of the chiefs, their retainers, and warriors of renown, sported body armor and wielded iron long-swords. It was they who boldly formed the front ranks in battle.

When the Cimbri and Teutones heard that the people of Noricum were friends of Rome, they sent word that they would leave them in peace. Carbo praised the barbarian envoys and in a gesture of goodwill, offered guides to take them back across the Noricum borders. In reality Carbo's guides led the Cimbri and Teutones into a Roman ambush. Carbo sprung his trap near Noreia but failed to scatter the barbarians, who rallied and viciously counterattacked. The Roman army was suddenly in very serious trouble. It would have been completely annihilated had it not been for a violent tempest that put an end to the battle. The clap of thunder drowned out the clashing of blades and the screams of death. In face of the disaster, Carbo took his life by poison.

After their victory the Cimbri and Teutones did not press on towards Italy; perhaps because remnants of Carbo's army still guarded the passes. They crossed the Alps, and skirting their northern reaches, marched into Gaul, by way of the lowlands between the Jura and Vosges Mountains.[5] En route, the Celtic Tigurini of western Switzerland gave the wanderers a warm welcome. The guests boasted of their triumph against the Romans and of the treasures amassed in their epic journey. Such tales whetted the Tigurinis' taste for adventure and they decided to join the Cimbri and Teutones in their travels.

For over a year the Cimbri coalition pillaged the southern Gallic countryside but lacked the siege know-how or the required patience of a blockade to take any of the walled towns. Powerless against the mighty Cimbri and Teutones, the besieged Gauls were reduced to starvation. With hunger gnawing at their ribs, some even resorted to cannibalism of their young and old.

By 109 BC the barbarians reached the northern border of Gallia Narbonensis where their progress was blocked by a Roman army under consul M. Iunius Silanus. Barbarian envoys arrived before Silanus and asked that "the people of Mars should give them some land by way of pay and use their hands and weapons for any purpose they wished."[6] Silanus referred the matter to the Senate. In another age, Roman Emperors who lacked the manpower to protect their crumbling frontiers might have accepted such an offer but in 109 BC it was a different matter. Victorious against the armies of Greece, Spain, Carthage and Asia Minor, Rome had no need to settle such barbarous folk within the borders of its rising empire. Silanus told the barbarians that "Rome has no lands to give, and desires no services."[7] He went out to engage the intruders and was promptly defeated.

Fortunately for Rome, the barbarians did not push onward into Italy. The Cimbri and Teutones turned north to plunder Gaul while the Tigurini continued westward. Led by their young chief Divico, the Tigurini raided Roman territories along the Rhône and in 107 BC incited a revolt among the Volcae Tectosages who placed the Roman garrison of Tolosa in chains. To suppress the uprising, consul L. Cassius Longinus, commander of Narbonese Gaul, confronted and initially routed Divico. However, the Tigurini withdrawal was but a feint to waylay the pursuing legions northwest of Tolosa (around

Agen on the Garonne). Longinus and a great part of his army were slain. The Tigurini chose to spare the survivors but demanded half their valuables and a number of hostages. The legionaries were further humiliated by being forced to crawl under the yoke.

To avenge these insults and restore order in Gallia Narbonensis, the Romans raised yet another army to be placed under the command of consul Quintus Servilius Caepio. In 106 BC, Caepio somehow managed to have Divico agree to a peaceful withdrawal. Caepio recovered Tolosa with the aid of traitors inside and looted the temple treasures of the god Belis (the Celtic Apollo). The fantastic amounts of gold and silver (rumored at 100,000 lbs of gold and 110,000 lbs of silver) would have been a welcome sight in Rome, whose own treasury was drained by the wars in Africa and Gaul. Mysteriously, the treasure disappeared while on its way to Massilia. The blame was put on bandits, but not everyone was convinced. Caepio himself fell under suspicion but the attention of Rome was diverted by the renewed appearance of the Cimbri and Teutones in Narbonese Gaul in 105.

Rome scraped together an additional army to rid itself of the barbarian menace once and for all. It was led by consul Gnaeus Mallius Maximus and accompanied by a separate strong corps under legatus Marcus Aurelius Scarus. By early October, all three Roman armies gathered to await the Cimbri and Teutones on the banks of the Rhône, near Arausio (Orange). Here the river made its way through a wide valley of marshy lowlands rising to the Massif Central to the west and the Alp Mountains to the east.[8] The total Roman forces were by far the largest assembled in the barbarian wars, numbering up to 80,000 men. Caepio, now proconsul, held the east bank of the river, Maximus the west. Well ahead of Maximus, Scarus and his corps occupied a vanguard position, perhaps some fifteen miles to the north, where the valley narrowed into the Donzere Gorge.

Scarus was the first to feel the fury of the Northmen. Led by the Cimbri king, Boiorix, the barbarians tore down upon the Romans in a rough square phalanx, relying on sheer speed and ferocity to overwhelm the enemy. Like Silanus before him, Scarus saw his legions crumble in the face of the barbarian charge. Scarus' vanguard was smashed and he was thrown into chains and dragged to Boiorix's feet. The latter held council with his chiefs, contemplating on whether or not to move on into Italy. Scarus defiantly cried out that they would learn of true Roman power if they dared to cross the Alps and set foot in Italy. In answer, the barbarians ran a blade through his body.

Back at the main Roman position, Maximus ordered a reluctant Caepio to cross the Rhône with his army and join Maximus on the west side of the river. The aristocratic Caepio resented having to serve under the humbly born Maximus. Their combined armies would have greatly outnumbered the barbarians, but Caepio's thoughts teemed with jealousy. Caepio set up his legion camp afar from Maximus' and refused to obey any more orders. So vehement became their discord that the matter had to be referred to the Senate. The incapable Maximus meanwhile failed to maintain discipline over his men, who turned the camp into a bazaar.

Onto this scene marched the army of Cimbri, Teutones, and a smattering of Celtic warbands. With them were the Ambrones, a people whose sudden appearance was as mysterious as their origin. They may have been Celts, who recently joined the Cimbri and Teutones, or a heretofore-unnamed subtribe of the Teutones. Possibly they were even distantly related to the Ligurians, an ancient mountain people of the Italian and French Rivieras.

Even with the Ambrones, Boiorix's army could scarcely have numbered over 30,000 warriors. Albeit outnumbered, the barbarians' morale was high: had not four prior Roman armies succumbed to their martial might? Past victories and raids also gave the Cimbri and Teutones access to better battle gear. Sharpened wood and bone-tipped spears were cast aside, their place taken by iron weapons. Helmets and mail cuirasses were no longer rare among the rank and file. Nevertheless, the formidable size of the Roman army deeply intimidated the barbarians. Boiorix again sent envoys to request land grants, but all Maximus offered them was scorn and ridicule. Back in his own camp, Caepio wrongly feared that the negotiations were making good progress. He teemed with envy of his hated rival Maximus who would surely get the credit for the barbarians' subjugation. On October 6th Caepio hastily flung his legions at the enemy to ensure that the glory of victory would be his.

The barbarians were ready for any unexpected move by the Romans and met Caepio with a terrific attack of their own. With the Ambrones in the lead, they burst asunder the Roman lines like a battering ram. The scheming Caepio managed to escape but behind him his army was destroyed. The survivors fled toward Maximus.

Their bodies and weapons splattered with Roman blood, the berserk barbarians threw themselves upon Maximus' legionaries who had readied themselves for battle. Ahead of the barbarians ran their war dogs, huge beasts akin to the 200 pound Mastiff "Mollassers" employed by Attila in later years. Their morale having withered in face of Caepio's defeat, Maximus' legionaries were unable to withstand the barbarian onslaught. Their ranks broken, the advantage of Roman discipline was nullified. Cornered against the Rhône, there was no escape for the Romans.

When the butchery was done, tens of thousands of Roman corpses littered the battlefield. In addition to Scarus' vanguard, two complete Roman armies were destroyed. Ancient sources claimed the entire Roman army and a further 40,000 camp followers perished with only ten men escaping the carnage.

An orgy of destruction followed the battle. The barbarians had vowed to sacrifice all loot to their gods should they grant them victory. Clothing was torn to pieces, breastplates smashed, weapons broken, horses drowned in the Rhône, gold and silver thrown into the river and captives hung from trees. Priestesses in garments of white linen dispatched prisoners from the land of the living and from their blood, divined omens of the future.

Arausio was the worst Roman military defeat since Cannae. On top of the prior defeats of Carbo, Silanus and Longinus' consular armies, Arausio sent shock waves of terror through Italy. The people's unconditional belief in Roman invincibility was broken. Gaul had become a giant meat grinder into which marched one Roman army after another.

After Arausio there was no Roman army left. The passes across the Alps lay open and nothing could prevent a barbarian advance into Italy. The catastrophe rekindled nightmare memories of that black day in Roman history, when nearly three centuries ago hordes of wild Gauls sacked and burnt Rome. To the Italians it seemed as if their civilization would surely be submerged in a tide of barbarianism.

The Roman apprehensions proved unwarranted; once again the barbarians did not descend into Italy. Perhaps awed by the size of the Roman army at Arausio, they feared that even larger forces awaited them closer to Rome, or possibly there were quarrels over command. Whatever the reason, the Teutones and Ambrones continued to ransack Gaul while the Cimbri moved toward Spain. Rome was given a respite and a chance to reflect on the failure of her armies. Clearly Rome needed not just another army but new tactics and able generalship. Rome got both in the person of Gaius Marius.

As a young soldier, Marius distinguished himself in the Spanish war against Numantia. A *novus homo*, Marius had no noble linage to gain him the attention of his commanding general; his parents were laborers in a village of central Italy. Nevertheless, through sheer courage and zeal, Marius became a favorite of his commanding general, Scipio Aemilianus. Scipio not only bestowed many honors on Marius but singled him out as his possible successor. It was Scipio's encouragements, which "like a divine admonition, chiefly emboldened Marius to aspire to a political career."[9]

In 119 BC, Marius attained the tribunate in Rome, followed by the praetorship in 115. Six years later Marius served under Q. Caecilius Metellus in the war against Jugurtha, King of Numidia. In 108, Marius sacrificed animals to the Gods at Utica. The soothsayer told Marius to tempt fortune; then marvellous things would come his way. In 107, at 50 years of age, Marius reached the consulship and superseded Metellus as commander of the African army.

While still in Italy, Marius instructed his lieutenant, P. Rutilius Rufus, to raise and train a new army of volunteers and begin a series of army reforms. Marius left for Africa, where he put Jugurtha on the defensive. In 106 BC Marius brought the war to an end when, by use of treachery, Jugurtha was delivered into Roman hands. The king of Numidia was paraded in Marius' triumphal march and then executed. The people hailed Marius as their savior, believing he would deal with the Northmen as he had with Jugurtha and would triumph where the Senate's blue-blooded representatives, like Caepio, had failed. In anticipation of the barbarians' return, Marius was re-elected consul in 104, an office he held till 100.

Taking command of Rufus' new army, Marius moved it to the Rhône delta. There he completed his army reforms. While Marius inspected his new legions, his thoughts may have reflected on Marcus Furius Camillus' army reforms nearly three centuries ago. From then, until this day, the legions fought in smaller, independent maniples of 60–120 men drawn up into three lines; the *hastati* and the *principes*, which were armed with javelins and swords, and the *triarii*, which wielded thrusting spears. No longer, thought Marius. He increased the size of the maniple and grouped three of them into the powerful 600-man-strong cohort. Marius was not the first to do so, Publius Scipio having formed a three maniple cohort in the Second Punic War, but beginning with Marius the cohort became the chief tactical unit of the Roman army. The three differently named and equipped lines were gone too, henceforth all his soldiers were armed with *pilum* and *gladius*. The Eagle, sacred to Jupiter, would be their sole and sacred symbol.

Legionaries no longer were expected to provide their own equipment: now the Republic issued them their uniforms and weapons. The old legions enjoyed the support of smaller contingents of Roman light infantry and Roman cavalry. These too, Marius had done away with. His new legion consisted virtually entirely of 6,000 heavy infantry.[10] From now on, the Roman army would have to depend on foreign auxiliaries for its light infantry and cavalry – a negligence that would have dire consequences in the future.

The changes in Marius' soldiers went deeper than their organization and their equipment. When Marius looked into the eyes of his legionaries, he knew their minds no longer dwelt on their families or civilian lives. No longer were the legionaries made up of conscripted militia who awaited their annual discharge. Marius' men had volunteered for a professional military career. Their minds were focused on battle and its grim rewards of rape and plunder. Discipline, physical fitness, entrenchment and sword fighting skills all were improved. The new legions were deadlier and more powerful. They were loyal not to Rome or to the Republic, but to Marius. Reluctant to commit the treasury to the retirement of the new soldiers or to fund their upkeep while not on campaign, the Senate foolishly left them in the care of their commanding general. This too was to have disastrous consequences for the Republic's future. Marius kept his soldiers busy with rigorous training and building projects. A fortified camp was built and a canal dug that bypassed the shallow Rhône delta, easing the transport of supplies to the army.

In the meantime, the Cimbri crossed the Pyrenees into Spain. Unable to subdue the tough Celt-Iberians, the Cimbri were sent reeling back north along the Bay of Biscay toward the Seine. At the border of the Belgae, the Cimbri rejoined with the Teutones, Ambrones and Tigurini. Although a few of the Cimbri and Teutones settled in the Belgae realm, the wandering barbarians were unable to gain more lands or loot from the powerful Belgic tribes.

In 103 BC the barbarian coalition once again advanced on Italy. This time the invasion was to be a two pronged attack. King Teutobod led the Teutones and Ambrones down the Rhône valley. A giant of a man, he towered over his own countrymen and was said to be able to leap over six horses tied breast to breast. Simultaneously King Boiorix and the Cimbri struck out for Italy via the Brenner Pass. The Tigurini remained behind as a reserve force in the Norican Alps.

Teutobod had the shortest route so that he was the first to threaten Italy. He crossed the upper Rhône in 102 BC, marching south until he found Marius waiting for him on the banks of the Isère. The latter had hastened there to entrench his army and prevent a barbarian breakthrough into Liguria and Etruria. Marius chose not to oppose the barbarian passage across the Isère and remained on the defensive. Once across the river, the barbarians wasted no time in assaulting the Romans. But the Romans held the higher ground and from their fortifications easily repulsed the headstrong barbarians with missile fire. Infuriated, the Northmen attacked twice more with no more success. Unable to dislodge the Romans or draw them into an open fight, Teutobod called off the attack.

The barbarian caravan ambled past the Roman camp, taunting their enemy for being cowards and shouting with laughter, "if the Romans had any messages for their wives for they [the barbarians] would soon be with them."[11] The insults were not without affect and Marius was hard put to restrain his men. Marius' defensive posture proved to be a prudent choice. Had he faced the barbarians in open battle, his untried soldiers may well have scattered at the first barbarian onrush. Instead he inflicted a few casualties and more importantly, familiarized his men with the enemy and showed them that the flaxen haired giants were not unbeatable.

The barbarians trekked down the Rhône toward the coastal road. On their heels came Marius and his legions. Each day, at the crack of dawn, the blare of horns awoke the sleeping legionaries. After a spartan breakfast of bread and water, the soldiers took down the tents and loaded up the wagons with equipment. Fully armored and armed, carrying a heavy pack with cooking gear and personal items, the legionaries were ready to march.

The legionaries' leather sandals ate up the miles. Thick soles, strengthened with 120 iron nails, protected the legionaries' feet as they walked over hard ground. After they waded through streams, the sandals quickly dried in the hot sun. Under good conditions Marius' legionaries could cover up to 15 miles a day, always entrenching themselves for the night.

Marius' legions easily outmaneuvered the cumbersome wagon train of the barbarians, so that they reached the neighborhood of Aquae Sextiae (Aix) before them. Here Marius occupied a strong position on the slopes of the Pourrières hills, about 13 miles east of Aquae Sextiae. Below him, to the south, the headwaters of the River Arc meandered through a plain. Soon after, the barbarians arrived and camped on the opposite side of the valley; the Ambrones aside the stream and the Teutones further away, near woodlands that reached down from the slopes.

Marius knew that with the Alps, and beyond them Rome, drawing closer, the time had come to confront the barbarians. Nevertheless, he still feared an open battle. To hold back his overeager men, Marius insisted that the camp first be properly fortified before any engagement. His men obeyed, albeit reluctantly. The day was hot and the proud Romans did not see why the barbarians should hold the stream while they themselves should suffer from thirst on the dry hillside.

The lack of water for both men and horses prompted a throng of camp servants to descend to the Arc. Here a multitude of barbarian families had waded to the Roman side, playing and bathing in the water. Upon the arrival of the Roman camp servants, a shouting match erupted. Lethargic from heavy drink and feasting, the barbarian warriors gathered their weapons. They rhythmically clashed their arms and leaping to the sound shouted their tribal name "Ambrones". Above on the hillside, the Romans worried about the safety of their servants, for large numbers of Ambrones crossed the stream to join their fellows. Disregarding Marius' orders his auxiliary Ligurian light infantry strode down to the stream.

A near comical situation now occurred. The Ligurians, who called themselves Ambrones by descent, resented the "barbarians" shouting "their" name and tried to outdo the latter by taking up the cry themselves! Both parties worked themselves to a pitch until the enraged Ligurians rushed upon the Ambrones. Abashed by the show of Ligurian bravery, the Romans joined the battle. Charging down the hillside, they plowed into the battle below and forced both friend and foe into the river. The barbarians were chopped down in droves so that the "Romans drank quite as much barbarian gore as water from the blood-stained stream."[12] The battle continued onto the far bank and beyond until the barbarians were driven back to their camp.

The Ambrones women cursed and yelled at their men for being cowards. With bare hands they futilely defended themselves against the Romans, trying to tear away their shields or grasp their swords while being hacked to pieces. After a great slaughter the Romans withdrew back across the stream to their original position on the hillside, presumably because of the approach of the Teutones.

Night shrouded the valley from which, like a banshee's cry, rose the haunting wailing of the barbarian women lamenting their dead. Their cries of grief and threats froze the blood of the Latins, who feared a night assault. But no attack came at night or the following day, which saw the barbarians marshal their forces.

Marius used the lull to send Claudius Marcellus[13] with 3,000 men to work his way around to the enemy rear. Marcellus' route would take him through the woodlands that grew behind the Teutones' camp. Accompanying Marcellus were camp followers and pack animals. When the time came, they would make Marcellus' small force seem larger than it really was. For now, however,

Marcellus wished to remain unseen and probably crossed upriver where glens and ravines hid his approach.

At dawn the next day, Marius sent his cavalry down into the plain to skirmish with the barbarians and to incite them into combat. Behind the cavalry, the legions left their camp and formed an orderly line along the hillside. The barbarians needed no further enticement than seeing their hated enemy in the open. The Teutones brushed aside the Roman cavalry and with a howl rushed towards the legions. The run uphill slowed down the Teutones' charge; a volley of Roman javelins stopped them in their tracks.

The Roman shield wall stood unbroken and the legionaries' short swords reaped a terrible toll. When the sheer strain of battle demanded a lull in the fighting, each side momentarily backed off to draw their breath. The Romans used such times to withdraw fatigued troops and feed fresh ones into the front lines, a task more difficult for their undisciplined and outnumbered foes. The merciless heat of the sun further sapped the strength of the Teutones. With Marius fighting side by side with his men, the Romans steadily pushed the barbarians down into the plain. Around midday the Teutones were about to reform their lines, possibly for another charge, when shouting and commotion erupted from their rear.

Marcellus had bided his time well, waiting in the woods for an opportune moment. Now with the barbarians pushed closer to the woods, Marcellus struck. Caught off guard, the rearward barbarians panicked and crowded into the front-line ranks. Teutobod's army collapsed into total confusion but nonetheless fought on to the bitter end.

Together with the Ambrones, over 50,000 barbarian men, women and children were killed or captured. Legend has it that the people of Massilia fenced their vineyards with the bones of the fallen and that the soil became rich with the putrefied matter that sank into it. Teutobod escaped but was later seized by vengeful Gauls. Turned over to the Romans, the tall king ended up a striking figure in Marius' triumphal procession.[14] After Marius' soldiers pilfered the barbarians' camp, the excess loot was piled according to Roman custom into a huge mound. Marius applied the torch, the flames leapt to the heavens, and his legions let loose a deafening roar of approval.

The Romans had won a great victory but their celebration was cut short. A few days later, news arrived of a second Roman army's inability to arrest the Cimbri's advance into Italy. Shrugging off snow storms and bitter cold, Boiorix had led his people unopposed over the Alps. In the spring of 102 BC, they descended toward the Italian plain along the valley of the River Adige (the Athesis). Ahead of the Cimbri moved the Roman legions, commanded by proconsul Quintus Lutatius Catulus. Catulus had foolishly abandoned the passes because he feared being outflanked in unfamiliar territory.

Below Tridentum, Catulus built strong fortifications on either side of the Adige to check the enemy's crossing. When the barbarians saw this they began to damn the stream.

> "Like giants of old, they tore away the neighboring hills and flung into the river fragments of cliffs and mountains of earth. Whole trees with their roots were sent whirling down the stream to pound against the bridge which quivered with their blows."[15]

The legionaries trembled in fear at the sight of the Northmen's display of primeval strength. Of the old school and unaware of Marius' victory at Aquae Sextiae, the Roman soldiers lost heart and fled. Unable to restore morale, Catulus decided to join them and at least ensure an orderly retreat. To cover the withdrawal, a small but determined rearguard remained to hold the Roman fort. They put up a gallant but futile defense. Deeply impressed, the Cimbri chivalrously not only spared the survivors but let them go free on parole.

Catulus continued his retreat, crossing the Adige near Verona. He did not halt until he reached the Po's southern shore, where he encamped for the winter. Although Catulus thus left Italy north of the Po at the mercy of the barbarians, his stand on the river effectively deterred their southward march. The Cimbri moved west along the Po's north bank, pillaging the rich countryside. Here they spent a carefree winter, enjoying the unaccustomed comforts of roofed shelters, warm baths and wine, along with plentiful bread and cooked meats.

When Marius arrived in Rome he refused his triumphal march in the light of the Cimbri's presence in northern Italy. He summoned his victorious legions from Gaul and joined them with Catulus' army. In the summer of 101 BC, the combined Roman armies of 52,300 men crossed the Po and moved westward to confront the Cimbri at Vercellae.

Boiorix, who at most had 20,000 warriors, did not know of the Teutones' defeat and was still waiting for them. To gain time he sent ambassadors to negotiate with Marius. The ambassadors demanded lands and cities for the Cimbri and their brethren, the Teutones. Marius retorted with a scoff: "Don't trouble yourself about your brethren, for they have land and they will have it forever – land which we have given them,"[16] and then called for the chiefs of the Teutones, laden in chains, to be brought forward. Angered by the show of Roman arrogance, Boiorix himself rode up to the Roman camp for "the barbarians had no trace of fear."[17] He challenged Marius to pick a time and place for battle and fight for the rule of the country. Marius answered that in three days the Romans would await the Cimbri on the Raudian plain.

The Romans were the first to arrive on the plain. Catulus' army of 20,300 men held the center and Marius' 32,000 men formed the left and right wings. The Roman army lined up facing west. The rising sun at their backs, "the sky seemed to be on fire with the glint reflected from the bronze of the Roman helmets."[18] Anticipating that the barbarians would charge straight for the Roman center, Marius planned for Catulus' less experienced men to fall back while his two wings would fold inward. The enemy would be caught in a gigantic Roman vice and eliminated.

The Romans remained in front of their camp to await the barbarians. The Cimbri were drawing nearer, with their infantry on their left and their cavalry on their right. The latter now formed a sizeable contingent and was splendidly equipped. Their helmets resembled the heads of wild beasts or creatures of legend and, adorned with crests of feathers, made them seem taller than they already were. Breastplates of iron protected their bodies and they carried gleaming white shields. Each cavalry man had two lances and a large, heavy sword.

Instead of their expected head-on charge, Boiorix came up with his own ruse. Assembled in a huge square, the Cimbri infantry slowly advanced toward Marius' right wing. The Cimbri cavalry now sprinted ahead of their infantry, then swerved right and skirmished along Catulus' lines. When the Romans in reply threw their javelins, the Cimbri cavalry hastily retreated to give the impression of a rout. Catulus' soldiers sensed an easy victory. They ignored the shouts of their commanders, who ordered them to hold ranks, and recklessly chased after the barbarian cavalry.

Boiorix's stratagem had worked, for by moving ahead of Marius' left and right wings, Catulus' center exposed its right flank to the barbarian infantry which now swerved right and broke into a charge. Marius at once perceived the danger and ordered the Roman wings forward.

The battle might have gone badly for the Romans but for the dry condition on the plains. The galloping of the horses and the march of thousands of infantry units stirred up tremendous clouds of dust, aggravated by a westward blowing wind. Blinded by the dust and the rising sun, the Cimbri infantry failed to scatter Catulus' units and a confused melee erupted.

Under the hot Italian sun, Catulus' legionaries held their ground against the Cimbri who soon sweated and breathed heavily. Marius' wings likewise lost themselves within the dusty haze and wandered aimlessly on the plain. The Roman left wing then came into contact with the Cimbri cavalry. The startled Cimbri horsemen were driven back upon the right flank of their infantry brethren. The resulting chaos decisively tipped the scales in the Roman favor.

Although the sources are unclear on the matter, it is likely that Marius' right wing joined the battle by striking the barbarian left flank. Within the Roman ring of iron, the exhausted barbarians were cut down to a man. Boiorix fell fighting at the forefront of his men, the slain Romans at his feet a grim testimony to his valor. The Cimbri war dogs valiantly stood guard over their master's bodies and continued the battle until they joined them in death.

A handful of Cimbri warriors who escaped the slaughter fled to their camp and, with their women, hastily erected a barricade of wagons. Onward came the legions, eager to claim their rewards of rape and plunder. But the barbarian women were no docile housewives or maidens of the civilized world. Like a lioness fights to the death for her cubs, so the Cimbri women fought for their children. From their higher positions, with axe and spear, they held the enemy at bay till at last the legionaries overcame the barricades. Mad with vengeance and bloodlust, the Romans scalped the women to mutilate their appearance. Terrified of the Roman brutality and a life of slavery, the women turned their swords on themselves and their infants. Others hanged themselves the night after they had passed into captivity.

When it was all over the slaughter equaled that of Aquae Sextiae. Tens of thousands of Cimbri lay dead and thousands were headed for the slave markets of Rome. As for the Tigurini, who were still in the Norican Alps, they abandoned their planned inroads into Italy and retired to their homelands. After twelve years of warfare and over seven major engagements, the northern menace was finally eliminated.

In Rome the significance of the victory was overshadowed by a renewal of the political quarrels between the Senate and the people. The aristocratic Catulus claimed that he, and not Marius, the "novus homo", brought about the Roman victory. The people would have none of it. To the vexation of Catulus and the Senate, Marius was hailed as the third founder of Rome and rewarded with his unprecedented sixth consulship. The people's sentiments were justified. It is doubtful that Catulus' men would have triumphed without the presence of Marius' forces and it was Marius who alone triumphed at Aquae Sextiae.

Remnants of both the Cimbri and the Teutones survived on the Danish coast and among the Belgae. They forever ingrained the Roman mind with a special dread of those savages lurking beyond the northern borders, waiting to breach the frontier defenses and to reduce the civilization of the Empire to ruins and ashes.

Chapter Eight

The Helvetii Invasion of Gaul, Caesar's First Great Battle

"It was the traditional custom of the Helvetii to demand hostages of others, but never to give them – as the Romans had good cause to know."[1]

Helvetii war chief Divico's warning to Caesar

After its belated triumph over the Cimbri and Teutones menace, the venerable Roman Republic entered into its twilight century. Rome's cold indifference to her Italian allies' demands for equality provoked the Italian Wars (91–88 BC) which in turn set the stage for a series of civil wars. Gaius Marius, once hailed as the third founder of Rome, besieged Rome in 87. His seizure of the city was marked by a reign of terror. Marius' men butchered Rome's leading aristocracy in a bloody frenzy. The bodies of the victims were decapitated and the heads displayed in the Forum. After declaring his seventh consulship in 86 BC, Marius died of an illness at the age of 70. Revolts in northern Italy and in Spain led by Roman generals and the slave uprising of Spartacus (including survivors of the Cimbri wars) in the 70s further tore at the withering spine of the Republic.

Externally, Rome triumphed in Asia Minor over the formidable Mithridates, King of Pontus, cementing her hold over the Mediterranean. Italian military pensioners settled on provincial land grants. The city of Rome swelled to a population of around 750,000, 100,000 of which were slaves. The numerous poor lived in squalid tenements, kept satiated physically with a free grain ration and mentally with the chariot races and the slaughter of the gladiatorial and wild animal fights. Lavish villas and building projects reflected the vast wealth concentrated into the hands of the first multimillionaires. These urban-based real estate tycoons appropriated the choicest land at home and abroad. The workers who toiled on the land were a combination of free men and armies of slaves captured during Rome's wars. Lesser family houses became the *clientela* of the greater ones. Corruption and violence in the streets became the order of the day.

It was in this period of political turmoil and in the beginning of the opulence and the grandeur of the future Imperial Rome that Gaius Julius Caesar became among the foremost politicians in Rome. Caesar's prestigious family claimed descent from the founder of Alba Longa, one of earliest and legendary settlements of the Tiber valley. His aunt was the wife of Gaius Marius, a relationship which gained Caesar political clout as well as enemies.

Surviving prosecution by anti-Marian factions, Caesar rapidly climbed the Roman political ladder. He served as quaestor (financial magistrate), aedile (temple, street and grain supply administrator), Pontifex Maximus (chief priest of Rome) and praetor (justice magistrate) before attaining the consulship in 59 BC at 41 years of age. That year he masterminded the first Triumvirate between himself, the affluent Marcus Licinius Crassus and the brilliant general Gnaeus Pompeius Magnus. The Triumvirate all but dictated the Senate of the Republic. However, its members were uneasy allies. Each suspicious of the others, all three were caught in a deadly power play to retain or extend their political influence in Rome.

To compete with Pompey and Crassus, Caesar needed troops loyal to him and also needed military triumphs. Although he had led victorious, albeit minor campaigns, against the hill tribes and pirates of Spain, his primary battlefield had been the political arena of Rome. His military exploits paled in comparison to those of Pompey. Caesar's chance came when the Helvetii appeared on the doorstep of Gallia Narbonensis, one of the three provinces, along with Gallia Cisalpina and Illyricum, of which Caesar currently was proconsul.

A Celtic people, the Helvetii originally hailed from southern Germany. Dislodged by Germanic tribes from the north, the Helvetii settled into the area of western Switzerland. But the German pressure did not cease so that in 61 BC the Helvetii towns and villages again stirred with talk of migration. One of their chiefs, the charismatic Orgetorix, proclaimed that all of Gaul would surely fall beneath the armed might of the Helvetii.

Orgetorix's words were no mere boasts. Much of Gaul, especially the lands that bordered Roman Narbonensis and Cisalpina Gaul, had become semi-civilized. Roman wine flowed north in exchange for raw materials and slaves. In the Gallic *oppida*, or fortified towns, pottery, glasswork and metallurgy flourished on an industrial scale. But the luxuries of civilization had softened the once barbaric Gauls. The Helvetii, by comparison, remained hardened due to their constant warfare with the Germans.

The Helvetii allotted themselves two years to gather provisions of wheat, draught-cattle and carts for the arduous journey. When the time came, in 58 BC,

Orgetorix was no longer with them. Overly ambitious, he aspired to become king, although the Helvetii, like most of Gaul, had come to despise monarchies and were now governed by elected tribal magistrates. Put on trial, Orgetorix chose to commit suicide rather than risk the punishment of being burnt alive.

Orgetorix's death did not dampen his peoples' resolve to find greener lands elsewhere. Billowing smoke clouds rose behind lumbering caravans of wagons, livestock, horsemen and foot folk. In a testament to their determination never to return, the Helvetii set fire to their own fortress towns and hundreds of their villages.[2] Their ultimate goal was the Atlantic coast and the fertile lands of the Santones.

The Helvetii would not be alone in their trek. Joining them were like-minded smaller tribes on the Helvetii border, the Rauraci, the Latobrigi and the Tulingi, and one of Rome's most stubborn foes, the Boii. The Boii had been fighting Romans since 283 BC when they began a bitter struggle with Rome from their Cisalpina homelands. Eventually driven out of their lands by the Romans, the Boii drifted east to Bohemia and the Danube. Over a century later, large numbers of them struck westward again to meet up with the Helvetii.

The exact numbers of the Helvetii confederation will never be known. Caesar claimed they consisted of 386,000 men, women and children with a fighting strength of 92,000; surely an exaggeration. Given the primitive roads through Gaul and the relatively sparsely inhabited countryside, this number is impossibly high. It would have necessitated a marching column over a hundred miles long, one that would have been utterly incapable of supplying itself by forage in the surrounding countryside. Other numbers, both of classical and modern historians, vary widely from an acceptance of Caesar's estimate to a mere fighting strength of 12,000 Helvetii warriors. The latter number seems too low, but it is doubtful that the Helvetii and their allies numbered over 90,000 people. Perhaps 25,000 would have been warriors, though not all in their prime years.[3]

The Helvetii could enter Gaul by the means of two routes. One way was the bridge across the Rhône at Geneva. Geneva dominated the lake outlet from a hill on the Rhône's southern bank. Dating back to back to pre-Celtic Ligurian times, Geneva had been a settlement of the Allobroges for five centuries. Near the end of the second century BC, Geneva became part of the Roman province of Gallia Narbonensis. The other route, between the Jura range and the River Rhône, into Sequani lands was narrow and mountainous and easily defended by the Sequani and by the large forces of Germans who had settled there.

The Helvetii choose to face the Romans rather than the Sequani and Germans. They hoped that the Allobroges would revolt against their Roman masters. If they did not, the Helvetii would simply intimidate the Allobroges into allowing the migrants passage through the land. On 28 March 58 BC, the Helvetii assembled on the Rhône opposite Geneva but to their dismay found the Romans prepared for their arrival.

Caesar heard of the imminent Helvetii invasion while at Rome. To counter their formidable army, Caesar had but a single legion in Gallia Narbonensis. This was the Tenth Legion, which was destined to become the most famed legion in Roman history. By litter or chariot, taking naps while on the road, Caesar hastened to Geneva from Rome in a single week. He recruited what auxiliary troops he could and ordered the Tenth Legion to destroy the bridge over the Rhône. Caesar was turning out to be as energetic a commander as he had been a politician. The military life in the crisp clean air of the countryside, away from the cluttered streets of Rome, toughened his tall gaunt frame.

At Geneva, the destroyed bridge and the presence of Roman troops came as a rude surprise to the Helvetii. On 5 April they sent embassies to Caesar requesting a peaceful march through the province. Caesar had no intention of granting their request. Whatever the true intentions of the Helvetii, to feed themselves and their livestock, they would have to plunder the countryside they passed through. Caesar shrewdly delayed his answer till 13 April. He used the time to block the Rhône valley with 19 miles of fortifications including a trench and a 16-foot high wall.

When 13 April arrived, Caesar flatly denied the Helvetii entrance. Consequently, by day and by night, the Helvetii attempted to ford the Rhône in the river's shallows. At other points they tied boats together to make crude rafts, but nowhere could they breach the Roman defenses. Although outnumbered, Caesar was able to rapidly concentrate his 6,000 troops at areas under attack. The Helvetii abandoned their plans to journey through Gallia Narbonensis. Instead they successfully appealed to the Sequani, and presumably their German overlords, to grant them safe passage through Sequani territory.

The new route took the Helvetii through free Celtic nations. Their ultimate destination, the lands of the Santones, was further away from the Romans than the original Helvetii homelands. The Helvetii migration was thus no longer of any concern to the Romans. Yet Caesar still coveted a decisive military confrontation. He preposterously declared that the Helvetii would end up dangerously close to the northwestern border of Gallia Narbonensis. To stop them, he left for Gallia Cisalpina leaving the Tenth Legion at Geneva under the command of legate Titus Labienus. In Gallia Cisalpina, Caesar enrolled two new legions and joined these with a further three stationed at Aquileia. In total, including Roman auxiliaries, this gave Caesar an army of over 30,000.

The Helvetii meanwhile had traveled through the Sequani territory. Probably because they were short on supplies, the Helvetii ravaged the Allobroges villages to the north of the Rhône and the Aedui lands on the Saône's (the Arar) eastern bank. To the rescue of these tribes came Caesar with his legions.

Caesar's journey was not without mishap. While taking the shortest route, the road from Ocelum across the Western Alps, his army was assailed by rebellious mountain tribes: the Ceutrones, Graioceli and Caturiges. Yet these minor tribes could do little more than harass the legions and were easily repulsed.

After crossing the River Isère, Caesar met up with Labienus and the Tenth Legion. At Lyon he received embassies from the Allobroges and the Aedui. They told him that the Helvetii were presently crossing the Saône River just north of the city.

At once Caesar set off towards the Saône. There his scouts reported that three quarters of the Helvetii coalition had already crossed the sluggish river. The section that remained was the bulk of the Tigurini, one of the four Helvetii cantons. Caesar was not about to miss an opportunity to catch a divided enemy. He sent Titus Labienus ahead with three veteran legions to hasten to the barbarian crossing. Labienus caught the Tigurini completely off guard. Heavily loaded with supplies and about to cross the river, the barbarians broke with barely a fight. Most were put to the sword while a few escaped into the nearby woods.[4]

Wasting little time Caesar had pontoon bridges constructed across the Saône, possibly with his three unengaged legions. The combined legions then set off in pursuit after the main Helvetii host, which headed north along the river. The Helvetii became alarmed at the speed of Caesar's approach, for it had taken him a single day to cross the river while they, with their noncombatants, cumbersome wagons and livestock, had required twenty days. Helvetii deputies arrived at the Roman camp led by Divico, the grizzled Helvetii war chief, who forty-nine years ago annihilated a Roman army near Tolosa.

Divico stated that if left in peace the Helvetii would settle wherever Caesar should desire. However, if the Romans sought war then they should not let the defeat of the Tigurini lead to overconfidence. The Tigurini, after all, were caught unawares and away from their countrymen. He advised Caesar "to remember the earlier disaster of the Roman people [their defeat near Tolosa] and the ancient valor of the Helvetii."[5]

Caesar was not about to be dictated by a barbarian. He replied that neither he nor the Roman people had forgotten their defeat by the Helvetii and the need for vengeance. If this were not reason enough to fight the Helvetii, then what of the atrocities inflicted upon Rome's friends, the Aedui and Allobroges? In spite of these ample reasons to make war on the Helvetii, Caesar swore that he would still accept a peace. In return the Helvetii would deliver hostages to him and make full reparations to the Aedui and Allobroges.

In essence Caesar demanded that the Helvetii submit to Roman authority. As for the loot taken from the Aedui and Allobroges, much of it was taken to fulfil basic supply needs and would be impossible to return. Predictably, proud Divico answered that the Helvetii received but did not offer hostages, as the Romans well knew.

Divico returned to the Helvetii who continued northward. Caesar sent his entire 4,000-strong cavalry to monitor their movements. Caesar's cavalry was made up of auxiliary troops drafted from the provinces, from the Aedui and from other allied tribes. Riding too close to the enemy, Caesar's cavalry enticed the Helvetii into a combat. Boldly, 500 horsemen of the Helvetii rearguard rode to meet the enemy and fighting on favorable ground routed Caesar's entire cavalry. Elated by their victory, the horsemen galloped on towards the main Roman army and skirmished around its perimeter. Caesar refused to give them battle and doggedly continued to follow the main Helvetii procession, which now moved westward and away from the Saône.

The commander who had begun the retreat of Caesar's cavalry in the engagement above was Dumnorix, the leader of the Aedui contingent. As it turned out, Dumnorix was actually a Helvetii supporter. A foresighted individual, Dumnorix felt it was better to be conquered by other Celts than Romans. He correctly feared that the Romans were a threat to all of free Gaul. Clearly Dumnorix's presence jeopardized the reliability of Caesar's entire cavalry corps. However, because Dumnorix's brother was Diviciacus, an influential and pro-Roman Chief of the Aedui and druid (high priest), Caesar could do little but keep a close eye on Dumnorix.

A fortnight later, the Roman scouts reported that the Helvetii had camped below a hillside. Caesar attempted to surround the enemy at night. The initial deployment went well. With two legions, Caesar crept around one flank of the Helvetii. Labienus with another two legions ascended the summit of a hill that overlooked the other barbarian flank. At dawn, a Roman scout commander from Caesar's legions spotted Labienus' legions holding the high ground on the hill.

The commander mistakenly thought that Labienus' legions were enemy troops and informed Caesar that the Helvetii held the hill. Due to this misinformation the attack was called off.

The Helvetii moved on, closely shadowed by Caesar. The next night the Romans camped near today's Toulon-sur-Arroux, while only separated from the barbarians by a few miles. The following day Caesar decided to veer off toward Bibracte, the main Aedui town. His Gallic allies had failed to bring him promised supplies and he desperately needed to restock on wheat.

To the Helvetii it seemed that the confidence of the Romans was wavering. Perhaps they were aware of Caesar's supply problems and wished to cut off their foes from Bibracte. The Helvetii now decided to give battle and caught up with the Romans in the valley of the Auzon Brook, around present day Amercy. They began to skirmish with the Roman rearguard but were temporarily checked by the Roman cavalry. Meanwhile Caesar drew up his four veteran legions in three echelons half way up the western slope of the valley. To his rear, on the ridge, he stationed the two newly enlisted legions and behind them the untrustworthy auxiliaries. To equalize the danger to all and prevent any thought of flight, he sent away his own horse and those of his lieutenants. Like common soldiers, the legati and the tribunes would fight on foot.

At the same time the Helvetii set up camp in the valley bottom, to the right of the Romans on the hillside. Leaving their women and children behind a barricade of wagons, the Celtic warriors assembled in a dense line. A feeble charge by the Roman cavalry was easily brushed aside. The Helvetii, Rauraci and Latobrigi led the attack. The Boii and Tulingi remained as a reserve in front of the wagon camp. Onward the barbarians marched until they faced the awaiting lines of Roman infantry on the hillside above.

Those legions presented a daunting sight for the motley barbarian horde. Drawn up in lines of centuries (usually 80 strong), maniples (two centuries) and cohorts (three maniples) the legion was the epitome of military discipline. They were armed to the teeth with the Spanish short sword (the gladius), two javelins (the pila), their oval laterally-curved shields, a bronze plumed helmet and a mail hauberk. Mounted on a standard, their silver Eagle, "the god of the legions," soared above the men. The eagle was the physical embodiment of their strength and courage and served as a focal point for the lesser bronze animal standards of the cohorts.

The close-cropped and clean-cut legionaries were not only well armed and disciplined but also superbly drilled in the use of their weapons and kept fit through excruciating forced marches, running and swimming. On them hinged

Caesar's fate as a commander and his future in Rome. This would be his first major battle, one that would make or break his reputation. Fortunately for him, the odds were slightly in his favor. He had four veteran legions of 20,000 men who occupied the higher ground and together with his two green legions and auxiliaries enjoyed at least a marginal numerical superiority.

Compared to the enemy on the hill, the Celtic rank and file was poorly equipped. They had little protection other than wattle shields, although their chiefs sported bronze cuirasses and helmets adorned with extravagant horns or feathers. Many Celts fought stripped to the waist, in a show of true bravery and oneness with the elements of nature that figured so prominently in Celtic spirituality.

For the Helvetii the battle decided their future as a people. The warriors who faced the Romans knew that defeat would mean almost certain death or life long slavery, not only for themselves but also for their families.[6] But the Helvetii had vanquished Rome's legions before and they could do so again. The legionaries might have been drilled into the finest heavy infantry of the ancient world but they were still civilized men. In their hearts lurked a primeval fear of the tall and brawny barbarians who in the past had humbled Rome's might.

In a huge disorderly phalanx the Helvetii, accompanied by wild shouts and boasts, moved uphill against their foes. A volley of javelins erupted from the Romans. The javelins tore into the Helvetii masses and stopped the barbarian advance cold. The din of the Roman trumpeters and horn blowers resounded along the Roman lines. With a shout, Caesar initiated the advance. He fought on foot, alongside his legionaries who drew their swords and charged. Many a barbarian faced them bare-bodied and unprotected, forced to cast away his javelin-pierced shield. Slowly the iron line of the Roman legions pressed back the barbarians, trampling the bodies of the fallen, across the Auzon and up the opposite side of the valley.

For a short while the battle calmed down as the exhausted barbarians retired further up the hillside. But now the fresh Boii and Tulingi surged at the exposed Roman right flank. Their attack revived the morale of their kinsmen on the hillside, who pressed forward with renewed vengeance. In a brilliant display of Roman discipline, the first two lines of the legions faced the oncoming main body while the third wheeled to engage the Boii and Tulingi.

The battle on the hillside was long and hard, lasting from noon until dusk. Urged on by their unforgiving and battle hardened centurions, the legionaries firmly held out against the barbarian wave that bore down the hillside. Fighting in line, with their short cut-and-thrust swords, two or even three Romans were able to engage a single barbarian, who needed more room to swing his longsword. When the legionaries in combat began to tire, fresh ranks from the rear would take their place. With such training and tactics, the legionaries slowly but surely forced the enemy back up the slope.

The Boii and Tulingi put up an equally tenacious fight. But like their brethren on the hillside, they could not breach the Roman lines and slowly battled their way back to the wagon camp. Here from behind the wagon barricades, the women and children joined the fray and hurled spears and darts upon the Romans. The cries and heroism of their women and children reinvigorated the Boii and Tulingi warriors who fought on with desperate courage. Not until midnight did the Romans take the last of the wagon ramparts.

When finally Celtic resistance broke on both fronts, less than half of them were left alive. The remainder withdrew from the battle but there was no panic-stricken rout. The survivors force-marched through the rest of the night, till three days later they reached the borders of the Lingones. They had left behind their wagons and belongings. No Roman followed them. The Romans were too busy healing their wounded and burying their dead who littered the valley, the hillsides, the brook and the destroyed wagon barricade. Amongst them lay some 40,000 dead Helvetii, men, women and children.

Caesar sent messages to the Lingones that they were to give no assistance to the Helvetii or face the wrath of Rome. Without supplies the Helvetii were soon reduced to misery. With tears in their eyes, these once proud people begged Caesar for peace. This Caesar granted, on his original demand of hostages and that the Helvetii turn in deserters, presumably from his auxiliaries, who had run over to the Helvetii. The bulk of the Helvetii agreed, with the exception of the Verbigene canton. Mistrustful of the Romans they made an unsuccessful dash for the German border. Caesar ordered the Gallic tribes that lay on the Verbigene path to the Rhine to catch the escapees. The hapless Verbigene were brought before Caesar who now treated them as enemies, which doubtlessly meant slavery.

Caesar was unusually generous to the remainder of the Helvetii. The Helvetii, Tulingi and Latobrigi were to return to their homelands and were to be provisioned by the Allobroges. There the Helvetii were to rebuild their burned homes. Caesar's leniency was partially due to his fear that German tribes would occupy the empty Helvetii lands. It also increased his prestige among the Gauls.

Remarkably, the Aedui petitioned Caesar to let the Boii contingent settle among them and this Caesar granted.

Caesar's victory over the Helvetii was well received by the bulk of the Gallic tribes. Envoys arrived from all over Gaul, who wholeheartedly thanked Caesar for saving Gaul from the scourge of the Helvetii. Caesar claimed and widely publicized that he had destroyed nearly a quarter of a million of the enemy. To many a Gaul he appeared not as a conqueror but as their savior. Notably, he achieved this victory with only his four veteran legions. His two green legions and the auxiliaries remained in reserve during the entire battle, although their mere presence must have weighed on Helvetii morale.

When he had first received the proconsulship of Gallia Narbonensis and Gallia Cisalpina, Caesar by no means envisioned himself as a conqueror of all of Gaul. It was during his battles with the Helvetii, that Caesar's shrewd opportunistic mind realized that Gaul was ripe for the taking. Beset with internal squabbles and external enemies, Gaul cried out for a savior and unifying force. His victory over the Helvetii put Caesar in a perfect position to become that savior and bring Gaul under Roman rule. Unconquerable in battle and a wise and just victor, Caesar won the respect and admiration of many Gallic tribes.

Yet the conquest of Gaul was anything but assured. Other tribes, especially those farther away from the Roman borders, would offer bitter resistance. Nor was Caesar the only one who desired the lands of Gaul. Soon after the Helvetii crisis, a delegation of Gallic chieftains led by Diviciacus pleaded with Caesar to deliver them from the tyranny of the German king Ariovistus.

While Caesar marched on to new martial glories, the Helvetii, as a free people faded from the limelight of history. Upon the remnant Helvetii Caesar bestowed the title "allies of the Roman people". Roman colonies and subjugation soon followed. In time Rome pushed her frontiers north across the Alps to the Danube, absorbing the Helvetii, once among Rome's staunchest foes, into her empire.

Chapter Nine

Ariovistus, King of the Suebi

"No one has ever fought me without bringing destruction upon himself."[1]
Ariovistus, King of the Suebi

East of the Rhine the horizon melted away in a dark green sea of trees upon which, so the legends told, giants piled up ranges of rugged hills. The pastures and ploughed fields, the scattered homesteads and hamlets, that marked the hand of man, were islands in a seemingly unending wilderness of swamps and forests. Only the raven's caw, the grunt of a bear, the howl of the wolf, or the bellow of the "aurochs", the great wild bull, broke the silence of the primordial forest.

A deer in a meadow stomped its hooves to warn the rest of the herd, and then bolted into the safety of the thickets. A handful of tall men filed into the clearing. Furs or short rectangular cloaks covered the chest and shoulders of their near-naked bodies. In their tribal tradition, they wore their flaxen and red hair sideways, in a stiff backward knot. The spears and shields they carried marked them as warriors and everything in their lithe stride, their appearance and their bearing marked them as much part of the natural world as the wild beasts with which they shared their domain.

The above scene of warriors recreates what part of the vanguard of 15,000 Germanic Suebi may have looked like. Along with warriors from lesser Germanic tribes and perhaps the odd Celtic or even Slavic tribes, they gathered from their villages to wander beneath green boughs to the banks of the Rhine. They were Suebi, and their mighty tribal confederation stretched from between the Rhine and the Danube, east all the way to and up the Elbe River, exerting pressure on Gaul and on the Alpine Helvetii.

Although Germanic tribesmen were known, and feared, by the Romans ever since the invasion of the Cimbri and Teutones over half a century earlier, it was Caesar's writings which first provided a clearer picture of the tribes and their homeland. Unfortunately, that picture was purposefully distorted by Caesar for his own political ends. Caesar deliberately accentuated the savage, warlike nature of the Germanic tribes and continually inflated their numbers. His propaganda, coupled with the still relatively recent memories of the Cimbri and Teutones, drew on and heightened Rome's fear of the Germans. More importantly for Caesar, it helped secure funds for his campaigns in Gaul. Not only did Caesar have to fight the Germans to protect the Gauls, but Caesar justified his conquest of Gaul as a necessity in creating a buffer province that would protect Italy against future German invasions.

To make them more of a threat than they were at the time, Caesar collectively referred to all the tribes east of the Rhine as Germans who lived in an endless wilderness called Germania. This clear distinction has vexed modern historians because the geographical area Caesar labeled as Germania was peopled by culturally and political distinct tribes, whose true ethnic backgrounds, especially along border areas such as the Rhine, remain a topic of debate. Instead of a nation of Gaul bordered by one called Germania, it would be more appropriate to view the combined geographical area as being populated by semi-fluid tribal groups, whose political alliances and cultural identities were tribal and not at all national. Ever since the first millennium BC, Germanic and Celtic tribes had fought other Germanic and Celtic tribes. Through warfare or peaceful alliances, tribes were fragmented, joined and absorbed to create new tribes whose ethnic backgrounds became an intangible mess. Nevertheless, to give Caesar credit, tribes that considered themselves of Germanic background had steadily displaced Celtic tribes from their former homelands in central Germany. By Caesar's time, the middle of the 1st century BC, the Rhine did serve as a very rough dividing line between the poorer, more primitive Germanic tribes to the east and the wealthier Celtic tribes to the west.

Despite Caesar's propaganda leanings, we are indebted to him for much of what we know about the Suebi and other Germanic tribes east of the Rhine. In his *Gallic Wars*, Caesar wrote that their chief gods were the Sun, the Moon and the Fire god. Their whole life consisted of hunting and war. Chastity was held in great esteem. Both sexes bathed in the river with little else than small skins of hide or fur. Even in the coldest localities a great part of their bodies were left bare. The chiefs settled disputes amongst their people and in times of war elected a warlord from the aristocracy. As in early Celtic society, power and prestige lay with those who could claim victory in raids and battle and who could boast of the largest entourage of personal followers. The land was owned by no one and regularly assigned and rotated amongst the clans with no one abiding in their habitation for more than a year. Vast wildernesses surrounded the tribal lands, kept purposefully clear of human settlement by warfare. The Suebi traded chiefly to sell their booty, caring little for imports and forbidding the import of wine, thinking that it made them weak and womanish. Caesar added that of agriculture the Germans knew little and their main foods were milk, cheese and meat. Archaeology, however, paints a different picture, with agriculture more dominant and a diet heavily reliant on cereal grains. Caesar's view was likely heavily influenced by the fact that many of the tribes he fought and encountered were either in the midst of migrations or had only recently settled. Such tribes would have had little or no agriculture and would have relied almost entirely on herds of livestock.

Representatives of the Suebi chiefdoms met once a year in a sacred grove of the Semnones. It may well have been here that the Suebi discussed whether or not to aid the powerful Gallic Arverni of south-central Gaul and their allies the Sequani. As will be remembered the Arverni had already clashed with Rome some five decades earlier and met with a crushing defeat at the confluence of the Rivers Rhône and Isère. The battle was followed by the Roman conquest of Mediterranean Gaul and an alliance with the Aedui of Burgundy. The Aedui were old enemies of the Arverni and it was them who the Arverni petitioned the Suebi to attack.

Despite the Aedui's close relationship with Rome, the Suebi needed little convincing to make war. The tribes of what Caesar called Germania were poor and primitive. West of the Rhine, however, the forest fragmented into the rich and comparatively densely settled Gallic countryside. The Gallic realm burgeoned with potential loot, the acquisition of which would bring martial glory to the Suebi warrior.

In 71 BC, the Suebi army crossed the fabled waters of the Rhine to strike into Aedui territory via the lands of the ostensible Suebi allies, the Sequani. When word spread back to their homelands of the bountiful life in Gaul, more Suebi decided to trek westward. Between 70–65 BC, 120,000 Germans, including women and children, settled among the Sequani and continued to assault the Aedui.

Both the German and Gallic rank and file enjoyed no more than a shield for protection. The Germans were iron-poor, however, and the Gallic swordsmen's yard-long blades were superior to the bone or fire-hardened, wood-tipped, spears wielded by the more savage of the German warriors. But the Germans enjoyed a fearsome reputation and, although the population of Gaul was more than six times larger than the estimated three million souls of Germania, the invading Suebi tribes likely held a numerical advantage over the Aedui. Although the Aedui summoned their satellite tribes to their aid they suffered nothing but defeats at the hands of the Germans. All the Aedui nobles, councilors and knights were killed and their power in Gaul was shattered.

The Arverni had achieved their goal of crushing their Aedui enemies, but at an unexpected price. The Suebi turned out to be no dogs to fight and heel at their master's call, but rather wolves, which would do and take as they pleased. Thus, the new power in Gaul was not the Arverni but the Suebi under their dynamic king Ariovistus. A man born before his time, he was carved out of the same wood as the Germanic warlords who centuries hence would claim the withering West Roman Empire for their own. Ariovistus seized a third of the land from the erstwhile allied Sequani, reckoned among the best in Gaul. From his new domain, Ariovistus addressed Gallic tribal envoys in their own tongue, for he became fluid in the Gallic language. He demanded and received distinguished Gallic hostages.

The Gauls, however, were not about to take the Germanic incursion without a fight. All of central Gaul united against the Suebi at the legendary 61 BC battle of Magetobria. It was the Germans who were now likely outnumbered but the result was the same. Ariovistus smartly remained on the defensive within his camp flanked by marshes. When the investing Gauls fractured into scattered groups due to supply shortages, Ariovistus sallied forth and crushed them. No doubt there was much celebration among Ariovistus' warriors. At banquets, his champions drank from prized aurochs horns inlaid with silver and hailed their victory!

Before striking into Gaul Ariovistus had allied himself to Voccio, King of the Celtic Alpine realm of Noricum, by marrying Voccio's sister. Now undisputed master of central Gaul, Ariovistus further consolidated his position by being proclaimed a "friend of Rome" in 59 BC by Metellus Celer, the proconsul of Gallia Narbonensis and by the rising Roman politician, consul Julius Caesar.

Caesar had proved that he could excel on the real battlefield as well as he did on the political one when he put an end to the Helvetii intrusion into Gaul in 58 BC. His victory tremendously increased his prestige among the Gauls. If he had defeated the feared Helvetii then perchance he could also deliver them from the greater menace of Ariovistus' Germans? A delegation of notable chiefs appeared before Caesar, led by none other than Diviciacus the chief druid. Diviciacus told Caesar how Ariovistus' Suebi had come to hold sway over the Gauls. Ariovistus was a cruel tyrant, "ill-tempered, headstrong and savage"[2] who demanded noble children as hostages and inflicted torture upon whoever did not instantly comply with his wishes. And as if matters could not get any worse, Ariovistus was now demanding that the Sequani evacuate another third of their land to make room for another 24,000 Germanic Harudes who had joined Ariovistus a few months ago. Soon all of Gaul would be under the dominion of the tyrannous Germans. Only Caesar and the Roman army could save Gaul from Ariovistus. Diviciacus fearfully continued that by no means should Caesar speak of this meeting to Ariovistus, lest he put to death all the Gallic hostages in his keeping.

Caesar weighed the words of Diviciacus carefully. The great Druid and chief of the Aedui, Diviciacus was respected as a man of cunning who had survived his tribes' devastating war with the Suebi. Diviciacus had been to Rome to speak before the Senate and was a guest of the great philosopher, orator and statesmen, Cicero. The two had discussed divination by conjecture and augury. Caesar noticed that there were Sequani envoys amongst the Gallic chiefs, but that they had not spoken a word having "hung their heads with dejection with their eyes fixed on the ground."[3] When he inquired as to their silence, Diviciacus replied that their fear of Ariovistus and his possible retributions on their lands was so great that they dared not even speak against him in secret.

To calm the Gauls, Caesar promised that he would confer with Ariovistus and put a stop to the German King's outrages. The matter put Caesar in a bit of a bind since he himself was the co-author of the senatorial decree that recognized Ariovistus as a friend of the Roman people. However, now that Caesar's victory over the Helvetii opened the door to Roman expansion in Gaul, Caesar saw Ariovistus in a different light. Caesar sent deputies to Ariovistus in order to arrange some neutral ground for a parley.

Ariovistus' envoys replied that Caesar should come to him. Furthermore, he had not ventured out of his homelands as a conqueror but was invited by the Gauls. He had beaten every army the Gauls sent against him and now it was his right as a conqueror to rule as he pleased. The Romans of all people should know this! And what business were his conquests to the Romans, whom he considered his friends? Caesar answered that the Aedui were the friends of the Romans and that if Ariovistus wished to remain the same he would restore all hostages to the Gauls and refrain from bringing any more reinforcements across the Rhine.

Ariovistus replied that he would refrain from attacking the Aedui and their allies if they paid their tribute; if not, the title of "brothers of the Roman people would not save them. I am not impressed by Caesar's threat to punish my 'oppression' ... No one has ever fought me without bringing destruction upon himself. Let him attack whenever he pleases. He will discover what German valor is capable of. We have never known defeat ... and for fourteen years have never sheltered beneath a roof."[4]

From a contemporary standpoint, Ariovistus rightly told Caesar and Rome to mind their own business. Virtually the whole history of Roman expansion was built upon waging a war in behalf of a third party. This was exactly what Caesar intended to do in Gaul but Ariovistus had beaten him to it. Since neither side was going to back down, the only possible outcome was war. To justify his confrontation with a "friend of Rome", Caesar declared that Ariovistus' Germans were a danger not only to Gaul but also to Rome. At the time this was pure propaganda, but from a long-term historical perspective it was Caesar who couldn't have been more right.

Along with the last messages from Ariovistus came news from the Aedui and from the Treveri. The Aedui complained of the latest violence and of looting by the Harudes. More alarming was the Treveri news. The Treveri dwelt north of the Sequani on the Rhine border. They reported that another large Suebi force, under the brothers Nasua and Cimberius, stood ready to cross the river. Caesar knew he had no time to lose and had to engage Ariovistus before the German King met up with the newcomers.

Both sides now pushed toward strategic Vesontio (Besançon), the largest Sequani town. Rich in supplies and surrounded by the Doubs (the Dubis) River and a hill, the town was fortified with a wall and a citadel. The stride of the Roman iron-hobnailed sandals ate up four to five miles an hour, as Caesar force-marched his legions and reached the town before the Germans. Once there he occupied it with a garrison.

While laying in supplies of grain and other provisions at Vesontio, the Roman soldiers heard of their German enemy from the locals. The Germans were said to be of enormous physical stature, "incredible courage and splendid military training."[5] The Gauls admitted that the fierce glance of the Germans' eyes was too much for them to endure. These rumors alarmingly spread through the Roman ranks, from the tribunes, the prefects of the auxiliary troops and the fresh recruits, to even the hardened veterans and centurions. Most came up with urgent excuses to leave the camp. Others stayed out of shame for cowardice but unable to hide their feelings swelled up with tears, bewailed their fate or stayed sulking in their tents. Some hid their real fear of the Germans by blaming their reluctance to fight on the terrain of gullies and forests and on the difficulty of ensuring supplies. Commanders confided in Caesar that their troops would panic if ordered to advance.

To revive the dangerously sagging morale, Caesar rallied his centurions and reprimanded them for questioning his orders. Furthermore, he doubted that Ariovistus would break his friendship with the Romans. Even if he did, had not the legions of Marius defeated the Cimbri and Teutones, and had not his own legions been equally victorious against the dreaded Helvetii ? If no one followed him then he would go to face Ariovistus with only his favored Tenth Legion. A natural orator, Caesar's speech humbled the ranks and instilled them with newfound courage to meet the Germans.

Caesar marched forth from Vesontio and after six days came within 23 miles of Ariovistus' camp. Ariovistus now agreed to a parley in five days time. Accompanied by a corps of cavalry, he rode towards a knoll that rose midway between the opposing armies. Approaching from the other way was Caesar. He had brought with him not his Gallic cavalry, which he did not trust against the Germans, but mounted infantry from his Tenth Legion. At a distance of 600 yards, both leaders took but ten men with them and rode towards each other.

Accentuated by his fair complexion, Caesar's piercing dark eyes sized up the barbarian warlord. It was clear that like himself, Ariovistus was a natural leader of men. The German king likely sported a fine corselet of mail and gilded Gallic bronze helmet, decorated with stylized animal motifs. A masterpiece Gallic longsword dangled at his side. To Ariovistus, Caesar looked tall for a Roman and in superb physical condition. He might have even noticed that the Roman leader combed his short hair backward to conceal his premature balding. But if Caesar appeared a bit of a vain fop, there was no way Ariovistus mistook him for anything other than the most formidable enemy he ever faced.

Caesar spoke of the gifts that the Senate had lavished upon Ariovistus. He reiterated about Rome's long standing friendship with the Aedui and his demands for Ariovistus to restore hostages, to cease his raids and to bring no more Germans across the Rhine. Ariovistus retorted with his earlier demands, stating that "this part of the country [Gaul] is my province, just as the other part is yours." He showed a keen knowledge of Roman politics when he took a verbal jab at Caesar, "If I killed you, there are plenty of nobles and politicians in Rome who would thank me for it."[6]

The parley was going nowhere, with Ariovistus skirting around the immediate issues in a sort of ritual warrior challenge. He probably was negotiating for time, in the hopes that Nasua and Cimberius' warriors would arrive to join the battle.

At this point a scout galloped up to Caesar. Ariovistus' remaining horsemen were seen riding towards the mount. Overeager they pelted the Romans with stones and javelins. The skirmish ended the conference, with Caesar and his men leaving the field. The next day more of Ariovistus' envoys arrived, asking for another meeting between their king and Caesar. In light of the previous day's events, Caesar prudently declined to come himself. When Ariovistus saw that Caesar had sent some other Romans, he spat "What are you coming here for? To play the spy, I suppose?"[7] Ariovistus promptly threw Caesar's envoys in chains.

On the same day Ariovistus broke camp and marched his army to within six miles north of the Roman encampment. Close by, the Vosges Mountains rose above the two armies. The next day Ariovistus' warriors, wagons and non-combatants, rumbled up and along the lower slopes of the Vosges. He circled around the Romans and camped two miles behind and to the south of them. From here Ariovistus was in a position to cut the Roman supply road to the Sequani and Aedui. Caesar could see them, of course, and he guessed perfectly well what Ariovistus was up to, but would not risk engaging the enemy on the hillside. For the next five days, Caesar led his legions out in front of the barbarian wagon barricades but was unable to entice the Germans into anything more than cavalry scuffles.

With Ariovistus' infantry refusing battle and the Roman supply situation worsening, Caesar ordered the construction of a secondary camp a thousand yards behind that of the Germans. To protect the laborers, Caesar wisely drew up two legionary lines. Ariovistus was not going to let the building go uncontested. The legionaries gritted their teeth and braced themselves as the ground shook beneath the thundering hooves of the whole German cavalry, some 6,000 strong, sallying forth from their camp. Many of the barbarians rode bareback, thinking it unmanly to use a saddle. At their sides, like mad dogs of war, ran thousands of half-naked foot men, armed with shields and spears and hanging onto horses' manes to keep up with the advance. Strong arms sent javelins whistling through the air. German warriors leapt from their steeds to do combat on foot. Their pony-like mounts obediently remained on the battlefield to carry their masters to safety if needed. But in face of the nerve-racking barbarian charge, the Roman lines did not falter, and after a skirmish the Germans withdrew.

Caesar now once again drew up his legions for battle but Ariovistus still refused to be drawn into the decisive engagement. However, as soon as Caesar retired to his main camp, Ariovistus launched an assault on the secondary Roman camp in order to re-sever the Roman supply line. The Germans fought with their usual ferocity, but behind their ditch, earth rampart and palisade of stakes, the legions proved invincible. The Germans did their best to retrieve the bodies of their fallen comrades, as was their custom even in the midst of battle. When at sunset the Germans withdrew, many of them limped from serious wounds. Back among their camp, the women tended and bandaged the wounded. The Roman medics too were busy that night, though many a soldier, his vitals pierced by a spear or javelin, was beyond help.

The Romans took some prisoners, and through them Caesar found out why Ariovistus refused a general engagement. To Germans and Romans alike, the world abounded with spirits and gods. To them the supernatural was very real and could be consulted by individuals skilled in the art. Soothsayers, Germanic priestesses, saw the future in the way streams swirled and by the noises of the water. They took rune-marked twigs and tossed them upon a white cloth. Raising them to the heavens, they cried that if Ariovistus fought before the rising of the full moon, he would go down in defeat! The German warriors, who held women in high esteem, believed "that there resides in women an element of holiness and a gift of prophecy."[8] The advice of a priestess was not taken lightly.

The following day, on 10 September 58 BC, Caesar left a garrison to hold each fort and drew up his auxiliaries in front of the lesser camp, in full view of the Germans. Caesar claimed he did this to give an impression of strength. Evidently, however, he did not trust the auxiliaries to hold their own against the Germans since he did not call upon them even in the critical moments of the coming battle.

With his six legions, around 24,000–30,000 men, he advanced in triple line upon the enemy camp. The Germans reluctantly came out to meet him, their wagons drawn up in a semicircle to protect their flanks and rear. As the historian Delbrück pointed out, Caesar does not mention the German cavalry in the ensuing battle, because Ariovistus, now on the defensive, had probably dismounted most of them to fight together with the infantry. His own forces probably numbered 20,000–30,000 warriors.[9]

Ariovistus decided to give battle because the supply situation had swung in the Romans' favor and he could not afford to wait till the full moon. By doing so, Ariovistus gave the psychological edge to the Romans as fears of ill omens gnawed at the German warriors.

The barbarians arranged themselves in rough tribal groups as related by Caesar: "Harudes, Marcomanni, Triboces, Vangiones, Nemetes, Eudusii, and Suebi."[10] The tribes that fought that day for Ariovistus hailed from lands near and far; the Triboces, Vangiones and Nemetes from the upper Rhine, the Harudes and Eudusii all the way from Jutland. The Marcomanni were Suebi from the Main Valley, powerful enough to form their own contingent, separate from others of their tribal confederacy.

Behind the warriors, on the wagon wall, teary-eyed women stretched out their hands and bared their bosoms, pleading for their men to save them and their children from a life of slavery. To the German warrior, "enslavement was a fate they feared more desperately for their women than for themselves."[11] On the Roman side Caesar took personal command of the right wing, where the opposing barbarian faction seemed the least steady.

When the blare of the Roman horns and trumpeters signaled the advance of the Roman lines, the Germans sprang forward with such swiftness that the legions had no time to discharge their devastating javelin barrage. Still, the Roman shield wall bristled with the blank blades of the gladius. The Roman right methodically forced back the weaker German left wing. For a time though the German shield wall kept the Romans at bay, as Paulus Orosius relates:

> "A battle took place, very severe on account of the phalanx of the Germans, which, with their battle line drawn close together and their shields locked over their heads, safe from all sides, they had prepared for breaking the attack of the Roman battle line."[12]

When, as Caesar described, the legionaries were "brave enough to leap on the masses of the enemy, tear the shields from their hands, and deal a deep wound from above,"[13] the German left wing collapsed in mad flight.

On the Roman left wing, however, it was the barbarians who threatened to crush the Roman lines. There, the first two legionary lines were already committed and only barely managed to remain in formation. It was Publius Crassus, commander of the Roman cavalry in the rear who noticed the dire situation. Publius was none other than the younger son of Caesar's fellow triumvir, Marcus Licinius Crassus. He galloped up to the third legionary line and personally led it into battle to join their hard-pressed comrades. The third line turned the tide against the barbarians.

The whole disorderly German mob vainly tried to reach the banks of the river Rhine, some fifteen miles distant. Those miles were strewn with the bodies of dead Germans, hunted and cut down by the Roman cavalry at their heels, led by Caesar himself. At the river a few of the barbarians managed to commandeer boats. Those not so fortunate dove into the water. Some reached the eastern side; others, too exhausted or heavily wounded, the river pulled down into its gloomy depths. Ariovistus himself managed to seize a skiff and gain the other side. Two of his wives died in the rout, as did one of Ariosvistus' daughters, while another daughter was captured. According to Plutarch total German losses were said to have numbered over 80,000, a figure that included tens of thousands of women, children and old as well as the bulk of Ariovistus' strike force.

With the destruction of Ariovistus' army, the Suebi reinforcements on the east bank of the Rhine vanished into the vastness of the German forests. Other tribes along the Rhine perceived their weakness and like sharks, which turn upon their wounded, attacked the Suebi and slew a great number. The Suebi, however, were far from finished, and continued to be the dominant German tribal confederation. Over a century later, Tacitus described their confederacy as covering half of Germany. They would continue to haunt Rome for a long time to come.

For the moment, Caesar was free to establish Roman hegemony over much of central Gaul. Indeed, to many Gauls, Caesar appeared as an invincible savior. Others thought otherwise, like the formidable Belgae who resented Roman intrusion. In Rome, Caesar's enemies called him a traitor for making war on Ariovistus, "a friend of Rome". As for Ariovistus, after the battle little is known of him other than that he died sometime later. In another age he might have carved out a kingdom for himself, but for now it was Caesar's time to shine.

Chapter Ten

Caesar Against the Belgae, the "Bravest of the Gauls"

"Live up to your tradition of bravery, keep your nerve and meet the enemy's attack boldly."[1]

Caesar addressing the 10th Legion

The gray skies of winter still shrouded the Gallic town of Vesontio (Besançon). The wooden palisade that enclosed the thatched huts of the Sequani capital lay nestled between an oxbow of the River Dubs (the Dubis) and the mountain side. To the south, when not obscured by mist and rain, rose the Jura Mountains, and beyond them the lofty peaks of the Alps and the nearest Roman Province, Gallia Cisalpina. Roman patrols strode by Sequani farmers tending their pigs, cattle and sheep. Off-duty legionaries gathered around a dice-game, haggled with Gallic merchants or flirted with local buxom women. It was early in the year 57 BC, and within Vesontio and the nearby villages of east-central Gaul were billeted the legions of Gaius Julius Caesar.

To the north, along the North Sea coast and west of the Rhine, one of the three large tribal groups of Gaul, the Belgae, did not appreciate the Roman meddler in Gallic affairs. They feared that a man and a nation which could defeat both the Helvetii and Ariovistus' Suebi would clearly not stop until all of Gaul was theirs. As it turned out their fears were not unwarranted. Councils were held and hostages exchanged. The kings and chiefs of the Belgae readied their people for war!

Caesar's newest foes consisted of Germanic tribes which, two centuries earlier, overran the older Celtic population. The Belgae adopted Celtic culture but, far removed from the borders of Rome, they remained little tainted by its civilization. The Belgae retained their ancient monarchies of tribal kings, who lorded over a predominantly rural people. In contrast, the Gallic tribes that bordered the Roman provinces were ruled by elected magistrates, after the fashion of the Roman Senate. The Belgae took great pride in the fact that half a century earlier they alone managed to keep the powerful Cimbri and Teutones from ravaging their lands. Belgic tribes also held sway over southeast Britannia (Britain). Continually at war with their German kinsmen to the east, the valor of the Belgae was of great renown. They won Caesar's admiration. He called the Belgae the bravest of the Gauls.

It did not take long for rumors of the Belgae's activities to reach the ears of legate Titus Labienus, the Roman commander in charge at Vesontio and Caesar's most able general. Labienus conveyed the news to Caesar who presently attended his duties as proconsul in Gallia Cisalpina. Labienus' messages must have delighted Caesar. If the Belgae conspired against him, then all the better, it would give him a legitimate excuse to make war on them. Once the Belgae were subdued, Gaul's border with Germania would be secured. Then Caesar could safely turn his armies west to conquer the remaining tribes of Gaul.

For the coming campaign, Caesar enrolled two more legions in Gallia Cisalpina; the Thirteenth and Fourteenth. In the spring, they were sent to join his other six legions at Vesontio. Caesar arrived later, when the fresh grass had grown up to supply forage for his campaign.

Caesar's return was no doubt welcomed by the troops. Tall, gaunt and physically fit, the stylish 43-year-old Julius Caesar provided a charismatic figurehead. He cared for his men dearly and always addressed them as his "comrades," instead of his "soldiers". In battle he had proven to be a shrewd commander who could inspire the troops with his personal courage. It was to Caesar, not the state, to whom the legionaries had taken their oath of loyalty and it was to Caesar to whom they looked for pay, booty and provisions after eventual demobilization.

Caesar's army was an imposing force. Alongside his eight legions, each fielding over 4,000 men, the army included auxiliary Numidian light infantry, Cretan archers and Balearic slingers for a grand total of more than 40,000 combatants. The Roman cavalry, 4,000 strong, was made up mostly of allied Gauls who had dispersed to their homelands during the winter but now reassembled to rejoin the Romans.

The allied Gallic cavalry included the Treveri, renowned for their courage and horsemanship, who boasted of their Germanic ancestry but spoke a Celtic tongue. The Treveri may also have taken pride in the fine weapons they carried. From above-ground clay mines around the Dollberg Mountain, the Treveri extracted iron ore. Forged in temperatures of up 1,000 degrees Celcius and repeatedly heated and cooled, the Treveri sword and spear blades could have reached steel-like quality. Besides the Treveri, Caesar's cavalry also included smaller permanent Gallic, Spanish and Germanic bodyguard-type detachments.

Caesar instructed allied Gallic tribes along the Belgic border to inform him about the happenings among the Belgae. When they confirmed Labienus' reports, Caesar secured his wheat supply and marched his army toward the Marne River (the Matrona). A fortnight later he arrived at the Belgae frontier.

At first the Belgae's reputation for bravery seemed unfounded. So rapid was Caesar's approach that the nearest tribe, the Remi, was taken completely off guard. They quickly surrendered to the Romans and all but groveled at Caesar's feet. The Remi pleaded that they had no wish to make war on Rome and that they were ready to give hostages. Their towns stood open to the Romans and they would obey Caesar's commands and supply his army with grain.

In marked difference to the Remi, the rest of the Belgae were up in arms! King Galba led a mighty alliance of his Suessiones, alongside the powerful Nervii and Bellovaci, and a host of lesser tribal contingents, as well as German mercenaries from across the Rhine. The exact number of Belgic troops at Galba's disposal can only be guessed at. On previous occasions the Roman army had faced invasions of barbarians which came as whole tribes, with their families and belongings. These barbarian armies were forced to pillage the land for supplies. The Belgae, by comparison, fought on home ground. Unburdened by civilians and with short supply lines, they would have been able to maintain an army of unusual size. Caesar tells us that the various tribes promised to muster some 306,000 warriors to fight for Galba. This is certainly an exaggeration but Galba's army could well have been over 75,000 warriors strong, still twice the size of Caesar's fighting strength.

If Galba could force Caesar into an open battle, then the Romans might have been swept away like leaves in the wind. Caesar knew this and convinced Diviciacus, the pro-Roman chief of the Aedui, his staunchest Gallic allies, to come to his aid and ravage the lands of the Bellovaci to the west. Such a two-pronged offensive, it was hoped, would force the Belgae to split their forces. But it took time for Diviciacus to gather his army and arrive at the scene – time during which Caesar alone would have to face the awesome might of Galba's army, which was rapidly approaching the borders of the Remi.

Caesar crossed the Aisne River (the Axona) by means of a bridge and went on the defensive. He built a fortified camp on a hill, with his back close to the river. To the front, the hill formed a slight ridge and then sloped down gently to a brook (La Miette) that meandered through a swamp. The slopes on the right and left sides were steeper. To ensure the safety of the Roman supply line across the Aisne, Caesar protected the bridge by means of another redoubt on the south bank, held by six cohorts under Quintus Titurius Sabinus. Sabinus' stronghold boasted twelve-foot ramparts and an eighteen-foot wide ditch.

Eight miles distant from the Roman fortifications on the Aisne, Galba placed Bibrax, a town of the turncoat Remi, under siege. The hapless citizens cried to Caesar for aid. In answer he sent some of his auxiliary troops, who crept into the town at night to reinforce the defenders. Infuriated, the Belgae left the town and set aflame every Remi village and farmstead in their path as they marched off to meet the Romans. Less than two miles from Caesar, they set up their camp on the north bank of La Miette. The smoke and watch fires of the Belgae camp extended for more than eight miles.

Due to the enemy's great numbers, Caesar continued to avoid a direct confrontation between his legions and the Belgae. Instead he sent his cavalry to keep the enemy occupied. Galba seemed equally reluctant to cross the swamp and likewise only sent his cavalry to skirmish with the Romans.

Caesar used the time to further fortify his troops with two lines of trenches. The trenches ran parallel to the left and right sides of the main camp and protected the legions, when drawn up in front of the camp, from being enveloped from the flanks. Each trench was 650 yards in length and crowned at both ends with forts holding the artillery. The artillery probably included javelin and stone-shooting *catapulta* and *ballista* and the "heavy howitzers" of the ancient world, the boulder-hurling *onager* or "wild ass".

When the fortifications were completed, Caesar left the newly enrolled Thirteenth and Fourteenth legions to hold the main camp and drew up his remaining six legions along the swampy shore of La Miette. His actions roused the Belgae who assembled to face the Romans across the swamp.

It is difficult to say whether the Belgae warriors' arms and armor resembled more that of their German kinsmen or that of their Celtic Gaul neighbors. Certainly, compared to the Romans the Belgae were a motley lot. Their oblong oval or hexagonal infantry shields and their round cavalry shields were probably brightly painted with animal and geometric designs. For many, their shield would have been their only defense. Others would have had iron helmets, perhaps plumed and with cheek guards, while chiefs and distinguished warriors sported corselets of mail. The most common weapons were spears, longswords, javelins and possibly bows and slings.

The cavalry of both sides splashed across the swamp, in wild but indecisive charges and countercharges that tended to favor the Romans. Caesar probably hoped that the presence of the legions would entice the barbarians to attack. However, Galba had been unwilling to cross the swamp with only the Roman cavalry facing him. He certainly wasn't going to cross with the Roman legions on the other side, ready to hack down his warriors as they made their way through the swamp. Outflanking the legions was out of the question due to Caesar's new forts and ditches. Caesar withdrew his legions to his camp when no barbarian attack materialized by the end of the day.

During the night, the Belgae decided to make their way across the swamp. No Romans stood guard on the opposite bank, as the Belgae skirted the Roman fortifications to head south for the Aisne. The Roman ramparts and towers were faintly silhouetted against the night sky, but in the dark the Belgae remained undetected. Within their eight-man tents, the legionaries tried to catch what sleep they could. Their comrades on sentry duty peered into the darkness from the camp parapets. Although they failed to hear or see the skulking Belgae, the Romans were safe enough inside their fortifications. The Belgae heading for the Aisne had no hope of taking Caesar's main camp. The plan of the bold Belgae was to cross the Aisne, then assault Sabinus' redoubt on the south bank of the river and destroy the bridge. If successful, the Roman supply line to allied tribes would be severed. And even if they failed, the Belgae would still remain in a position to devastate the surrounding Remi lands and deprive Caesar of a nearby source of supplies.

However, the vigilant Sabinus espied the barbarians fording the Aisne. He at once sent word to Caesar, who hurried to his aid across the bridge with the Numidians, the slingers, the archers and the cavalry. Seeing that they had only a few cohorts, Caesar's light troops and cavalry to deal with, the Belgae continued to wade through the shallows of the river. They were met by a storm of stones and arrows, perishing in droves till their corpses choked the river. Over the bodies of their fallen comrades others strove to gain the far side only to be chopped down by the Roman cavalry.

After the attack petered out, the Belgae found themselves in a dilemma. The Romans refused to fight them on favorable ground and their own grain reserves were running low. Although the homelands of the individual tribes were relatively close by, the barbarians simply lacked the infrastructure and organization to supply their army. A council was held and it was decided that the tribes would return to their lands. The recent news of Diviciacus' Aedui approaching the Bellovaci homelands provided further impetus to break up the Belgic army. If the Romans attacked any tribe, the other tribes promised to come to its aid. This proved to be little more than a face saving gesture.

Some time before midnight, with much uproar and commotion, disorganized groups of disgruntled Belgae departed for their homes. Their retreat was forthwith reported to Caesar by his scouts but Caesar would not believe his good fortune. He remained skeptical and feared an ambush. Not until dawn, when further reconnaissance confirmed the truth, did Caesar send his cavalry, followed by Titus Labienus and three legions, to harry the rear columns of Belgae. The pursuit went on until sunset, over many miles. Isolated throngs of Belgae fought to the last man but were surrounded piecemeal and annihilated.

The campaign now began to resemble more of a Roman triumphal march than a war. At the town of Noviodunum, the Suessiones were overawed by the array of Roman siege engines. They surrendered and offered the sons of King Galba as hostages. In the territory of the Bellovaci, Caesar had not even reached Bratuspantium before the town elders came out to submit to the Romans. At the town, the women and children lined the walls, pleading for peace. Diviciacus, who had disbanded his Aedui army and joined Caesar, supported their supplication. Caesar agreed, but to assure that the powerful Bellovaci remained peaceful, confiscated their weapons and took six hundred hostages. After the Bellovaci, the Ambiani surrendered unconditionally. But in the lands of the Nervii, the picture changed.

Fiercely proud of their native ways, the Nervii scorned all trade with the civilizations of the south. They even forbade the import of wine, which they thought lessened their courage, and in this way resembled the Germanic Suebi. Disgusted by the cowardice of their Belgae kinsmen, the Nervii were determined to cast out the Roman invaders. Along with their like-minded neighbors, the Atrebates and Viromandui, the Nervii awaited the Romans in the Sabis[2] river valley. Furthermore, the Aduatuci, descendents from a splinter group of Teutones and Cimbri who had settled in the area, were coming to their aid.

Some of the Belgae hostages managed to sneak away from their Roman captors at night. They visited the Nervii and told them that the Roman army was vulnerable if attacked on the march. At such time, the legions were strung out, not in their battle formations, and separated from each other by each legion's baggage train. The legions' only protection was a small screen of Roman cavalry. The Roman legions on the march were therefore dangerously exposed to large cavalry attacks or ambushes. Unfortunately the Nervii spurned the use of cavalry and had only the horsemen of their allies to rely on. However, the Nervii excelled in concealing themselves within woods and thickets. Thus they decided to prepare an ambush.

For three days Caesar pressed deeper and deeper into Nervii territory. It was at this point that prisoners told him of the Nervii army awaiting him on the far side of the Sabis, little more than ten miles from his present camp. In light of the near vicinity of the enemy, Caesar changed his regular marching order. Instead of each legion being followed by its baggage train, he advanced with six legions in field order and placed the entire baggage in the rear followed by a guard of the Thirteenth and Fourteenth legions. Reconnaissance units were sent ahead to chose a suitable campsite on the near side of the Sabis.

The shallow but broad Sabis was flanked with slopes on both sides. The Roman side was fairly open, with sparse tree growth but uneven ground. Beyond the opposite bank, 300 yards of open terrain sloped up to dense wood lands and thickets. A number of enemy cavalry held the open ground near the river.

Caesar unleashed his cavalry along with the slingers and archers, which splashed across the stream and drove the Belgae horsemen back into the woods. Caesar's cavalry did not follow into the depth of the forest, so that the Belgae cavalry was able to reassemble and charge again. Caesar's horsemen and a barrage of missile fire once more held them at bay.

Caesar seemed confident that his cavalry, slingers and archers sufficed as protection for his legions. While surveyors used instruments and flags to mark out the camp on the ground, the legions tramped down the valley side. Before long, the legionaries of the first *contubernium*, or eight-man squad, marched into their allotted section. The men lifted poles strapped with palisade stakes from their shoulders. At the end of the poles were tied bags with their personal belongings, a sickle, mess kits and cooking kettles. Javelins were stuck into the ground, to prop up shields and hold helmets. The legionaries also carried their entrenching tools, probably in leather satchels. Soon they got busy cutting turf and shoveling earth to erect the usual camp entrenchment. No doubt they kept an eye out on the occasional Belgae horsemen seen across the stream, on the other side of the valley. Officers barked orders, to remind the soldiers to keep working and to leave the lookout to the sentries.

The presence of the Belgae cavalry should have forewarned Caesar that the entire Nervii coalition might be nearby, just like the prisoners had told him. Despite such knowledge Caesar considered his cavalry sufficient cover for his toiling legionaries. After all, other than some cavalry units, the enemy seemed nowhere close by. He was wrong. From beneath the emerald foliage of the woods on the far bank, the eyes of some 30,000 Nervii, Atrebates and Viromandui, watched the oblivious Romans with anticipation.

As soon as the Roman baggage train appeared over the hillside, the entire Belgae army broke out of the woods. The Nervii formed the left wing, the Atrebates the right and the Viromandui in the center. The barbarians poured down the hillside like a human avalanche, unstoppable in its fury. The Roman cavalry and light troops were completely overwhelmed and scattered, barely even impeding the enemy charge. So fast were the barbarians that Caesar wrote, "almost at the same moment they were seen at the woods, in the river, and then at close quarters!"[3] The three-foot deep river proved scarcely more of an obstacle than the Roman cavalry. In no time the barbarians gained the river's farther side to continue with seemingly unbroken momentum up to the entrenching Romans.

The barbarian ambush would have sealed the doom of almost any other army caught in the same situation. But this was not just any army; it was the Roman legion in its prime, under the generalship of one of the great captains of history! The *vexillum*, the red flag of battle, rose high accompanied by the drone of trumpets. Everywhere the men threw down their tools and rushed to their weapons, which each *contubernium* stacked close to its worksite. Wisely Caesar had ordered his generals to remain with their respective troops during the entrenching. Without waiting for Caesar's orders they at once assembled their men as best they could. The legionaries, many half-armed or donning helmet or shield while on the run, hastened to whatever standard was nearest, regardless if it was of their own unit or not.

Caesar was everywhere, first at the Tenth Legion and then at the others. He yelled out orders, and with words of valor encouraged the men to withstand the enemy assault. There was no time to draw up the regular tactical formations. Separate clumps of legionaries formed a rough line, against which was about to burst the barbarian tide.

The Ninth and Tenth legions, under legate Titus Labienus, formed the left wing of the Roman army. The *optiones* struck unruly legionaries with their staffs, to keep order and silence in the ranks, while closer and closer rushed the howling Atrebates warriors. Only when the barbarians closed within 30 yards did the circular bronze cornu horn drone across the Roman lines, the signal for the legionaries to let loose a murderous volley of javelins. The 7-foot pilum, with its entire weight concentrated behind a small triangular point, easily penetrated the wooden shield of the barbarian and could reach the man behind. The pila volley broke the momentum of the Atrebates. With a yell the legionaries drew their swords and counter charged. Breathless and wounded, the Atrebates were pushed back downhill into the river. On the far bank, the Atrebates rallied and desperately tried to throw the Romans back but to no avail. The men of the Ninth and Tenth legions carried the assault up the bank and routed the Atrebates up the hill. The battle between the Ninth and Tenth legions and the Atrebates swung up and down the valley like a giant pendulum.

Likewise in the center, the Eleventh and Eighth legions withstood and broke the initial onslaught of the Viromandui. They too carried the fight downhill to engage the Viromandui on the river's bank. This proved to be a serious error for it opened a huge gap between the Eighth and the Twelfth Legion, which along with the Seventh Legion had remained up slope to the right.

Into the gap poured the bulk of the Nervii led by Boduognatus, their commander in chief, right towards the Roman camp and baggage. At the same time other Nervii warriors ran to envelop the exposed Twelfth and Seventh legions. Milling around the camp were the remnants of the routed Roman cavalry and the Roman auxiliary light troops. At the sight of the oncoming Nervii they fled in wild panic. Their fear spread among the Roman camp followers, some of which were prematurely looting the battlefield in the wake of the victorious Roman left and center. Camp followers, horsemen and slingers scattered in all directions. The auxiliary Treveri cavalry did not cease their flight till they arrived back in their homelands! There they heralded that the Romans had been overcome.

On the Roman right wing the situation looked dire indeed. The men of the Twelfth Legion huddled around their standards. Attacked from both the front and flanks, the legionaries were so closely jammed together that they hampered each other while they desperately tried to fend off the assailing Nervii.

Behind their large rectangular shields, the legionaries exposed as little of their bodies as possible to the enemy. Horsehair-crested helmets, with cheek and neck guards, protected their heads, and for some, mail hauberks their torsos. Yet their armor was not invulnerable. The yard-long sword of the tall and powerful Belgae warrior slashed down with terrific force, to cleave through the Roman helmet and into the skull beneath.

All the centurions of the fourth cohort lay slain, as was the *signifer*, his bronze animal standard lost among the barbarians. The other cohorts fared little better, their centurions dead or wounded, including the chief centurion Publius Sextius Baculus of the first cohort who no longer could stand on his own accord. The Nervii unrelentingly pushed uphill and against the flanks. All of the legionaries were tiring and many of those in the rear, who were mercilessly being hit by a hail of enemy missiles, retired from the battle while they still could.

To the rescue came Caesar, who snatched up a shield from a soldier in the rear. He shoved his way through to the front lines, rallied the centurions by name and cheered on the rank and file. The knowledge of his presence spread through the ranks and like a tonic instilled the men with renewed vigor. Caesar called for the lines to advance a little, so as to give them more space. At the same time he ordered the tribunes to close the space between the Twelfth and the Seventh Legion. The Seventh Legion was to the right of the Twelfth and it too was hard pressed. Slowly the two legions inched together to form a square. With his rear and flanks now protected, Caesar called for the front lines to charge.

At this moment the Thirteenth and Fourteenth legions of the Roman rearguard finally appeared over the crest of the hill. Meanwhile, Titus Labienus had led the victorious Tenth, and presumably the Ninth Legion, all the way into the Belgae camp. From there he beheld the arrival of the Roman rearguard and the fierce battle raging on the Roman right wing. At once he ordered the Tenth Legion to hasten to the aid of their commander in chief.

With breakneck speed the Tenth Legion ran down the hillside and across the river. The Ninth Legion likely remained behind to occupy the enemy camp. The arrival of the Tenth Legion so revived the Roman morale that even wounded legionaries heaved themselves up with their shields in an effort to rejoin the battle. So, too, the remaining Roman cavalry, in an effort to undo their earlier cowardice, returned to ride down enemy stragglers.

Although Caesar's account of the battle now becomes muddled, it is clear that the Romans surrounded the Nervii. With Caesar and the Twelfth and Seventh legions striking the Nervii left flank, the newly arrived Thirteenth and Fourteenth legions engaged the enemy from the front. The Eleventh and Eighth appeared to have remained on the river's bank and thus on the Nervii right flank. Most devastating of all, the Tenth Legion charged right into the Nervii rear.

Outnumbered and surrounded, their allies slain or routed, the Nervii fought on with unparalleled courage. When their front ranks lay dead, others took their place to fight upon the bodies of the fallen. Here and there, Nervii warriors stood defiant upon mounds of corpses, deflecting spears and missiles and hurling them back at the Romans below. But all their desperate fury could not save them from bitter defeat. Caesar wrote, "The tribe of the Nervi was almost annihilated and their name almost blotted out from the face of the earth."[4] When calm descended upon the hillside, a pitiful 500 Nervii remained alive.

Deputies of the Nervii elders, who along with the women and children had sought refuge in nearby marshlands, arrived at the Roman camp and formally surrendered. Caesar proved to be a merciful victor. The Nervii were to keep their lands and settlements. Caesar also commanded their neighbors not to make war on the weakened and now vulnerable Nervii. Among the Atrebates, he installed as king Commius. Commius was a courageous man in whose loyalty Caesar had great faith and who would become one of the more notable characters of Caesar's Gallic wars: though ultimately not in a way Caesar would have hoped for.

The battle of the Sabis proved the climax, but not the end of the Belgae campaign of 57 BC. As will be recalled the Aduatuci were on their way to aid the Nervii. However, upon hearing of the disaster on the Sabis, they retired to their homelands and prepared for the inevitable Roman invasion. The Aduatuci abandoned all of their towns and gathered their entire belongings in a single heavily fortified stronghold (south of Thuin).[5] The stronghold boasted steep cliffs on all sides except one, where a lofty double wall defended a gently sloping approach. Sharp stakes and heavy stones lined the parapet. The Aduatuci light troops skirmished with the approaching Roman army but had they had no way of stopping it before it arrived at the gates of their stronghold.

Caesar surrounded the Aduatuci stronghold with five miles of 12-foot-high earthworks, strengthened with redoubts. Next the Romans began to construct a siege tower some distance from the walls. This provided great amusement for the Aduatuci, who laughed at the Romans, for how would so puny and short a people as the Romans hope to move so mighty a tower?! However, when the tower began to roll onto the walls, the barbarians were so dumbfounded that they appeared to surrender without a fight.

The gates were flung open and in exchange for Roman "protection" the Aduatuci delivered their weapons into Caesar's hands. To prevent looting, Caesar forbade his troops to remain in the town; unaware that the Aduatuci had yet to play their last card. Drawing on a hidden stockpile of weapons, they sallied forth from the town some time after midnight in hopes of catching the Romans unawares. But the ramparts and towers of the Roman camp proved impregnable.

Some 4,000 Aduatuci were left behind dead before the remainder retired to the town. In the morning the Roman battering ram crashed in the gate. The whole town was looted and the population marched into slavery.

The enslavement of the Aduatuci ended the Belgae campaign. Caesar had won more renown. He had now defeated three of the most dreaded and feared warrior tribes, the Helvetii, Ariovistus' Suebi, and the Belgae. If they could not defy the might of Rome then who could? And if this were not enough, Caesar's cavalry commander, Publius Crassus, the hero of the Ariovistus battle, during the same season brought the maritime tribes along the channel, from the Seine to the Bay of Biscay, under Roman dominion.

The bulk of the legions now got some well deserved rest as they went into winter quarters in central Gaul. For the Twelfth Legion and a detachment of cavalry, however, there was more immediate battle ahead. Under the command of legate Servius Galba they were dispatched to secure a trade route from Lake Geneva through the Alps. Inadequate manpower and supplies, as well as the determined resistance of local hill tribes, forced Galba to abort the campaign. After the Twelfth Legion went into winter quarters among the Allobroges, Caesar left his loyal legions behind and departed for Illyricum. Justifiably proud of his accomplishments for the year, his mind soon teamed with thoughts of a new adventure: the invasion of Britannia!

In Rome the scale of Caesar's victories caused unprecedented jubilation amongst the people, much to the chagrin of Caesar's political enemies. Merchants boasted of 53,000 Aduatuci slaves sold at auctions! Even Gnaeus Pompeius Magnus, Caesar's partner in the all-powerful Triumvirate, along with the multi-millionaire Marcus Licinius Crassus, was most impressed. Pompey sponsored an unheard of thanksgiving of sacrifices and public feasts fifteen days long in honor of Caesar; five days longer than one previously given to himself and three times as long as the usual duration. Caesar's star continued to rise but both in Gaul and in the political arena of Rome storm clouds gathered.

Chapter Eleven

Caesar's Grip Tightens

"We could not injure them by ramming because they were so solidly built, and their height made it difficult to reach them with missiles or board them with grappling-irons."[1]

Caesar comments on the advantages of Celtic ships

Before Caesar could continue his military campaigns in 56 BC, he had to deal with the intrigues of his political opponents. The prominent statesmen Marcus Tullius Cicero and Marcus Porcius Cato "the Younger" rightfully saw the Triumvirate of Caesar, Pompey and Marcus L. Crassus as a threat to the Senate and to the Republic. In the spring of 56 BC, Cicero and Cato sought to lessen the powers of the Triumvirate and of Caesar in particular, by driving a wedge between its members. The timing seemed favorable as Pompey was already at odds with Crassus over their mutual desire to hold command in Egypt.

To alienate Caesar from Pompey and to win over Pompey, Cicero tried to deprive Caesar of the land grants promised to his veterans; grants that Pompey had already received. Furthermore, Cato's brother-in-law, Domitius, claimed that if he gained the consulship in 55 BC he would recall Caesar from his command in Gaul. Caesar summoned Pompey and Crassus to a conference at Luca in Cisalpine Gaul, where the Triumvirate resolved their differences, at least for the present. Pompey and Crassus returned to Rome to protect their own and Caesar's interests, leaving Caesar free to return to his legions.

With Pompey and Crassus looking out for him in Rome, Caesar planned to invade Britannia in 56 BC. But events transpired in Gaul that had to be taken care of first. Not only did the conquests of Marcus L. Crassus' eldest son, Publius, in Aremorica (northwestern Gaul) prove too easy to be of lasting impact, but the rest of Gaul turned out to be not nearly as pacified as Caesar had hoped.

The rumors that Caesar set his sights on Britannia were not at all to the liking of the most powerful Aremorican coastal tribe, the Veneti. The Veneti feared that Roman ambitions would threaten the Veneti's grip on Britannia's tin trade and the toll they collected from ships that sailed the Channel. To top it off, the presumptuous Romans demanded that the coastal tribes furnish the grain supplies for the legions.

The Veneti excelled as sailors and possessed the most powerful fleet among the Gauls. When the Veneti griped about their misgivings, their fellow coastal Gauls listened. Convinced that they submitted to Roman sovereignty too hastily, the tribes of Aremorica joined the Veneti in a full-blown uprising. Ready to fight with them were tribesmen from Britannia and the Morini and Menapii from the Belgae coast. It was the beginning of what Caesar termed the first rebellion.

When Caesar heard of the alarming turn of events, he ordered a fleet of ships to be built along the River Loire (the Liger), and rowers, sailors and steersmen to be drafted. The rumors that he was contemplating an invasion of Britannia were true. To do so, Caesar had to have absolute command of the Channel. To get control of the channel, he had to make sure that the Aremorican tribes were completely subdued. In the campaign against them, Caesar would lead the land force. Young Decimus Brutus, a distant cousin of Caesar who he loved like a son, was put in command of the fleet.

Caesar was not such a fool as to believe that the Veneti were the only ones that resented Roman rule and yearned for their erstwhile freedom. Quintus Titurius Sabinus was sent with three legions to keep in check the Lexovii, the Venelli and the Curiosolites, who were not initially involved in the revolt. Furthermore, to safeguard eastern Gaul, Caesar dispatched Titus Labienus with the cavalry to the Treveri on the Rhine. From the Treveri lands, Labienus was to keep an eye on the Belgae and the Germans. Caesar also decided to expand the campaign and ordered Publius Crassus, with twelve cohorts and some cavalry, to head into Aquitania (Gascony) to prevent possible reinforcements coming from that part of Gaul.

The Veneti were not idle either. Their confederate fleet assembled on the Veneti coast, correctly reckoning that Caesar would begin his campaign there. They gathered in the grain stocks and awaited the coming of the legions from within their fortified towns. To ward off invaders, these strongholds were built at the end of promontories and tongues of land which where flooded with the incoming tide. Approach by foot and by siege engines was nearly impossible. At the same time ships could be stranded and damaged in the shallow water during ebb.

Caesar attempted to counter these difficulties with gigantic moles that stretched along the tidal causeways, from the shores up to the level of the town walls. With such laborious and time-consuming methods, several Veneti towns were captured. The inhabitants nevertheless gave Caesar the slip, as they simply hopped on their ships with all their valuables and retired to the next town. After a while Caesar had enough. He decided to await the arrival of his fleet.

Along the cliff tops of Morbihan Bay (Quiberon), Caesar and his legions watched as below them Brutus' fleet plowed through the waters to collide with the 220 Veneti ships sailing forth from their harbor. In almost every aspect the Gallic ships were superior to those of the Romans. The keels of the Gallic ships were flatter and able to navigate shoals and low tidal areas. Instead of ropes, iron chains attached the ships' anchors and their sails were of leather. The ships were built entirely of oak with the beams of the crosspieces a foot thick, secured with iron nails as thick as a man's thumb. They were so sturdy as to be nearly invulnerable to the ram. Their high prows and similar sterns towered over the Roman galleys even when these were equipped with turrets, making it difficult to assault the Gallic ships with missiles or to grip them with grappling hooks.

The Romans overcame their ships' inferiority with typical ingenuity. The swifter Roman galleys rowed close to the bulky ships of the Gauls and used hooks on long poles to grab hold of the halyards, the ropes used to hoist or lower the sails. The Romans then rowed away at maximum speed to tear apart the halyards and bring down the sails. The Gauls no doubt frantically tried to dislodge the hooks and pelted the Romans with whatever they could hurl at them. But lacking archers, the Gauls were unable to do any real damage. One after the other, the massive Gallic ships were immobilized, surrounded by two or three Roman galleys and taken by assault. To avoid having their whole fleet thus destroyed piecemeal, the unengaged Venetian ships hoisted their sails and attempted to flee.

On the open sea, the Gauls should have been able to evade the Romans. The fragile Roman galleys were of little use in the foul weather that normally plagued the coast while the Romans themselves were poor navigators on open seas. As fate would have it, calm weather descended upon the area, leaving the Gauls at the mercy of the swift Roman oarsmen. By the time the fiery sun dipped beneath the waves, the Veneti fleet was destroyed.

With no means to evacuate the besieged towns, the whole of the Veneti and coastal tribes surrendered to Caesar. Their punishment was severe. Their political leaders were executed and the bulk of the male population sold into slavery.

While Caesar dealt with the Veneti, his lieutenants, Q.T. Sabinus and Publius Crassus, met with varying success elsewhere in Gaul. Sabinus found himself shut up in his camp by the rest of the rebellious Aremorican tribes, headed by the Venelli under Viridovix and reinforced by Gallic freebooters from the rest of Gaul. The slurs of the barbarians from outside the ramparts failed to goad Sabinus into sallying forth against a numerically greater foe but they stung his legionaries' proud hearts.

With his men muttering of their "cowardly" leader, Sabinus refused to let his vanity get the better off him and be tempted into a hopeless battle in the open. Instead he came up with a ruse. One of his Gallic auxiliaries went to the Gallic camp, pretending to be a deserter. The "deserter" told the Gallic chiefs that the Romans were trembling in fear, that Caesar was hard pressed against the Veneti, and that Sabinus planned to evacuate his camp secretly at night. Coaxed by the false prospect of an easy victory, the hot-blooded Gauls refused to let Viridovix and the other chiefs step away from the assembly unless they promised forthwith to attack the Roman camp!

With bundles of firewood to fill the Roman trenches, the Gauls rushed a mile up a gradual slope to the Roman camp. The ecstatic Gauls maintained no order and ran as if the battle had already been won and all that remained was to collect the spoils. By the time they reached the Roman ramparts, the Gauls were already breathing heavily. While they were still catching their breath, the gates suddenly opened. Out charged the legionaries, straight at the disbelieving and startled Gauls. The Gauls immediately broke in panic. Most of them were cut down then and there, and even those that managed to flee the initial slaughter were caught and finished off by the Roman cavalry. The aftermath of the Gallic debacle was that all the tribes surrendered to Sabinus.

While Aremorica was brought firmly under Roman control, further south the 25-year-old Publius Crassus was determined to do the same to Aquitania. In the territory of the Sotiates, his twelve cohorts, cavalry contingent and allied Gauls were ambushed *concursare* style. The fighting was hard but the Romans and their allies persevered in the end. The reduction of the Sotiates' strongholds proved no easy task either. The prevalence of local copper mines made Crassus' foes skilled sappers, who threatened his siege terraces and mantlets. Even so, Crassus overcame the Sotiates' fortifications.

A greater challenge lay ahead after Crassus crossed the borders of the Vocates and Tarusates. Reinforced from neighboring tribes and even from nearer Spain, the native army severed Crassus' supply line by constructing a camp to his rear. Before the enemy grew too strong, Crassus decided to assault the enemy camp. When the Romans attacked from both sides the Gauls panicked and attempted to flee. But on the plains there was no shelter from the Roman cavalry. Only a quarter of the tribesmen survived the disaster. Crassus' victory was followed by the general surrender of Aquitania, with the exception of a few distant tribes who could not be reached due to the onset of winter.

Only the Morini and Menapii left the string of Roman conquests in Gaul incomplete. If Caesar envisioned a quick and easy campaign against these still defiant Belgae tribes, he was sorely mistaken. The Morini and Menapii decided not to meet Caesar in open battle and neither did they retire to their strongholds. Instead they withdrew into the vast forests and swamps of their country from whence they set ambushes. Although Caesar cut and burnt down tracts of forests and destroyed fields and villages, the enemy continued to elude him.

With the onset of heavy autumn rains, the damp and cold legionaries shivered beneath their drenched canvases. The campaign was called off, and the army placed into winter quarters amongst the recently conquered tribes while Caesar, as usual, set out for Cisalpine Gaul. Although the Morini and Menapii and some of the Aquitania tribes remained free of Roman sway, the summer campaign on the whole had been a success.

Early in the next year, 55 BC, more good news for Caesar arrived from Rome. By means of bribery, political bullying and bloodshed, Pompey and Crassus made good on their agreements reached at Luca the previous year. Cicero was cowed into dropping his attacks on Caesar's veteran land grants and even went on to publicly praise Caesar's achievements in Gaul. Domitius, who had threatened to take away Caesar's armies, continued to run for the consulship but was defeated by Pompey and Crassus who ran against him and assumed a second joint consulship. Despite the continued opposition of Cato, Caesar's pro-consulship in Gaul was forthwith extended for a second five years. Pompey and Crassus in turn gained five-year pro-consular commands in Spain and Syria, respectively.

Encouraged by the extension of his command in Gaul, Caesar used his own funds to raise a new legion, probably designated the Fifth, in Transalpine Gaul. It was the first legion to be composed of barbarians and raised in a foreign country. The recruits were trained and equipped in Roman fashion and would later be rewarded with full Roman citizenship. Caesar named the legion the "Alauda", a Gallic name for the small bird, the Crested Lark, in reference to the plume on the Roman helmet. The new recruits would have a chance to see combat soon. The next upheaval in Gaul did not even wait until the spring. During the winter of 56/55 BC, German tribes crossed the Rhine near the mouth of the river.

Ousted from their tribal homelands by Rome's old enemy the Suebi, the Usipetes and Tencteri wandered the German hinterland for three years before reaching the Rhine opposite the lands of the Menapii. Alarmed by the approach of the Usipetes and Tencteri, the Menapii abandoned their villages on the river's east bank. On the western bank, however, they put up a stout defense. The Germans were unable to ford the river and for three days withdrew; or so it seemed. When the Menapii crossed back over to their villages on the eastern side, the Germans' cavalry quickly doubled back and put the startled Menapii to the sword. The Usipetes and Tencteri crossed the river on the Menapii's boats. Once across, the large German tribes were unstoppable. They lodged themselves in the farm houses of the Menapii and took what food they needed.

More supplies for the Germanic immigrants were forthcoming from Gallic tribes to the south, which in Caesar's opinion they were all too eager to give up. Suspicious that the Gauls wished to ally themselves with the Germans against the Romans, Caesar returned to Gaul where he assured the Gallic chiefs that the Romans would take care of the Germans. Early in spring 55 BC, Usipetes and Tencteri envoys arrived at the Roman camp near the River Meuse (the Mosa). They declared that they did not seek war with the Romans and had only invaded Gaul because they had been driven from their own lands. The Romans should grant them lands or let them live in peace in their conquered territories. However, if it was war the Romans sought then war they should get. The Usipetes and Tencteri yielded only to the mighty Suebi, against whom even the gods could not stand in battle!

Caesar's reply was that he would settle them in the territory of the Ubii, a German tribe whose territory lay on the eastern side of the Rhine. The Ubii, who were friendly with the Romans, were also hard pressed by the Suebi. The Usipetes and Tencteri delegates declared that they needed three days to consider Caesar's offer and sent their own delegates to the Ubii. This Caesar refused for he feared that the Germans only wished to gain time for the return of their main cavalry force, which was busy pillaging abroad. He pressed the issue by advancing closer to the barbarian camp and demanding a personal visit from their chiefs.

The two forces were now so close that a confrontation between patrolling cavalry was nearly inevitable. Caesar's cavalry consisted largely of allied Gauls. Among them was the gallant Aquitanian nobleman, Piso, whose grandfather was once king of his tribe and had been granted the title of "Friend of Rome" by the Senate. Piso, alongside his brother, likely joined Caesar's forces in the aftermath of Crassus' recent campaign in their homelands. The two Aquitanians and the rest of the Caesar's 5,000-strong cavalry were under orders not to entice the enemy, but approached too close to the enemy camp. When they were spotted by the 800 remaining German cavalry, the Germans boldly attacked. Before colliding with Gauls, many of the Germanic warriors jumped of their steeds. Spear in hand, they bolted forward on foot and sliced through the mass of startled Gallic horsemen. The Usipetes and Tencteri tribesmen lunged at the Gallic horses, impaling them with their spears. The Gallic riders were thrown to the ground and quickly dispatched. Everywhere around him, Piso watched the Gauls scattering in flight. A number of Germans closed around him and cut off his own escape. Suddenly his brother galloped into the fray, holding off the Germans so that Piso could get away. When he had reached a safe distance, Piso turned to look for his brother. The latter was thrown to the ground when his horse was wounded. Although surrounded, Piso's brother resisted bravely. He was bleeding from multiple wounds before being slain by the Germans. When Piso beheld what had happened, he dashed back to his brother's side and to his own death. The whole melee was quick and furious. Piso and his brother were counted among seventy-four dead.

The incident suited Caesar just fine for it gave him an excuse to accuse the Germans of treachery. The next morning when the German chiefs and their retainers arrived to express regret for the engagement and to continue the peace talk, Caesar put them all under armed guard. Caesar formed up his army and advanced towards the German camp in triple-line battle formation. The eight-mile march was covered in great speed as Caesar pushed his legions hard.

So sudden was the Roman attack that the Germans were overwhelmed. Without their leaders, chaos reigned in the barbarian camp. Women and children bolted in all directions. There was little time to take up their arms although a few of the men made a brave but futile stand among the wagons and carts. It was less a battle than sheer butchery. Everywhere the barbarians, regardless of age and gender, were impaled by the pilum or the gladius, or were trampled under the hooves of the Roman cavalry. Those Germans that managed to reach the nearby junction of the Rhine and Meuse dove into the water. They escaped their executioners but not the current of the river. Too weak to swim, the barbarians were pulled under to drown in the river.

Probably over a hundred thousand barbarian men, women and children were killed without any real loss to the Romans. A boastful Caesar wrote that an enemy of 430,000 people was annihilated. It was perhaps his most complete victory but also his most shameful. The massacre shocked the Roman intellectuals. Cato the Younger proclaimed that the honor of the Republic could only be reclaimed if Caesar surrendered to the Germans. In contrast, the Roman mob, which gleefully cheered at the butchery of the gladiatorial games and beast "hunts," was no doubt thrilled by the news of the slaughter.

Caesar now decided to cross the Rhine in a show of force, to teach the Germans that nowhere were they safe from the arms of Rome. When he heard that the Sugambri[2] sheltered the Usipetes and Tencteri cavalry, he demanded that they hand them over. The Sugambri retorted that the Rhine marked the limit of the Roman Empire. If Caesar thought it unfair for the Germans to cross into Gaul, then why should it be fair for the Romans to cross the other way?

Such a challenge could not go unheeded by Caesar. To impress the barbarians, he rejected offers by the Ubii to ferry the Romans across and instead decided to build a bridge. After ten days, the legions had completed yet another near miraculous feat of engineering with a 40-foot wide wooden bridge that spanned the 400-yard wide and 16-foot deep river.

Over the bridge and into the territory of the Sugambri marched the legions, only to find the villages abandoned. The Sugambri had heeded the advice of the Usipetes and Tencteri cavalry. Like the Belgae Menapii, the Sugambri took to the woods with their women, children and belongings. Caesar tarried for a few days, burning villages and wheat crops, and then moved south into Ubii lands.

The Ubii welcomed the Romans, hoping that Caesar would deliver them from their hated enemies the Suebi. The latter, however, did not remain unprepared for Caesar's coming. Their women, children and old had sought shelter in the forests, while from everywhere their warriors had assembled into a mighty army. Deep within their forested heartland, the Suebi awaited Caesar's coming.

Since a forest battle was not at all to Caesar's liking, he forthwith announced that he had accomplished all he intended and withdrew to the western bank of the Rhine. To the Germanic tribes, it showed that Caesar's Romans were reluctant to meet the Suebi on their own ground. Even so, Caesar made it clear that his legions could cross the Rhine any time he wished. Caesar would not tolerate any Germanic intrusion into Gaul. Gaul was to be Caesar's and his grip on it had tightened.

Chapter Twelve

Caesar in Britannia

"Jump down, comrades, unless you want to surrender our eagle to the enemy; I,
at any rate, mean to do my duty to my country and my general."[1]
Eagle-bearer of the 10th Legion

Caesar followed up his conquest of Aremorica in 56 BC with his defeat of the invading Usipetes and Tencteri in the spring of 55 BC. In spite of Caesar's latest victories, by now he should have realized that the spirit of the barbarians could not easily be subdued. It seemed that every time the Roman legions knocked them down, the barbarians sprang right up again, ready for another beating. Nevertheless, as the 55 BC campaign season neared its end, Caesar considered Gaul sufficiently subjugated to allow him to cross the channel to invade Britannia. Ostensibly Caesar set out to punish the Briton tribes for aiding the Gauls in the past, but the real reason was more likely Caesar's lust for even more martial glory. Since there was little time before the onset of the winter, he decided to limit the expedition to a reconnaissance to find out more about the strength of the tribes and of the local geography.

During the ensuing campaigns, Caesar learned much of Britannia. His anecdotes left a picture of the land and people he was about to invade. At the time of Caesar, Britannia's southern maritime tribes consisted of Belgae who had migrated to the island in search of lands and booty at the end of the second century BC. Like the Celts of Gaul, the Briton Belgic tribes were primarily an agricultural and cattle rearing society. They brought to Britannia town-sized settlements, with wealthy chiefs who patronized skilled metal smiths and potters. The clusters of Briton farms south of the River Thames yielded a population density comparable to Gaul. In contrast, the tribes north of the River Thames were mostly of older Celtic stock. Their ancestors arrived on the island sometime after 900 BC, long before the Belgae. The northern tribes were more primitive, according to Caesar, who wrote that they subsisted primarily on meat and milk. Peculiar customs among the Britons included the sharing of wives between male family members and disdaining the meat of hare, fowl and goose, which were kept as pets. The maritime districts produced tin and the midland region iron, while bronze was imported.

To begin with, however, Caesar knew very little of Britannia: "the Gauls knew next to nothing; for in the ordinary way traders are the only people who visit Britain, and even they know only that part of the coast which faces Gaul."[2] To find out more, Caesar sent ahead one of his officers: Gaius Volusenus. Known for his courage and wise council, Volusenus had served as a military tribune under legate Galba in the ill fated Alps mountain campaign of 57 BC. With a single warship, Volusenus explored the Britannia's coastline for suitable landing sites.

Caesar assembled the fleet he had used in the Veneti war at Portus Itius, in the territory of the Morini. From here the journey across the Channel was the shortest. Fortunately for Caesar, several cantons of the Morini, which earlier had defied Roman annexation, now had a change of heart and offered hostages.

More good news came with the arrival of Briton tribal envoys. Having heard of Caesar's intentions through traders, they offered hostages as well. Caesar in turn made them promises of goodwill. When the envoys were ready to return to Britannia, Caesar asked for Commius the Atrebatean, one of the continental Belgae kings, to accompany them and spread word of Caesar's friendship. Commius owed his kingship to Caesar and enjoyed the Britons' respect. Unfortunately, Commius was sailing into trouble as the show of Briton goodwill proved to be an illusion. Once in Britannia, poor Commius and his 30-man-strong advance troupe were thrown in fetters.

At midnight of August 25th, a flotilla of warships escorted 80 transports as they sailed into darkness from Portus Itius for the mysterious shores of Britannia. The weather seemed favorable and justified the late hour of the departure. On board were Caesar with the Seventh and the Tenth Legions. He had sent the cavalry to another port, a few miles to the north. There they were to embark on eighteen cargo ships and follow the main fleet. Nine hours later, Caesar and the men aboard the first ships beheld the coast of Britannia. The white cliffs of Dover towered far above the narrow shoreline below. Not one of the legionaries knew anything about the size of the land they were about to invade. Indeed, some scholars speculated that the isle was a figment of the imagination. But the cliffs were real, as were the rows of Britons gathered on top of them.

The Britons stood ready to greet the Romans, not with open arms but with stones and javelins! Caesar gathered his legates, tribunes, centurions and all the other major commanders of his legions and auxiliaries, for a *consilium* (a war council) on his ship. He listened carefully to their opinions and wisely decided against a landing on the narrow beach below the cliffs. Based on information gathered by Volusenus, Caesar hugged the coastline for some miles until the cliffs gave way to open shores at Deal.

The Britons, however, would not be avoided so easily. Their cavalry and charioteers, with their infantry in their wake, shadowed Caesar's fleet. With the Britons milling along the beach, the great Roman ships dropped their anchors. Centurions shouted orders to their aides, the optiones, who gestured with their staffs. Circular horns blared and legionaries leapt into the water.

Burdened by their heavy arms, pounded by waves and pulled by the suction of rip currents, the legionaries were barely able to keep themselves upright as they waded to the shore. The javelins and sling-stones of the Britons rained among them. Exhausted and wounded, many Roman soldiers drowned in the waist-deep water, the blood of their limp bodies clouding the water. Those legionaries that neared the shore got ready to exert their last ounces of strength. Britons urged on their steeds, splashing through the waves. Horses reared and salty water sprayed into the legionaries' eyes. To the legionary, exhausted and dazed by fear, the Britons appeared as horrifying apparitions, with their long wild hair and mustaches, their bodies completely shaved and dyed a startling blue. Instinctively, the legionaries lifted their shields to block spear thrusts and swords swinging at them from above. The strain proved too much even for Caesar's iron legions. Unable to press forward, their characteristic resolve began to waver and turn into fear.

Caesar watched anxiously as his amphibious assault became bogged down and was critically close to turning into a rout. To bolster his hard-pressed legionaries, he ordered the marines on the warships to provide support fire. Horns blew and hundreds of sweat-drenched seamen[3] bent to multiple banks of oars thrashing the water. Onward sped the galleys until, like wooden whales, they beached themselves upon the enemy's right flank. From their decks spewed forth a devastating array of sling stones, arrows and catapulted rocks.

Shocked and frightened by the imposing Roman landing, the natives momentarily pulled back from the beach. This was enough for the legionaries, who stormed forth with renewed vigor. The Eagle bearer of Tenth Legion prayed to the heavens and cried, "Jump down, comrades, unless you want to surrender our eagle to the enemy; I, at any rate, mean to do my duty to my country and my general."[4] With those words he cast himself into the sea, to bear the gold-plated, eagle-topped standard forward against the Britons.

The she-wolf suckling the twins Romulus and Remus, the mythical founders of Rome. The bronze she-wolf was probably cast by the Etruscans of Veii (550 BC) and is based on a Hellenistic-Ionian model. The twins were added during the Renaissance. Location: Musei Capitolini, Rome. *(Erich Lessing, Art Resource)*

Woe to the Vanquished. (Courtesy of Heritage History)

'Dying Gaul', Roman marble copy of a Hellenistic original of 230-220 BC. *(Erich Lessing, Art Resource)*

The Barbarians before Rome by Evariste Vital Luminais (1822–96). *(The Bridgeman Art Library)*

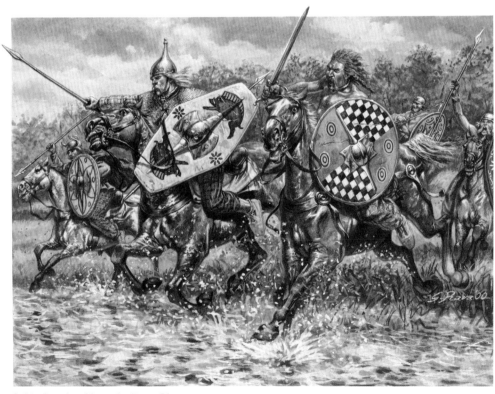

Celtic Cavalry Charge by Rava Giuseppe.

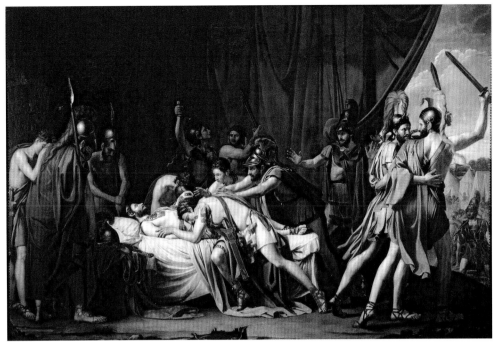

The Death of the Rebel, Viriathus, Raimundo de Madrazo y Garetta, (1841–1920), Prado, Madrid. *(The Bridgeman Art Library)*

The Teutones Wandering in Gaul. (Courtesy of Heritage History)

Gaius Julius Caesar – Battle of Bibracte 58 BC by Mark Churms.

Caesar's 10th legion lands in Britain by Peter Connolly. *(akg-images)*

Vercingetorix throws down his arms at the feet of Julius Caesar, oil on canvas (1899) by Lionel Noel Royer (1852–1926). *(Musee Crozatier, Le Puy-en-Velay, France, Giraudon, The Bridgeman Art Library)*

Arminius' Triumph over the Romans. *(Courtesy of Heritage History)*

German, called Arminius.[1]

Arminius, Roman Bust, marble,
Capitoline Museum, Rome.
(Bridgeman Art Library)

Hermann's (Arminius') Monument, Teutoburg Forest,
North-Rhine Westphalia. *(Photo by author)*

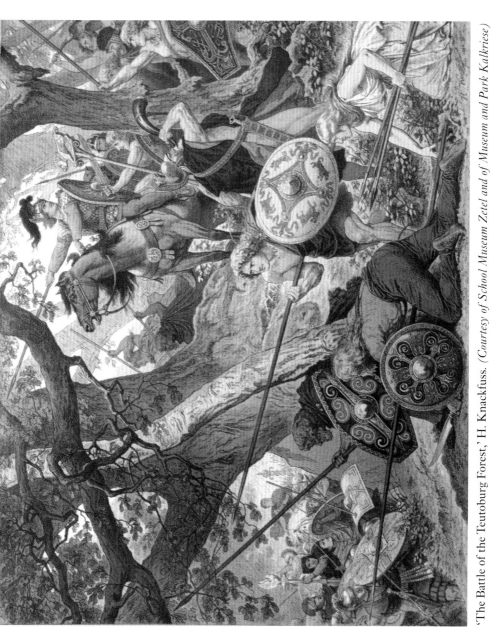

'The Battle of the Teutoburg Forest,' H. Knackfuss. *(Courtesy of School Museum Zetel and of Museum and Park Kalkriese)*

Fighting Scene during the Retreat of Germanicus by Ferdinand Leeks (1874–1923). *(Art Resource)*

Portrait of Germanicus, (15 BC–19 AD), marble bust, Louvre, Paris. *(Art Resource)*

Everywhere, the Romans gained the beachhead only to be met with a renewed charge of the Britons. Unable to form up in proper formation, the legionaries were hard pressed. Isolated Romans were surrounded and cut down in the shallows, the salty foam turning red. Again Caesar reacted quickly, ordering the warships' boats and scout ships loaded with troops and sending them to critical points. Once the legionaries gained the dry ground and formed up in numbers, the tide turned against the Britons who fled for their lives. Regrettably for Caesar, he had no cavalry to pursue the Britons because unfavorable winds delayed the arrival of his cavalry transports.

Envoys arrived from the Briton tribes, seeking pardon and asking Caesar for forgiveness. Caesar demanded that Commius be freed and that the Britons would give Caesar hostages. In return Caesar accepted their renewed offer of peace. However, Caesar was no doubt fully aware that the Britons, like the Gauls, would take up their arms at the slightest favorable opportunity.

Such an opportunity developed when a furious storm broke upon the area, at the very moment when the cavalry transports were finally seen offshore from Caesar's camp. The latter were unable to make a landing and blown off course ended up back in Gaul. During the night the storm played havoc with the Roman warships. These had been pulled upon the shore but due to unusual high tide were violently tossed about.

The ships' groaning and creaking timbers broke through the din of the storm. The Romans helplessly watched their transports and great galleys alike torn to pieces. Even those that made it through the night were severely damaged and unable to sail. The morale of the army sunk like its ships. The legions were effectively stranded in Britannia, on unknown shores, and without any wheat supplies for the coming winter.

The Britons welcomed the misfortune of the Romans by renewing hostilities. They were intent on prolonging the fighting into the cold season when hunger would force Caesar to succumb. Caesar confronted his plight with his characteristic zeal. Timber and bronze from the most damaged ships was used to repair the rest. Thus all but twelve of the ships were made seaworthy again.

To deal with his supply problem, wheat was collected by the legions from the nearby fields. Using sickles, the legionaries collected bushels of wheat. Back at the camp, the grains would be ground into flour and baked into bread. At first the harvest was carried out with little opposition by the natives, some of whom became regular visitors to the Roman camp. However, one day, the guards in front of the camp gate noticed a massive dust cloud in the distance. The cloud arose from the direction in which the Seventh Legion had marched to confiscate wheat. It could only mean one thing: a battle.

Caesar spat out orders, quickly collected some cohorts, and sped towards the commotion. Sure enough he beheld the Seventh Legion, hard pressed from all sides by Britons who pelted the legionaries with missiles. The Britons had approached the area at night to hide in a wood. Whilst the legionaries were spread out and busy cutting wheat, the barbarians suddenly burst upon them in an ambush. Briton javelins whistled, Roman mail was punctured and a few Romans fell dead. The remainder hastened to form rough ranks.

All around the legionaries galloped the Briton cavalry and chariots. Superb charioteers, the Britons raced wildly about. Their horses and chariots raised a terrifying ruckus. One Briton steered the team while another hurled javelins at the Romans. The latter Briton then sprang to the ground, to fight alongside his cavalry and infantry.

The arrival of Caesar with reinforcements caused the Britons to halt their attack. Caesar used the opportunity to withdraw his ambushed troops back to his shore-side camp. For several days stormy weather prevented hostilities but at least it gave both sides a break from the constant fighting. While the legionaries waited out the rains huddled in their waxed and waterproof goat hide tents, Briton messengers rallied support in the outlying farmsteads. The messengers cried out that only a few Romans held the camp and that much booty and freedom was at stake!

As soon as the skies cleared up the Britons attacked again and in greater numbers. Unshaken, the legionaries formed up their unbreakable ranks and, aided by thirty horsemen of Commius, repulsed the Britons. The legions harried after their beaten foes, swords and spears cutting them down on the run. Outlying homes were set to the torch. Flames flickered from timber beams and straw roofs. Spirals of smoke marked the path of the victorious Roman army.

Once again the Britons came to offer peace and surrender hostages. But Caesar had had enough. The storms were followed by a spell of fair weather. After all the rain and storms, the legionaries basked in the warm rays of Sol, their sun god. With the fall equinox fast approaching, Caesar decided to leave Britannia while he still could. At midnight he weighed anchor and set sail for Gaul.

Caesar was gone from Gaul less than three weeks yet in his absence the Morini revolted again. They gave Caesar a rude surprise by contesting his landing. Only after hours of battle were they driven off. There followed the usual Roman reprisal raids after which Caesar stationed his entire army in winter quarters among the troublesome Belgae.

When the Senate got ear of Caesar's latest victories, they decreed an extraordinary twenty days of public thanksgiving. In retrospect though, did Caesar really deserve his latest acclaim? His expedition to Britannia was even more of a farce than his conquest of Gaul and his reprisal against the Suebi. For putting himself and two of his best legions at risk, he merely familiarized himself with the country and with the tactics of the natives. The numerous rebellions of the year showed that the Gallic tribes only remained "conquered" as long as large Roman forces were stationed among them. In other words it had been a year of tactical but not strategic victories. Napoleon Bonaparte called Caesar's Britannia campaign a "second class operation".[5] Nevertheless, to his credit, Caesar became the first Roman commander to set foot on Britannia.

Caesar was well aware of the shortfalls of his first Britannia campaign. Accordingly, before he left for Italy, he ordered the construction of new ships. Based on his recent experience, the ships would be built for a beach landing, quick loading and disembarking, and would better be able to deal with the local tides. As a result the new ships were smaller, while those for the cavalry, draught animals and cargo were broader. Both could be propelled by oar or by sail.

Caesar was not idle during the winter. There were assizes to be held in northern Italy and in Illyricum. There were barbarian raiders along the Illyricum border and an anti-Roman faction among his Treveri allies to be taken care of. In between dealing with all these problems, Caesar toured his army's Belgae winter quarters. With materials brought from Spain and through the nearly superhuman efforts of his legionaries, there were built 600 of the new ships and 28 of the traditional war galleys.

In the fading light of an early July day in 54 BC, Caesar's armada weighed anchor at Portus Itius. The sails of 800 ships billowed in the wind. It was the largest fleet to be seen crossing the channel for the next two millennia. On board were five legions with a total of around 25,000 troops and an additional 2,000 cavalry. Remaining on the continent were Labienus with three legions and 2,000 cavalry to protect the ports and the supply route and to keep an eye on Gaul.

This time the mere sight of Caesar's mighty armada so intimidated the Britons gathered on the shoreline, that they withdrew. At midday, the *caliga* legionary boots stepped unopposed onto the sandy beach. Caesar left 10 cohorts and 300 cavalry behind under Quintus Atrius, and with the rest pressed on after the enemy. The legions marched past patches of wheat fields, round huts, and forests of ancient giant oaks. Sometimes a hilltop fortress rose up in the distance. Now and then a herd of elk browsing near the forests, or perhaps even a brown bear, was seen by scouts.

After a night march of 12 miles, the Romans sighted the enemy the next day. Near a river the Britons attacked with cavalry and chariots but this time Caesar had his own cavalry handy and they easily routed the Britons back into a nearby wood. Amidst the trees and foliage the Britons sought safety behind ramparts made of felled trees. The soldiers of the Seventh Legion countered the Briton fortification by throwing up their own earthen ramp. With shields locked above their heads, the legionaries formed the classic "tortoise" maneuver. Missiles struck into the double layers of the 4-foot-by-2-foot scutum, or ricocheted off its iron boss. The Romans breached the Briton ramparts and drove the enemy out of the woods. Although Roman casualties were light, Caesar postponed a pursuit since he was unsure of the terrain ahead and because night was fast approaching.

When at daybreak bad news arrived from the fleet, Caesar returned to his coastal camp. Storms had struck again, ripping apart another forty ships and damaging most of the remainder. Messages were sent to the continent for replacements while the legionaries, many of whom were skilled craftsmen, carried out repairs. To prevent further damages, Caesar beached all the ships and connected the landing to the camp by an entrenchment. Surveyors marked off the corners with big flags. Pioneers and legionaries dug trenches and threw the soil up to form a rampart. Wooden stakes were hammered into the rampart and lashed together to form a palisade. After ten days of round-the-clock Herculean labor, the legions completed the work.

With the same forces as before, Caesar set out to once more confront the Britons. The Britons had used the time to reassemble with additional reinforcements. Having put aside the wars amongst each other, they elected Cassivellaunus, King of the Catuvellauni, to lead them. The Briton warlord unleashed his cavalry and chariots upon the marching Roman columns. Javelins hurled through the air, skewering Roman shields or thudding into the ground. Expert marksmen, Briton slingers dashed in Roman helmets with their stones. When the Roman auxiliary cavalry bolted into action, the Britons reined in their own horses and whipped their chariots back for the cover of nearby woods and highlands. There a number of individual combats broke out while the bulk of the Britons dispersed into the wilderness. Longswords parried and slashed as a few of the Britons turned on their over-eager pursuers.

Another surprise attack came from the woods while the legions were setting up camp. Caesar sent his elite, and possibly larger, first cohorts of his two legions to confront the attackers. Very nearly, the Britons got caught between the shield walls and blank sword blades of the cohorts but a mad Briton dash unnerved the Romans. The Britons broke through and got away unhurt. More cohorts had to be rushed up to clear the field.

The Briton reluctance to fight was not cowardice but clever tactics. Each time the Britons struck, and quickly disengaged, the Romans took casualties. During the last engagement, a Roman tribune was counted among the dead. The skirmishing tactics were disadvantageous to the legionaries who preferred a set battle, and dangerous to the undersized Roman cavalry, which could be lured away into an ambush.

The next day, Gaius Trebonius left the camp to collect food from the countryside with three legions and the cavalry. Suddenly throngs of blue-painted barbarians swept down upon Trebonius from all sides. With wild, howling savages all around them, a lesser army would have panicked. But hard training and discipline paid off for the Romans. The legionaries stoutly formed their lines, swords rasped from scabbards, and in a countercharge completely scattered the Britons. The nimbler Britons tried to reform but the Roman cavalry gave them no chance. The Roman horse kept on their heels, hacking and slashing away. The field was left strewn with Briton dead and wounded.

Caesar pushed on toward the River Thames. Near Brentford, the river was shallow enough to cross by foot. The Britons held the opposite bank behind rows of sharp projecting stakes. Undaunted, the legionaries and cavalry plunged into the river. Incredibly, although weighed down by 30-pound mail shirts and by their shields and helmets, the legionaries waded through water that at times rose to their necks. The Romans' speed and aggression terrified the Britons who took to flight without much of a fight. After this setback, Cassivellaunus disbanded the greater part of his army and returned to his harrying tactics with his 4,000 remaining charioteers.

Celtic disunity now once again played in Caesar's favor. With Cassivellaunus unable to defeat the Romans, the powerful Trinobantes tribe sought an alliance with Caesar. The Trinobantes lived just north of the Thames estuary and to the east of Cassivellaunus' territory. Cassivellaunus had formerly slain the king of the Trinobantes but the king's son, Mandubracius, escaped his father's fate. He fled to Rome and currently was with Caesar's entourage. The Trinobantes wished for Caesar to reinstate Mandubracius as their head of state. Caesar complied and was rewarded by the submission of most of the maritime tribes, except those of Cantium (Kent). Furthermore Caesar was told of the location of Cassivellaunus' stronghold. A sort of guerrilla base, the stronghold lay in thick woods near Wheathampstead and boasted a formidable rampart and trench. Inside, the Britons herded large numbers of cattle. Caesar was impressed by the defenses but they quickly fell to his legions' violent two-pronged assault.

Meanwhile Cassivellaunus had ordered the four kings of Cantium to assault the Roman naval camp at Sandwich. However, not only were the Britons unable to overcome the Roman defenses but they were easily dispersed by a Roman sortie. The murderous blades of the 16-inch gladius exacted a terrible toll. No Romans were lost and a noble Briton named Lugotorix was captured. Ever since Caesar crossed the Thames, the Britons' will to fight had been lackluster. Their morale was broken.

Without allies and with nothing but defeats to show for his troubles, Cassivellaunus decided to sue for peace. Luckily for Cassivellaunus, the usual rumors of unrest in Gaul induced Caesar to return his army to Gaul for the winter. With Commius acting as an intermediary, all Cassivellaunus had to do was to give hostages, promise to not make war on Mandubracius and agree to pay a tribute to Rome. In time, Cassivellaunus resumed to extend his sway over Britannia. His dynasty came to rule over much of the southern isle, ironically profiting from the flourishing trade with the Roman world that sprang up in wake of Caesar's expeditions.

When, at summer's end, Caesar's entire army returned to Gaul, his second expedition to Britannia proved no more successful than his first. With no Roman garrisons in Britannia, the alliances and submissions of the tribes were meaningless. Although Cassivellaunus paid "a large sum of money,"[6] it is doubtful whether any subsequent tribute was ever paid to Rome. The looting too had been meager. "The islanders were so miserably poor that they had nothing worth being plundered of,"[7] wrote Plutarch.

Still, the legionaries had fought with their usual valor and Caesar added more victories to his military fame. More of Britannia was explored and hostages were taken. If the ultimate aim was to deter further Briton aid to their cousins in Gaul, then Caesar's expedition was likely a success. Plutarch praised Caesar for "his expedition to Britain" being "the most famous testimony to his courage,"[8] and lauded Caesar for invading an island whose extent and nature were still a mystery to Rome.

Among the Britons too, the effect was profound. After Caesar's incursion into Britannia, trade with the Roman world, in wine and pottery, began to flourish.

In Rome, however, at least among the Senate, the reaction was mute and there were no public thanksgivings. The prominent politician Cicero noted the lack of war booty. And booty after all, in precious loot and slaves, was what fed the Roman war machine. The Roman Eagle fastened its talons on Britannia only to release them again. It would be another century, during the reign of Emperor Claudius, before Britannia would again feel the talons' grip.

Chapter Thirteen

The Belgic Tribes Revolt

"Perhaps there is nothing very surprising in their readiness to revolt; among many other reasons, tribes which were considered the bravest and most warlike in the world naturally felt bitter resentment at the complete loss of this reputation which submission to Rome rule entailed."[1]

Caesar on the Second Gallic Rebellion

In 54 BC the plight of war-ravaged Gaul worsened, as nature too took no mercy on her people. There was precious little rain and the crops withered in the face of Belis, the Celtic sun god. The people's discontent manifested itself into a growing hatred of the Roman occupiers, who confiscated what grain they needed from the supplies desperately saved up by the Gauls. Before winter blanketed the land in frost, insurrection resurfaced in Gaul.

The seeds of what Caesar referred to as the second rebellion[2] were sown by Indutiomarus, a noble of the Treveri. The Treveri dwelt in the lower valley of the Moselle and, as mentioned earlier, were renowned for their courage and for their cavalry.[3] Under Indutiomarus' rival and son-in-law, chief Cingetorix, the Treveri had been allies of Rome and had provided cavalry for Caesar's war against the Belgae in 57 BC. Even then, however, there were signs that their support was half-hearted, for they were quick to abandon the Romans when the battle turned against them.

Before Caesar headed off on this second Britannia expedition in July 54 BC, he had to personally intervene with no less than four legions to reaffirm Cingetorix's position. When he brought with him such imposing military might, Caesar almost certainly had the Treveri's massive Dollberg fortress on his mind.[4] The 18-hectare fortress was one of the largest Celtic fortifications ever built. Glacial moraines from the mountain provided handy building material for the massive 60-foot-high and equally wide walls which ringed it. If Caesar rode through the stronghold's double gateway, he would have noticed that it was topped by a wooden battlement. Since the walls projected outward from the gate, any attack on the gate would have met with resistance from three sides. As events turned out, any thoughts that Caesar may have harbored on laying siege to the Treveri stronghold proved unwarranted. Cingetorix and most of the other tribal leaders re-affirmed their loyalty to Caesar. Humbled and isolated, Indutiomarus was left boiling in hatred and forced to give hostages which included his own son. Now, late in 54 BC, Indutiomarus again turned large numbers of the Treveri against the Romans.

Indutiomarus' schemes found fertile ground among the Belgic Eburones and their two chiefs, the younger Ambiorix and the elder Catuvolcus. The Eburones were a relatively minor tribe and subordinate to the Treveri. However, what they lacked in numbers they made up in resilience. Ambiorix would prove to be a brilliant guerrilla warfare leader, a type of fighting in which the Eburones excelled and which would earn them Caesar's hatred. From the lands between the River Meuse and the River Rhine, Ambiorix and Catuvolcus marshaled their warriors and advanced on Atuatuca, the military camp of the Fourteenth Legion. Atuatuca stood in Eburones territory, near modern Tongeren. When the Eburones cavalry surprised a party of unfortunate Roman wood cutters outside of Atuatuca, the second rebellion had begun.

Ambiorix and Catuvolcus marched their Eburones army right up to the gates of Atuatuca. There the Gallic cavalry was bested by the Roman Spanish auxiliary cavalry, which made a dashing sortie out of the camp gate. The valiant Spaniards retired back into the camp. Even though the Fourteenth Legion had been reinforced by five cohorts (half a legion), its generals Quintus Titurius Sabinus and Lucius Aurunculeius Cotta were not about to risk an open attack on the Eburones army. For their part, Ambiorix and Catuvolcus wisely reckoned that any attack on the strong Roman fortifications would be hopeless.

Ambiorix decided to parley and win Sabinus and Cotta's trust. Ambiorix thanked them for all that Caesar had done for him in the past. After all, Caesar's enslavement of the Aduatuci three years ago freed Ambiorix of the tribute he had to pay to them. And did not Caesar return to him Ambiorix's son and his brother's son, who had been kept as hostages by the Aduatuci? Ambiorix maintained that he was no enemy of Rome. He blamed Indutiomarus for causing all of Gaul to rise up against the Romans. Now, or so he claimed, Ambiorix had no choice but to attack the Romans as well or risk the wrath of the other tribes. Indeed, at this very moment, Ambiorix warned, large numbers of German mercenaries had crossed the Rhine and would arrive in a few days. The Romans were in grave danger and their only hope lay in escape. To repay Caesar's kindness, Ambiorix and his Eburones would allow the Fourteenth Legion safe passage through their lands.

The lives of some 6,000 soldiers and a multitude of camp servants, slaves and traders depended on the decision of legati Sabinus and Cotta. Both were veterans who had fought together before, although Sabinus was likely the senior commander.[5] During Caesar's 57 BC battle against King Galba on the River Aisne, Sabinus helped prevent a dangerous outflanking attempt. When Galba retreated from the Aisne, it was Cotta with the Roman cavalry who hunted down and killed large numbers of fleeing Belgae. A year later, Sabinus won a great victory over the Venelli, when he lured them into a disorganized attack on his camp. In 55 BC, Sabinus and Cotta burnt and looted the lands of the Menapii.

The legati held a council of war, attended by the tribunes and centurions. The officers shook their fists at each other, uttered oaths, argued and swore. The decision whether to stay or go was "hotly debated".[6] Cotta argued against leaving without Caesar's approval and most of the tribunes and centurions agreed with him. "We can resist any number of Gauls … and Germans into the bargain, in this fortified camp."[7] Furthermore, the Romans had plenty of grain stored away to resist a siege. "Besides," Cotta finished, "who would follow the advice of an enemy?"[8] Sabinus retorted that the Eburones were too weak a tribe to risk a bluff. Surely all of Gaul must be in revolt. If the Germans too were coming to aid the Gauls, then the camp will be doomed for sure. "Our only chance of escape is to act quickly. The men will understand: if disaster follows, it is you Cotta that they will hold responsible," Sabinus loudly implored, raising his voice so that the soldiers could hear him as well."[9] The debate became so heated that at one point officers had to hold back the two generals. Not until midnight did Cotta finally give way to Sabinus' plan. At least it was preferable to dividing the forces, which would mean certain disaster for both. The Fourteenth Legion would evacuate Atuatuca at dawn.

The legionaries marched into the brisk fall morning. Their sandal-boots crunched through the thick leaf-litter of the forest floor. The soldiers looked tired. Many were raw recruits, robbed of sleep by fear and worry. They felt the sting of the morning cold on their hands and faces. At least their woolen cloaks and tunics gave some protection from wind and cold. The baggage train followed the legion, with its hundreds of servants, pack mules and two and four wheeled carts that carried the heavier equipment. After two miles the path descended into a wooded defile. All around the legionary column, hidden behind trees and shrubs, the Eburones watched and waited.

The legionaries in the vanguard looked up; ahead the path led up and out of the defile. Their eyes widened as Eburones appeared from behind the trees that grew on either side of the path. All of a sudden, the forest ahead was alive with Eburones, blocking the only way out of the defile. Fighting erupted, but the Eburones held the higher ground and with spears, swords and slingshot, vexed any Roman attempt to break out to the front. A cry then came up from the rearguard that they too were under attack; the entire Roman column was trapped!

Sabinus ran around in near panic, desperately trying to arrange the cohorts. Considering his past combat experience, Sabinus' deteriorating morale was a sign that the situation was dire indeed. Cotta, on the other hand, retained his composure and discipline. He expected treachery from the Gauls. Now, the best that Cotta could do was to shore up the fighting spirit of his men. He shouted words of encouragement and fought among the ranks. At last, the order was given to abandon the baggage and form up in a defensive circle.

Although surrounded by Gauls, the legionaries fought on bravely. Individual cohorts charged through the Eburones' ranks like a battering ram, then fought their way back into the protection of the legion's defensive circle. Their sorties inflicted heavy wounds and killed many Eburones. Seeing that he was losing too many men, Ambiorix wisely decided to wear the Romans down by skirmishing tactics. When next the Romans charged, the lightly-armed Eburones ran out of harm's reach and pelted the Romans with a barrage of javelins and slingshot.

The battle went on for one long hour after another. Javelins pierced both thighs of centurion Titus Balventius. Another centurion, Quintus Lucanius died trying to rescue his surrounded son. Cotta was wounded by a sling stone that hit him full in the face.

From dawn until two in the afternoon, barbarian skirmishers steadily wore down the hard-pressed legionaries. Fear of the inevitable death gnawed at Sabinus. In a last hope to save his own life and the lives of his men, Sabinus sent his interpreter to ask Ambiorix for quarter. When Ambiorix asked to speak to Sabinus himself, the latter asked for Cotta to accompany him. The wounded Cotta refused, considering it folly to bargain with an enemy. Accompanied by his tribunes and senior centurions, Sabinus walked up to Ambiorix who demanded that the Romans lay down their weapons. Sabinus and his men did as they were told and were promptly surrounded. Brawny barbarian arms lifted long slashing blades and spears and killed the defenseless Romans.

At the death of Sabinus and his officers, a blood-curdling shout of triumph erupted from the Eburones. With renewed vigor they stormed upon the Roman defensive circle and shattered its ranks. In a savage battle, Cotta was slain alongside most of the soldiers that were with him. The legionaries that weren't cut down then and there fled for their lives; a handful into the woods and the rest back to their original camp.

The Eburones hotly pursued the legionaries back to Atuatuca. The standard-bearer of the legion threw his eagle over the rampart lest it fall into the hands of the Eburones. He turned to face his pursuers and died fighting. From inside the camp, the remaining legionaries defended the ramparts until nightfall. Seeing that there was no escape, the defenders fell into utter despair and committed suicide. Only a handful of men of the Fourteenth Legion reached Labienus' camp, located over fifty miles away. Virtually the entire Fourteenth Legion and its reinforcements were destroyed.

Ready to capitalize on his good fortune, Ambiorix and his Eburones cavalry galloped for the territory of the Aduatuci to enlist them as allies. This was astonishing not only because the Romans had freed the Eburones from the tribute they had to pay to the Aduatuci, but also because Caesar claimed to have enslaved virtually the entire Aduatuci tribe three years prior. Apparently, Caesar exaggerated; there were enough Aduatuci left for Ambiorix to set aside tribal differences and make a special effort to recruit them. With his infantry following behind, Ambiorix's horsemen pressed forward through day and night to reach the Aduatuci. When Ambiorix proclaimed his great victory, the Aduatuci swore to renew their war against the Romans. They had not forgotten the long columns of their people dragged into Roman slavery.

Ambiorix wasted no time. The day after he won over the Aduatuci, he stood among the Nervii. Here once again, Caesar's narrative disagrees with himself. When he defeated them in 57 BC, Caesar boasted that the Nervii were reduced to a pitiful 500 fighting men. Now, only three years later, the allegedly nearly vanquished Nervii were not only able to rally an army of warriors to support Ambiorix but also retained their control over many lesser tribes. The Ceutrones, the Grudii, the Levaci, the Pleumoxii and the Geidumni, all mobilized their forces. No doubt though, the ranks of the Nervii and allies were filled with young men in their late teens ready to prove their valor in war against the Romans.

The Belgae coalition of the Nervii, the Eburones and the Aduatuci swooped down upon the nearest Roman camp, that of the Eleventh Legion, along the River Sambre in Nervii territory. Ambiorix was still with the army, but overall leadership of the Belgae coalition was now taken over by the Nervii chiefs.[10] Their adversary was Quintus Tullius Cicero. The 48-year-old Cicero was the younger brother of Marcus Tullius Cicero, the famous orator and philosopher.

The younger Cicero held a number of governmental positions before first serving under Caesar in his second Britannia expedition. Cicero had personally picked the site for his camp on the Sambre and was not going to give it up without a fight.

In a replay of the attack on Sabinus and Cotta's camp, the Belgae cavalry initiated the hostilities by surrounding a party of Roman wood cutters outside of Cicero's camp. Not long after, the legionaries on the ramparts and towers espied the Eburones horsemen[11] galloping out of the bleak autum woods. Trumpets and cornets resounded from inside the camp. Legionaries hastily threw on their mail shirts, donned their helmets, and with callused hands grasped spear shafts and sword handles. Everyone rushed to the ramparts and not a moment too soon. In wake of their cavalry, the Nervii infantry poured into the open field between the ramparts and the woods. The young warriors of the Nervii and their allies stormed upon the ramparts to clash with the legionaries. The fighting lasted until the night and was particularly desperate because Cicero had been unable to complete the camp fortifications.

During the night, the attacks ceased but there was little rest for Cicero's legionaries. In the dim light of the torch, spades dug into the earth and axes chopped through timber. Luckily the latter had been gathered into the camp prior to the Nervii attack. By sunrise and not a moment too soon, the camp defenses were complete and over 120 towers were built. The Belgae renewed their attack with reinforced strength, but by evening the Romans still held the ramparts. Again, the Romans rebuilt and added to the fortifications in the night. Siege spears and stakes charred at the point were added, as were extra stories for the towers and wicker breastworks. Even the sick or the wounded could not get much sleep, including Cicero. Although ill, Cicero refused to rest at night until he was forced to do so by a crowd of persistent soldiers.

Seeing that they were unable to break the resolute Roman defense, the leaders of the Nervii asked to speak to Cicero. Their request was granted and Cicero heard their terms. Perhaps on Ambiorix's advice, the Nervii chiefs tried the same deception that Ambiorix had used on Sabinus and Cotta. They swore that all of Gaul had risen in war, that they themselves had no quarrel with the Romans and that the Romans could leave the camp unmolested. Unlike Sabinus, Cicero proudly countered by saying that the Roman people did not accept terms from an armed enemy and that the Belgae, not the Romans, should lay down their arms and surrender to Caesar's mercy!

Their dubious offers having been rejected, the Nervii resorted to another strategy. Many times the Belgae had watched the Romans erect massive siege works; now the Belgae would do the same. Although the Belgae lacked the proper siege know-how, their Roman prisoners were forced to help them while the sheer numbers of Belgae made up for the lack of proper tools. Sod was cut with swords and earth carried in cloaks. So numerous were the Belgae that in only three hours they built up a rampart three miles in circumference. During the next few days towers grew up on the rampart, higher than those of Cicero's camp. Aided by their Roman captives, the Celts even built movable siege-towers.

On the seventh day of the siege, it must have seemed to the Belgae that even Taranis, the Celtic god of thunder, was coming to their aid. A great gale sprang up just as the Belgae launched their assault by slinging bullets of red-hot clay and incendiary darts into the Roman camp. The missiles blazed across the ramparts to land on the thatched huts of the camp. The huts burst into flames which were fed into an inferno by the strong wind. Sensing victory, the emboldened Belgae lifted their siege ladders and pushed their towers toward the rampart. With the Belgae spurred on by the belief of certain victory, the fighting reached new levels of intensity. The legionaries refused to give up and hewed down great numbers of barbarians trying to gain the parapet. One of the Belgae siege towers rumbled right up to the wall. The warriors inside expected the Romans on the rampart to run in fear but were met by the gathered centurions of the 3rd cohort. The centurions dared the Belgae to come out of their tower and fight them. The Belgae declined and were driven away by a volley of stones. Their tower was set on fire.

During the fiercest point in the battle, two centurions distinguished themselves in their valor. Titus Pullo and Lucius Vorenus always argued amongst themselves as to who was the better soldier.[12] Pullo challenged Vorenus, "Why hesitate Vorenus? What better opportunity do you want to prove your courage?"[13] Pullo did not wait for an answer and rushed outside the ramparts, right towards a large number of Belgae warriors. Not to be outdone, Vorenus immediately followed behind. Pullo hurled his spear, transfixing one of the barbarians. As their impaled comrade sank to the ground, the other barbarians hurled their javelins at Pullo. A javelin pierced Pullo's shield and another knocked his scabbard out of place. Pullo reached for his sword but was unable to grasp the handle. Vorenus arrived just in time to draw the enemy away from Pullo. With his sword Vorenus killed one of the barbarians and drove the rest back a bit, but then stumbled down a slope. Instantly the Belgae warriors were upon him and now he would have died had not Pullo appeared in the nick of time. Side by side, Pullo and Vorenus slew more of the enemy before fighting their way back into the Roman camp.

Despite the heroic Roman defense, there was no denying that the situation grew worse for the Romans day by day. The critically wounded grew in number while fewer and fewer legionaries manned the ramparts and towers. Cicero made more attempts to get messages through to Caesar. So far, all his messengers had been caught by the Belgae who tortured them in full sight of the legionaries on the ramparts. Luckily there was a Nervii deserter, a nobleman named Vertico, who volunteered to send his Gallic slave through the lines. The slave tied the message around his javelin and passed undetected through the ranks of his countrymen. Late in the afternoon, the message reached Caesar who was staying with general Gaius Trebonius and his legion at Samarobriva (Amiens).

Samarobriva was the main *oppidum* of the Ambiani, a Belgic tribe which had surrendered to Caesar after his victory over King Galba in 57 BC. The fortified town was named after a bridge, *briva*, over the River Samara (the Somme). Close to the sea and connected to the main road of Gaul, Samarobriva grew rich through trade and provided a strategic military base for Rome.

Caesar's stay at Samarobriva turned sour when he heard of the massacre of the Fourteenth Legion. He "swore neither to cut his hair nor to trim his beard until they had been avenged."[14] Caesar lost no time and on the same day sent a messenger to mobilize the nearest legion, that of questor Marcus Crassus, elder son of the triumvir, which was camped among the Bellovaci. Crassus was ready to march at midnight. Likewise Caesar summoned the aid of general Gaius Fabius' legion and of Labienus' legion from the lands of the Morini and the Remi, respectively. The other legions were stationed too far away to be of immediate help.

News arrived that large numbers of the Treveri, formerly allies of Rome, had risen in arms against the Romans. Led by Indutiomarus, the Treveri army had crossed into Remi territory and was closing in on Labienus' border camp. With the Treveri army only three miles from his camp, Labienus thought it wiser to stay put and defend. Caesar agreed with Labienus' decision; leaving Caesar with three legions, one of which, that of Marcus Crassus, he ordered to garrison Samarobriva. With only the two legions of Trebonius and of Fabius, Caesar would face the Nervii, Aduatuci and Eburones coalition.

On the way to the land of the Nervii, Caesar captured and interrogated some locals who told him of the desperate state of Cicero's camp. Back in Cicero's camp, he and his men desperately scanned the horizon for any signs of Caesar. Two days later they were rewarded by the sight of dark smoke clouds.[15] It could only be Caesar's nearing army, burning the outlying farms and villages. The Belgae noticed Caesar's approach as well. They raised the siege of Cicero's camp and marched to meet Caesar, expecting to engage his army in the open. To their disappointment they found Caesar's two legions fortified in a marching camp. The camp stood on the other side of a wide valley with a stream running through it. Because Cicero was no longer in immediate danger, Caesar thought it wiser to go on the defensive. After all, Caesar's 7,000 legionaries were grossly outnumbered. Even if Caesar's narrative of 60,000 Nervii and allies is exaggerated, the Belgae must have outnumbered him by several times.[16]

After the hard fighting at Cicero's camp, the Nervii and their allies were unwilling to attack another fortified Roman position; especially one defended by Caesar with fresh legionaries. For the remainder of the first day, the cavalry of both sides skirmished along the stream with indecisive results. At dawn of the next day, the Belgae cavalry rode up to the ramparts of Caesar's camp where they fought and routed the Roman cavalry. With the Roman cavalry back inside the camp, the Belgae cavalry was free to scout out the Roman position. They saw that a pitiful number of legionaries manned the ramparts, who were frantically trying to strengthen the fortifications.

Elated by the apparent dire predicament of the Romans, the Belgae infantry crossed the stream. In a disorganized manner the barbarians tried to fill up the Roman trenches and even used their bare hands to dig openings in the earth rampart. They had fallen for Caesar's sham, for he had pulled back his cavalry on purpose and manned the ramparts with a skeleton guard. Suddenly, the Roman cavalry and the infantry poured out of all the gates. Caught off guard by an enemy they had believed were cowed and defeated, the Belgae threw down their arms and fled. The Romans killed many but many others escaped into the woods and marshes.

Lacking the manpower for a vigorous pursuit of the Belgae, Caesar pressed on toward Cicero's camp. He was amazed at the ramparts and towers erected and left behind by the Nervii and their allies. Caesar praised Cicero, his tribunes and his centurions, and the cohorts of the Eleventh Legion for their hard-fought defensive victory. More good news soon came from Labienus, who reported that Indutiomarus and the Treveri had called off their attack on his camp and fled back to their own lands. With the initiative back in Roman hands, Caesar sent Fabius' legion back to their camp among the Morini. Caesar returned with Trebonius' legion to Samarobriva. The situation remained so volatile, however, that for the first time Caesar decided to break his custom of returning to the Roman provinces for the winter. He stayed at Samarobriva, correctly anticipating more troubles among the tribes.

Despite the failure of the Nervii to capture Cicero's camp and thwart Caesar's relief attempt, the news of Sabinus and Cotta's annihilation continued to incite the tribes. Throughout the winter of 54/53 BC envoys passed back and forth, as the tribal leaders forged new battle plans. Indutiomarus continued his tireless efforts to rouse additional tribes into open revolt. All across Gaul, the tribes were showing growing defiance to Roman authority. The powerful Senones of central Gaul deposed their pro-Roman King and completely ignored Caesar's summons. Caesar also received word that Aremorican tribes had only called off an attack on the Thirteenth Legion's camp when they heard about Caesar's victory. When Caesar called the leading men of the tribes to appear before him, he had to resort to diplomacy as much as to intimidation to keep the peace. A few tribes, most notably the Remi and the Aedui, remained loyal to the Romans. Even among the Treveri, Indutiomarus' own son-in-law, Cingetorix, stayed faithful to Caesar. An infuriated Indutiomarus branded Cingetorix a public enemy.

At an assembly of tribal leaders, perhaps within the confines of the mountain stronghold on the Dollberg, Indutiomarus proclaimed that the Senones and Carnutes had invoked his help. He would march to their country and on the way ravage the lands of the traitorous Remi. First, however, he intended to attack Labienus' camp. Indutiomarus' grandiose boasts were easier said than done because he clearly lacked the manpower to take Labienus' camp by assault. Nevertheless, Indutiomarus became so contemptuous of the Romans that he and his cavalry daily skirmished in front of the camp ramparts. The Treveri taunted the Romans and pelted them with missiles. No doubt Indutiomarus was trying to lure the legions into the open, where his horsemen would have the advantage. At night or whenever they felt like it, Indutiomarus' cavalry split into smaller groups and retired into the forest.

Labienus could do little other than have his legionaries throw javelins at the Treveri galloping around the ramparts. Lacking the cavalry to counter the Treveri horsemen, Labienus would not risk his heavy infantry in an open ground engagement. Fortunately for Labienus, Cingetorix came to his help. Indutiomarus' bitter rival gathered Roman-friendly cavalry from his tribe and sneaked them into Labienus' camp. The next time Indutiomarus retired into the woods, Labienus sent Cingetorix's cavalry to hunt him down. Just to make sure, Labienus put a big price on Indutiomarus' head and sent a few cohorts in support. Forsaken by many of his followers, Indutiomarus was caught and killed while fording a stream. Indutiomarus' bloodied, severed head was delivered to Labienus' camp.

After Indutiomarus' death, a false lull of peace returned to the lands. The rebellious Nervii, Eburones and Aduatuci smoldered in their frustration of being unable to defeat Caesar. To make sure the rebels stayed subdued, Caesar sent his generals to recruit new troops. Before the spring of 53 BC, two new legions were enrolled in northern Italy: a new Fourteenth Legion to replace the one destroyed by the Eburones, and the Fifteenth Legion. Caesar also borrowed Pompey's First Legion and renamed it the Sixth.[17]

His army reinforced by three legions, Caesar took four legions and pillaged the Nervii lands and forced them to give hostages. Early in spring, he marched upon the Senones and the Carnutes and they too had to provide hostages. Next he returned to Belgic Gaul and built causeways into the swamp hideouts of the Menapii. In a triple pronged advance, with general Fabius and questor Marcus Crassus leading the other two detachments, Caesar's army of five legions burnt farms and villages and took prisoners until the Menapii sued for peace. Caesar left Commius the Atrebatean King, who had served him so well in Britannia, with some cavalry to keep watch over the Menapii.

Among the Treveri, Indutiomarus' kin continued to lead the resistance against Rome, and with Ambiorix's assistance were trying hard to recruit German mercenaries. Ambiorix had faded from Caesar's narrative after he rallied the more powerful Nervii against the Romans in the previous year. However, he was the one rebel that remained at large and a troublesome thorn in Caesar's side. It was partially because of their close ties to Ambiorix that Caesar pillaged the lands of the Menapii and threatened them with more reprisals if they gave Ambiorix shelter or aid.

Large forces of Treveri cavalry and infantry meanwhile moved on Labienus' camp for a third time. They were still two days march away when they heard that Labienus had just been just reinforced with two legions. Three fortified Roman legions were too daunting a foe for the Treveri, who decided to forestall their attack until the Germans arrived. Labienus, however, decided not to let them wait that long. With twenty-five cohorts, plus a powerful contingent of Gallic cavalry, he sallied forth to confront the Treveri. A mere five cohorts remained behind to defend the camp.

Labienus' legions marched until they came to the steep banks of a river, on the other side of which, a mile away, lay the camp of the Treveri. Labienus was not about to have his men fight an enemy who held the high ground. Instead, the clever Labienus would trick the Gauls into attacking him. At night, he ordered his men to hastily break camp, so as to appear frightened. The Treveri patrols noticed the increased commotion and racket coming from the Roman camp. Riding back to their countrymen, the Treveri scouts exclaimed that the Romans were fleeing in panic. There was no time to wait for the Germans and let their prize slip away. The Treveri gathered shields and weapons and in a disorganized mob crossed the river. They hurried up the opposite slope just as the last Romans cleared their entrenchments. Labienus turned to his soldiers, "Here is your chance. You have got the enemy where you wanted them – in a bad position … Fight as bravely under me as you often have under the commander-in-chief."[18] As one, the legionaries "raised a shout and launched their spears."[19]

The Treveri warriors advancing up the hill caught their breath; bewildered, they beheld the cohorts charging downhill to meet them. The first of the scattered Treveri were already being cut down. Soon the whole lot of them fled for the woods, the Roman-allied Gallic cavalry on their heels. The disaster broke the back of the Treveri resistance. The family of Indutiomarus fled to the Germans who, hearing of Labienus' victory, hightailed it back across the Rhine. The Romans appointed Cingetorix as new leader of the Treveri.

In his continuing efforts to deprive Ambiorix of any safe haven and to teach the Germans not to send any help to Gauls, Caesar re-crossed the Rhine. He did this by means of a bridge, completed by his able soldiers in only a few days. Not long after Caesar's cohorts and his entire cavalry had marched into the lands east of the Rhine,[20] envoys of the Ubii came cowering. They told Caesar that it was not they who had sent help to the Treveri, that they remained loyal to Caesar, and that they would even offer more hostages if spared Caesar's wrath. The culprits turned out to be, not surprisingly, the Suebi, whose warriors were gathering from all their villages and subject tribes. Anticipating an attack on the Ubii lands, Caesar told the Ubii to gather all their grain and flee into their strongholds. The Suebi did not attack, however, and awaited Caesar far inside their lands, on the edge of the Silva Bacenis, a vast beech and pine forest.[21]

Just like in 55 BC, after his defeat of the Usipetes and Tencteri, Caesar again declined to take the fight to the Suebi. He feared that he would be unable to properly supply his army. According to Caesar the Germans paid scant attention to agriculture, and subsisted mainly on milk, cheese and meat, so there was insufficient grain for Caesar to confiscate. Besides, it was a long march through difficult terrain ideal for ambushes, such as the one that annihilated the Fourteenth Legion. With Gaul not completely subdued, it would have been unwise to launch a campaign deep into Germania. Accordingly, Caesar broke down the part of the bridge that touched the Ubii shore of the river. At the

Gallic end, Caesar erected a heavily fortified four-story tower garrisoned by twelve cohorts; a warning for the Germans to stay out of Gaul.

The time had come to hunt down Ambiorix, a task to which Caesar appointed Lucius Minucius Basilus and the entire cavalry. Basilus raided into Eburones territory, where he happened upon farmers working on the fields. Fearful for their lives, the Eburones farmers betrayed Ambiorix's location in a house in the woods. Basilus' soldiers broke into the house but Ambiorix was not alone and his followers put up a ferocious fight. The cramped quarters worked to the advantage of the defenders, and for a time evened the odds against Basilus' superior numbers. While his friends fended off the Romans, Ambiorix slipped out of the building, jumped on a horse and eluded the Romans in the woods.

The Roman commando raid nevertheless spelled the end of Ambiorix's resistance movement. He sent messengers to all his allies, telling them that they were on their own and that they should flee from the Romans. Ambiorix's old ally and co-chief, Catuvolcus poisoned himself with an extract from the yew tree. At least he would not be there to witness the campaign of terror that Caesar was about to unleash.

Caesar placed the Fourteenth Legion and the baggage and loot of his entire army, from all ten legions, at Atuatuca under the command of Cicero. He then ordered Labienus and Trebonius, with three legions each, to devastate the lands of the Menapii and the Aduatuci, respectively. Caesar himself took his remaining three legions to set out after Ambiorix. The latter was said to be hiding out with some cavalry among his Eburones, at the western end of the Ardennes Mountains.

The Eburones had pulled off a great victory against Sabinus and Cotta's reinforced legion but they were no match for Caesar's three legions in a set battle. So the Eburones fought back with guerrilla warfare. The Eburones killed any Romans they found separated from the main army. When the Romans went on patrol, when handfuls of individuals went out to loot the farms, when small groups got separated from their column due to the rough terrain, they were always in danger of Eburones ambushes. So effective were the Eburones guerrilla tactics that Caesar proceeded to take "the most careful precautions" and "let the enemy off lightly".[22] In other words, he forbade individual looting, tightened security and concentrated on his search for Ambiorix. Even these measures did not wholly prevent more Roman casualties, nor did they produce Ambiorix. A frustrated Caesar pulled his legions out of the Eburones lands. Preferring to shed Gallic blood to "exterminate this race of criminals,"[23] Caesar invited allied Gallic tribes to devastate the Eburones. Drawn by the lure of easy looting, large numbers of Gauls assembled to attack the Eburones lands from all sides.

With all this plundering going on, the Germans could hardly be left out. When the Sugambri heard "all comers were invited to share the spoil,"[24] they gathered 2,000 cavalry and crossed the Rhine thirty miles below Caesar's bridge fortifications. The Sugambri took a number of Eburones captive and stole a lot of cattle, which were highly valued by the barbarians. A greater prize, however, was revealed to them by one of the captured Eburones, "Why go after this paltry miserable loot … in three hours you can reach Atuatuca, where the Romans have stored all their property."[25]

A week had passed at Atuatuca, where Cicero awaited Caesar's return. Cicero's men were grumbling that they had been cooped up too long. No doubt the legionaries and auxiliaries felt envious of the other legions which were plundering the rebels. Accordingly, Cicero sent five cohorts and his 200 allied Gallic cavalry, to gather grain from the nearest fields, behind a hill outside the camp. Another 300 recovered wounded from the other legions and large numbers of servants were to go with them. The latter took with them much of the livestock, presumably to let the animals graze.

The Sugambri gathered at the edge of the woods that grew close to the back gate of Atuatuca. Calming their sturdy ponies, the Sugambri peeked through the foliage to see the tents of the traders outside the rear ramparts. The Sugambri burst out of the trees and fell upon the traders. So sudden was their appearance that the raw recruits remaining inside the camp were struck with fear. They dreaded that they would end up like Cotta and Sabinus' ill fated legion. Rumors broke out that the Germans had destroyed the entire Roman army and the commander in chief. Cicero still had over 2,000 legionaries but lacked the cavalry to engage the Sugambri, whose strength the Romans over-estimated. The Sugambri, in turn, wrongly thought Atuatuca barely defended and attacked with unrelenting vigor.

Roman morale was sagging until uplifted by the heroic example of chief centurion Publius Sextius Baculus. Baculus was in his tent, recovering from a wound. Like all centurions he enjoyed the comforts of a personal tent, furnished with loot he had acquired during his years of service. The servants who tended to his injuries likely told Baculus of the dire situation outside. Even without their update, he could hear the sounds of battle well enough, the desperate Latin calls for reinforcements, the guttural war cries of the Sugambri and the clash of sword and spear. Baculus had fought under Caesar in the great battle of the Sabis. He was not going to languish in his bed, not as long as he could stand and still wield a weapon. Despite his injuries, Baculus walked out of his tent and borrowed arms from the nearest soldier. Side by side with the cohort centurions, Baculus fought off a critical Sugambri assault on the gate. During the fight Baculus was again severely wounded. He would have perished if not dragged out of the fray by his comrades.

All the commotion at the camp was heard by the foraging party, which had just finished its work. Soon the Sugambri spotted the Roman standards of the foraging party coming around the nearby hill. The sight of the feared barbarians, who Caesar called "born fighters and bandits,"[26] filled the young Roman recruits of the foraging party with panic. There were no fortifications to shield them; they were in the open at the mercy of the Sugambri cavalry. For their part, the Sugambri at first feared that Caesar's legions had returned. When they saw that the numbers were even, they spat in contempt at the Romans.

With the Sugambri galloping at them from all directions, the new recruits were all for making a stand on the hill. A number of veterans and their leader, the Roman knight Gaius Trebonius, swore that the only chance was a bold dash to the gate. While several cohorts made for the hill, Trebonius' men charged for the gate. Not only did Trebonius' entourage reach the camp without casualties but they cleared the way for the cavalry and for the camp servants who safely followed in their wake. The Sugambri concentrated on the bigger prize by catching the remaining cohorts on low and unfavorable ground. The legionaries of the latter cohorts had wasted precious time arguing and had not been able to reach the high ground in time. Their centurions made a brave last stand, enabling a few more legionaries to reach the camp. The rest of the legionaries fell to the spears and swords of the Sugambri.

Satisfied with their booty, including the Roman livestock, and convinced that further attacks on the camp would prove fruitless, the Sugambri returned to their lands across the Rhine. Even after the barbarian's departure, the Romans in Atuatuca continued to be gripped with fear. "Fear had so completely possessed them all that they nearly took leave of their senses,"[27] related Caesar; fear which did not leave them until Caesar returned to Atuatuca with his legions. Caesar did not pursue the Sugambri into their forested wilderness; judging by past experience he probably knew it was futile to do so.

Instead of setting out to punish the Sugambri, Caesar set out on a renewed terror campaign against the Eburones. As before, the actual dirty work was done by allied Gallic cavalry. "Every village and every building they saw was set on fire; all over the country the cattle were either slaughtered or driven off as booty;

and the crops, a part of which had already been laid flat by the autumnal rains, were consumed by the great numbers of horses and men."²⁸ The Eburones were completely eradicated as a people, the few pockets of survivors that survived Caesar's wrath being eventually absorbed by other tribes.

When the autumn of 53 BC drew to a close, Caesar set out for the lands of the Remi to hold a general Gallic council. Although the uprisings of the year had taken part chiefly among the Belgae parts of Gaul, anti-Roman factions among the Gallic Senones and Carnutes had made common cause with Indutiomarus of the Treveri. Acco, the chief instigator among the Senones and Carnutes, was put to death in the Roman manner, by flogging and beheading.

The one chief rebel that continued to defy Caesar's efforts to capture or kill him was Ambiorix. Time and time again, people swore they saw Ambiorix in flight. Ambiorix's entourage was reduced to a mere four horsemen. Hiding in ravines and deep woods, he slipped into the night to elude his pursuers and was never caught.²⁹

Caesar left to hold his assizes in northern Italy for the winter of 53/52 BC. He left six legions in winter quarters among the Senones, another two on the Treveri frontier and two among the Lingones. The year since the previous winter of 54/53 BC had been a turbulent one. There had been Roman setbacks, the destruction of the Fourteenth Legion by the Eburones and the loss of two cohorts to the Sugambri. Roman casualties, however, were more than replaced by the enrollment of new legions. The Romans won victories against the Nervii and the Treveri, and so thoroughly devastated the lands of the Belgae, especially the Eburones, that the Belgic tribes ceased to be a serious threat to Roman hegemony.

Chapter Fourteen

Vercingetorix, the Last Hope of the Gauls

*"The Romans have not won by superior courage or in a fair fight ... but by their
expert knowledge of siege craft, a special technique that we were unacquainted
with."*[1]

Vercingetorix, Warlord of the Gauls

After six years of relentless war, Caesar had killed hundreds of thousands
of Gauls and Germans by war and by starvation. Yet the more he
tightened his grip, the more Gaul seemed to slip through his fingers.
Gaul continued to seethe with hate and resentment for their Roman occupiers.
With the Belgae too devastated by Caesar's terror campaign, the next seeds of
rebellion grew in Gallia Celtica, Celtic Gaul.

Secretly the Gallic chiefs gathered in hidden wooden glades, to curse the
Romans for reducing their lands to misery. They speculated that victory
might be possible if Caesar were cut off from his legions. During the winter of
53/52 BC, Gaul was a landscape of snow-covered woods and frozen rivers and
marshes. Vast areas of the low country lay under seasonal floods. With Caesar in
northern Italy, separated by inhospitable terrain from his legions stationed in
Gaul, the time was ripe to strike. In a solemn rite the Gallic chiefs bound their
standards together and took an oath to stand by each other in the coming fight
for liberation.

Implicated in these intrigues was none other then Caesar's old friend
Commius, King of the Atrebates. For Commius, who had served Caesar loyally
for five years, to turn against Caesar showed how bad the Gauls suffered and
how desperate they became to rid themselves of their Roman masters. When
Labienus, who remained on the Belgae border, got word of Commius' deceit he
decided to get rid of the traitor. The task was allotted to Gaius Volusenus, the
veteran commander who had scouted out Britannia's coastline. Accompanied
by a number of centurions, Volusenus paid a visit to Commius. Commius was in
the presence of his friends when he was confronted by the Romans. Volusenus
grasped Commius' hand: the pre-arranged signal for his centurions to begin the

attack. Swords rasped out of scabbards, blades flashed and a centurion struck at Commius. The iron Roman blade bit Commius' skull but failed to kill him outright. His head a bloody mess, Commius fell into the arms of his attendants. Thinking Commius mortally wounded, the centurions drew back. Fearing that more Romans were on the way, Commius' friends were anxious to escape with their wounded friend. After both sides parted, Commius recovered. If he had not yet fully decided to join the rebels, after that day Commius made up his mind "never again to come into the presence of any Roman."[2]

Despite all the oaths taken by the Gallic chieftains, and a massacre of Roman merchants at Cenabum by the Carnutes, the Gallic rebellion showed no great promise until the emergence of a remarkable leader. He was called Vercingetorix and his very name meant king-over-warriors.[3] Still a young man, Vercingetorix was the son of the influential Arverni chief, Celtillus. However in 80 BC, when Vercingetorix was but a baby, Celtillus' ambitions had reached too high. He tried to become King and for doing so was sentenced to death by the tribal elders. It may well have been his father's legacy that caused the leading men of the Arverni stronghold of Gergovia to turn a cold shoulder to Vercingetorix. The chiefs, including his uncle Gobannitio, had no wish to rally the population against the Romans and to face Caesar's wrath.

Vercingetorix's resolve did not falter. A man of boundless energy, he wandered through the villages of the barren winter countryside. Vercingetorix raised an army from the common folk who among the Gauls were little more than slaves. Everywhere he went, the Arverni flocked to his standard. Vercingetorix returned to Gergovia with an army and ousted those who opposed him. Triumphantly, he was declared King by his countless followers. Vercingetorix achieved his father's dream.

Embassies were sent to the rest of Gaul and before long, the Senones, Parisii, Cadurci, Turoni, Aulerci, Lemovices, Andes, Pictones and many others, elected Vercingetorix to be their warlord. To ensure their loyalty, which was always fickle among the Gauls, Vercingetorix demanded hostages and threatened with torture and execution those who disobeyed. He ordered the tribes to supply troops at once, to forge swords and spear blades, to make shields and helmets, and to raise a great host of cavalry. Vercingetorix was aware that Caesar faced political opposition by the *optimates,* the aristocratically aligned party of Rome. Caesar was still busy in Italy, cut off from his legions stationed in their winter quarters along the Belgae border, just as the Gauls had originally planned.

Although by now Caesar should have known better, Vercingetorix's uprising caught him by surprise. Caesar was separated from his legions by towering mountains in the depths of winter with potentially hostile tribes in his path. To get there would be to risk capture since even formerly friendly tribes could not be trusted. Events did not allow Caesar to contemplate, as a strong force of Gauls was already approaching the Roman province of Gallia Narbonensis, straddling the Mediterranean Sea.

Leading the Gallic force towards Narbonensis was one of Vercingetorix's lieutenants, Lucterius the Cadrucan. Lucterius had just swelled his ranks with fresh recruits from among the Ruteni, whose lands bordered Narbonensis. The people of the coastal city of Narbo were understandably frightened and only calmed down by Caesar's swift arrival. He re-deployed part of the garrison troops in areas bordering the Gallic advance, threatening to outflank Lucterius who aborted the attack. Caesar assembled the rest of the garrison troops, his bodyguard and fresh levies he had brought with him from Italy, in the foot hills of the Cevennes Mountains. On the other side of the mountains sprawled the lands of the Arverni.

The Arverni thought the Cevennes Mountains impassable in winter. Caesar thought otherwise. His men shoveled snowdrifts that covered the passes up to six feet deep, opening the way for Caesar to reach the Arverni lands. Once there, Caesar sent his cavalry out to raid a wide area and to create as much terror as they could. Vercingetorix was winning over the Bituriges when he heard the news of Roman cavalry running amok in his homelands. He hurried back to the Arverni lands but by the time he got there Caesar had again given him the slip. Leaving his troops in the Arverni lands under the command of Decimus Junius Brutus, Caesar had gone to gather some cavalry he had stationed in Vienne. From Vienne he marched to the Aedui, who, so far, remained his loyal allies. Caesar pushed onward to the Belgae border until he stood reunited with his legions. With speed and daring, Caesar had outmaneuvered Vercingetorix.

Attempting to regain the initiative, Vercingetorix laid siege to Gorgobina, a stronghold of the Boii in Aedui territory. After Caesar defeated the Boii in conjunction with the Helvetii in the beginning of his Gallic wars, the Boii were settled among the Aedui. With all of Gaul watching to see if Caesar would aid or desert his allies, Caesar had little choice but to come to their aid. Leaving two legions at Agedincum (Sens) in hostile Senones territory, he set out with eight legions for Gorgobina. Lacking the proper siege know-how, Vercingetorix was unable to take Gorgobina. In contrast, on his way to Gorgobina, Caesar captured, burnt and looted towns among the Senones and the Carnutes, appropriating supplies for his army.

Vercingetorix raised the siege of Gorgobina and marched to meet Caesar. By now, Caesar had entered Bituriges territory, bordering the Boii lands, where his army lay in siege around the town of Noviodunum Biturigum (Neuvy-sur-Barangeon). Envoys from the town negotiated a peaceful surrender. They promised to provide hostages, horses and deliver their weapons and armor to Caesar, in turn for which their town would not be sacked and burnt. A few centurions were already in the town, collecting horses and weapons, when Vercingetorix's cavalry vanguard appeared on the horizon. Caesar ordered his auxiliary Gallic cavalry, consisting mostly of Aedui, to engage them. The Aedui, however, were no match for Vercingetorix's horsemen, prompting Caesar to send his 400 German horsemen into the attack.[4] The handful of Germans scattered Vercingetorix's cavalry to the winds.

Either because his cavalry was unable to best Caesar's German horsemen or because he did not have enough infantry to fight the Roman legions, Vercingetorix retreated. He held a council of war and told his followers that, with three towns already fallen to Caesar, a new strategy was needed.

> "We must prevent the Romans from obtaining forage and supplies. This will be easy, since we are strong in cavalry and the season is in our favor. There is no grass to cut; so the enemy will be forced to send out parties to get hay from the barns, and our cavalry can go out every day and see that not a single one of them return alive … What is more … be prepared to sacrifice our private possessions. Along the enemy's line of march we must burn all the villages and farms. We can rely upon the resources of the people … but the Romans will either succumb to starvation or have to expose themselves to serious risk by going far from their camp."[5]

In a single day, the fires and smoke clouds of more than twenty Bituriges towns spiraled into the sky. They were joined by settlements in neighboring lands, until all the land surrounding Caesar and his legions seemed aflame. The one Bituriges town that was left intact was the nearly impregnable Avaricum (near Bourges). Upon an 80 foot hill, the 26 hectare town lay at the confluence of five rivers. Surrounded by marshlands and the Avara (Yèvre) River, the only access was a narrow land bridge. Avaricum was considered the finest town in Gaul and its inhabitants refused to set it aflame. Neither would they surrender to Caesar.[6]

Caesar shrugged off the losses that Vercingetorix's cavalry inflicted on Roman foraging parties and advanced steadily on Avaricum. Once there, Caesar wasted no time in building a siege terrace and erecting mantlets and two towers within the meager space that gave access to the town. Although his supply situation rapidly deteriorated, the legionaries grimly hung on and maintained the siege.

Prisoners told Caesar that Vercingetorix had left the Gallic army to lead the cavalry and light troops in an attempt to ambush any Romans who left Caesar's camp. Apparently, the main Gallic army was camped some fifteen miles nearby and was also suffering from supply shortages. Marching to the Gallic camp at night, Caesar planned to attack while the Gauls were separated from their leader. However, the Romans were spotted by Gallic scouts. By the time Caesar approached the Gallic camp the Gauls had hidden their baggage in the woods and formed a strong defensive position on a hill surrounded by boggy ground. Despite the eagerness of his legionaries to take the fight to the enemy, Caesar thought it unwise to risk such an unfavorable attack and pulled back to Avaricum.

So fickle were the Gauls that when Vercingetorix returned to his main army, they blamed him of desertion with the cavalry and conspiring with Caesar! He reminded them that he had chosen a natural defensive position for them where the cavalry was not needed. Disappointed in his men's loyalty, Vercingetorix produced some prisoners who were primed to complain of starvation and the near collapse of Caesar's legions. Suddenly, the Gauls had only praise for Vercingetorix, calling him a great leader and swearing their unwavering loyalty!

Back at Avaricum the harder the Romans tried to take the town, the harder the Gauls tried to defend it. Roman terraces were sent crumbling by Gauls who mined under them, wall hooks were pulled aside with lassoes, sallies were made to attack the Roman workers and to set fire to the siege works. The Gauls threw boiling pitch and boulders into the Roman subterranean galleries, and countered Roman towers by adding towers and platforms, protected by hides, to the town walls. The Gallic walls themselves were built of interlocking timbers, stones and rubble, protecting them from fire and the battering ram.

Though drenched by incessant rain, in twenty-five days the legions raised a terrace over three hundred feet wide and eight feet high. When it almost touched the city walls, the Gauls launched one last desperate night sally to burn down the Roman terrace. From Caesar's narrative:

"There was a Gaul standing before one of the gates and throwing into the flames, opposite one of our towers, lumps of tallow and pitch that were passed along to him. An arrow from a catapult pierced his side and he fell dead. Another near him stepped over his prostrate body and took over his job. When he likewise was killed by the catapult, a third took his place, and so they went on."[7]

The Romans counterattacked and extinguished the fire. The end for Avaricum was near. In a heavy downpour, on the twenty-seventh day of the siege, the Romans finally breached the walls. There was no fight left in the defenders and no mercy left in the victor. A red haze of hate, raised to a pitch through the horror of the siege, clouded the legionaries' eyes. They were no longer men but mindless killing machines. For hours, men, women, children, the old and the young, all were cut down, till the streets ran crimson and echoed with the agonized cries of the victims. Caesar wrote that of the 40,000 inhabitants, a mere 800 escaped to join Vercingetorix.

A well-earned rest at Avaricum, with its stockpiles of supplies, allowed the legionaries to recover from their combat fatigue. Caesar used the time to settle a dispute among the Aedui, who had split into a pro and an anti-Roman faction. He used the occasion to levy the rest of the Aedui cavalry, which forthwith joined him, as well as 10,000 infantry from amongst their ranks, who were to follow later.

The day after the massacre at Avaricum, Vercingetorix held a council of war. He showed shrewd insight into the tactics of the enemy, reminding his men that the Romans had not won through valor but only due to their knowledge of siege craft. Vercingetorix promised success that would more than make up for the defeats. He would win over the tribes, so that: "The whole of Gaul will then be united, and when we are all of one mind the entire world cannot stand against us."[8] Vercingetorix's resolve uplifted the sagging spirits of his men. Even in defeat, his renown grew so that his losses were more than made up for by new recruits and new allies. Large numbers of archers were summoned from all over Gaul.[9] Teutomatus, King of the Nitiobroges, saddled up his cavalry and raised mercenaries in Aquitania to come to Vercingetorix's aid.

Both Gauls and Romans could feel the warmth of spring in the air. The grass was greening and soon the cavalry horses and the thousands of draught mules and oxen that accompanied the armies would be able to graze on the fields. With the supply situation improving, Caesar sent Labienus, with four legions and part of the cavalry, to move against the Parisii and the Senones. Caesar took the remaining six legions and cavalry and struck for the Arverni town of Gergovia, to the west side of the River Allier. Vercingetorix demolished the bridges over the Allier and by holding the opposite bank blocked Caesar's crossing over from the east. Caesar used a diversionary maneuver to lure Vercingetorix's blocking army away, while two legions hidden in the woods repaired a destroyed bridge. The two legions crossed the river and held the far bank with a marching camp until they were joined by the other four legions. With Caesar likely holding a large numerical advantage, Vercingetorix avoided a pitched battle and fled towards Gergovia.

When Caesar reached Gergovia, he beheld the fortified town, perched on a plateau in a wide hilly valley. The River Auzon flowed to the south of the hill, winding its way east and north where it emptied into the River Allier. Like two mighty arms, the northern ridges of the Massif Central climbed upward to the west and east of Gergovia. To the west, the nearby volcanic summit of Puy de Dôme dominated the landscape. To the east, across the Allier, the valley sprawled farther to climb up through fir and beech forests to the high meadows of the Forez Mountains.

Caesar was faced with another tough siege. Vercingetorix's main camp was on the high ground in front of the town, facing Caesar who was camped to the southeast. Directly opposite the town, to the south, the Gauls occupied another steep hill. In a night attack Caesar dislodged the Gauls from the hill and erected a secondary camp to be held by two legions. Furthermore, a 12-foot-wide double trench was dug to connect both camps. The Roman fortifications were meant to deprive Vercingetorix of his water supply, presumably the Auzon River to the south.

Bottled up in Gergovia, and besieged by Caesar and his legions, the situation looked dire for Vercingetorix. He needed a lucky break and got it when Litaviccus, the leader of the Aedui infantry marching to aid Caesar, succumbed to bribes offered by the agents of the Arverni. Thirty miles from Gergovia, Litaviccus turned to face his men and with tear-stained eyes implored, "Soldiers, where are we going? All our cavalry and all our men of high rank have perished."[10] He then produced some men who verified the fib, claiming that Caesar had treacherously executed the Aedui leaders, Eporedorix and Viridomarus, alongside the entire Aedui cavalry. In anger the Aedui infantry turned upon the few unlucky accompanying Romans. They were tortured and killed. When Caesar got word of this, he took four legions, the allegedly murdered Eporedorix and Viridomarus and their Aedui cavalry, and marched towards the incoming Aedui infantry. He left the Roman camp under the command of the veteran general, Gaius Fabius.

Vercingetorix, who watched Caesar depart, lost no time in sallying forth from his camp in front of the town and assaulting the remaining two legions in the Roman camp. With the tables turned on them, the defenders of the Roman camp found themselves under siege by superior forces. Unable to replace his tired troops with fresh ones, Fabius' legionaries were nearly overwhelmed. A hail of Gallic arrows, spears and slingshots, inflicted serious casualties, but supported by heavy caliber fire from their catapults, the legionaries persevered.

Caesar meanwhile sent his Aedui cavalry ahead to intercept the Aedui infantry. Upon seeing their tribal leaders and cavalry alive, the Aedui infantry surrendered and begged for quarter from Caesar. He spared them but was dismayed to find that Litaviccus had already slipped away to the enemy. Unfortunately for Caesar, Litaviccus' clever propaganda flamed up the Aedui countryside with anti-Roman sentiment. The Aedui killed, enslaved and looted whatever Romans they could get their hands on.

Caesar returned to Gergovia with the Aedui reinforcements, which currently remained loyal. Nevertheless, it was clear that even Caesar's staunchest Gallic allies were showing signs of wavering. Caesar was beginning to think it wiser to break the current siege and to reunite with the legions of Labienus. So as to not boost Gallic morale further, Caesar hoped for at least a tactical victory before withdrawing. He noticed that Vercingetorix was building up the fortifications on another hill west of Gergovia, which connected to the town by a ridge. At midnight several squadrons of Caesar's cavalry galloped to the area and made as much commotion as possible. During the day, they were joined by a "cavalry" contingent of mules and packhorses, ridden by their drivers who wore helmets to appear like proper soldiers. Next, one legion marched into a wooden area below the hill.

The Gauls beheld the apparent Roman build-up below the hill to their west. Alarmed, they shifted the bulk of their forces to finish the fortifications on the hill at the expense of their position in front of Gergovia; just as Caesar had planned. Caesar told his generals to have their men cover their helmet crests and hide their standards, and in small unassuming groups, move their legions from the larger Roman camp to the smaller one opposite the town. The Gauls, who were still expecting the attack on the hill to their west, remained unaware of the Roman preparations right below their town. When all was ready, Caesar gave the signal to attack and the legionaries sprang into action. At the same time he sent the Aedui uphill to the far Roman right.

Although as the crow flies the legionaries had little more than a mile to cover, the steep ascent to the town necessitated switchbacks. Half way up, the Romans encountered a six-foot high stone wall following the contour of the mountain. Between that wall and the town ramparts, lay Vercingetorix's main camps. There was virtually no opposition. The legionaries clambered over the stone wall and captured three Gallic camps. Teutomatus, the Nitiobroges King, was surprised taking a nap in his tent. Virtually naked, he jumped on a horse, escaping by a hair's breath.

Caesar achieved all he hoped to do and ordered the retreat.[11] At the sound of the Roman trumpet, the Tenth Legion, which was near to Caesar, came to a halt. The others, however, elated by their easy victory, were unable to hear the blaring trumpets. They continued to storm up towards the town walls. Inside the town, fears of another Avaricum worked the people to a frenzied panic. Women threw clothes and coins down the walls and bared their breasts, begging the Romans not to slay them or their children. An eager centurion of the Eighth Legion clambered up the walls, boasting of the rewards he would gain from Caesar.

The commotion in the town did not go unnoticed by the Gallic army to the west of the town. Men shouted that Gergovia had fallen to the Romans! The Gallic cavalry followed by a horde of angry foot soldiers, came streaming around the town ramparts to dash into the Roman troops. It was chaos, but the Gauls continued to feed more numbers into the mad melee while most of the Romans were still strung out on the hillside. From above the women urged on their men, flinging their long hair in the air and holding up their children.

Caesar was worried, for he feared that his legions would be driven down the hillside. He called out the remaining cohorts of the smaller camp and readied his Tenth Legion to cover the retreat. The Aedui now appeared on the Roman right flank, their right shoulders left uncovered to distinguish them as Gallic troops friendly to the Romans. They were too late. Hemmed in, the legionaries at the town walls were cut down by the mob. Those that managed to get inside the town were flung back over the walls. A centurion of the Eighth Legion, Marcus Petronius, held back the enemy at the gates. Bleeding from a score of wounds, Petronius cried for the others to run and save themselves. He killed at least two of the enemy, and gained time for his men to escape, before he disappeared under a mass of Gauls.

Forty-six centurions perished as the Gauls forced the legionaries at the camp ramparts down the hill. The rout did not stop until the defensive line of the Tenth Legion, reinforced with the extra cohorts, allowed the fleeing legionaries to reform. Vercingetorix called his men back to redeploy behind their fortification.

Instead of a tactical victory, Caesar barely averted a tactical disaster. According to him, Roman casualties were less than 700. Probably they were considerably higher. He reprimanded his troops, praising their valor but condemned them for disobeying and for their rashness. Twice more Caesar tried to goad Vercingetorix into an open battle but to no avail. Caesar broke off the siege and headed toward the Aedui country. The initiative was back into Vercingetorix's hands.

Caesar got more bad news when he heard that Litaviccus, with Vercingetorix's cavalry, had sped ahead of Caesar's forces to further win over the Aedui. When the two leaders of Caesar's Aedui cavalry, Eporedorix and Viridomarus, heard this, they asked Caesar to be allowed to ride ahead and convince their kinsfolk to stay loyal to Rome. Caesar reluctantly let them go. He feared more treachery and rightly so. Instead of securing the loyalty of the Aedui, Eporedorix and Viridomarus set upon Caesar's supply depot at the Aeduan town of Noviodunum (Nevers). They freed the Gallic hostages that Caesar kept there, killed the Roman merchants, and looted and burnt the town to prevent the Romans from retaking it. The seventy-year-old alliance of the Aedui and the Roman Republic was broken.

Gallic morale was at an all time high, and Caesar found himself in the middle of an enemy country with few allies left. There had been revolts before, but never like this. Roman authority in Gaul was swept away as if it all had been for nothing. Many a commander would have given up long ago but not Julius Caesar. Confident in his own genius he resolved to meet up with Labienus as fast as he could and somehow snatch victory from looming defeat.

Day and night, virtually without rest, Caesar's legions marched on to the River Loire. The cavalry entered the water first, using the bodies of the horses to break the current's force to ease the crossing of the infantry. Swollen with snow melt, the icy waters of the river nearly reached the shoulders of the infantry, who carried their shields and weapons above their heads. After crossing the River Loire, Caesar let his men pillage grain and cattle. When his army was freshly supplied, Caesar marched toward the north. Caesar was hoping to join Labienus, whose legions were at Agedincum in the territory of the Senones.

Labienus had won victories against the Senones and Parisii strongholds, when a false rumor of Caesar retreating back to Narbonensis reached him. Accordingly, Labienus decided to fall back toward Agedincum. On the way, Labienus annihilated a Gallic army blocking the River Seine crossing. At Agedincum he joined back up with Caesar. Caesar could still count on his ten battle-hardened legions. The campaign losses incurred from Gallic raiders, and suffered at the brutal siege of Avaricum and at the battle of the Gergovia entrenchments, left the legions wounded but not mauled. He still had his auxiliary German and Spanish cavalry but otherwise there were no more reinforcements. If anything it seemed that his last allies would desert Caesar and leave him and his legions standing alone in a whole country bent on their destruction.

Chapter Fifteen

Decision at Alesia

"On that day, he said, on that very hour, depended the fruits of all their previous battles."[1]

Caesar encouraging his soldiers at the siege of Alesia

The warrior stood up and examined his sharpened sword. Campfire flames danced in the polished iron of the splendid yard-long blade. The others muttered their approval. One took a deep swallow of wine. Red liquid dripped down his ample beard as he bellowed praise to the war gods. A few of his comrades shook their heads. They refused to give way to the lure of the wine. Their tribal tradition taught them that it made men soft and weak.

The warriors were tall men, gigantic by the standards of the time. Their skin was scarred and leathered, their limbs gnarled with muscles. A lifetime spent under sun, rain and snow, on the hunt and on the field of battle, had made them so. Some wore their long blond or red hair combed sideways and done up in a knot, after the fashion of their people, the Germanic Suebi. But there too was a sprinkling of adventurers from farther afield. One might see a Harii, who blackened his shield and dyed his body, preferring to fight in the dead of night, or an Aestii who wore a protective emblem of the wild boar, symbol of the Mother of the Gods.[2] In the night shadows that grew behind the barbarians' fire one might hear the snort of a horse and now and then, the Latin tongue. The German band was camped right among Caesar's legions![3]

Among the Germans, the retainers (*comitatus*) of a chief were drawn not just from his own tribe but from warriors that wandered the land in search of martial glory and plunder. To such men it mattered not if they served a German chief of a different tribe, a Gallic lord or even a Roman consul. Germans even served as bodyguards for Cleopatra and for Herod the Great. Among both Germans and Gauls, the mercenary career was not only acceptable but deemed honorable.

Some of the Germans around the campfire scene recreated above were former hostages, mostly well-armed chiefs and their attendants. They were part of the 400 cavalry recruited by Caesar after he beat back German tribal intrusions into Gaul in 58 and 55 BC. Recently, their small contingent had been joined by another 600 Germanic cavalry and light troops. Still, the Germans must have asked themselves if they were wise to fight for Caesar. For at the moment, in mid-52 BC, things did not look promising for the conqueror of Gaul.

Nearly all of Gaul was in full-blown rebellion. After reuniting his own legions with those of his talented legate Labienus at Agedincum, Caesar marched south into Lingones territory. The Lingones remained his allies, as did the Belgic Remi. The Treveri remained neutral, being too occupied with their hostile German neighbors across the Rhine. All the other tribes had gone over to the charismatic young warlord, Vercingetorix. Even now, his lieutenants were striking across the southern frontiers, at the Allobroges, the Helvii and the Volcae Arecomici, tribes living within the Roman province of Gallia Narbonensis.

With all of Gaul defecting from Roman rule, Caesar's inferiority in cavalry became critical. This was because since the turn of the first century BC, the "Roman" cavalry was made up entirely of foreign auxiliaries. For Caesar those auxiliaries were mostly allied Gauls. But the largest contingent of allied Gallic cavalry, those from his erstwhile allies the Aedui, had just defected. Although he also had with him a handful of Spanish horse, probably enlisted during his prior Spanish campaign, Caesar must have put high hopes on his Germans. He valued them so highly that he replaced their hardy pony-like horses with the larger steeds of his bodyguard, tribunes and knights. How the Germans made do with Caesar's larger and faster steeds is unclear. Possibly they continued to use their highly trained ponies in most combats unless speed was of the essence, as in a quick pursuit, in which case they used the Roman horses.

Near Dijon, Vercingetorix's cavalry attacked Caesar's legions which were strung out on the march and out of battle position. In a three pronged attack the Gauls targeted the Roman vanguard and the flanks of the main body. Vercingetorix hoped that the Romans would panic and abandon their baggage train. Surprise was achieved but the Gallic cavalry failed to close with the enemy and skirmished about instead. Caesar managed to draw up his own cavalry to keep the Gauls at bay while his legionaries formed a defensive square around the baggage.

Caesar's German cavalry, however, was not content with being on the defensive. They gained the summit of some rising ground, dislodged some of the enemy, and chased them back upon Vercingetorix's nearby infantry. Seeing their comrades being chased, cut down and skewered by the berserk Germans, the rest of Vercingetorix's cavalry took to flight. The remainder of Caesar's cavalry bolted after them and inflicted more losses. With his cavalry in shambles, Vercingetorix ordered a retreat towards the stronghold of Alesia (Alise Sainte Reine, on Mont Auxois). Caesar immediately led his legions in pursuit, engaged the Gallic rearguard and inflicted up to 3,000 casualties.

The battle completely reversed the situation of the war. The Gauls placed the greatest reliance on their cavalry arm and with its defeat their spirits sank. Vercingetorix found himself shut up in Alesia. Perched on a plateau and surrounded by hills and streams, to Caesar the city seemed impervious to assault. Below the town ramparts, a hastily constructed six-foot wall and trench enclosed a Gallic camp.

Caesar decided on a blockade and began to surround the entire city with two massive lines of fortifications. The fortifications consisted of two concentric rings of earthworks, ditches, ramparts, spikes, stakes, covered pits, forts and camps. The inner ring, the line of contravallation, some 10 miles long, faced the defenders of Alesia while the outer, the line of circumvallation, over 12 miles long, protected the Romans from anticipated relief forces.

Barely had the siege commenced when Vercingetorix's cavalry, some 10,000 to 15,000 strong, assailed Caesar's horsemen, presumably to reduce the Romans' foraging capability. When Caesar's auxiliary Gallic and Spanish cavalry had the worst of it, Caesar unleashed his Germans and drew up his legions for support. Bolstered by the Germans, Caesar's cavalry turned the tide. The Germans harried the Gauls back against the rampart and trench the Gauls had erected before the town walls. Frantic Gauls jammed up the narrow gates or abandoned their mounts in order to scramble through the trench and up the rampart. The Germans wantonly slaughtered those caught outside and captured a number of horses.

With the failure of his cavalry, Vercingetorix changed his strategy. Deciding to remain on the defensive, he sent his mauled cavalry to infiltrate the Roman lines at night. They were to ride abroad and raise a relief army among the rebellious tribes. Vercingetorix would hold Alesia until help arrived. Caesar claimed that Vercingetorix had some 80,000 picked men to defend the city, but in reality the number was surely far less and closer to 25,000.

Vercingetorix's heralds rode their horses through the countryside, into the villages and gated towns of Celtic central Gaul. From out of their A-frame thatched huts, and from the farm fields that surrounded them, men, women, young and old, gathered to hear the call to arms. To the chiefs, magistrates and people, the messengers declared that Vercingetorix, who fought so hard for their national liberty, "ought not to be abandoned to the cruel vengeance of the enemy."[4] Moreover, if they did not hurry, they would condemn Alesia's defenders to their death. The heralds rode further, to call to arms the seafaring Aremorican tribes, the Spanish Celtic-Iberian Aquitani and the Germanic-Gallic Belgae.

The army that mustered to Alesia's aid included contingents from almost every conceivable part of Gaul. The largest numbers of warriors came from the Aedui and from the Arverni with their dependent tribes. Caesar neatly listed every tribe and the numbers each of them supplied, for a grand total of 8,000 cavalry and 250,000 infantry. Again the real number must have been much less, perhaps around 120,000, but regardless it was the greatest show of pan-Gallic unity ever.[5] The bulk of them were not much better than armed riffraff, the serf-like common class that Caesar described as having little more value than slaves. Spirits were high and every man was confident that the mere sight of their enormous host would "be enough to make the enemy turn tail."[6]

Under the command of Commius, the Atrebatean king, the noble Aeduans Viridomarus and Eporedorix, and Vercingetorix's cousin Vercassivellaunus, alongside a host of other nobles and chiefs, the huge Gallic army arrived at Alesia. Notably, the first three mentioned leaders were all former allies of Caesar. One can only imagine the joy of the besieged at Alesia when they beheld the appearance of the mighty relief army. Supplies within the fortress town had been used up and hunger gnawed at the defenders. So bad had the situation become, that one noble Arvernian counseled eating the flesh of those too old or too young to fight as had been done in the days of the Cimbri and Teutones invasion. Thankfully, this cruel and desperate measure was not taken. The local population, with their women and children, had left the town and walked to the Roman ramparts. With tear stained eyes, they begged to be taken as slaves and to be relieved from their hunger. But there was no mercy in Caesar's heart and he turned them back.

The relief army set up camp a mile from the Roman lines. Around noon the Gauls reopened the battle. Commius sent forth his cavalry, archers and light armed troops to assault the outward facing Roman line of circumvallation. Vercingetorix's infantry simultaneously readied themselves to storm the inward facing line of contravallation. Caesar was hard pressed; his eleven legions were weakened from the heavy fighting in the campaign against Vercingetorix and he only had a handful of auxiliaries left. Although Caesar still had some 35,000 soldiers, he had to keep at least minimal garrisons along his miles of fortifications. Nevertheless, Caesar did his best to concentrate his legions against Vercingetorix's men while he sent his cavalry to engage Commius' cavalry.

The spectacle of the cavalry melee on the plain was visible from Caesar's main camps. It was also watched by the Gauls in Alesia and by the infantry of Commius, which was deployed on the slopes of a hill. Shouts of encouragement echoed from the ecstatic Gallic spectators. It seemed certain that their own, more numerous, cavalry would have the best of Caesar's horsemen. The hard fought battle lasted until the sun dipped near the horizon. It was then that the Germans massed all their squadrons for a charge that struck Commius' cavalry like a thunderbolt. Commius' cavalry was hurled back and fled the field, exposing his archers. The horrified bowmen watched as Caesar's cavalry galloped around them. Surrounded, their fate was sealed. Caesar's cavalry closed in and chopped down the bowmen with swords or impaled them on spears. With Commius' cavalry bested and his archers decimated, Vercingetorix abandoned his current breakout attempt and retired back into Alesia. Morale among his men was at an all time low.

After a day's lull, the Gauls were ready for another try. Carrying fascines, ladders and grappling hooks, the infantry of the relief army assaulted Caesar's outer wall at midnight. Under a barrage of arrows, sling shot and stones thrown by hand, they attempted to fill up the Roman trench. Roman commanders shouted for reinforcements. Legionaries rushed from redoubts to buffer threatened sectors. In the dead of night, the fighting was chaotic and costly on both sides. Legionaries plunged over the walls or collapsed with Gallic javelins skewered through their mail. Gauls tumbled into pits, impaled themselves on spikes, or were mowed down by the devastating fire of Roman siege engines. Trumpets sounded within Alesia and from out of its gates poured forth the besieged. Unfortunately for the Gauls, Vercingetorix's warriors wasted too much time filling up the outer Roman trenches. By the time they reached the main Roman fortifications it was too late; the relief army on the other side was already in retreat. The rising sun revealed a beaten Gallic army limping away in defeat.

But the Gauls were not finished yet. The next day saw the Roman fortifications under a coordinated attack. Vercingetorix made another sortie from the inside while the relief army's cavalry rode closer to the outer Roman wall and its infantry drew up in front of their own camp. Under cover of missile fire, Vercingetorix's men succeeded in filling a trench with earth and fascines. Grappling hooks were hurled at the palisade and bit into the breastwork. The

Gauls grunted and sweated as they pulled the ropes of their grappling hooks and tore down the palisade.

Caesar was at his best, hurrying around the defensive lines, redirecting reinforcements and personally urging his men to hold on, telling them that "on that day, on that very hour, depended the fruits of all their previous battles."[7] When two sets of reinforcements failed to stem Vercingetorix's Gauls who had breached the defenses, Caesar personally led up a fresh detachment and repulsed the attackers.

While Vercingetorix struck from the inside, Vercassivellaunus the Arvernian, with the best of the relief army's infantry, assailed a weak point in the Roman outer defenses. Due to the wide sweep of a hill, the Romans had been unable to connect a legionary camp within their line of circumvallation. Vercassivellaunus' men were able to assault the camp from a position of higher ground. The unrelenting hail of Gallic missile fire forced the Romans to take cover. Other Gauls advanced with shields locked above their heads. Labienus was sent to the rescue with six cohorts but even these did not suffice to hold back the furious Gallic onslaught.

Labienus was able to rally up eleven more cohorts. He sent a message to Caesar that the time had come for the decisive action. Caesar collected four more cohorts and part of his cavalry and hurried to confront Vercassivellaunus. He sent the other part of the cavalry around the outer defenses to strike Vercassivellaunus' Gauls in the rear. Both the Romans and Gauls recognized Caesar's arrival by his scarlet cloak, worn only by the commander-in-chief. The legionaries gave off a shout, dropped their spears, drew their gladii, and flung themselves into close combat with a vengeance. Suddenly, the Gauls heard the thunder of the enemy cavalry behind them. Surrounded, they panicked and ran for it. Few escaped and most were cut down. King Sedullus, who had led several thousand of his Lemovices from central Gaul, was killed in battle. Vercassivellaunus was taken prisoner and seventy-four standards were captured and presented at Caesar's feet. The rout did not stop at the Gallic camps as the survivors of the relief army fled back to their homelands and villages.

The relief army was crushed and with it went the hopes of the besieged. Even Vercingetorix's spirit was broken: "I did not undertake the war for private ends, but in the cause of national liberty. And since I must now accept my fate, I place myself at your disposal. Make amends to the Romans by killing me or surrender me alive as you think best."[8] Draped in his best armor, Vercingetorix mounted his splendidly adorned steed and rode out of doomed Alesia's gates. He was brought before Caesar and circled the Roman warlord before dismounting.

Proud even in defeat, the great Gallic king spoke, "Receive these spoils: thou thyself, bravest of men, hast conquered a brave enemy."⁹ Vercingetorix took off his armor and threw it to the ground, then seated himself at Caesar's feet and waited until he was led off into captivity. The siege of Alesia was at an end. Caesar spared the Aeduan and Arvernian prisoners, in hopes of regaining their tribal allegiance. The rest were handed out as slaves to his soldiers.

Even the capture of Vercingetorix and his resounding defeat at Alesia, did not wholly quell Gallic resistance. During the winter of 52/51 BC, rumors surfaced that the tribes planned multiple rebellions in so many places that would stretch the Roman resources beyond their limits. To prevent rumors from turning into reality, Caesar launched a pre-emptive attack on the Bituriges. He enslaved thousands of farmers caught on the fields and in their villages, until the Bituriges pleaded for peace and surrendered more hostages. Caesar next set out to punish the Carnutes. His cavalry raided at will, returning to the Roman camp laden with the spoils of war. The terrified Carnutes scattered into the barren woods, where they perished in droves due to the severe winter conditions. A more serious revolt broke out among the Bellovaci, led by their chief Correus and by Commius the Atrebatean. The revolt necessitated four legions and the levy of additional auxiliary cavalry from among the Remi, the Lingones and other tribes. It involved a lengthy stand-off between the fortified Roman and Gallic camps. For the most part, however, the campaign consisted of cavalry engagements. Correus was slain in a heroic last stand, smiting his foes until shot off his horse. When the Bellovaci surrendered hostages and sued for peace, Commius again eluded the Romans by finding shelter among German tribes from whom he had received reinforcements.

After re-subduing the Bellovaci, Caesar unleashed the final terror campaign on the hapless Eburones. Whatever homes remained after the devastation two years prior were burnt to the ground and whoever survived was killed or enslaved. Thereafter the Eburones were completely eradicated as a people, the few pockets of survivors that survived Caesar's wrath being eventually absorbed by other tribes.

Relatively minor revolts continued to erupt in the rest of Gaul, particularly among tribes in the western part of the country which had only marginally been involved in the previous fighting. The Pictones, who were allied to the Romans, were attacked by the Andes. General Gaius Fabius marched to aid the Pictones and in a hard fought battle his cavalry annihilated the enemy, slaughtering thousands. Fabius next joined up with general Gaius Caninius Rebilus, to track down the brigand leaders, Drappes and Lucterius the Cadrucan. Drappes had preyed on Roman foraging parties and supply convoys ever since the beginning of Vercingetorix's rebellion when Lucterius, as will be recalled, nearly invaded Gallia Narbonensis. Although Lucterius managed to escape Roman persecution, Drappes was captured and their forces were defeated. Hirtius' account praised the fighting powers of the auxiliary cavalry, especially the Germans and their accompanying light infantry, which "were very fleet on foot."[10]

Caesar meanwhile further browbeat the Carnutes. After flogging to death and beheading a rebellious ringleader of the Carnutes, Caesar joined Fabius and Rebilus at the Cadurci town of Uxellodunum. The two Roman generals had laid siege to the town because it had aided Lucterius. By cutting off the town water supply, Caesar forced its inhabitants into submission. He spared the surviving defenders' lives but to make an example of them ordered their hands cut off. While Caesar was busy at Uxellodunum, Labienus fought a successful cavalry engagement against the Treveri and some German allies. Thereafter, the legions were strategically deployed throughout Gaul. Caesar spent the winter visiting the various states. After showing the wrath of Rome, Caesar showed that Rome too honored her allies. He addressed the chiefs in honor, lavished upon them presents and imposed no new burdens.

The only one who carried on the fight was Commius who, reduced to a brigand, raided Roman supply convoys. Commius' old enemy Volusenus, who had once given Commius a near fatal head wound, was dispatched to hunt him down again. Commius was riding, accompanied by his entourage of warriors, when Volusenus sprung his ambush. The startled Gauls bolted at the sight of the Romans. Suddenly, Commius reined in his horse. Filled with hatred for Volusenus, Commius rallied his men to charge at the pursuing Romans. When the Romans saw the Gauls so valiantly charging at them they had a change of mind. The pursued became the pursuers.

Commius raced up behind Volusenus and jabbed his spear clean through his enemy's thigh. The danger to their leader gave the Romans new heart. They reversed their steeds and crashed into the pursuing Gauls. A fight ensued in which the Romans gained the upper hand. Knocked off their steeds, a few of the Gauls were trampled by the horses. Others were taken prisoner. Commius, however, made a clean getaway due to the speed of his horse.

After this latest harrowing encounter with the Romans, even Commius had had enough. He sent hostages to the Romans, telling them that he would let them be in peace if they would do the same to him. His only request was not to be required to come into the presence of any Romans. His request was honored and he too kept his word. Incredibly, even this was not the end of the adventurous Commius. In 50 BC, he decided to leave the land of Roman occupation and sailed for Britannia. There he settled on the River Thames and founded a new dynasty.

Caesar's Gallic wars were over. According to Plutarch, in less than ten years Caesar "had taken by storm above eight hundred towns, subdued three hundred states, and of the three million men, who made up the gross sum of those with who at several times he engaged, he had killed one million and taken captive a second."[11] Although Plutarch's figures are almost certainly inflated, there is little doubt that hundreds of thousands died in battle, were butchered in raids or were enslaved. How many more hundreds of thousands, if not millions, died of famine and cold, as conquering armies burnt villages and confiscated food supplies, can only be guessed at. For reasons unknown, even the 400-year-old Treveri stronghold on the Dollberg was abandoned sometime after Caesar's wars. Despite the hardships of the Gauls, Caesar demanded a punitive annual tribute of 400,000 gold pieces from the defeated tribes. The Gallic war had made Caesar a very rich man. According to Suetonius, in Gaul Caesar "had plundered large and small temples of their votive offerings, and more often gave towns over to pillage because their inhabitants were rich than because they had offended him. As a result he collected larger quantities of gold than he could handle."[12] Gaul remained utterly cowed and weakened for years to come.[13] Gallic pride in their war for freedom, however, did not diminish entirely. At a later date Caesar was shown a short sword hanging in a temple of the Arverni. Caesar smiled when the locals told him that it was the sword that had been taken from Caesar. Although his friends urged him to have it taken down, Caesar would not permit it.

Even the Germans kept quiet across the Rhine, which was fortunate for Caesar who, in 51 BC, right after the Gallic war, marched his legions across the Rubicon. By doing so he violated Roman law which made it illegal for a Roman general to lead his armed forces into Italy. The law sought to prevent a military takeover by a general and by breaking it Caesar plunged the Republic into civil war. Opposing him was Pompey. The Triumvirate was broken, friends turned into enemies. The third Triumvir, Crassus, who might have acted as a mediator between Caesar and Pompey, was dead. Two years prior, Crassus foolishly instigated a war against the powerful Parthian Kingdom. Crassus was killed by the Parthians after his crushing defeat at the battle of Carrahae. The battle claimed the lives of 25,000 legionaries, among them Crassus' son, Publius, who had served Caesar so valiantly during the Gallic war. After Crassus' death,

Pompey was turned against Caesar by the Senate. For four years Caesar's Gallic and German cavalry accompanied the legions through the war against the Pompeians and through the interludes of the Egyptian and Pontic wars. Caesar emerged victorious, crushing Pompey and his supporters.

In 46 BC, Caesar held four triumphs within one month, celebrating his victories over the Gauls and those of his civil war. Vercingetorix was led forth from the notorious dungeons of Tullianum, which was reserved for high profile captives. The once former king of the Gauls had languished six long years within its six-hundred-year-old walls. Bound in chains, Vercingetorix followed his conqueror in Caesar's Gallic triumphal march, "the first and most magnificent"[14] of his triumphs.

In a golden chariot drawn by four horses, Caesar led the procession, flowers strewn in front of his path. He wore the robes of Jupiter Capitolinus and a purple tunic and held an ivory scepter crowned with an eagle. Following Caesar were the columns of his legions and auxiliaries and the spoils of war: prisoners, sacrifices and effigies, and wagons brimming with 60,500 silver talents and 2,822 gold crowns. Along the way, the legionaries broke out in soldiers' songs, two verses of which were noted down by Suetonius:

"Home we bring our bald whoremonger;
Romans, lock your wives away!
All the bags of gold you lent him.
Went his Gallic tarts to pay."[15]

"Gaul was brought to shame by Caesar;
By King Nicomedes, he,
Here comes Caesar, wreathed in triumph
For his Gallic victory!
Nicomedes wears no laurels,
Though the greatest of the three."[16]

The second verse referred to an early time in Caesar's career when, uncharacteristically, he was rumored to have been bedfellow of Nicomedes, King of Bithynia.[17]

The triumph began on the Campus Marius and filed through the Porta Triumphalis, the Circus Flaminius and the Circus Maximus. It ended at the Capitol Hill, which Caesar ascended flanked by "two lines of elephants, forty in all, which acted as his torch bearers."[18] On the Capitol two white bulls were sacrificed. Vercingetorix was executed. With him died the best and perhaps the only real hope for Gallic independence.

Caesar handsomely rewarded his soldiers. Each legionary was given a bonus of 240 gold pieces, the equal of thirteen years pay. To the commoners of Rome, Caesar dealt out grain and oil rations and four gold pieces each. Days of lavish games followed his triumphs, with gladiatorial fights and beast hunts on the arena sands and a naval battle on a flooded Campus Marius. Several thousand men, alongside hundreds of lions, scores of elephants and for the first time, a giraffe, killed each other for the amusement of the Roman populace. So many people showed up from all directions to witness the bloody spectacles that tents were pitched along the streets, roads and on roof tops. The crowds became so ecstatic that people were crushed to death, including two senators. "This horrifying and wanton display of power exceeded anything as yet seen in Rome, and it revealed a side of Caesar's character which did him little credit,"[19] noted Fuller.

In 44 BC, Caesar became dictator for life and in the same year, on the fateful Ides of March, was assassinated. The death of Caesar caused another civil war which ended with the rise of Caesar's nephew and close disciple, Gaius Octavian, to the title of Augustus, the semi-divine, first Emperor of Rome, on 16 January 27 BC. The reign of Augustus heralded a new chapter in Rome's war against the barbarian peoples. The Gauls were a conquered people, but across the Rhine, the free Germanic tribes were about to bear the full brunt of Rome's conquering legions.

Chapter Sixteen

Onward to the River Elbe

"Whither, pray, art thou hastening, insatiable Drusus? It is not fated that thou shalt look upon all these lands. But depart; for the end alike of thy labors and of thy life is already at hand."[1]

Cassius Dio

Gaius Octavian (63 BC-AD 14) possessed none of his great-uncle Caesar's charisma, natural leadership or soldierly qualities. And yet it was Octavian who became not only Rome's first Emperor but also undeniably one of its best. Although handsome and bright-eyed, he suffered from ill health and neglected his personal appearance. Octavian commanded absolute power but he never abused it and lived a relatively modest life style. Octavian was a Republican at heart. His down to earth nature prevented the power he held from going to his head, and enabled Octavian to resolve problems in a practical manner and to delegate duties to capable individuals. Much of his success was based on good luck for he inherited Caesar's fame and fortune and could count on the unwavering loyalty of his champion Marcus Vipsanius Agrippa. An outstanding commander, Agrippa defeated the imperial aspirants Mark Antony and Cleopatra, at the fateful 31 BC battle of Actium, setting up Octavian as "Augustus", the sole master of the Roman world.

The empire of Augustus' time boasted a population of more than 50 million.[2] Up to a million of them, including 200,000 slaves lived in Rome alone, most of them crowded into densely packed, dim and squalid, tenements. Rents were high, hunger, unemployment and crime rampant. But the bellies of the mob were kept satiated by free grain rations and their vulgar minds occupied by pompous triumphal marches, by the thrill of chariot races and by the bloodshed of the gladiatorial fights and beast hunts.

In contrast, the white-marbled limestone forums, temples, theaters and country villas of the upper class, reflected the spoils of war concentrated into the hands of a few. While the turmoil of the civil wars disturbed provincial manufacturing, it allowed wealthy Romans to acquire bargain real estate and cropland. Vast numbers of slaves toiled on the large estates. It was the first age of the Roman millionaires who, in stark contrast to their emperor, lived a life of unbridled opulence. Augustus was nevertheless the richest Roman of them all and it was he who carried out many of the startling building projects, monuments to Roman history and heroes, which graced the central area of the Eternal City. He boasted "I arrived in a city of brick and I created a city of marble."[3]

Augustus maintained security in Rome through the Urban Cohorts and his creation, the imperial Praetorian Guard. Abroad, order was maintained by his iron legions on whose unwavering loyalty he depended. Both the Praetorians and the legions swore allegiance to Augustus and looked to him for their material rewards. Every year, every legion in mass assemblies renewed their oath to obey the emperor, to never desert and to be ready to sacrifice their lives for Rome. Discipline was fostered through a combination of unit pride and draconian punishment. A cohort that broke in battle drew lots; every tenth man was executed. Centurions who abandoned their posts shared the same fate. Lesser punishments included standing all day whilst carrying ten-foot poles or clods of earth. All legionaries continued to be heavy infantry but unlike in Caesar's day, a contingent of 120 Roman cavalry had been added to each legion.[4]

During the civil wars the numbers of legions had grown to 60. Augustus brought the number back down to a more reasonable 28, closer to what they had been in Caesar's day. This left Augustus with 250,000 to 300,000 soldiers equally divided between the legions and the auxiliaries. The auxiliaries were no longer the tribal irregulars but foreign troops organized and armed in the Roman manner, who would earn their citizenship after twenty-five years of service.

The legions and the auxiliaries guarded 4,000 miles of frontier, in addition to enforcing order within the provinces. Augustus knew well enough that idle legions, deprived of loot, could turn against him. Likewise, the spoils of war were what fed his popularity among the war-hungry Roman mob. War too, provided slaves to work the estates of the wealthy. The problem was that there were few lucrative lands left whose conquests justified the required military expenditure. Augustus faced the daunting task of maintaining stability in the provinces of his empire, keeping the loyalty of his legions, retaining his political clout among his peers and insuring the adoration of the Roman masses. He accomplished all these tasks by a wisely applied combination of diplomacy and military action that varied with each province.

Augustus nurtured friendly trade relations with Britannia. In North Africa, the flexing of Roman military muscle secured the wheat basket of the Empire. Roman military strikes cowed hostile Berber tribes, ensured peace with the Ethiopians and safeguarded the Indian and Somali trade routes from Ethiopian and Arabian threats. Augustus curbed Roman aggression in the Near East. A show of Roman power in Armenia sufficed to ensure Armenia's subservience and to maintain peace with Parthia. Northern Spain, however, felt the full might of the Roman war machine, when Augustus finally conquered the area in a fierce war that lasted from 26 to 19 BC.

Although minor rebellions were put down in Aquitania in 39 and 30 BC, Gaul as a whole remained peaceful. Augustus divided Caesar's conquests into three Imperial provinces. Gallia Aquitania bordered Spain, while Gallia Lugdunensis, the most Celtic of the three, was in the center. Gallia Belgica, with the sub districts of Germania Inferior and Germania Superior, ran along the left bank of the Rhine down to the Alps.

In 38 BC, the Germanic Ubii pleaded with Agrippa to be allowed to immigrate into Germania Inferior. There the Ubii would be safe from the feared Suebi. Agrippa knew well that the Ubii had been faithful friends of Rome for the past seventeen years, ever since they swore fealty to Caesar. He granted them settlement on the left bank of the lower Rhine. Their main town *Oppidum Ubiorum*, the future Cologne, served as an important Roman military base.

Although relative peace reigned for nine years, the barbarian Alps and Balkans, and the endless forests east of the Rhine, in Germania Magna, loomed over Gaul and northern Italy like some dark, fearsome cloud. Running north to south along the Rhine, and west to east along the Danube, the Roman border with the barbarian tribes formed a giant, triangular salient. It was here that Augustus' legions would see their largest and hardest fought campaigns.

In 29 BC, the Roman army put down a rebellion by the Belgic Morini and arrested minor Suebi inroads across the Rhine. The Suebi prisoners ended up in the arena where they were pitched in battle against Dacian prisoners. The Dacians had the misfortune of having fought for the Roman enemies of Augustus in the last civil war. In the Danube lands, the legions repulsed the Bastarnae, a fierce Germanic-Celtic tribe from the eastern Carpathians, who raided across the Danube. A more serious foray occurred in 17 BC, when the Sugambri led by Melo, brother of Baetorix, defeated Marcus Lollius' Fifth "Alauda" Legion and captured its Eagle. Melo's victory marked the onset of continuous strife along the border. "Different peoples at different times would cause a breach, first growing powerful and then being put down, and then revolting again, betraying both the hostages they had given and their pledges of good faith,"[5] noted Strabo.

It would not be Agrippa who would lead the legions of Augustus against the barbarian tribes. After bringing the war against the Spanish Cantabrians to an end in 19 BC, Agrippa went on to serve as governor of the eastern provinces. He was now in his forties and increasingly estranged from his old friend Augustus, whose jealous wife, the Empress Livia, resented Agrippa's influence over her husband. It would be the sons of Livia by a former marriage who would become the new champions of Augustus. Fortunately for Augustus, his stepson Drusus Nero Claudius proved to be a capable commander and Roman hero. Not only that, but Drusus' elder brother, Tiberius Claudius Nero, was no military slouch either, though, as shall be seen, of a very different character than Drusus. Conveniently, both stepsons had just reached the right age to take over command.

The first military test of the imperial princes was against the Rhaeti, an Illyrian Alpine people, who dwelt between Germania Superior and Noricum. The latter Celtic Kingdom had a very long tradition of friendship with Rome and in 16 BC peacefully accepted Roman provincial status. The Rhaeti, however, preyed on Roman travelers and plundered into Gaul and even into northern Italy. Allegedly, they killed all male prisoners. In 15 BC, the 23-year-old Drusus and his four years older brother Tiberius set off to deal with these troublemakers. The two Roman princes rampaged through the country and deported a large number of captured males. The area became the new province of Rhaetia. In honor of the Roman victories the Senate financed the building of a gigantic 150-foot tall monument on the Mediterranean coastal road between Italy and Spain. A bronze statue of Augustus stood on top with captive figures at his feet.

East of Noricum lay Pannonia (roughly Slovenia and Croatia), inhabited by a mix of mostly Illyrians and a few Celts and Thracians. They had a habit of wearing apparel called *panus* or patch, made up of strips of cloth. Centuries later, many of Rome's most formidable emperors would hail from the area. In the late days of the Republic and early days of the Empire, however, the Pannonians were more of a scourge to Rome. Already in 35 BC, Augustus skirmished with Pannonian bandits.

Now Augustus decided on a full Pannonian conquest. Despite his stepsons' success in Rhaetia, Augustus at first gave the Pannonian command to his old champion Agrippa. The Fates however, decreed otherwise when Agrippa succumbed to an illness. Agrippa had been a man of impeccable morals. Never once had he been a source of scandal in a city infamous for it. Loyal Agrippa symbolized the Rome of an earlier age.

It was a time for Drusus and Tiberius to further show their worth. Tiberius accordingly assumed command in Pannonia, subduing the tribes in a tough war from 12 to 8 BC. While Tiberius did his best in Pannonia, Augustus entrusted a more prestigious task to Drusus. The Emperor much preferred the dashing Drusus to his brooding, tongue-tied brother. Unlike Tiberius, who opposed any major operations across the Rhine, Drusus urged the conquest of the German tribes. Inspired by Drusus, Augustus figured that if the Roman frontier was pushed east to the River Elbe (the Albis), it would be shortened and the security of Gaul and Italy assured.

The conquest of the Germanic tribes would also ensure more slaves for the markets of Rome and open a vast reservoir of the vital commodity of timber. By the first century AD, Italy was already nearly stripped bare of its accessible forest and most of the timber was imported. Much of the wood fed the fires of Roman metallurgic industries. Due to lack of wood for charcoal, these industries increasingly moved to areas outside of Italy. Wherever they went the land was deforested. More wood was to be consumed by the empire's growing number of public thermal baths, where beneath the floors giant fires burnt day and night, heating the water to 37 degree Celsius.[6]

The Roman naturalist and philosopher, Pliny the elder, held the forests of Germania in awe: "gigantic oaks, uninjured by the lapse of ages, and contemporary with the creation of the world, by their near approach to immortality surpass all other marvels known."[7] The Germanic tribes were a materially poor people, but the Romans would profit from the people themselves and from the land.

Just as Gaul had done for Caesar, the conquest of Germania would solidify Drusus' renown in the Empire. The legions adored Drusus and they were ready. So was Drusus. Long ago, in 283 BC, the first Drusus gained his surname by slaying a Gallic chieftain named Drausus. Drusus Nero Claudius likewise was eager to slay a German chieftain in single combat and win his foe's armor, the "Noblest Spoils".[8]

In 13 BC, Drusus prepared Gaul against German counter raids by building a line of fifty wooden forts along the Rhine, the two major ones at Vetera (Xanten) and, covering 90 acres, at Moguntiacum (Mainz). In later ages these forts, often situated at older Celtic settlements, grew into the most famous towns along the Rhine, including Bingen, Spires, Worms and Strassburg. In 12 BC, the

Sugambri again invaded Germania Inferior. Drusus drove them back across the Rhine and devastated their villages. He was now ready to launch the first stage of his conquest, which was to establish Roman supremacy along the North Sea coast and thereby isolate the interior tribes from their coastal resources.

Sailing down the Rhine, he dug a series of canals, the *fossa Drusiana*, connecting the river with Lake Flevo and the North Sea. At the time the lake was part of a series of lowlands, lakes and channels that now lie submerged beneath the Ijsselmeer.[9] The route through Flevo allowed Drusus to shorten the distance his flotilla had to travel along the more treacherous North Sea coast. The Roman ships headed east toward the mouth of the River Ems (the Amisia). In lagoons along the way, Drusus visited the villages of the Frisii.

In typical Germanic fashion, the Frisii dwelt in rectangular longhouses, with walls of mud and wood and thatched roofs. A new recruit among Drusus' bodyguard might have reflected how differently the German tribes lived compared to his own Latin people. Unlike the Romans, the Frisii built each house separated from all the others. Not only that but the Frisii, as was common for all the tribes, shared their home with their livestock, albeit in separate quarters. Then again, the young recruit's eyes might have wandered to some fair Frisii maidens among the crowd of bearded men, who along with their wives and their naked, dirty children, gathered to see the Roman visitors. The local maidens let their hair fall loose, to signify their unmarried status. For such important visitors, they must have donned their most beautiful, ornately woven, crimson and purple garments. Drusus, for his part, had little time to dwell on local maidens while he finished his fruitful negotiations. The Frisii did not seek war and readily submitted to Drusus. A seafaring people, they saw in Rome a lucrative trading partner. In return for their goodwill, Drusus made the Frisii pay only a paltry tribute of hides.

From the River Ems it was off to the mouth of the River Weser (the Visurgis). Here the ebb of the ocean stranded the Roman fleet. The area was Chauci territory. Though known for fair play and not for aggression, the Chauci were quite ready to defend their lands. Drusus would have been in trouble if not for the Frisii, who came to his aid with their infantry. Possibly he built forts at both the River Ems and the Weser mouths, before withdrawing for the winter and heading back to Rome.

In 11 BC, Drusus returned to subjugate the Usipetes and thereafter ventured up the fertile valley of the River Lippe (the Lupia). His route took him through Sugambri lands and as far as Cherusci territory on the banks of the Weser.

Unlike Caesar, whose incursions barely penetrated the lands east of the Rhine, Drusus had ventured far into the hinterland. The philosopher Seneca the Younger went so far as to claim that "Drusus set up military standards where the people did not even know Rome existed."[10] Seneca's words highlight the sense of the remoteness into which Drusus had ventured. Nevertheless, it is hard to believe that even the most distant Germanic tribes did not at least hear of Rome. Tales of Caesar's war with the Gauls and Germans were likely told in song and verse. Indeed, it was Caesar's conquest of Gaul that had forced many Germanic tribes to abandon their movements to the west. As a result the Germans encountered by Drusus had become more settled than they were in Caesar's day and had become almost entirely dependent on agriculture.

Villagers gathered in astonishment and apprehension, as heralds reported of an approaching mighty army of armored infantry, accompanied by a great host of cavalry. At the sight of Drusus' cavalry, women and slaves working in the field or tending cattle fled to their longhouses. The villages, clusters of houses, lay scattered around fields of cleared forest, where cattle roamed and grain blew in the wind. The cleared land surrounded patches of woodland, where Drusus' legionaries may have come upon holy groves. To the Romans, such places were filled with dreadful, unfamiliar gods and spirits. Here the tribes ritually butchered and ate cattle and horses. Skulls and extremities of the animals were left as offerings to Nerthus, mother earth, in hopes that she would bless the land with fertility. Strange pillar idols to represent the Germanic gods, stylistically endowed with male or female genitals, ominously leered down upon the Romans.

So far, there was no real opposition to the Roman invaders. The Sugambri were busy making war on the Chatti, who refused to join a Sugambri-Cherusci alliance against Rome. The Cherusci retreated into their woods to assemble their army. Drusus, like Caesar before him, was unable to confiscate sufficient grain from the tribal farms to feed his legions. Even though the tribes tilled the soil, their population density remained very low. The patchworks of farmsteads, woods and fields of cleared land, remained surrounded by vast wilderness areas. Short on provisions, Drusus was forced to return to the Rhine. On the way he was attacked by the Cherusci who relentlessly harried the Roman columns, nearly eliminating the legions in a defile. But when the barbarians pressed in for the kill too soon, the legions hit them hard and thereafter the Germans dared little more than petty annoyances.

Drusus established a fort at Oberaden, just south of the Lippe, in Sugambri lands, and another fort among the Chatti, on the banks of the Rhine. The camp at Oberaden held no less than three of Drusus' legions. There the soldiers, who hailed from northern Italy and from Gallia Narbonensis, enjoyed some of the luxuries of Roman civilization. Figs and olives were imported from the Mediterranean, and even pepper, originating all the way from India. Drusus returned to Rome, riding into the city on horseback to celebrate his latest triumphs.

On his return to Moguntiacum in 10 BC, Drusus headed up the Lahn valley. Here he fought the Chatti, who had been subjugated by the Sugambri. Tacitus described them as a nation "distinguished by hardy bodies, well-knit limbs, fierce countenances and unusual mental vigor."[11] Their strength was in their infantry and they were among the most disciplined of the Germans. Among them the legionaries encountered young men, whose beards and hair had never been cut, for it was their custom to stay unshorn until they had killed their first enemy. Weakened by their recent war with the Sugambri, the Chatti valor was not enough to defeat Drusus, who brought them under Roman control. As a reward, Drusus became an honorary Imperator and received his first consulship.

The next summer, in 9 BC, Drusus undertook his most ambitious campaign. From Moguntiacum he marched over Chatti lands and squared off, indecisively, with the powerful Marcomanni in the River Main valley. Shortly thereafter, Augustus sent a Suebi noble, Maroboduus, to win over the Marcomanni as a client state. Maroboduus had been but a child when he was given to the Emperor as a hostage after the reduction of the Rhaeti. Growing up at the Imperial court, he keenly absorbed Roman ways, especially those pertaining to warfare. Just as Augustus hoped, the Marcomanni accepted Maroboduus as their king.

Drusus pillaged the Cherusci to the north. He crossed the Werrer, a headstream of the Weser, at the ford of Hedemünden,[12] establishing a fort, and from there advanced all the way to the Elbe. Time and time again, Drusus partook in personal combat but his wish to slay a chieftain was to remain unfulfilled. What happened next is shrouded in mystery and legend. He was just about to cross the Elbe when a giant woman appeared and spoke to him, "Whither, pray, art thou hastening, insatiable Drusus? It is not fated that thou shalt look upon all these lands. But depart; for the end alike of thy labors and of thy life is already at hand."[13] Unnerved, Drusus turned from the Elbe and crossing its western tributary, the Saale, hastened back to the Rhine. Wolves howled and prowled around his camp at night. Someone heard a woman lamenting and there were shooting stars. According to one tale Drusus was thrown off his horse, in another he contracted a disease. Whatever happened, he died after suffering for thirty days.

Tiberius received the news of his brother's accident while at Ticinum on the River Po. Tiberius immediately mounted a horse and galloped off to the Rhine. He reached his beloved brother just before Drusus breathed his last. Tiberius accompanied Drusus' body, walking in front of it, all the way back to Rome. Drusus' body was fittingly cremated on the Campus Martius, the plains of Mars, god of war. For his victories in Germania, Drusus and his descendants were bestowed with the honorary title of Germanicus. Back at Moguntiacum the troops erected a 64-foot high cylindrical monument to Drusus, overlooking the Rhine.

Tiberius assumed Drusus' command of the Rhine army. The German tribes sent envoys to Augustus, who remained nearby in Roman territory to keep an eye on his stepson. Augustus rejected all the peace offers from the German tribes, unless the Sugambri yielded as well. Possibly in wrath over Drusus' death he imprisoned the Sugambri envoys, who took their own lives in despair. Between 9 and 7 BC, Tiberius took 40,000 Sugambri prisoners. The men, women and children were settled on the western side of the Rhine, leaving only a remnant in their homeland.[14] During this time, the Romans pulled back from their fort on the Werrer at Hedemünden. The military camp at Oberaden was likewise abandoned, though a new and better camp was built, 20 miles further westward, at Aliso (Haltern).[15] The new camp was built on the slopes of Silver Mountain. Merchant ships from Gaul docked in its port and wharves on the banks of the Lippe. Unlike Drusus' temporary camp at Oberaden, which held three legions, the 19-hectare fortress at Haltern was only large enough for one legion, the Nineteenth. However, the Haltern fortress was a more permanent settlement, fortified with a masonry wall and surrounded by a double ditch. It even included a sewer system.

In 6 BC, Tiberius retired to his private retreat on Rhodes. Augustus had forced Tiberius to divorce his wife, Agrippina, in favor of Julia, the daughter of Augustus. The problem was that Tiberius loved his wife and hated Julia. Coupled with Augustus' continuing lack of faith in him, Tiberius' troubled love life dragged his mind into a mire of depression.

Tiberius' replacement in Germania was the arrogant Lucius Domitius Ahenobarbus, whose wild animal hunts and gladiatorial fights were so cruel that they warranted a cautionary edit from the emperor. In 3 BC, Ahenobarbus built a wooden causeway, the 'Long Bridges', through a swamp between the Rhine and the Ems, and led a Roman campaign up to and across the Elbe. He marked the crossing with an altar to Augustus. As usual however, the campaign had no permanent results. The next year the Cherusci were back up in arms against the Romans. Overall though, the Roman legates did their best to encourage good relations with the tribes. The political climate remained relatively subdued until AD 4, when minor revolts prompted the return of Tiberius.

Tiberius suppressed the Bructeri, a tribe living north of the River Lippe. He subjugated the Cherusci, the most powerful German tribe outside of the Marcomanni and Suebi. After winning the allegiance of the Cherusci nobility, he gave their tribe the status of a federated state within the Empire. Unlike Drusus in his prior campaigns, Tiberius did not return to the Rhine that year. He quartered a Roman army in the middle of Germany at a new fort at Anreppen. The next year saw Tiberius reach the lower Elbe. Aided by supplies brought in by sea, he established Roman supremacy over the Chauci and Langobardi. From the north of the Elbe, from the Charudes and from the remnants of the Cimbri, came tribal envoys bearing words of friendship. The Cimbri even presented their most treasured cauldron as a gift to Augustus.

Altogether, the conquest of the Germanic tribes, who had so long terrorized Gaul and even threatened Rome in the past, was proceeding without any major mishaps or even any major engagements. Yet the Roman forts remained isolated in the midst of vast untamed forests and swamps. From out of the wilderness, tribesmen trickled in to visit the Roman towns and markets and there was a great deal of trade going on. The Germans traded food, local pottery and furs, for Roman glass beads, jewelry and pottery. The blond hair of the German women too was eagerly sought after by fashionable, wealthy, Roman women. The Romans felt secure enough to establish entire towns east of the Rhine, one of which was discovered on the outskirts of the modern village of Waldgermis on the River Lahn. Founded in 4 BC, the town was laid out in the Roman pattern, with a forum, bath houses, flowering gardens and atriums. A gilded bronze statue of the divine Augustus mounted on a horse served as a reminder of the Empire's omnipotence. Farther west, on the Rhine, at *Oppidum Ubiorum*, a Germanic priest worshipped at Augustus' altar. The altar looked out toward Germania, where its chieftains likewise honored the Emperor. It was their sons who held command over the Roman auxiliaries. The Germans were being conquered and assimilated into the Empire without even realizing it. It all went too easy, much too easy.

The problem was that the Romans considered the Germans conquered but not all the Germans considered themselves conquered. After all, what exactly did the Romans conquer? In Gaul, Caesar was at his most successful when he captured enemy strongholds. When he burnt and looted the countryside and the natives scattered into their wilderness hideouts, he rarely achieved lasting victory. In Germania, which was much less civilized that Gaul, there were no large urban centers or strongholds to capture and all Drusus and Tiberius could do was to march around in a demonstration of Roman power. The roads, if any were available, were much poorer than in Gaul and the terrain more difficult. Campaigns, Roman forts and towns were usually confined to river valleys and along the coast, where supplies could be brought by ships. Many interior villages probably remained relatively unaffected by the Roman demonstrations.

Ranke and Delbrück have also suggested that many German tribes saw the Romans not as conquerors but rather as allies against a potential mutual threat, Maroboduus, the new King of the Marcomanni. Maroboduus had taken his people from the Main valley to Bohemia (now the Czech Republic), where he absorbed or displaced Rome's old foes the Boii. There, in the footsteps of Ariovistus, Maroboduus forged a powerful Germanic kingdom. A large part of the mighty Suebi federation, which had given Caesar such trouble, went over to his side. Maroboduus extended his sway to the upper Elbe. He drilled his 75,000 warriors with Roman type discipline and armed them in the Roman way.

Although there is every indication that Maroboduus desired friendly relations with Rome, his realm remained a thorn in the new Roman frontier line. Maroboduus' kingdom formed a potentially highly dangerous salient between the upper Elbe and Rhaetia. In AD 6, Tiberius advanced on Maroboduus with no less than twelve legions plus auxiliaries. But before Tiberius' legions clashed with Maroboduus' tribesmen, a serious rebellion broke out in Pannonia that spilled over into the Roman province of Illyricum. The ostensible reason was forced recruitment among the Pannonians. Tiberius and his legions left to deal with the insurrection. Maroboduus was only too happy to agree to Roman terms and in turn be recognized as King and friend of the Roman people.

When rumors spread that the Pannonian rebels numbered over 200,000 and that some of them were moving on Italy, even Augustus was thrown into a panic. In Rome there were no reserves left to stop such an army and no recruits could be found to raise new legions. In desperation, Augustus requisitioned slaves from the wealthy, granting the slaves freedom in return for military service. The freemen 'volunteer' cohorts temporarily buffered the Illyrian defense. More substantial reinforcements arrived in AD 7, bringing the army of Tiberius up to an astonishing 100,000 men. With such incomparable might at his disposal, Tiberius crushed the Pannonian insurrection in two brutal campaigns. Germanicus Julius Caesar, the 24-year-old son of Drusus, fought at the side of

Tiberius, subduing the Illyrians in AD 9. Thereafter, Pannonia became a separate province while Illyricum was renamed Dalmatia.

Even through all the turmoil of the Pannonian war, the Germans remained peaceful. They were watching, however, and the bravery of the Pannonians made them ponder and think. And when a new governor, Publius Quinctilius Varus, arrived in Germany, their thoughts bore crimson fruit.

Chapter Seventeen

"Death March of the Legions"
The Battle of the Teutoburg Forest

"At that time among the Germans there was a young man of noble family, of courageous hand, quick mind, and wisdom such as one would not believe possible of a barbarian. His name was Arminius"[1]

Velleius Paterculus

Born c. 18 BC, Arminius, a prince of the Cherusci nobility, eldest son of Chief Segimer, became one of Rome's most bitter and most respected foes. To begin with however, Arminius was a friend of the Romans. He considered them not as conquerors of his people but more as equals. Arminius' Cherusci were allies of the Romans and received federate status within the Empire. To secure peace between his tribe and the Romans, it is quite possible that Arminius was sent as a child hostage to Rome. Rome demanded noble child hostages from conquered tribes and nations, both to ensure that her former adversaries remained loyal and to ingrain the hostages with Roman values. Such hostages were treated well and raised as members of the upper class, being tutored in Latin, in Roman customs and in Roman warfare. We can imagine how Arminius beheld Rome for the first time as a young boy. Back in the Cherusci lands, his princely longhouse was no doubt the envy of the village but compared to the marbled palaces of Rome it must have seemed like a hovel. When Arminius sat among 270,000 cheering spectators in the Circus Maximus, he must have thought that here were more people than in all of Germania.

While Arminius' childhood remains a matter of speculation, what is known for certain is that the young prince and his brother Flavus sought glory fighting under the Roman banner. Arminius and Flavus led Cherusci cavalry and lightly armed auxiliaries, probably fighting side by side with Tiberius' legions through the Pannonian and Illyrian revolts.[2] The Cherusci horsemen and light troops saw action against the enemy cavalry and hunted down straggling enemy infantry. Doubtlessly, Arminius and Flavus' horsemen carried out more sinister deeds as well, setting villages to the torch, looting and pillaging, and spreading misery and famine in the name of Rome.

As part of the Cherusci nobility, Arminius had been granted Roman citizenship. For his services in battle he was further awarded *equestrian* "knightly" rank. Respected by both his countrymen and the Romans, Arminius' career in the "Roman" Germania was on the rise. Just under 26–years-old, lean and fit, in the physical prime of his life, Arminius returned to Germania in AD 8. A contemporary Roman bust[3] shows him with stubble beard and thick, wavy hair that covered his ears and fell to just above his shoulders. Posted to the headquarters of the Roman governor Publius Quinctilius Varus at Vetera, Arminius continued to lead a troop of allied Cherusci and acted as a liaison between Rome and the Cherusci chiefs. Arminius' brother Flavus continued to serve Rome abroad for he is not mentioned at Varus' court. Flavus may well have remained in Illyria, helping Rome defeat the last of the insurgents and winning further battle honors.

It would be hard to imagine two men of more different temperaments than Arminius and Varus. Whereas the first was a natural leader of men, used to hardships of war, of life under the sun and stars, the other was a pen and scroll-pushing bureaucrat without an inkling of the harsh conditions of the northern frontier.

Born around 46 BC, into a respected family, Varus entered the inner circle of the Emperor when at thirty-three years of age he married the daughter of Augustus' trusted general Agrippa. Later, a second marriage to the daughter of the Emperor's grand niece, and the marriage of Varus' sister to a friend of Augustus, gained him the Emperor's confidence.

In 13 BC Varus served as consul, along with the Emperor's stepson Tiberius. Although the consulship no longer wielded the royal authority as in the days of the Republic, it remained a glamorous position. Varus wore a ceremonial toga and walked around attended by twelve *lictors*. The *lictors* were high status bodyguards that carried bundles of rods and axes, the *fasces*, symbolic reminders of the lesser punishment by the rod and of the ultimate penalty with the axe. Varus judged on certain criminal cases, such as those pertaining to slaves and, more important, presided over the games and the many festivals of Rome.

From his relatively frivolous days as a consul, Varus went to serve as proconsul of Roman Africa in 7–6 BC and from there to the important job of provincial governor of Syria. Syria was the axis of Far Eastern trade routes and of the Roman position in the East. It encompassed the territory from Cappadocia to Arabia and included Judea. Velleius Paterculus, historian and veteran of the Pannonian and German wars, probably met both Arminius and Varus in person. He sums up Varus' Syrian government: "when he [Varus] went to Syria, he arrived as a poor man in a rich province, and when he left, he was a rich man leaving behind a poor country."[4] Paterculus further wrote of Varus, "somewhat slow in mind and body, he was better suited for the quiet camp life than for fighting … a man of moderate ideas and calm temperament."[5] Varus did not hesitate to use his legions to spill blood for him. He squashed the unrest in Judea that followed the 4 BC death of the Roman client King Herod and crucified 2,000 of the rebellious Jews. Varus maintained order among the many different secular and religious factions but his brutal methods fostered anti-Roman sentiment that was only suppressed through fear of punishment. Nevertheless, Augustus was sufficiently impressed with Varus' record to appoint him governor of Germania in AD 7 and commander of its five legions and auxiliaries, perhaps a fifth of Rome's frontline strength.[6] Varus' mission was to turn the apparently pacified area of *Germania Magna* (Greater Germania) into a full-fledged province.

At the time of Varus' arrival in Germania, relations between the tribesmen and the Romans proceeded amiably. At the Roman outposts, the locals bartered milk and cheese, game meat, fowl, cattle, sheep, goats and hides. In return they received the luxuries of Roman civilization; glassware, silver cups, bronze trays and more than anything, wine. The Germans, however, paid no tribute to speak of, retained their uninhibited lifestyle, their laws and customs, and their weapons and military power.

The continued independence of the Germans did not sit well with Varus. If Germania were to be a Roman province, the Germans would have to pay tribute in silver and gold! After all, how could Varus line his own pockets if there were no taxes to be collected? Accordingly, Varus decided to govern the Germans as he had done the Syrians. To Varus the Germans were little better than animals, humans in appearance only, to be ordered around like slaves and kept in line with Roman law. Varus held an assembly and boasted that he would control the "savagery of the barbarians with the lashings of the lictor and the voice of the herald."[7]

When the Germans got wind of Varus' new ways, they were dumbstruck. There were only a handful of Roman outposts in Germania Magna and now those haughty Romans had the nerve to treat the Germans as a subjugated people! Precious metals were rare in Germania and the nobles were loath to part with them. Common goods and livestock seized as tribute in lieu of coins impoverished the already poor tribesmen. Villagers cursed and spat at Roman rule, chiefs met and reminisced of the freedom too easily given away. The barbarians "sadly watched their swords rusting and their horses unexercised, when they realized that the toga and court were worse than weapons."[8] Ridding themselves of the Roman presence, however, would be no easy task. Although the Roman outposts were few, they were strongly held. The Germans decided to bide their time and outwardly yielded to the demands of Varus.

As was common practice, after overwintering at the Roman towns on the Rhine, Varus planned to spend the summer of AD 9 at an advance post deep inside the barbarian wilderness. Varus would take with him the Seventeenth, Eighteenth and Nineteenth Legions from Germania Inferior. The First and the Fifth Legions under the command of Lucius Nonius Asprenas, Varus' nephew, remained in Germania Superior. From the plateau of Moguntiacum, Asprenas kept watch across the river. Asprenas was ready to defend not just the middle Rhine but also the lower Rhine of Germania Inferior, which after Varus' departure would only be held by a few legionary detachments and auxiliaries.

Several hundred auxiliary cavalry, quite possibly Ubii, in Roman mail and bronze helmets, lances and swords at their sides, trotted over a narrow pontoon bridge to the east side of the Rhine. The first shoots of green foliage and a warm wind heralded the end of winter's cold grasp and the approach of spring. It was early March, the beginning of the Roman campaigning season.[9] The Ubii were scouting ahead of Varus' army which had left Vetera.

In the wake of his scouts, Varus' army entered Greater Germania, following the traditional route along the Lippe River valley through Sugambri territory. The Roman column stretched mile after mile, shadowed by a small fleet of boats carrying the heavy supplies. On the first night they probably set up a fortified camp on the site of the earlier marching camp of Holsterhausen; during the second night they reached Rome's main base on the Lippe at Aliso. Varus conferred with the Nineteenth Legion's camp prefect Lucius Caedicius whose detachment held the fort, the likely topic: tribal relations. Perhaps Varus stayed a few days at Aliso, reorganizing the forty tonnes of daily grain and fodder consumed by his army. From Aliso, Varus struck farther east along the meandering Lippe. Setting up camp at the site of Oberaden, he pressed onward to the fort at Anreppen. The legions had now marched over 100 miles since they left Vetera. East of Anreppen, the Lippe turned south toward its headwaters in the uplands of the western Teutoburg Forest.[10] At Anreppen, Varus left the Lippe and made his way north through the Teutoburg and the western reaches of the Weser Hills. Upon reaching the upper Weser, Varus built his summer camp on the western bank, smack-dab in the middle of Cherusci territory.[11]

Varus was confident in his ability to control the natives. His summer camp dwarfed any of the local settlements and his army was more than sufficient to deal with any local uprisings. Compared to the Germanic villages, the largest of which had some 20–30 houses, Varus' summer camp was gigantic. In addition to the 12,000[12] or so soldiers of his three legions, it was defended by three auxiliary *alae* (cavalry squadrons), and six cohorts of auxiliary light troops. The auxiliaries likely included strong elements of Rome's staunch allies, the Ubii and Frisii, and numbered around 4,000 men.

Attending the soldiers were several thousand servants, not to mention the illegal[13] wives and children of the legionaries. Hoping for a profitable summer, a few hundred of the more adventurous merchants that lived in small communities beside the Rhine bases had followed Varus' army as well.

Varus' legions were well trained, among the best units in the Roman army. Paterculus praised their "outstanding discipline, courage and combat experience."[14] First raised in 49 BC, by Julius Caesar during the beginning of the civil war, the Seventeenth, Eighteenth and Nineteenth Legions consisted of Italians, Gauls and a few Syrians and North Africans. Most of the legionaries had seen combat in Germania under Drusus and Tiberius and were about half way through their twenty years of service.

The Germans had little chance of breaching the ditch and the rampart of the well-defended summer camp. Not that Varus ever imagined they would try. After all, Arminius' family was thoroughly integrated into the Roman military and government. His brother Flavus continued to serve Rome abroad. Their father, Segimer and his brother, the renowned warlord Inguiomerus, as well as another Cherusci noble, the huge and physically powerful Segestes, were respected allies of Rome. Segestes' son, Segimundus, even served as a priest at the altar of Augustus in the Ubii capital of *Oppidum Ubiorum*. Varus' entourage included nobles from other pro-Roman tribes as well, such as a young Boiocalus from the Ampsivarii on the middle Ems River. Like Arminius, Boiocalus had served under Tiberius.

Arminius and Segimer feasted at Varus' table and assured him that all was well. Cherusci tribesmen came to Varus' court, asking him to dispense Roman justice on complicated trials and replace might with right. Varus felt as if "he were the city praetor meting out justice in the Forum rather than commanding an army in the middle of Germany."¹⁵ Believing the land to be at peace, Varus risked splitting the troops, sending them out to deal with petty robbers and to protect and improve the supply route back to Anreppen by working on roads and bridges.

Paterculus wrote of the Germans that they were, "with all their wildness extremely sly and born liars."¹⁶ Indeed, beneath Arminius' reassuring goodwill to Varus there lurked a deep hatred of everything Roman. During the Pannonian war, Arminius might well have been inspired by the Pannonians who fought so hard for their freedom. When he returned home, he realized that the plight of the Pannonians was the same as that of his own people. To Rome the German tribes were not equals, as he once thought. Germania's sons fought and died for Rome while her daughters served the conquerors and her wealth fattened the pockets of men like Varus, who knew nothing of honor and battle.

Arminius was not alone. Together with his father, Segimer, he met with other tribal chiefs to forge plans on how to rid themselves of the Roman despots. The chiefs and their retainers arrived fully armed, their place of assembly perhaps a circle of standing stones in a forest glade. With the arrival of a priest, who commanded silence, the crowd seated itself. Arminius spoke and the chiefs weighed his words. When he saw the Romans triumph in Pannonia, Arminius learned much of their strengths and of their weaknesses. His knowledge would be the best weapon against the Romans. Arminius knew that an assault on Varus' camp was out of the question. Likewise, when drawn up in proper battle formation, the legions were near unbreakable.

An old chief may have reminded Arminius that since the days of Caesar, the tribes had become wiser in the ways of war, and fielded more and better swords and spears. Another chief might have retorted that this was true only for the elite warriors of the chiefs' personal entourage. The bulk of the tribal army consisted of farmers and many of them could afford little more than wattle shields, woodman's axes, clubs and bone-tipped spears. Overall, both in equipment and discipline, the average German warrior remained inferior to his Roman counterpart. Furthermore, Arminius knew that his Germanic warriors remained difficult to control on the battlefield since they were not enlisted soldiers. The Germanic warrior fought purely out of personal choice, for martial glory, for vengeance, to gain loot or due to social pressure. The only real power that Arminius possessed to make them obey was his personal charisma.

A few of the chiefs disagreed and shouted in anger, but most showed their approval of Arminius' call to rebellion. All would have looked to Arminius, how could they defeat the Romans? Arminius' answer was that to negate the legions' superior equipment and training, the tribes had to attack under favorable conditions. When strung out on the march, in difficult terrain that favored the quick and nimble, lightly armed Germanic warrior, the legions could go down in defeat. The leaves rustled in a cool wind, heralding the coming of fall. Soon Varus and his legions would return to Vetera on the Rhine for the winter. The time for the Cherusci to strike was drawing near. Arminius spoke with conviction and fiery passion blazed within his eyes. The chiefs wholeheartedly clashed their weapons to show their unanimous approval.

Despite Arminius' efforts to keep his plans secret, word about his impending treachery leaked out and reached Varus' ears. Not all the Cherusci chiefs were ready to abandon their flourishing careers in the Roman Empire, most notably Segestes. Segestes divulged the news about a brewing conspiracy to Varus after a banquet. Segestes urged Varus "to arrest Arminius and the other chiefs, and also himself, on the grounds that their removal would immobilize their accomplices and Varus could then take his time in sorting out the guilty from the innocent."[17] Varus had heard it all before. Even though Segestes seemed more anxious than usual, Varus would not listen. Arminius had his eye on Thusnelda, the daughter of Segestes, who, as fate would have it, was betrothed to another. Varus accused Segestes of slander. He likely thought that Segestes' was only being a protective father and acting out of his personal dislike of Arminius.

Almost immediately after Segestes' latest accusations of Arminius, Varus received the news that a few distant tribesmen, perhaps among the Angrivarii to the north-west, had rebelled. For Varus the timing was less than ideal, for his army was ready to begin its late summer march back to Vetera on the Rhine. Arminius advised Varus that to deal with the rebels, Varus should lead his army back to Vetera on a different route from the usual military road. The detour would take Varus along the northern edge of the Weser Hills and the Teutoburg Forest, where the highlands descended into the swamps and forests of the North European Plain. Varus agreed; his legions would set out at once to crush the insurrection before it could grow any larger. Word was sent to the Roman detachments that were strung out along the supply route back to Anreppen, or were chasing robbers in local villages. The detachments were ordered to catch up with Varus' slower main column.

Varus was confident that Arminius would be there to support and guide him through the wilderness. Arminius and his Cherusci contingent joined the legions marching out of the camp gates. Above each legion bobbed its Eagle standard, proudly carried by the first cohort. Wings spread, talons gripping thunderbolts, it was an icon of near religious nature, representing the invincibility of Rome. No doubt, the soldiers who marched beneath those proud standards thought that the rebels would easily be dealt with. The legionaries were in good spirits. Although their summer duties had been relatively lax and many had gotten along well with the locals, even made a few sweethearts, they were glad to see the last of the camp in the middle of the Germania wilderness. If things worked out, the legionaries would be back in "civilization" at their Vetera winter base in no time. Their pockets were full too, having just received the third installment of their *stipendium*, their annual salary, which they could top off with loot and slaves from the rebels.

The clatter of armor and iron-nailed sandals resounded through the woods. Arminius and his entourage galloped along the long Roman column. Possibly the Cherusci warriors rode right by Marcus Caelius of the Eighteenth Legion. At fifty-three years old, the tough, weathered curly-haired native of northern Italy's Bononia (Bologna) had seen his share of combat. For valor in battle, Caelius won two golden torcs. After serving his full term, Caelius re-enlisted. The transverse crest on his helmet distinguished Caelius as a centurion, but as first-rank centurion, *primi ordines*, he led his entire cohort. Caelius likely guessed that Arminius was heading to the front of the column to confer with Varus.

Reigning in his steed at Varus' position, Arminius exclaimed that he and his men must dally behind. More tribal reinforcements were on the way. Once assembled, Arminius and his Cherusci would hasten to catch up with Varus' convoy. Varus agreed. For some distance, his path led through friendly Cherusci territory. Varus thought he would have no need for extra precautions or for the help of Arminius' auxiliaries.

Arminius and his attendants rode off to muster the other Cherusci chiefs. Segestes, however, at first refused to join the rebellion. Hoping to avert disaster at the last minute, Segestes' men seized Arminius and threw him into chains. The debacle only delayed the inevitable, for Segestes had no support from the other chiefs who soon freed Arminius. Perhaps out of consideration for Thusnelda, Arminius gave Segestes another chance, who, having really little choice, threw his lot in with the rebels.

True to his word to Varus, Arminius led an army of 10,000–17,000 warriors back to Varus. Perhaps some two to three times that number were still on the way.[18] Word of the impending attack on the Romans continued to spread from one farmstead to the next. Not just among the Cherusci did warriors gather but also from their allies the Marsi and the Bructeri, who dwelt south and north of the River Lippe, respectively, and possibly from the Angrivarii, Chauci, Chatti and Sugambri as well. The Roman patrols and work parties along the route to Anreppen and in the countryside never made it back to Varus. Caught off guard, they were easily slaughtered by Cherusci whom they at first thought to be allies. The Ampsivarii noble Boiocalus likewise was taken unawares and imprisoned when he refused to break his Roman allegiance.[19] As for Arminius' uncle, Inguiomerus, he apparently stayed out of the conflict, for now.

Out on the farmsteads, the tribal families prepared themselves for battle. The Germanic women did not forget the bond between them and their husbands. In the mystic rites of their weddings witnessed by their gods, they had interchanged sacred gifts. No gleaming jewelry of amber or fancy dress had the young brides received, but oxen and horses, spears and shields, to remind them of the toil of daily life and the hardships of war. The women raised the children, took care of hearth and home, worked in the fields and gathered nuts, berries, herbs and mushrooms in the forest. In battle, the women served as nurses and medics, applying medicinal herbs like mugwort, the knowledge of which was passed down from one generation to the next.

Provisions of food were gathered, mainly millet, barley and livestock. Ordinarily meat was too precious to be eaten on a daily basis. Now, however, the warriors would need all the strength they could get. Those too old would stay behind, to look after the very young and the remaining farm animals. Aged grandparents bid emotional farewells to sons, grandsons and daughters-in-law, who they might never see again. They trusted in their gods to give them courage and good fortune. Priests took sacred emblems from their holy groves and carried them into battle. The Germanic warriors would fight side by side with their family members. Fathers, sons and brothers were comrades in arms, families were their squadrons and clans were their divisions. From thousands of tiny settlements, bands of warriors hungry for loot and vengeance gathered and followed in Arminius' wake.

Varus' army meanwhile made good progress, by evening covering some fifteen miles over relatively open country, before setting up its first marching camp.

Trumpets signaled when it was time to sleep. In the middle of the camp, torches flickering off the silver and golden eagles planted in sacred ground. Early in the morning, trumpets called for the soldiers to wake. By the time they sounded twice more, the packing and loading was completed and the legions stood ready to march off.

The path to the rebels led through heavy woods. Ahead, the dark clouds of the northern fall hovered over the horizon. Soon, Varus had his hands full just moving his army ahead. Oak and birch, beech and alder, boulders and rocks, hemmed in the legions as if the very woods and mountains were turning against the Romans. There were no real roads by Roman standards. Legionary pioneers wiped beads of sweat from their foreheads as they lifted axes to hew into trees blown onto the trail, which hindered the passage of the convoy wagons. Above them, tree limbs groaned and leaves rustled in the wind. Rain belted down and somewhere in the distance thunder burst and flashes of lighting cut the sky.

Tired feet stumbled over slippery roots. The seventy pounds of armor and forty pounds of camp gear, carried by each legionary, got heavier and heavier with each mile, with each step. The officers were luckier, many rode horses and most of their gear was in the baggage train. The wooden wagons slid into swampy pools. Men groaned and whips lashed at sweat coated mules, as both strained to free wheels embedded in mud. Treetops broke and fell upon the Romans. Streams, swollen by the rain, had to be forded. The convoy became more and more stretched out. The legionaries hopelessly intermingled with the accompanying camp followers and with pack animals and the herds of livestock. Everything slowed to a snail's pace. Women whined, children cried and servants and soldiers asked themselves into what kind of hell Varus was leading them. Barking orders to his subordinate centurions, the veteran first-rank centurion Caelius likely managed to maintain formation. Not all were such old warhorses, however. With the forest closing in around them, the inbred fear of the northern wilderness and its people re-emerged in the hearts of the civilians and of the new recruits. Surely native forest spirits aided the Germans! The legionaries prayed to their own deities and grasped spiritual amulets and tokens.

Whistles cut through the air. Startled legionaries watched in horror as a javelin suddenly protruded out of a comrade's back. Here and there, all along the convoy, javelins and slingshot showered upon the Romans. The Romans damned the enemy, whom at first they could not even see. The wind carried guttural bellows: the barbarians calling upon their spirits and their gods. Ghostly figures, pale-skinned, near-naked bearded giants, appeared and disappeared among the trees.[20]

The barbarians, lightly armed, carrying naught but large oval shields were at home in the woods. They struck at will, wherever the Romans were at their weakest. With no time to draw his gladius, a legionary chopping away at a fallen tree instinctively raised and swung his pioneer's axe. The axe split the hairy face of a barbarian. More barbarians leapt out of the woods like panthers. A wooden club smashed against a legionary's helmet. The legionary staggered in a daze. Another barbarian, the muscles of his arms gnarled like an oak, powered his iron-tipped spear through the Roman mail hauberk. Overwhelming numbers of Germans hewed down half a dozen legionaries. A centurion, perhaps Caelius, personally led a century of legionaries to rally to their comrades' aid, but before they arrived, the Germans fled back into the impenetrable thickets. In their heavy mail or the newer segmented armor, the legionaries were too slow.

Slowly, painfully, the Roman convoy dragged itself onward. The barbarian attacks never let up, striking at man, woman and beast alike. The enemy was everywhere and to the Romans, their numbers seemed without end. It was like a pack of wolves, their jaws nipping at the heels and flanks of a bull moose, waiting till exhaustion and bleeding took their toll, before they closed in for the kill. Arminius, the other chiefs and their personal guards, distinguished by mail shirts and iron helmets, as befitted their ranks, were likely in the thick of it. They raised their longswords into the air and rallied and inspired their men with personal valor. The Romans suffered mounting losses without being able to seriously harm the enemy. The only blessing was that at least the rain stopped for a while.

At last, Varus' battered convoy reached an acceptable place to set up camp. Despite the physical strain of the march and fighting, the legionaries' iron endurance enabled them to dig a deep ditch and pile the excavated soil into a rampart. Many remembered their training days, when they cursed at having to carry equipment that was twice as heavy as their regular issue. Now that training paid off.

The two servants that attended to each *contubernium* of eight legionaries brought up their pack mule, to unload the tent and the heavier baggage. Caelius was luckier, as befitted his rank he had his own tent and two servants. Fires sprang up between the ordered rows of gable roofed tents. The legionaries baked bread and cooked freshly butchered meat. Unfortunately, a lot of oxen, pigs or sheep had been lost during the harrying attacks of the day. For many legionaries the only meat to chew on was perhaps a strip of dried bacon. The legionaries huddled around the fires, wrapped in their red military cloaks, the *sagum*, enjoying a last few swigs of cheap wine. At least two of each *contubernium* prepared for sentry duty, the others retired to their tents. The woolen *sagum* probably doubled as their blanket. In many tents, the legionaries looked at empty spaces beside them, spaces where once slept friends. Lucky were those whose exhaustion carried them into slumber. The nightmare thought that on the morrow the march would continue, robbed others of a well-deserved rest.

The groans of the heavily wounded broke the still night air. Ordinarily, the skill of Roman medics was such that despite their dangerous profession, Roman soldiers enjoyed a longer life span than their civilian counterparts. In the Teutoburg however, it was difficult to keep wounds clean and to administer the required help. Many of the wounded, victims of shock and blood loss, would never awake.

Somewhere deep in the forest, the Germanic warriors too took their rest. Their woolen trousers, tunics and cloaks dried quickly beside smokeless fires. The Germanic women bandaged open wounds and applied healing herbs. They also provided moral support, praising their men who risked their lives for their families and who fought with courage. Alongside their usual porridge of barley and millet, the warriors ate pork and beef, some of the latter having no doubt come from the Roman column. As they wrapped themselves in blankets and furs and drifted into slumber, the Germans too thought of sons, fathers and friends lost in battle.

The Germans could see clouds of smoke spiraling into the air from the location of the Roman camp. The Romans were burning any surplus equipment and most of the wagons. They left behind their heavily wounded, doubtlessly killing many to spare them capture and torture by the enemy. It wouldn't have taken long for the Romans to identify their attackers of the previous day as Cherusci and Arminius were likely spotted in the fighting. Clearly, the initial news of a rebellion had been a sham, meant to lure Varus and his army into the wilderness and into disaster. The question for the Romans was how to proceed. As the crow would fly, the untried route ahead to the Ems and beyond to friendly Frisii territory or to the lower Rhine was far shorter than backtracking to the Lippe road. Their load lightened, the Romans pushed on northwest the next morning.

The barbarian attacks continued and their numbers grew. From everywhere tribesmen came to slay the hated Romans. At times the road improved and led through cleared areas of pasture meadows, barley and wheat fields. *Grubenhauser*, simple timber structures erected over shallow hollows, and the larger tribal long-houses, were seen in the distance. Yet even in these open areas the Romans faced ambushes by barbarians hidden in the long grasses. And thereafter the track always led back into the foreboding woods.

One agonizing day dragged on into the next. Roman attempts to lash back at the barbarians in close infantry and cavalry ranks faltered as the trees jumbled up their formations. On the third day the overcast sky erupted anew, drenching the legions. Tired feet stumbled and slipped, exhausted limbs no longer had the strength to hack a way through the wilderness. Weapons, shields and clothes were soaked.

As if in answer to their prayers, the legions came upon good defensive ground for another marching camp.[21] They were now skirting the northeasterly to northern side of the 350-foot high Kalkrieser Berg.[22] The hill protruded from the Wiehengebirge, on the northern extremity of the Weser Hills, into the Great Moor. Behind the mauled convoy, back along its 12–20 mile passage to the southeast, lay 13,000 dead; left as food for flocks of ravens and for packs of wolves.[23] The heaviest casualties were among the thousands of servants, slaves and civilians, who would have made the easiest targets. The fatigued legionaries must have been ready to drop, but training and discipline paid off, enabling them to set up a defensive barrier.

In his command tent, Varus held his nightly council with his remaining senior officers. With two of his legion commanders having fallen in battle, Varus relied on his remaining legate Vala Numonius and his two camp prefects, the third-in-command of a legion, Caeonius and Lucius Eggius.[24] Arminius' treachery roused strong feelings but in the end there remained only one choice. There was no going back and with no supplies they could not hold out. Plunging north or south into the even harsher terrain of the swamp or hills was tantamount to suicide.

Perhaps sitting by a fire, Arminius conferred with his chiefs as well. The battle had gone well, the Romans were beaten and many called for an assault on the camp. Likely against Arminius' wishes, who probably saw no point of risking his warriors on a premature attack, the loot hungry council overruled him.

Either at night or in the haze of early morning, trumpets blared. The general's banner, a large square identifying the commander and his army, was raised to signal the call for battle. From all directions, barbarians charged at the camp, plunging through the shallow ditch and storming the ramparts.[25] Volleys of

Roman arrows swooshed into the howling masses but the barbarians came on with a fury. Now the legionaries were able to fight in formation and defend from above, behind earthen ramparts and walls of sharp stakes. Released of their penned up frustration, of not being able to come to grips with their foes, the legionaries fought with renewed vigor. The barbarian waves pounded against the Roman shield wall, to be gutted and stabbed from above by Roman swords. Though swaths of tribesmen lay at their feet, with each assault, the Roman lines became thinner until they gave away. The Roman breastwork half torn to pieces, the tribesmen burst into the camp like a breach in a dam.

Droves of barbarians sensed easy spoils and started to plunder. Arminius desperately tried to maintain order and concentrate the attack on the standards of Varus. Wounded in battle, Varus knew the end was near. Shamed by the disaster he had brought upon his legions, Varus chose the honorable death of suicide. In the footsteps of his father who met defeat at Philippi when Varus was but a child, Varus and his highest ranking officers fell on their swords. Word of Varus' death caused the troops to lose their last hope. A few imitated Varus and took their own lives. Others threw away their arms.

Chaos reigned. The last legionary line protecting Varus' body collapsed while his men tried to burn his body. Camp prefect Caeonius decided to surrender; he was killed. Legate Vala Numonius, the last legion commander, took command of the Roman cavalry. Vala, otherwise a brave man, decided that his only chance was to abandon the infantry and with his cavalry vanished into the forests. They were never heard of again. The remaining camp prefect, Lucius Eggius, alone retained composure.[26] Perhaps it was he who retained order among his own cohorts, rallying fleeing legionaries to him. Gathering what provisions they could on mules and taking with them their wives and closest servants, the legionaries of Eggius' ad hoc battle group fought their way out. Probably they faced only sporadic opposition as the bulk of the barbarians were busy ransacking the Roman tents.

When the spoiling attacks on Eggius' retreating battle group abated, his men proceeded in silence. Hoping to elude their pursuers, Eggius' men even muffled the bells attached to the mule harnesses with tuffs of grass and earth. Their hopes were dashed when the way ahead narrowed into a choke point between deep swamp to their right and an earth embankment to their left. A waist high palisade of stakes, interlaced twigs and branches, ran along the top of the embankment, and behind it lurked more tribesmen. The legionaries may have tried to force the barrier, locking their shields above their heads in tortoise formations to ward off a deluge of barbarian missiles. The wooden mesh bent but did not break easily under the blows of Roman axes and entrenching tools. When the Romans faltered the barbarians sallied forth. Groups of Romans died fighting to the end, including brave Eggius. Others finally panicked, risking all for a mad dash into the swamp. Speared in the back, their blood turned the water crimson. Only a very few lucky legionaries managed to make a heroic escape to the Rhine.[27]

Possessed by the fury of their war gods, Tiwaz, Wodan and Thunar, a red haze clouded the barbarians' eyes and they "struck down man and beast."[28] Somewhere on the battlefield, men draped in lion and bearskins lay dying. They were the Roman standard bearers and out of their hands slipped the gilded silver or golden Eagle Standards. Two Eagle Standards, the physical embodiments of the legions, fell into barbarian hands. One was claimed by the Cherusci, another was taken into the land of the Marsi. The third Legionary Eagle was broken off its shaft by its bearer, who hid the Eagle under his clothing and disappeared into the swamp.

The Germans dug up the hastily-buried, half-burnt body of Varus. One of them walked up to the ghastly, blood and mud soaked corpse. He lifted his blade, and swooped off the head. No doubt a wild cry went up from the bystanders; this was the fate of the Roman "conquerors"! From a platform, Arminius addressed his exuberant warriors, who cheered his mocking of the Eagles and of the Roman standards. The grim trophy of Varus was eventually sent to Maroboduus, a sign of the power of Arminius and the Cherusci.

First-rank centurion Marcus Caelius' long military career came to an end in the Teutoburg.[29] If he was lucky he died in battle, for the Cherusci and Marsi took cruel vengeance, especially on the leaders, the stripling thin-stripe tribunes[30] and the hardened first-rank centurions. "They pierced out the eyes of some and cut off the hands of others. In one case, they cut out the man's tongue … and the barbarian who held it in his hand shouted at him: 'Now, snake, your hissing is finished.'"[31] The merciless Germanic gods too demanded their due. Several hundred Roman prisoners were sacrificed, dragged to altars in forest groves. The Romans had their throats slit or they were hanged from oak trees. Weapons, armor and ornaments were thrown into sacred ponds.

Others were dragged into slavery, a fate that the Romans had meted out to so many other people. "Men who might have hoped to enter the Senate someday spent the rest of their lives as shepherds or doorkeepers."[32] Although the lot of a slave was never an enviable one, the Romans who became slaves of the Germans were nevertheless relatively lucky. After the rage and anger felt in the aftermath of battle subsided, the Germanic warrior harbored little resentment against his captives. Unlike slaves in Rome, slaves of Germanic tribesmen did not have to carry out regular duties. Their slaves gained homes and fields of their own, from which their master demanded a tribute of grain, clothing and livestock as if they were his tenants. Physical punishment of slaves was very unusual. Sometimes slaves were killed, but mostly in fits of anger that were little different from the deadly brawls that erupted between quarreling freemen. Amazingly, some forty years after the battle, a few Roman survivors were recovered by allied German tribal levies who intercepted a party of Chatti raiders into Upper Germania.

Since ambushes and javelin barrages killed the majority of Romans in the Teutoburg, German casualties probably numbered less than 4,000 killed and wounded.[33] Of the wounded a few hundred more died days or weeks later, from the common battle ailments of tetanus, gangrene bacterium infections and blood poison. The bodies of the German dead were placed upon funeral pyres, alongside the warrior's weapons. If the fallen was a famed warrior or chief, then special wood was gathered for the pyre. As flames engulfed the fallen, women wailed in anguish and sorrow while the men held back their tears. The ashes and charred remains were gathered, placed in urns and buried beneath mounds of soil. No rocks were placed upon them, for the Germans did not want rocks to lie heavy upon their dead.

The destruction of Varus' legions was not the end of it. The barbarians pressed onward to Aliso on the Lippe, where Arminius displayed the heads of slain legionaries in front of the besieged Roman garrison. Unintimidated, camp prefect Lucius Caedicius replied with volleys of Roman arrows that mowed down the assaulting barbarians. Caedicius held the walls until his provisions were used up and most of the tribesmen had moved off. During a stormy night his garrison made its way west, reaching the Rhine but abandoning a large number of civilians. Further south, on the Lahn, the Romans burnt down their town at Waldgermis and fled to the Rhine.

On the Rhine, Asprenas' two legions had their hands full as German tribes on the river's west side were causing trouble. At *Oppidum Ubiorum*, Segestes' son Segimundus removed his insignia of the Roman priesthood and ran off to join his father who sided with the rebels. Allegedly, Segimundus even desecrated the corpse of Varus. Everything that had been gained in nearly 30 years of campaigning had been lost in a single battle.[34]

The news of the disaster reached Augustus at Rome along with the head of Varus, courtesy of Maroboduus, which the Emperor honorably laid to rest in Varus' family vault. Augustus disbanded his German bodyguard and sent patrols into the streets to prevent an uprising. To maintain stability abroad he prolonged the terms of the provincial governors. As in the crisis of the Illyrian insurrection, Augustus requisitioned slaves for freedmen cohorts as a stopgap measure. The freedmen reinforced the Rhine defense until the arrival of six additional legions and large numbers of auxiliaries transferred from the barely ended fighting in Dalmatia. Augustus promised the people games in honor of Jupiter, the father of the Roman gods. Tiberius, who had just brought the Illyrian revolt to an end, respectfully postponed his triumph in light of the *glades Variana*.

It was the first time that the barbarians had destroyed a whole Roman army since the Cimbri and Teutones invasion a century ago. The numbers of the lost legions, the Seventeenth, the Eighteenth and the Nineteenth, were never re-allocated. It was unquestionably a major setback for the Roman conquest of Germania, one that became the turning point in the Germanic wars.

The 72-year-old Augustus let his beard and hair go untrimmed for months. He beat his head on a door and like some madman shouted, "Quinctilius Varus, give me back my legions."[35] The anniversary of the *glades Variana* remained a day of mourning. More importantly, it convinced Augustus to abandon his whole plan for extending the Roman frontier to the Elbe.

Why the change in Augustus' policy? After all, the Roman Republic had absorbed greater losses against the Cimbri and Teutones and against Hannibal; even though theoretically the Republic had a much smaller recruiting base than Augustus' huge empire. Augustus even retained the state's right to recruit by compulsion and extended it to the provinces. In reality, political considerations likely limited the ability of Augustus to conscript citizen troops.

Two new legions were raised, the Twenty-first and the Twenty-second. The Twenty-second was probably made up of Galatian troops, recently granted citizenship. The Twenty-first was made up of the *sentina*, literally the "dregs" of the population of the city of Rome, who had never before been a source for the legions. The Twenty-first was sent to Germany. No wonder Tiberius complained of the poor quality of available recruits.

Roman citizens who lived the good life saw no reason to risk life and limb – let others do the fighting for them! This was a far cry from Republican days, when serving in the legions was the right and duty of the Roman citizen and the only recruits normally passed up were the poor. The startling conclusion is that in an Empire of over 50,000,000 people, the loss of three crack legions could not easily be made good.

Likely another reason for Augustus' turn about was that the conquest of Germania was the brainchild of Drusus and not of Augustus. The *glades Variana* confirmed that the cost of a German conquest far outweighed the benefits. Henceforth, the Rhine was to remain the eastern border.

In AD 10, Tiberius returned to the German frontier to carry out some raids into Germania. Tiberius' campaign had a different character than the pre-Varian Roman campaigns. Aware that the disaster was due to Varus' rashness and lack of caution, Tiberius no longer trusted his own judgment and relied heavily on the advice of his military council. To lighten the load and increase the speed of his legions, he strictly forbade any surplus supplies. Officers in doubt about anything were required to consult him at any time of day or night. Discipline, always harsh in the legions, became even more severe. Tiberius' paranoia proved not entirely unfounded. Near the end of his campaign, a Bructeri assassin infiltrated Tiberius' quarters but revealed himself through his nervousness. The assassin confessed under torture.

Two years later Tiberius returned to Rome, to hold his postponed Illyrian triumph. His recent German campaigns had been half-hearted and subdued. Notably, there was no triumph *de Germania*. Neither Aliso, nor any other Roman presence in the German interior, had been restored. In face of his stepfather's old age, Tiberius was more worried about ensuring his accession than to press the conquest of Germania. Others in the upper military echelons thought otherwise. Drusus' young son, Germanicus Julius Caesar, who inherited his father's spirit and popularity, was calling for vengeance. The German wars were not over; they had just begun.

Chapter Eighteen

Germanicus and Arminius

"Assuredly he was the deliverer of Germany, one too who had defied Rome, not in her early rise, as other kings and generals, but in the height of her empire's glory."[1]

Tacitus on Arminius

Born the son of the dashing general and Imperial Prince, Drusus, in 15 BC, Germanicus Julius Caesar was groomed to become a Roman hero: a legacy that came as naturally to him as it had to his father. Having lost his father in Germania in 9 BC, Germanicus was eventually adopted by his uncle Tiberius in AD 4. Fighting alongside the somber Tiberius from AD 7 to 10, Germanicus won his first laurels by suppressing the Pannonian and Dalmatian insurrections. From there he followed Tiberius on his half-hearted German campaigns of AD 11 to 12. Upon Tiberius' return to Rome, Germanicus remained behind to command the two armies that guarded the German frontier. Tiberius needed to be in Rome to assure his succession to the throne, for his own aged stepfather, Emperor Augustus, was of failing health. At the same time, however, Tiberius feared that Germanicus would use the Rhine legions to make his own bid for the throne. Germanicus, after all, was much more popular among the people than Tiberius.

The monumental four-decade reign of Rome's first emperor ended in AD 14, when Augustus passed away at the age of 76 years. Justifiably worried about unrest, Tiberius immediately ordered the Praetorian Guard to protect him wherever he went. He wrote to the legion commanders in the provinces, commanding them to affirm their loyalty. The legions had their own ideas. The three legions in Pannonia mutinied. They called for pay and service conditions akin to that of the Praetorians, who were paid more and saw less action. Among the most telling episodes of the revolt, a camp prefect was ridiculed by being forced to carry heavy loads at the head of a column. The legionaries also killed a hated centurion, nicknamed "Bring another",[2] for his habit of calling for another vine stick after having broken one on a soldier's back. Attended by Praetorian cohorts and by units of Tiberius' German bodyguard, Tiberius' own blood son, Drusus II, quelled the Pannonian rebellion. He shrewdly drew on the legionaries' fear of superstition. When an unexplained dimming of the moonlight foreshadowed ill omens, the legionaries suddenly felt afraid that the heavens "frowned on their deeds."[3] Drusus promptly made use of their hesitancy to execute the ringleaders of the revolt and to restore order.

More worrisome were revolts among the four legions of Germania Inferior under the command of general Aulus Caecina Severus. During the late fall of AD 14, the legions were still stationed at their summer camp of Vetera (Xanten). The revolt began there, among the fresh recruits of the Fifth and the Twenty-first Legions. Many of the soldiers had been recently levied from the rabble of Rome's most unsavory and destitute neighborhoods. Unused to a life of military hardship and hard work, their whining about the harsh and long service conditions and poor pay affected even the veterans. From the Fifth and the Twenty-first Legions, the mutiny spread to the First and the Twentieth Legions, which were made up of Syrians and Spaniards. The common sentiment of the mutineers, as Tacitus tells us, was "The Roman world was in their hand ... it was from them that emperors received their titles."[4] The first to feel their wrath were the centurions. "They were hurled to the ground and given the lash, sixty strokes each, one stroke for each of them in the legion. Then, broken and mutilated, they were cast outside the lines or thrown into the Rhine, more dead than alive. One, Septimius, took refuge on the general's dais and fell at Caecina's feet. But he was shouted for so violently that he had to be given up to his fate."[5] Intimidated by the blind rage of his soldiers, their army commander, Aulus Caecina, did not dare raise his hand against them. The whole army of Germania Inferior was now in revolt and it remained to be seen if the legions to the south, in Germania Superior, would be affected as well. For now the soldiers of general Caius Silius waited to hear of events to the north with unease, unsure what course to take.

Germanicus was busy collecting taxes in Gaul when he heard about the trouble in Germania Inferior. At once he hurried to Vetera to confront the mutineers. When Germanicus reprimanded the soldiers for dishonoring their colors, the men bared their wounds and scars, some having served in 30 campaigns. Many were ready to follow Germanicus, if he proclaimed himself emperor. The road to civil war, and the throne, lay before him but Germanicus chose not to take it. He drew his sword and threatened to plunge it into his breast, "protesting that he would rather die than cast off his loyalty."[6] Not all the soldiers were enamored with Germanicus. One offered his sword, "saying that it was sharper than his [Germanicus'] own."⁷ Germanicus retired to his tent, considering what was to be done. Word was that the rebels wanted to sack the Ubii capital at *Oppidum Ubiorum*, 60 miles south of Vetera, and thereafter turn to pillage the unprotected towns of Gaul. *Ubiorum* was expecting the arrival of two legions; the town would be caught totally unawares. Only a puny Roman garrison protected Gaul. Even more catastrophic, the frontier would be open to barbarian invaders.

Germanicus ended up having to pay money, out of his own purse, and to grant concessions to regain the legions' oath of loyalty. Only then was general Caecina able to march the First and the Twentieth Legions to their winter quarters at *Oppidum Ubiorum*. Germanicus left for the army of Germania Superior, where he re-affirmed the oath of loyalty from its four legions. Germanicus then returned to *Oppidum Ubiorum*, where he paid his respects at the altar of Augustus.

More violence threatened to erupt when the legionaries bullied delegates of the Senate who they feared would nullify the concessions gained through mutiny. Germanicus had to use his auxiliary cavalry to protect the delegates. The situation remained so critical that Germanicus sent his pregnant wife and her young son, Gaius Caesar, for safekeeping to the lands of the Treveri. Born and raised amidst the legionary tents, the soldiers affectionately nicknamed Gaius "Caligula", after the like-named boots he wore. No one would have guessed at the time, that the young lad would one day become one of Rome's worst despots.

Germanicus finally restored order in *Oppidum Ubiorum* by accepting the surrender of the chief mutineers as proof of the legions' loyalty. Among the First Legion, the rebels were paraded before the rest of the soldiers. "If they shouted 'Guilty,' he was thrown down and butchered. The soldiers reveled in the massacre as though it purged them of their offences."⁸ The mutiny met its most gruesome end among the Twenty-first and the Fifth Legions that were still at Vetera. Loyalists turned upon rebels and "uproar, wounds, bloodshed, were everywhere visible."⁹ When Germanicus returned to Vetera he burst into tears and cried, "This is no cure, this is a catastrophe."¹⁰ Germanicus ordered the bodies of the dead to be cremated.

Germanicus channeled the legionaries' frustrations against the enemy. With the mutiny taken care off, Germanicus was free to do what he really wanted: carry on his father's legacy and make war on the German tribes. With eight legions holding the Rhine frontier and another seven on the Danube line, fifteen out of the twenty-eight legions available at the time of Augustus' death stood guard against mostly Germanic barbarian tribes. By comparison, the rich Roman province of Syria, which faced Rome's other main enemy, the Parthians, had to make do with just three legions. A mere 1,200 men at Lugdunum (Lyon) sufficed to ensure Roman control over all of southern and central Gaul. The fact that nearly half of Rome's entire armed might faced the Germans, gives ample enough evidence of just how much of a threat the Romans considered the German tribes.

According to Tacitus, the goal of Germanicus was purely to avenge the humiliation of the *glades Variana* and not a second attempt of expanding the empire to the Elbe. In the fall of AD 14, Germanicus commanded a field army of 12,000 men in 4 legions, plus 26 auxiliary cohorts and 8 *alae* of cavalry, troops who had proven most loyal during mutiny, presumably leaving the less reliable on garrison duty.

Although usually performed in spring at the beginning of the campaign season, perhaps now, more than ever, there was need of the symbolic *lustratio exercitus*, the purification of the standards. Adorned in garlands, sprinkled with perfumed oil, the standards were further honored with animal sacrifices. Even so, for many soldiers "honorable wounds ... were the only means of appeasing the ghosts of their fellow soldiers."[11]

Germanicus launched his retribution campaigns by laying waste to the Marsi villages south of the River Lippe. The legions surrounded the Marsi villages. The clear and bright night sky revealed no sentries, or signs of life. Blank gladius and pilum held ready, the legions entered to find the inhabitants passed out on beds and tables. During the evening, the Marsi had celebrated what was likely a fall harvest festival, with ceremonial banquets and performances. Germanicus was unopposed and his victims were scattered, unarmed and half-asleep. He spared no one. "Neither sex nor age moved his compassion. Germanicus divided his enthusiastic army into four detachments and pillaged an area some 45 miles wide. Everything, sacred or profane ... was leveled to the ground," including the sacred temple of the goddess Tanfana, relates Tacitus.[12]

Alarmed by reports of the massacres, the neighboring Bructeri, Tubantes and Usipetes tribes rallied their warriors and set off after Germanicus' army. Germanicus was already on his way back to the Rhine when his scouts reported large numbers of barbarians in the woods ahead. Tribesmen from north of the Lippe had crossed the river. A nervous tension gripped the Roman troops. Warned of imminent ambush they marched into the forest battle-ready. Cavalry and auxiliary troops held the vanguard, with the legions abreast in the center and more auxiliary cohorts in the rear. The barbarians did not attack until the whole Roman column was stretched out in the woods. German skirmishers nipped at the flanks and vanguard while the main body struck at the rear of the Roman column. They scattered the lightly armed Roman auxiliary troops and charged at the Twentieth Legion on the left flank. The barbarian assault might have ended in another Roman disaster, but this time it was Germanicus and not Varus who held command. Putting the heels to his charger, he galloped up to the Twentieth Legion and cried "Forward, hasten to turn your guilt into glory."[13] Eager to wipe out their shame, the legionaries dashed forward and drove off the enemy. Once back on the Rhine, the legions went into their winter quarters. Germanicus had successfully carried out his raid on the Marsi and won a defensive victory against their allies, but in doing so he more angered than cowed the tribes.

The next year, in AD 15, the Romans returned to attack Germania with two powerful armies, one commanded by Germanicus and the other by general Caecina. Germanicus pillaged Chatti territory and crossed the River Eder in central Germania. It was a campaign without mercy, as defenseless women, children and old people were at once slaughtered or enslaved. Germanicus had with him even more troops than in the previous year, doubling the number of auxiliaries. To support them and the additional thousands of camp followers and servants, he made use of the waterways just as his father Drusus had done before him. The whole expedition lasted five to six weeks and included the rebuilding of a destroyed fort. The fort lay in the Taunus Mountains and had first been built by Germanicus' father.

At the same time as Germanicus' campaign, a second Roman army under Aulus Caecina Severus, marched up the River Lippe. Caecina had with him four legions, 5,000 auxiliaries and additional levies from allied Germans, probably Ubii. Caecina rebuilt Aliso and continued the war with the Marsi, who remained defiant enough to launch offensive operations but were again defeated.

So far there had been no sign of Arminius and the Cherusci. The reason was revealed by a party of envoys sent by Segestes to Germanicus. As will be remembered, Segestes had tried to warn Varus of the impending treachery of Arminius but Varus ignored him. The strong support among the Cherusci for Arminius forced an isolated but reluctant Segestes to join the war against Rome, alongside his more enthusiastic son Segimundus. Welcomed back by the Romans, Segimundus spoke among Segestes' envoys and appealed for help. With Rome's return, Segestes had broken away from Arminius and was ready to rejoin his old allies. Somewhere on the western border of the Cherusci lands, Segimundus' father was presently besieged by Arminius. Germanicus was not going to leave a valuable Roman ally in danger. The Roman legions marched to Segestes' aid and drove off the besieging Cherusci. A grateful Segestes thanked his Roman rescuers:

"This is not my first day of steadfast loyalty towards the Roman people. From the time that the Divine Augustus gave me the citizenship, I have chosen my friends and foes with an eye to your advantage, not from hatred of my fatherland (for traitors are detested even by those whom they prefer) but because I held that Romans and Germans have the same interests and that peace is better than war."[14]

Segestes and his family were escorted back to the safety of the Roman Rhine forts where they were given amnesty, although there was to be some hesitation about Segimundus. Among Segestes' family was his pregnant daugter Thusnelda. Against her father's will, she had married Arminius and carried his child. Segestes, who hated Arminius and called him "ravisher of his daughter,"[15] admitted that she had to be forced to come with her father and the Romans. Like her husband, she remained defiant; "subdued neither to tears nor to the tones of a suppliant, her hands tightly clasped within her bosom, and eyes which dwelt on her hope of offspring."[16]

Tacitus leaves us with a stirring description of Arminius' reaction to the loss of his pregnant wife:

"Arminius, with his naturally furious temper, was driven to frenzy by the seizure of his wife and the foredooming to slavery of his wife's unborn child. He flew hither and thither among the Cherusci, demanding 'war against Segestes, war against Caesar.' And he refrained not from taunts. 'Noble the father,' he would say, "mighty the general, brave the army which, with such strength, has carried off one weak woman. Before me, three legions, three commanders have fallen. Not by treachery, not against pregnant women, but openly against armed men do I wage war. Let Segestes dwell on the conquered bank … one thing there is which Germans will never thoroughly excuse, their having seen between the Elbe and the Rhine the Roman rods, axes, and toga. If you prefer your fatherland, your ancestors, your ancient life to tyrants and to new colonies, follow as your leader Arminius to glory and to freedom rather than Segestes to ignominious servitude."[17]

Arminius' emotional appeals ensured the support of the chiefs of the Cherusci and of neighboring tribes, including his uncle, Inguiomerus. Since Inguiomerus had long been a friend of the Romans, his defection was not taken lightly by Germanicus.

Germanicus and Caecina next concentrated their forces for a crushing attack on the Bructeri. With four legions, Germanicus sailed up the Rhine, entering the North Sea via the Drusus canal. As he sailed up the River Ems, his force struck at the Bructeri from the north while Caecina came up from the south with forty cohorts, from the Lippe route. The cavalry moved along the Frisian North Sea territory. Another mobile column under Lucius Stertinius went around killing and looting.

Between them the Roman armies laid waste to the Bructeri country. Stertinius recovered the lost Eagle of the Nineteenth Legion. Although the standard bearer escaped the Teutoburg disaster he must haven been hunted down by the Bructeri who found the Eagle hidden in his clothing. At the extremity of the Bructeri territory in the Teutoburg Forest, Germanicus' legions stumbled upon a field of bones. They had found the *glades Variana* battlefield. Thousands upon thousands of human bones, bleached stark white in the sun, sprawled amidst wildflowers, green grasses and brown and beige leaf litter.

With Germanicus himself taking the lead, the legionaries did their best to bury the remains of their slain comrades. They buried the bones in pits and placed weapons beside them. Other bones they piled in great heaps and covered them with mounds of earth. The task was too monumental even for the hard toiling legions. After half a day, Germanicus ordered the work to be stopped. The time for vengeance was at hand. United with Caecina's legions, Germanicus moved against the Cherusci.

East of the River Ems, Arminius fell back before Germanicus' overbearing might to lead him on a chase through trackless wilderness. Arminius feigned a retreat, luring Roman cavalry into an ambush and nearly forcing them into a perilous morass. They were saved by the timely arrival of the legions, which drove back the enemy. Following the indecisive engagement, Germanicus broke off the pursuit of Arminius and returned to the Ems. His supply had probably run out.

Unable to sustain the campaign, Germanicus sailed back down the Ems while Caecina took the land route back to Vetera. To avoid grounding his ships at low tide, Germanicus lightened their load by dispatching two of his legions to make the journey on foot. The two legions got caught up in severe floods and storms along the shoreline, but their hardships were nothing compared to those of Caecina's corps. Germanicus had warned Caecina to move as quickly as possible along the familiar but swampy route of 'Long Bridges', laid out eighteen years ago by Lucius Domitius Ahenobarbus. Indeed, as soon as the Roman army split, Arminius struck at Caecina.

At first it looked like Caecina would share the fate of Varus. The Germans attacked Caecina's army while it was trying to repair a causeway over a swamp. Fighting in waterlogged ground, the larger Germans, with the long reach of their spears, enjoyed an advantage over the heavily armored Romans. A veteran of forty years service, Caecina bravely led his beleaguered army to a confined area of level ground. There he entrenched for the night. It must have been obvious to Caecina that the morale of his legions was dangerously low. The Romans had suffered casualties and inflicted few. Outside the camp the Cherusci waited to kill more Romans. It is not surprising that Caecina drifted into nightmare-haunted sleep; "Varus, covered with blood, seemed to rise out of the morass, and call him: but he would not obey; and when Varus held out his hand he pushed it back."[18]

At dawn, the morale of the legions holding the flanks of the Roman position broke. When they retreated in fear, Arminius saw his chance and personally led another attack. During the confused fighting in the bog, Caecina's horse was killed under him. He was nearly captured before being rescued by men of the First Legion. Fortunately for the Romans, the German warriors got distracted by looting the baggage. By evening, Caecina managed to reach dry and open ground. Although they had lost most of their equipment, including their tents, the soaked, wounded and tired legionaries built up earthworks.

Arminius wanted to wait until the Romans were forced to leave their defenses and then renew the successful harrying attacks. His wise words were overruled by Inguiomerus who was eager to collect more prisoners and the rest of the loot. Inguiomerus rallied the enthusiastic Cherusci warriors for an immediate assault on the camp. Caecina's legions stormed out of the gates at the exact time of Inguiomerus' attack. The unexpectedness and viciousness of the Roman sally scattered the Germans who thought their enemy near defeat. Many of the Germans were killed and Inguiomerus was wounded, but both he and Arminius escaped. Caecina's column finally returned to the bridge across the Rhine. He and his men were welcomed by Agrippina, the wife of Germanicus. She helped tend to the wounded and dispersed clothing to needy soldiers. For its heroism in the battle, the First Legion thereafter earned the title of 'Germanica'.

For six years Germanicus had rampaged through Germania but, so far, had nothing concrete to show for it. The problems were, as he saw it, his vulnerable long overland supply routes, the difficult terrain and the short summers that restricted campaign time. Gaul too was being exhausted from having to supply horses for the Roman expeditions. Accordingly in AD 16, Germanicus decided to embark not just part, but all of his army on a fleet, thereby gaining surprise and allowing for faster transfer of troops and supplies to the river mouths and channels of the campaign area.

A thousand vessels were needed. Many of them were specially constructed for the upcoming invasion. To endure the waves, some had a small draught, a narrow stem and stern, and a broad center. Others were flat bottomed for shallow areas and still others had rudders at both ends to enable them to run ashore from either direction. Decks were built to hold siege engines and to carry horses and supplies.

While the fleet rendezvoused at the Rhine Island of the allied Batavi, Gaius Silius undertook another raid on the Chatti. Sudden rains slowed down Silius troops and he only gained a little loot but he did manage to capture the wife and the daughter of Arpus, one of the Chatti chiefs. Germanicus' campaign plans were further delayed when news arrived that a fort on the Lippe, probably Aliso, was under siege. Likely it was Arminius trying to gain the initiative in the war. The Roman garrison held out until Germanicus came to its relief with six legions. Confronted with such military might, the tribesmen had little choice but to lift the siege and pull back into the wilderness. On the way, they leveled the *glades Variana* burial mounds.

Finally Germanicus was ready to launch his amphibious invasion. He prayed to his father Drusus to aid him. Reinforced with a cavalry corps commanded by the Batavi chief Chariovalda, the Roman fleet arrived at the River Ems after an uneventful voyage. Possibly due to low water in the tidal flats of the Dollard Bay, Germanicus was forced to disembark his troops on the western side of the bay. A camp was set up and a bridge built to reach the eastern shore. Once across, Germanicus marched south.[19] Leaving the Ems, Germanicus then headed east towards the Weser and Cherusci territory. Passing through Angrivarii lands, Germanicus was setting up camp when reports arrived of trial unrest. In wake of the Roman advance, Angrivarii tribesmen were causing trouble. Lucius Stertinius needed to be sent with the Roman cavalry and light troops. Burning and killing, he quieted the rebels.

When Germanicus' army reached the Weser, Arminius and the Cherusci appeared on the far side of the river. Arminius asked whether Germanicus was with the Roman army. When he was told that he was indeed there, Arminius asked to see his brother Flavus. Unlike his older brother, Flavus had continued to loyally serve Rome. An empty eye socket and scar were the mementos which Flavus gained fighting under Tiberius a few years ago. When he saw his brother step forth, Arminius saluted him. He ordered his guards to draw back and requested for the Roman archers to do the same. From along the shore, Arminius called to his brother across the river, "whence came the scar, which disfigured his face,"[20] and asked what reward he got for it! Flavus told him of the battle and of a neck chain, a crown and other gifts he had received. Arminius jeered; this was all he got for slavery? Proud of this service, Flavus spoke of the glory of Rome. He warned of the punishment of those that earned her wrath and praised her mercy for those who surrendered. Had not Arminius' wife and son, both in Roman captivity, been treated with honor? Arminius retorted with words of ancestral freedom, of the gods of the north and of their mother, who shared his prayers that Flavus might come back to their side.

Each brother was deaf to the other's words. Rage built up within them and curses and insults were hurled across the water. Flavus called for his weapons and charger. He would have plunged into the water to cross blades with his brother, had not Stertinius hurried forth to restrain him with his own hands.

Germanicus meanwhile contemplated on how to engage the Cherusci. Their numbers were probably not very great at his point but they did hold the opposite bank, making it difficult for the legions to cross. Accordingly Germanicus sent forth his cavalry under Stertinius, Aemilius and Chariovalda to cross at a different river ford, presumably further up or down stream, to confuse the enemy. The snorting horses splashed through the fast flowing river. After the Roman cavalry safely gained the east bank of the Weser, they doubled back to take the Cherusci from the flanks and rear. Chariovalda with his Batavians charged ahead of the rest of the Roman cavalry. He drove the Cherusci into a meadow surrounded by woods. There the Cherusci rallied and burst upon the Batavians from all directions, hurling missiles and pressing them with shields and lances. Chariovalda heartened his men's courage with shouts of valor. With a berserker's daring, he spurred his horse into the midst of the enemy. A lethal rain of javelins and spears struck at Chariovalda and his steed. The unfortunate beast collapsed beneath its mortally wounded master. Many of Chariovalda's retainers died fighting by his side and the rest of his men nearly shared their fate, had not Stertinius and Aemilius arrived with the Roman cavalry. Stertinius and Aemilius beat back the attackers who made a hasty retreat into the thickets.

With the enemy routed, Germanicus' legions reached the eastern shores of the river. Soon after, word came to him from a German deserter that the Cherusci tribes were assembling in a forest sacred to Hercules, the Roman name given to the Germanic god Thor or Donner. The deserter's words rang true; scouts who crept close to the enemy reported "the neighing of horses and the hum of a huge and tumultuous host."[21]

At night, Germanicus draped a wild beast's skin over his shoulders and so disguised left his tent by a secret exit. He wished to find out about his soldiers' honest state of mind. Mingling among them, he heard them praise his looks and superb physical condition and his generous nature and even temper. Above all, the troops were ready to fight for him and for Rome.

Suddenly the clatter of a horse's hooves resounded outside the camp. In a booming voice, speaking Latin, a barbarian rider "promised in the name of Arminius to all deserters, wives and lands with daily pay of a hundred sesterces as long as the war lasted."[22] Angered at the barbarian's arrogance, the Romans spat "Let battle be given. The soldiers will possess themselves of the lands of the Germans and will carry off their wives."[23]

At midnight, the Roman sentries spotted large numbers of tribesmen in the dark, possibly massing for an attack. The Germans were looking for any weak points in the Roman defenses but found their enemy vigilant everywhere. That night, Germanicus dreamed of himself carrying out a sacrifice. His robe splattered in blood, he was handed a fresh and finer one by his mother. To Germanicus the dream seemed favorable, as did the auspices taken the next day. The latter usually consisted of interpreting the feeding of sacred chickens. The chickens were brought forth by their special keeper, the *pullarius*, who opened their cage and fed them. If the birds fed eagerly then it was taken as a good sign. If they squawked and flapped their wings in alarm or cowered in the cage, then it was a bad sign.[24]

Enthused by the good omens, Germanicus rallied his troops with a speech. He talked of the poor quality of armor worn by the enemy, of the enemy's inability to withstand wounds and of the River Elbe, which lay ahead, and with it the end of the war. He further assured the men that even in the woods, the thickets would work against the huge barbarian shields and lances and favor the shorter Roman swords and javelins. Germanicus' words, true or not, did the job of instilling confidence in the hearts of the legions.

In the sacred wood of Thor, Arminius gave his own inspirational speech to his warriors. Standing beside his uncle Inguiomerus and the other chiefs, he called Germanicus' legionaries runaways, who abandoned Varus, some of whom bore wounds on their backs. The Romans had only managed to escape in the past because of their fleet. But winds and oars would not help them in battle. "Is there anything left for us but to retain our freedom or die before we are enslaved?"[25]

On horse and on foot, the Cherusci and allied tribesmen filed out from the open forest floor, beneath the lofty branches of towering tree trunks. Before them, grasslands sloped down from the great forest to the Idistaviso plain. An outward bend in the winding River Weser skirted the far side of the plain.[26] Towards one of the barbarian flanks, the hills and forest drew closer to the river.

While Arminius and the Cherusci held the higher ground, the allied tribes spilled forward onto the plain itself. The barbarians watched as the Roman army drew up. Older, grizzled veterans stared with thoughtful eyes, reflecting on the horror of past battles, while the young and unproven recklessly boasted of their coming deeds.

First the Cherusci saw hundreds of horses, with bearded, mustachioed and longhaired riders, armed with spears and round shields. The barbarians heard the neighing of horses, the trampling of hooves of the auxiliary Germans and Gauls who fought for Rome. The auxiliaries with their array of animal standards, like the boar and the lion, were followed by lines of archers. Then came the tightly ordered cohorts of four legions; row after row of plumed bronze helmets, shields displaying the legion emblems, and armored infantry in red tunics.[27] The signiferi held high the legionary eagles. The stamp of hobnailed sandals resounded up the slope. Trumpets blew to signal orders.

There were murmurs among the barbarian ranks, as seasoned warriors pointed at the unfamiliar standards and troops that appeared after the legions. White were the tunics under their mail shirts and white were the horse tail plumes of their bronze helmets. Their centurions' colors were red and in addition they wore greaves to distinguish their ranks. Marching beneath a standard of Victoria, the goddess of victory, they were the two cohorts of Praetorians and among them, accompanied by some elite cavalry, rode Germanicus himself. Even this was not the end of the Roman host. Four more legions reinforced with light infantry and archers followed after the Praetorians, and after them came more auxiliaries.

The Roman army was a formidable array. A Roman legion of the early Imperial period numbered anywhere from 3,000 to over 5,000 men[28] and there were usually equal numbers of auxiliaries. The grand total of Germanicus' army thus was at least 60,000 soldiers. It was probably in moments like this, when the odds were against them and they needed all the courage they could muster, and when the silence of ambush was not required, that the Germanic warriors began their well known battle chant, the *baritus*. By holding "their shields in front of their mouths, so that the sound is amplified into a deeper crescendo by the reverberation,"[29] the chant built to a powerful roar. No doubt it terrified the raw Roman recruits and even intimidated the veterans who had heard it before. As the chant grew louder it built up the barbarians' courage until, like a dam ready to burst, they were ready to hurl themselves against the shields and spears of their foes. Led by their bravest, the barbarian horde roared down upon the Roman lines. At once, on Germanicus' signal, the Roman and auxiliary cavalry led by Stertinius and others, bolted forward, not directly at the enemy but circling around. There was no German cavalry to oppose them, probably because it was needed to fight with and bolster the German infantry storming at the main Roman body.

According to Tacitus, Germanicus at this very moment beheld eight eagles in the sky, flying towards the forest; eight eagles for eight legions. "Follow the birds of Rome, the Roman army's protecting spirits!"[30] cried Germanicus. Trumpets blared and with a yell the Roman infantry charged forward. Both sides collided on the plain like two titanic waves. The Roman cavalry then tore into the barbarian flanks while Stertinius attacked from the rear. Droves of barbarians fled back into the woods while at the same time fresh contingents were still emerging out of the trees. It was hellish chaos, but one warrior, by the strength of his voice and his bravery, stood out amongst the many. It was Arminius, who though wounded, led his Cherusci to slice through the lines of Roman archers. Hacking away to his right and left, he was about to rupture the lines when cohorts of allied Roman Rhaeti, Vendelici and Gauls rallied to the archers' aid. Beset from all sides, his face smeared with blood, Arminius put the heels to his horse. The faithful beast broke through and carried its master to safety. Inguiomerus made a similar escape.

Many of Arminius' soldiers were not so lucky. They fled and met their death in every direction. Some threw themselves into the Weser, only to be pierced by Roman missiles or to be dragged under by the current. Others, caught in a mad rush, were crushed by their own kind. A few barbarians even tried to climb trees from where the Romans shot them as if for sport. The slaughter began at nine in the morning and it did not end until nightfall, when the Romans gave up their hunt for German survivors. Roman casualties were reportedly light. The soldiers gave a hearty hail to Tiberius the Imperator, and "raised a mound on which arms were piled in the style of a trophy, with the names of the conquered tribes inscribed beneath them."[31]

The Roman victory did not dampen the fighting spirit of the Germans. On the contrary, from everywhere, the "common people and chiefs, young and old,"[32] took up what arms they had and rushed to rally against the invaders. Joined by the Angrivarii, the Cherusci infantry awaited the Romans behind a broad earthwork, which in times past had been raised as a boundary between the two tribes.[33]

Unfortunately, Tacitus' account of the battle is extremely muddled and often contradictory, possibly because the fighting became so confused that the Romans themselves did not know exactly what was going on. The impression is that unlike the prior battle where the Romans apparently held the numerical advantage, the two sides were now more evenly matched. Accordingly the fighting was hard.

The battle stretched over many miles of varied terrain. Roughly, the Roman flanks and rear were hemmed in by a river to one side and by hills to their other. Guided by tribal scouts, Germanicus probably rode up to a good vantage point on the higher ground from where he surveyed the terrain below. Ahead, towards their hilly flank, the Romans faced open ground leading up to open woodland. The woods stretched towards a narrow swampy open space between the woods and the river. The earthwork spanned the open space, blocking passage along the river. Further beyond the wood and the narrow space the land turned to a morass.

Within the trees waited the German cavalry. Anticipating that the Romans would enter the forest in order to outflank the rampart, the German cavalry hoped to ambush the Romans from behind. Through scouts or traitors, Germanicus was aware of his enemy's deployment. Germanicus divided his army into three corps. The cavalry with Lucius Seius Tubero was to lead the attack across the open ground and into the wood. They were to be followed by part of the infantry, the rest being ordered to storm the rampart. Germanicus kept the Praetorians as a reserve.

Tubero's cavalry and following infantry marched into the woods without opposition. Once inside, chaotic, indecisive fighting broke out against German cavalry. The heaviest fighting, however, was at the ramparts. The Germans refused to give way, their long lances thrusting downward, stabbing Roman mail and flesh. With the numbers of Roman dead and wounded growing and no breach of the Germans defenses in sight, Germanicus wisely ordered his legions to pull back. It was not easy for the proud legionaries, so unused to defeat, to be hounded by jeers and missiles from the enemy.

Mortally wounded soldiers, trampled by their comrades, crawled and groaned among the Roman dead that were left sprawling in front of the ramparts. If the Germans did not dispatch the wounded Romans then and there, they would soon be killed by friendly fire. Germanicus ordered the auxiliary slingers and Roman siege engines to be brought up. A hurricane of sling stones and catapult spears hit the ramparts with such relentless fury that the defenders scattered. The ramparts conquered, Germanicus led his Praetorians in a charge into the woods.

Shields at their breasts, swords in their hands, the Romans formed impenetrable walls that slowly squeezed the barbarian multitudes toward the morass. Hampered by the wound sustained in the previous battle Arminius was less active, his place taken by Inguiomerus. Inguiomerus galloped around with little thought to his own safety, trying hard to restore the situation. But it was Germanicus' day to shine. Tearing off his helmet so that all might behold him, he led his men into the fray, calling for no prisoners and for the utter destruction of the whole enemy nation.

The enemy was again routed. The captured weapons were piled up with the inscription "The army of Tiberius Caesar, after thoroughly conquering the tribes between the Rhine and Elbe, has dedicated this monument to Mars, Jupiter, and Augustus."[34] As usual, Germanicus entrenched his legions for the night. The inscription on the monument may have boasted of complete Roman victory but in reality, the enemy was by no means decisively defeated.

Germanicus' next course of action was to send Stertinius to punish the Angrivarii for helping the Cherusci. No battle was necessary, as the Angrivarii promised to abide by whatever the Romans wished and were given a full pardon. The Roman leniency towards the Angrivarii was at least partly due to the continued threat of the Cherusci. The fighting had been hard, the legions were worn out and they had suffered heavy casualties. Without fresh reinforcements, Germanicus had no desire to prolong the fighting.

Although summer was at its height and there was plenty of campaign time left, Germanicus decided to call it quits. Marching back to the Ems, Germanicus met up with his fleet. A rise in the tide had likely allowed the fleet to navigate the troublesome tidal flats and meet Germanicus' army farther up river. While a handful of legions continued the trek west on foot, the majority boarded the fleet and sailed down river for the ocean.

The quiet waters resounded with the thrashing of thousands of oars before a wind picked up. Whitecaps appeared, the sails billowed, and ominous black clouds darkened the horizon. Suddenly a hailstorm burst upon the fleet, shredding at the canvases, riddling the planks. Men prayed and clutched sacred icons to ward off the anger of the gods. Beat to a fury, the waves contemptuously tossed the ships about. Though rain and saltwater stung their faces and blinded their sight, though the waves threatened to sweep them off the decks, the sailors did their best to keep the ships afloat. Unfortunately the sailors were seriously hampered in their efforts by terrified soldiers who got in their way or offered clumsy aid.

Deep from the hills and rivers of Germania, a wind rolled like some vengeful spirit onto the hapless fleet. The neighs of frightened mules and horses, thrown overboard with baggage to lighten the load, cut through howling wind and cracking timber. But nothing satiated the remorseless wrath of nature. Ships smashed into the hazy cliffs of unknown shores. Rocky shoals raked wooden hulls. Ships and crews were swallowed by the open sea. Those that survived found themselves marooned on islands, to perish by hunger unless a horse's carcass washed up.

Tacitus tells us that at first Germanicus' trireme alone reached the coastline of the Chauci. When at last the storm died down, other vessels, some towed, some with clothing as sails, returned to land along the Chauci coastline as well. The ship oar banks and decks were filled with haggard crews. Germanicus had the ships repaired as quickly as possible and sent them back to search for other less fortunate survivors. One can only imagine the joy of the starved Roman soldiers upon espying the sails of their countrymen! Help was also forthcoming from the Angrivarii, who did not forget the recent show of Roman goodwill. Marooned Roman soldiers that had fallen into the hands of inland tribes were saved by the Angrivarii, who negotiated for their release. Some Roman ships even ended up in Britannia from where their crews were sent back by Roman-friendly chiefs. The Roman survivors told "of far distant regions, of wonders, of violent hurricanes, of unknown birds, of monsters of the sea, of forms of half-humans, half beast-like, things they had really seen or in their terror believed."[35]

While the disastrous loss of the fleet stirred the Angrivarii into compassion, it had the opposite effect on the other tribes. They laughed and gloated at the Roman's ill fortunes. Despite the heavy losses incurred in battle and by the storm, Germanicus still managed to send Caius Silius with 30,000 infantry and 3,000 cavalry to suppress the Chatti. Many of these troops must have been newly raised auxiliaries, since lost legionaries were not so easily replaced. Germanicus himself marched with an even greater army to invade the Marsi. The main

Roman objective was probably not to avert a threat to Gaul but to acquire booty and slaves for the troops to compensate for their earlier losses. Neither German tribe had any chance of seriously challenging such an army. Those that fought were instantly crushed. Most fled. The Romans rampaged at will, taking booty and slaves where they could. Informed by a turncoat Marsi chief, Germanicus even recovered another of Varus' lost eagles which lay buried in a grove.

When the legions went into winter quarters, Germanicus was sure that he could bring the war to an end in the next summer. Tiberius thought otherwise. He urged Germanicus to return to Rome for a triumph but reminded him not to forget the heavy losses taken at sea. Furthermore, Tiberius wrote in his letters, he himself had been sent nine times by Augustus into Germania and in the end achieved more by diplomacy than by the strength of arms. "The Cherusci too and the other insurgent tribes, since the vengeance of Rome had been satisfied, might be left to their internal feuds."[36]

Germanicus tried to gain another year on the front but Tiberius was obstinate, offering him a second consulship in Rome but requiring him to serve it in person. Tiberius also added that any further campaigns could be entrusted to Germanicus' stepbrother, Drusus II. The writing was on that wall. Tiberius either believed the war in Germania to be futile and not worth the vast expenditure it required, or he did not wish Germanicus to become too popular. Probably it was a bit of both. Germanicus on the other hand, seemed determined to finish the war that had been started by his father. But Tiberius was the Emperor and he had his way. As in the days of Julius Caesar, the Rhine remained the border between the Empire and the free German tribes.

Germanicus returned to Rome and was given a magnificent triumph in AD 17. Upon the appearance of Germanicus' chariot, the noise of the crowd crescendoed to drown out the heralding trumpets. White horses drew Germanicus' sacred golden chariot, which was otherwise kept in its own temple. A wreath of bay leaves crowned Germanicus' head, the golden palm of victory adorned his vest and a purple cloak draped his shoulders. The people smiled in affection when they saw that their hero had taken his five young children in his chariot. The populace marveled at the wagons of loot, the wheeled stages with dioramas depicting Germanicus' battles, the sacrificial oxen with their gilded horns. The cheers turned to booing and mockery at the arrival of the captives.

On display in Germanicus' triumph were droves of captured Bructeri, Usipi, Cherusci, Chatti, Chauci and other tribes, alongside an array of barbarian nobles. There was Libes, a priest of the Chatti, and Deudorix, son of Baetorix the Sugambri chief. The most notable prisoners though were those of the Cherusci nobles. Sesisthacus of the Cherusci, Segestes' nephew, walked into captivity with his wife, Rhamis, a noble daughter of the Chatti. Segimundus, Segestes' son, who had repeatedly switched sides, did not escape captivity either, although he had been promised Roman amnesty. In stark contrast to her spineless brother, proud Thusnelda never recanted her loyalty to her husband Arminius. Thusnelda's honor must have given her strength as she led her and Arminius' three-year-old son, Thumelicus, to be exhibited among the captives. Notably, the most notorious enemy warlords, Melo, Segimer, Inguiomerus and, above all, Arminius, all eluded capture.

Watching his enslaved family members as a guest of honor among the Romans was the Cherusci chief Segestes. Segestes had never flinched in his allegiance to Rome, and Rome, for all her cruelty, wisely rewarded those that stayed loyal. For loyalty to Rome and hatred of Arminius, Segestes had even betrayed his own daughter and grandson. Thumelicus, son of Arminius, ended up being sent to Ravenna, home of a famous gladiatorial school. It was the beginning of the end of the royal house of the Cherusci. In AD 47 the only member of the royal family to lead the Cherusci that remained alive was, ironically, Italicus, the son of Flavus. He was "born at Rome as a citizen, not as a hostage … Italicus was kept at Rome – a handsome man, trained to fight and ride in both German and Roman style."[37] By that time, Thumelicus may well have died a gladiator's death for he is not heard off again. Tacitus added that even if Thumelicus had been there to return to his people, "there would be reason to fear the contagion of foreign upbringing, slave-labor, dress, and everything else."[38]

Was Germanicus right, could Rome have eventually conquered Germania and absorbed its unruly peoples into her empire? Would Rome's military prowess and vast resources assure a decisive victory over the Germanic tribes and a lasting conquest? The answers to this must, of course, remain speculative. What had Rome achieved in three decades? Not only had Rome suffered one of the worst defeats in her entire history in the Teutoburg forest, but also, more importantly, none of her "victories" proved decisive. As already mentioned earlier, unlike in Gaul, there were no major strategic strongholds in Germania around which the Romans could consolidate their victories. In answer, Rome built her own strongholds but when she tried to actually impose suzerainty over the surrounding tribes this too failed. Of course more strongholds could have been built and more troops poured in to guard them. But given that defense against the barbarian tribes already absorbed over a third of the entire Roman army, it is questionable whether such resources were even available.

As Tiberius maintained, the greatest success had actually been by cooperative policies, in which the Germans were incorporated into the empire as allies and trade partners. This is exactly what happened centuries later, on a much greater scale, when lack of manpower forced Rome to rely on German recruits, first as individuals then as entire peoples, to fight her wars and protect her borders. The result of this, however, was not the assimilation of Germania into the Roman Empire, but rather the dismemberment of the Empire by German tribes. At the same time, Germanic culture became merged with Latin culture, although the degree of this merger varied with each tribe.

Another road to victory would have been to hammer the tribes so hard and so relentlessly as to break their spirit to resist. There was no indication that this was happening either. No amount of Roman propaganda could conceal that in 11 BC Drusus was fighting the Cherusci, and that 27 years later his son Germanicus was still fighting the Cherusci. All the wars, all the bloodshed, of the last three decades had achieved naught but to further militarize the already dangerous Germanic tribes. After contact with the Roman Empire, more bent swords and lances were placed among the grave goods that accompanied the ashes of cremated tribesmen.

The hardships that the Roman military endured in its wars with the Germanic tribes were aptly summed up by Tacitus who considered the Germans to be Rome's greatest foes:

> "Neither by the Samnites nor by the Carthaginians, not by Spain or Gaul, or even by the Parthians, have we had more lessons taught to us. After all, what has the East to taunt us with, except the slaughter of Crassus? But the Germans routed or captured Carbo, Cassius, Aurelius Scarus, Servilius Caepio, and Mallius Maximus, and robbed the Republic, almost at one stroke, of five consular armies. Even from Augustus they took Varus and three legions. And we had to pay a high price for the defeats inflicted upon them by Gaius Marius in Italy, by Julius Caesar in Gaul, and by Drusus, Tiberius, and Germanicus in their own country."[39]

The battle of the Teutoburg forest and the subsequent German resistance freed the tribes from Roman annexation and assimilation and enabled them to conquer Gaul and Britannia centuries later, giving birth to the countries of Germany,

France and England. It was one of those battles whose outcome changed the whole course of history.

The Roman wars of aggression left the German tribes polarized into two mighty tribal confederations. One was that of Arminius, the other that of Maroboduus. Notably, both were trained in Roman ways of war. That Germanicus' claim of soundly beating Arminius was just propaganda, is indicated by Maroboduus' plea for help from Rome against Arminius. Arminius, who was supposed to be a beaten man, was powerful enough to seriously threaten Maroboduus against whom in AD 6 the Romans considered throwing no less than twelve legions!

Maroboduus had fallen out of favor with many tribesmen who resented his authoritarian proclamation as King, as opposed to Arminius the "champion of freedom." Accordingly, the Suebi Semnones and Langobardi went over to Arminius. Arminius however, lost the support of his uncle Inguiomerus who along with his supporters sided with Maroboduus. Apparently, Inguiomerus resented having to follow Arminius' orders.

When the two opposing armies drew up in AD 17, there were none of the disorganized haphazard attacks by bands of overeager tribesmen, formerly so common among the Germans. "Prolonged warfare against us had accustomed them to keep close to their standards, to have the support of reserves, and to take the word of command from their generals,"[40] related Tacitus.

Both warlords rode along the lines, rallying the troops with words of valor. Arminius boasted of the slaughtered legions and called Maroboduus a traitor to his country. Maroboduus bragged that he had held off the legions of Tiberius. He held up Inguiomerus' hand and claimed that all of Arminius' victories were due to his uncle's council.

The shock of battle echoed across the wilderness as both sides fell at each other with a vengeance. For a while, victory hung in the balance as the right wings of both armies were routed. It was Maroboduus, however, who withdrew to the hills. Weakened by desertions, he fled to the homeland of the Marcomanni and was reduced to pleading to Tiberius for help. Tiberius' answer was that Maroboduus "had no right to invoke the Romans' aid against the Cherusci, when he had rendered no assistance to the Romans in their conflict with the same enemy."[41] Drusus II arrived to help negotiate a peace between the Cherusci and the Marcomanni; probably because he did not want the Cherusci to annex the latter's territory and become too powerful. The peace negotiations certainly were not for the benefit of Maroboduus. Thereafter, Drusus II lost no opportunity in encouraging the tribes to finish off the broken power of Maroboduus.

Word that Maroboduus was deserted by his allies came to the ears of Catualda of the Gotones. The noble youth had been driven into exile by Maroboduus. Now, Catualda judged, was the time for vengeance. At the head of a strong force, Catualda entered the Marcomanni lands and won over its nobles by corruption. He burst into Maroboduus' palace and surrounding fortresses and appropriated the treasures of the Marcomanni. Maroboduus was not there, having fled across the Danube into the Roman province of Noricum. He was given asylum and ended up being kept at Ravenna. Maroboduus never left Italy again. Clinging to life, he lived another eighteen years and reached old age before he passed away. Catualda shared a similar fate; being driven out of his holdings by the Suebi Hermunduri. Just like Maroboduus, Catualda found refuge within the borders of the Empire.

With the Romans driven out of Germania and his greatest tribal rival Maroboduus defeated, nothing seemed to stand in Arminius' way. Nothing that is, except the same spirit of freedom which had enabled Arminius to rally the tribes against Rome and against Maroboduus. As his status grew, Arminius suffered the same accusations as Maroboduus. His rivals cried that Arminius was making himself King. The tribesmen who refused to kneel to the authority of the Roman Emperor or of Maroboduus would not accept Arminius as absolute ruler either. The liberator of Germania did not live long to enjoy his newfound power and glory. In AD 19, a Chatti chief offered to Rome that he would kill Arminius with poison. The Roman answer was that "it was not by treason or in the dark but openly and in arms that the Roman people took vengeance on their foes."[42] Later that year, after a prolonged and undecided fight against his tribal foes, Arminius was betrayed by his relatives and killed. Arminius, Prince of the Cherusci, passed into legend. Tacitus, who admired and respected Arminius for his courage, vision and skill at arms, gave a fitting last tribute:

> "He was unmistakably the liberator of Germany. Challenger of Rome–not in its infancy, like kings and commanders before him, but at the height of its power–he had fought undecided battles, and never lost a war. He had ruled for twelve of his thirty-seven years. To this day the tribes sing of him. Yet Greek historians ignore him, reserving their admiration for Greece. We Romans, too, underestimate him, since in our devotion to antiquity we neglect modern history."[43]

Like Arminius, his Roman adversary Germanicus was not fated to die of old age either. He passed away in AD 19, the same year as Arminius's death. Germanicus fell ill after traveling through Egypt. He had been very popular with the people, being nearly mobbed to death by his admirers whenever he arrived in Rome. After he returned from Germania all of the Praetorian cohorts marched out to meet him, although only two had been ordered to do so. Almost all of Rome, young and old, rich and poor, flocked out to greet him at the twentieth milestone! He had spent his last years in the Roman east, accomplishing much. He helped turn Cappadocia into a province, stifled unrest in Armenia, improved relations with Parthia and relieved a famine in Alexandria. In the East, as in Rome, Germanicus became a hero to all.

At Germanicus' death there were riots in Rome and abroad, fueled by rumors that he had been poisoned. Among those implicated was Tiberius himself. It did not help matters that thereafter, the Emperor treated the wife and children of Germanicus unkindly. The mob threw stones at temples and overturned altars. "Give us back Germanicus,"[44] they shouted and scrawled on walls throughout Rome. Abroad, the Parthian King of Kings cancelled his hunting parties and banquets. Rumors told of German princes shaving their beards and their wives' heads, as a sign of grief and respect.

It was the dawn of a new era, that of Imperial Rome. Though there would be more battles and more wars and even a few more conquests, the Empire was increasingly locked into a deadly stalemate with the free tribes of the north. The shores of Britannia still beckoned, where a fiery warrior queen would lead her people against the heirs of Caesar. In the mountains of today's Hungary and Transylvania, Dacians would slice through Roman armor with fearsome two-handed scythes. Italy would only be saved from the Marcomanni by a great soldier emperor. Finally the great tribal confederations would arise: the Goths, the Vandals, the Saxons, the Angles and the Franks, which would migrate over the face of Europe, plunging the Empire into chaos and turning the tide from stalemate into the dismemberment of the Empire. The sack of Rome by the Visigoths in AD 410 heralded the final demise of the Roman Empire in the west. The deposition of the last Western Roman Emperor, Romulus Augustulus in AD 476, by the barbarian Odoacer, marked its end. For nearly five centuries after the Roman defeat in the Teutoburg forest, the Roman Empire would war with the barbarians. The great battles of those ages, the tribal warlords, the legion commanders and the emperors, the Roman soldiers and the tribes of the great migrations, are another story in the Roman barbarian wars.

Notes

Introduction

1. The main Roman writing tools were the reed or bronze pen for writing with ink on papyrus or vellum (hide) and the bronze, bone or iron stylus used for scratching on wax tablets (Matthew Bunson, *Encyclopedia of the Roman Empire*. New York: Facts on File Inc., 2002, p. 594–5).
2. Tacitus, *The Agricola and the Germania*, translated by H. Mattingly and S.A. Handford (Ontario: Penguin Books, 1987), G19, p. 117, 118.
3. N. Sekunda and others, *Caesar's Legions, the Roman Soldier 753 BC to 117 AD*, (Oxford: Osprey Publishing. 2000), p. 92.
4. At Cannae a Roman army of 50,000 was virtually annihilated (M. Cary and H.H. Scullard, *A History of Rome*, (London: Macmillan Education. 1988) p. 128–129). At Arausio, Roman casualties may have reached up to 80,000 (Paulus Orosius, *The Seven Books of History against the Pagans*, trans. Roy. J. Deferrari, (Washington: The Catholic University Press. 1961), p. 235). Of course both numbers are estimates. Cary and Scullard doubted that the Arausio losses were as high as stated (Cary and Scullard, p. 218).
5. Victor Duruy wrote of the Cimbri and Teutones migration, "They were perhaps a million of human beings when, thirteen years before, they had left the Baltic shore" (Victor Duruy, *History of Rome*, Volume II. (London: Kegan, Paul, Trench & Co. 1884), p. 506). When considering the low population densities of the time and the logistical problems of moving such a large population over a number of years, over mountains, hills and rivers and through relatively sparsely inhabited areas (by modern standards), Duruy's numbers become highly implausible.
6. Thucydides I. 22, as quoted by Michael Grant in his introduction to Tacitus' Annals of Imperial Rome (Tacitus, trans. Michael Grant, *The Annals of Imperial Rome* (London: Penguin Books. 1996), p. 12).

Chapter 1

1. Titus Livius, *The History of Rome*, trans. Roberts Canon (London: New York: Dutto & Co. Inc., 1927), V.I.5.21.
2. The classical histories themselves expressed different opinions on the origins of the Etruscans. Dionysius of Halicarnassus considered the Etruscans a very ancient people, native to Italy, with a unique language and culture (Dionysius, *The Roman Antiquities of Dionysius of Halicarnassus*, translated by Earnest Cary (London: William Heinemann LTD, 1960), Volume I. p. 97). Herodotus, the "Father of History," told of an Etruscan King who led his people from their home in Lydia (modern Turkey) to Italy (Herodotus, *Herodotus*, translated by William Beloe (London: Henry Colburn and Richard Bentley, 1830), Volume I. p. 79, 80).
3. H. Delbrück, *Warfare in Antiquity* (Lincoln: University of Nebraska Press, 1990) p. 260.
4. The Trojan War is best known from Homer's literary classic, *The Iliad*, which, however, covers only its dramatic last days. For the whole war see Apollodorus' *Epitome* 3–5 and Virgil's *Aeneid*. What really happened is a matter of speculation. There were no less than seven settlements at the site of Troy, some which archaeology shows were probably destroyed by natural disaster, such as an earthquake, others possibly by invasion (J.B. Bury and R. Meiggs,

A History of Greece (London: Macmillan, 1987), p. 42, 47, 48). Like that of Troy, the length of the Roman siege of Veii may have similarly grown in legend.

Chapter 2
1. Livy, *The History of Rome,* translated by Roberts Canon V.1.5.48.
2. Peter Wilcox and Trevino Rafael, *Barbarians against Rome,* p. 59, Strabo, *The Geography of Strabo,* translated by Jones L. Horace (London: William Heinemann Ltd., 1923) IV.4.2.
3. Livy, *The History of Rome,* V.1.5.33. Livy further claims that the initial Gallic inroads into Italy occurred 200 years before the Gauls were allegedly lured into Italy by the trade in wine. He blames the first great Gallic invasion on the overpopulation of their land and places it in the reign of the Roman Etruscan King Tarquinius Priscus (trad. 616–579 BC). Modern scholars generally reject this as 100–200 years too early when compared to archeological evidence (Cary and Scullard, p. 590). According to Livy, to find new homes for the growing population of Gaul, King Ambigatus of the powerful Bituriges asked his sister's sons, Bellovesus and Segovesus, to find new lands to settle. Leading a smattering of tribesmen from the Bituriges, the Arverni, the Senones, the Aedui, the Ambarri, the Carnutes, and the Aulerci, Bellovesus crossed the Alps into Italy. His brother, Segovesus led his Gauls east, toward the Hercynian (Harz) forest (Livy, *The History of Rome,* V.1.5.34).
4. Andrew Sherratt, "The Emergence of Elites: Earlier Bronze Age Europe, 2500–1300 BC, in *Prehistoric Europe,*" p. 261.
5. Brennus may be a general term for a Gallic chief or king, as opposed to a name of an individual (Theodor Mommsen, *The History of Rome,* Volume I (London: Richard Bentley and Son, 1894), p. 428).
6. Livy, *The History of Rome,* V. 1.5.36
7. Dio gives a number of 24,000 warriors for the Roman army and more than 70,000 for the Gauls (Dio. *Roman History,* translated by Cary Earnest, XIV. 114.2, 3). Plutarch says the Romans were not inferior in numbers to the Gauls and gives us a figure of 40,000 men (Plutarch. "The Life of Camillus," in *Plutarch's Lives,* translated by Perrin Bernadotte XVIII 4). Cary and Scullard estimate the Romans at 15,000 and the Gauls at 30,000–70,000 (M.Cary and H. H. Scullard, *A History of Rome,* notes p. 590). Ellis considers the Roman army to have been 24,000 men strong, the Gauls at only half that number (Peter Beresford Ellis, *Celts and Romans: The Celts In Italy* (London: Constable, 1998), p. 10).
8. Wilcox and Rafael, *Barbarians against Rome* p. 70–71.
9. Livy, *The History of Rome,* V.1.5.38.
10. Headhunting was a prevalent Celtic custom. Besides actual finds of skulls, images of severed heads remained behind on carvings.
11. Livy, *The History of Rome,* V.1.5.48.
12. Not to be confused with the Celtic, Aremorican coastal tribe of the same name.
13. Over the centuries the size of the *manipular* legion, which first arose sometime in the 4th century BC, was subject to change both in its overall strength and in the size and number of its subunits. Polybius in his *Histories* spanning the years 264–164 BC, describes the Roman *manipular* legion as fielding 4,200 infantry and 300 Roman cavalry but being increased in times of great danger to 5,000 (Polybius 6. 20–21). Livy, who wrote the entire history of Rome, from its foundation to his own time of Emperor Augustus, leaves an account of a larger Roman manipular legion, with fifteen maniples in each of the legionary lines, instead of the ten of Polybius, for a total of 5,000 men, each assigned 300 cavalry (Livy 8.8). On another occasion, Livy mentions 2,000 *hastati* in the 197 BC legion of Quinctius Flamininus (Livy 33.1.2) during the Second Macedonian War. During the Third Macedonian War (171–168 BC), legions reached 6,000 or even 6,200 men (N Sekunda and others, *Caesar's Legions, The Roman Soldier 753 BC to AD 117,* p. 86).
14. J.B. Bury and Russell Meiggs, *A History of Greece,* p. 447.

Chapter 3
1. Polybius, *The Histories*, II.27.
2. Ibid. II.21.
3. Ibid. II.22.
4. Archaeology reveals the presence of the Taurisci Celtic culture in Slovenia from around 300 BC (John T. Koch, *Celtic Culture a Historical Encyclopedia* (Santa Barbara: ABC-CLIO, 2006) p. 1663).
5. Most of the army sizes and casualty numbers in Chapter 3 are quoted directly from Polybius, *The Histories*, Book II.23, 24. His information appears entirely credible, the only possible exception being the size of the Roman allied contingents. According to Polybius, each of the two consular armies numbered 22,000 Romans and 32,000 allies. Polybius does not mention if the army under the praetor in Etruria was equally strong. However, as mentioned in the chapter, it must have been of fair size, for at first the Gauls decided to avoid an open battle and came up with a plan to ambush the Romans. Polybius does go on to list numerous other Roman allies, for an unbelievable total "seven hundred thousand foot and seventy thousand horse." But as Polybius mentions, they were men "able to bear arms," meaning they were likely to be the total number of men in Italy that could, in theory but not in reality, be armed to fight for Rome. I estimate the Roman and allied defenders in the three armies at somewhere above 150,000 strong. Cary and Scullard's estimate was "a force of not less than 130,000 defenders" (Cary and Scullard, *A History of Rome*, p. 122).
6. The Marsi were a mountain people of Italy. Their tribal name should not be confused with a Germanic tribe of the same name which fought Rome in the early first century AD.
7. Polybius, *The Histories*, II.29.
8. The inscriptions on the Acta Triumphalia stone tablets, dating from the reign of the first Roman Emperor Augustus, record that Marcus Claudius Marcellus gained the spoils of honor for triumphing over the Insubrian Celts and the Germans. Marcellus' victory in 222 BC at Clastidium is the earliest date that Germanic tribesmen are mentioned in the historical record (Ellis, *The Celtic Empire*, p. 41, A. Degrassi, *Fasti Capitolini* (Torino: G.B. Paravia, 1954)).
9. Livy quoted in King, *Kingdoms of the Celts*, p. 77.

Chapter 4
1. Polybius, *The Histories*, XXXV.1.
2. Cunliffe, Iron Age Societies in Western Europe and Beyond, 800 -140 BC, in *Prehistoric Europe*, p. 370.
3. Pro-praetors Postumius and Gracchus' armies advanced from the southeast and north, respectively, squeezing the Celt-Iberians between them. Their submission was followed by a long lasting settlement that established Roman dominion over all of Spain outside of the Atlantic coast. Gracchus left his stamp on Spain by founding the colony of Gracchuris on the Upper River Ebro.
4. Appian, *Appian's Roman History*, VI.X.59, 60.
5. Wilcox and Trevino, *Barbarians Against Rome*, p. 112.
6. Gades' chief deity was Melqart, usually depicted as a bearded man, holding in either hand an anhk and an axe, symbols of life and death, ("Melqart", *Encyclopeidia Britannica*, britannica.com).
7. Appian, *Appian's Roman History*, VI.XII.70.
8. Ibid.,VI.XII.72.

Chapter 5
1. Appian, *Appian's Roman History*, Book VI.XV.93
2. Gracchus' peace treaty included provisions for the poor, who were allotted land to settle on. Carefully crafted treaties with the tribes bound them to be friends of Rome with oaths

exchanged on both sides. "These treaties were often longed for in the subsequent wars. In this way Gracchus became celebrated both in Spain and in Rome." (Appian, *Appian's Roman History*, translated by Horace White, VI. 43).

3. From 179 to 154, complaints by the Spaniards of oppressive Roman governors were met by empty promises. As a result the Belli began to prepare for another possible war. In 154 the Belli induced settlers from smaller towns and from among the Titii to move to their city of Segeda and began to fortify it with a new wall. The Senate forbade this even though Gracchus' treaty had not forbidden the fortifications of existing cities, although it forbade the construction of new cities. Furthermore, the Senate demanded tribute and soldiers from the Belli, as per Gracchus' treaty. The Belli replied that the Romans had already released the Belli from these requirements. This was true but the Senate replied that these exemptions "should continue only during the pleasure of the Roman people." (Appian, *Appian's Roman History*, translated by Horace White, VI. 44, Cary and Scullard, *A History of Rome*, p. 143, Wilcox and Trevino, *Barbarians Against Rome*, p. 115).

4. Polybius, *The Histories*, XXXV.4.
5. Cary and Scullard, *A History of Rome*, p. 143.
6. Appian, *Appian's Roman History*, Book VI.XIV.85.
7. Ibid., VI.XIV.85.
8. Peter Wilcox and Trevino Rafael estimate 3,500 warriors (*Barbarians Against Rome*, p. 119). Appian gave a fighting strength of 8,000 (Appian, *Appian's Roman History*, Book VI. 97). Considering the heroic defense of the city and the tendency of classical historians to overstate the size of enemy armies, I would expect the numbers were somewhere in between.
9. Part of one of the largest and earliest remains of a Roman siegework, the ruins of Scipio's seven fortresses, can still be seen on the hills surrounding the excavated town of Numantia (S. J. Key, *Roman Spain*, p. 40).
10. Plutarch, *Greek and Roman Lives*, p. 194

Chapter 6
1. Livy, *The History of Rome*, V.5.XXXVI.39.
2. Cary and Scullard, *A History of Rome*, p. 13.
3. Livy, *The History of Rome*, V.5.XXXVI.39.

Chapter 7
1. Plutarch, "The Life of Marius," *Plutarch's Lives* XI.8
2. Their simple dress is based on descriptions in Tacitus' Germania (Tacitus, *The Agricola and Germania*, p. 115,116), written nearly two centuries later. If anything one would expect the Cimbri and Teutones attire to have been more primitive than Tacitus' Germans.
3. The question of whether the Cimbri and Teutones were Germans or Celts is a difficult one and one that caused me considerable difficulty during my research. Basically scholarly opinion appears to be divided with an apparent leaning toward the German side, the exception being Celtic historians.
4. Modern estimates of the numbers of Cimbri and Teutones vary greatly. Logistical considerations and the low population density of Germany, under 5 people per km2 (Pounds, *An historical geography of Europe, p. 111)* at the time, make the large numbers in the ancient sources impossible. Delbrück (Delbrück, *The Barbarian Invasions*, translated by Walter J. Renfroe Jr. (Lincoln: University of Nebraska Press, 1990, p. 298)) estimates a mere 10,000 warriors for the Cimbri. Kildahl, (Kildahl, *Caius Marius*, p. 99–100) believes that each tribe furnished 50,000 fighting men, and some authors (Duruy, *History of Rome and the Roman People*, p. 490) state larger numbers. I believe Kildahl's numbers are too high – it would have meant over 400,000 men, women and children! On the other hand, Delbrück seems too low considering the tribes' impact on Rome. The Cimbri and Teutones were probably the same size as the larger tribes

of the migration age, which according to Bury numbered from 80,000 to 120,000 people (J.B. Bury, *The Invasion of Europe by the Barbarians* (New York: The Norton Library, 1967), p. 42).

5. The route taken by the Cimbri and Teutones into Gaul is conjectural. Duruy proposed that after the Helvetii (the Tigurini) joined the Cimbri and Teutones, the tribes ventured down the Rhine crossing into Gaul in the Belgae lands (Duruy, *History of Rome and the Roman People*, p. 490, 491).

6. Florus, *Epitome of Roman History*, Book I. XXXVIII.

7. Duruy, *History of Rome and the Roman People*, p. 492.

8. The marshes have since been channeled by dams and cannals (*Encylopedia Britannica*, "Rhone River," britannica.com).

9. Plutarch, *Greek and Roman Lives*, p. 194.

10. Just as was the case in the pre-Marian reforms, the post-Marian legion size and structure doubtlessly changed over the decades. Keeping in mind Goldsworthy's "warning against rigid thinking concerning unit strength and internal structure," (Goldsworthy, *The Roman Army at War 100 BC-200 AD*, p. 13), many scholars believe that the Marian reforms resulted in a 6,000 infantry-strong legion (Stephen Dando Collins, *Legions of Rome* (New York: Thomas Dunne Books, 2010) p. 17, Cary and Scullard, *A History of Rome*, p. 219, J.F.C. Fuller, *Julius Caesar*, p. 80–81, Delbrück, *Warfare in Antiquity*, p. 263).

11. Plutarch, "Life of Marius," *Plutarch's Lives*, XVIII.

12. Florus, *Epitome of Roman History*, Book I. XXXVIII.

13. M. Claudius Marcellus was likely the grandson of his namesake who fought in the Iberian war (B.G. Niebuhr, *Lectures on Roman History Vol. II* (London: Henry G. Bohn, 1855).

14. No account of Teutobod's end remains, though he was almost certainly executed after Marius' triumph.

15. Plutarch, "Life of Marius," *Plutarch's Lives*, XXIII.

16. Ibid. XXIV.

17. Florus, *Epitome of Roman History*, Book I. XXXVIII.

18. Florus, *Epitome of Roman History*, Book I. XXXVIII.

Chapter 8

1. Caesar, *The Conquest of Gaul*, I.14.

2. Caesar's account tells of the Helvetii burning their twelve oppida and 400 villages. Like many of Caesar's numbers, their credibility is suspect. So far, archaeology has only revealed one of fifteen oppida destroyed by fire while many other excavated sites of the period in Helvetii territory have not shown any fire damage (Andres Furger-Gunti, *Die Helvetier: Kulturgeschichte eines Keltenvolkes* (Zürich: Neue Züricher Zeitung, 1984) p. 118ff).

3. For the size of the Helvetii army see, Caesar, *The Conquest of Gaul*, I. 29, Plutarch, The Life of Julius Caesar, *Plutarch's Lives*, XVIII, Orosius, *The Seven Books of History against the Pagans*, p. 242 (6.7.6), Delbrück, *Warfare in Antiquity*, p. 459–475, Furger Gunti, *Die Helvetier: Kulturgeschichte eines Keltenvolkes*, p. 102.

4. The deployment of Caesar's three unengaged legions during the battle with the Tigurini is unclear. Furthermore, Caesar claims he himself led his three legions against the Tigurini, while Plutarch and Appian say it was Labienus (Caesar, *The Conquest of Gaul*, I.12, Plutarch, "The Life of Julius Caesar," *Plutarch's Lives*, XVIII, Appian, *Appian's Roman History*, Book IV.XV).

5. Caesar, *The Gallic War*, translated by H.J. Edwards (London: Harvard University Press, 1970), I.13.

6. Slavery was the common fate of Rome's defeated enemies, such as the former allies of the Tigurini, the Cimbri and Teutons (Plutarch, "The Life of Marius," *Plutarch's Lives*, XXVI.5–XXVII.4).

Chapter 9

1. Caesar, *The Conquest of Gaul*, I.36.
2. Ibid I.31
3. Ibid I.32
4. Ibid I.36
5. Ibid I.39
6. Ibid I.45
7. Ibid I.49
8. Tacitus, *The Agricola and Germania*, p. 108.
9. Bunson estimates 75,000 men for Ariovistus and 50,000 for Caesar (Bunson, *A Dictionary of the Roman Empire*, p. 28), Delbrück echoes Napoleon I's sentiment, in that he estimates Ariovistus' army considerably smaller than Caesar's (Delbrück, *Warfare in Antiquity*, p. 481). Plutarch wrote that Ariovistus' dead numbered 80,000 (Plutarch, *Greek and Roman Lives*, p. 338). Since Caesar himself describes how Ariovistus' wives were counted among the dead in the general slaughter, the 80,000 likely includes the women, the children and the old. This gives 20,000–30,000 warriors for the battle.
10. Caesar, *The Conquest of Gaul*, I. 51.
11. Tacitus, *The Agricola and Germania*, p. 108.
12. Orosius, *The Seven Books of History against the Pagans*, VI.
13. Caesar, *The Conquest of Gaul*, I.52.

Chapter 10

1. Caesar, *The Conquest of Gaul*, II.21
2. The traditional identification of the Sabis as the Sambre has been challenged as being the Selle, near Saulzoir, instead (Kimberly Kagan, *The Eye of Command* (Michigan: University of Michigan Press, 2006) p. 226 and Plutarch, *Caesar*, translated and commentary by Christopher Pelling (Oxford: Oxfort University Press, 2011), p. 239.
3. Caesar, *The Conquest of Gaul*, II.19.
4. Ibid. II.28.
5. Jona Lendering, "*Caesar and the Aduatuci*," Livius, Articles on Ancient History, 2012, livius.org.

Chapter 11

1. Caesar, *The Conquest of Gaul*, III.13.
2. Like other tribes along the Rhine, the Sugambri were another Germanic-Celtic cross cultural tribe, usually classed as Germanic but with Celtic ancecestry as well (Carl Waldman and Catherine Mason, *Encyclopedia of European Peoples* (New York: Infobase Publishing, 2006, p. 786)).

Chapter 12

1. Caesar, *The Conquest of Gaul*, IV.25.
2. Ibid IV.21.
3. Roman seamen, manning oars and operating sails, were not slaves, as is commonly believed, but freemen (Richard Gabriel, *The Roman Navy, Masters of the Mediterranean*, Military History Magazine (Herndon: December 2007, p. 36)).
4. Caesar, *The Conquest of Gaul*, IV.25.
5. Fuller, Julius Caesar, Man, Soldier, and Tyrant, p. 123.
6. Suetonius, *The Twelve Caesars*, p. 24. Suetonius is doubtlessly referring to the tribute and hostages paid by Cassivellaunus.
7. Plutarch, *Greek and Roman Lives*, p. 341.
8. Ibid.p. 340.

Chapter 13

1. Caesar, *The Conquest of Gaul*, V. 54.
2. The first rebellion flared up in 56 BC, chiefly among the Aremorican and Belgic coastal tribes. See Chapter 11.
3. The Treveri gave their name to the city of Trier, which claims to be the oldest city in Germany (Stadt Trier, "History", redaction.trier.de.).
4. The probable site of Caesar's camp for his four legions has recently been discovered by archaeologists of the Johannes Gutenberg-Universität Mainz (JGU). The remains of the 26 ha earthworks near Hermeskeil are only 3 miles from and within sight of the Dollberg fortress (Sabine Hornung, Johannes Gutenberg-Universität Mainz, *Römisches Militärlager aus der Zeit der Eroberung Galliens erhellt ein Stück Weltgeschichte*, 28.08.2012. uni-mainz.de.)
5. Sabinus was given command over the six cohorts that defended the vital rearguard stronghold at the battle of the Aisne. He then held command over three legions with which he subdued a number of Aremorican tribes. By comparison, before being mentioned by Caesar in command with Sabinus, Cotta only led a cavalry detachment. More than likely, then, it was Sabinus who held senior command when he and Cotta raided the Menapii lands and it was Sabinus who held senior command at Atuatuca.
6. Caesar, *The Conquest of Gaul*, V.28–31.
7. Ibid.
8. Ibid.
9. Ibid.
10. Although Caesar's narrative makes it clear that the army of Gauls consisted of a coalition of Belgae tribes, from this point on his emphasis is on the Nervii and their leaders. This seems to indicate that both in leadership and in numbers, the Nervii and the tribes under their rule became the prominent force in the Belgae coalition.
11. Caesar does not specify which tribe led the initial cavalry attack on the woodcutters of Cicero's camp in Book V of his *Gallic Wars*. However, in Book II, he mentions that the Nervii virtually have no cavalry (Caesar, *The Conquest of Gaul*, p. 65) so the Eburones and others likely provided the cavalry.
12. The centurions Titus Pullo and Lucius Vorenus of the Eleventh Legion served as the inspiration for the fictional characters of the same name in the HBO television series *Rome*. In the series they are portrayed serving in the Thirteenth Legion.
13. Caesar, *The Conquest of Gaul*, V. 44.
14. Suetonius, *The Twelve Caesars*, p. 42.
15. Cicero and his men were notified of Caesar's coming by one of Caesar's Gallic cavalry horsemen. He infiltrated the enemy lines around Cicero's camp, tied the message around a javelin, threw the javelin into the camp and hit one of the towers. The javelin remained unnoticed for two days, until found at the time of Caesar's approach.
16. Not only were there several tribes involved, but the battle took place in or near to the tribal homelands. As such it would have been easy for the Belgae to raise large numbers of their men able to bear arms. Their ability to erect large siege works around Cicero's camp also points to a sizeable army.
17. Caesar, *The Conquest of Gaul*, p. 233.
18. Caesar, *The Conquest of Gaul*, VI. 8.
19. Ibid.
20. Roman camps dating to Caesar's time were discovered during bridge construction in Hesse, near Limburg, in 2013. The camps were probably built in conjunction with Caesar's crossing of the Rhine in 55 and 53 BC (Hr online.de, *Julius Caesar an der Autobahn*. 2.05.2013, hr-online.de.).
21. The Bacenis forest was also the territory between the Suebi and the Cherusci (Caesar, *The Conquest of Gaul*, VI, 10) a tribe which one day would became greater foes of Rome

than even the Suebi. Possibly the Bacenis was the Thuringinan-Franconian Forest, once covered in beech and pine but now dominated by planted fir (naturpark-thueringer-wald.eu, oekologische-bildungsstaette.de).

22. Caesar, *The Conquest of Gaul*, VI. 34.
23. Ibid.
24. Ibid. VI. 35
25. Ibid.
26. Caesar, *The Conquest of Gaul*, IV. 35.
27. Ibid. VI. 41.
28. Ibid. VI. 43.
29. A heroic statute of Ambiorix erected in 1866, stands in the great market square of Tongeren, Belgium.

Chapter 14

1. Caesar, *The Conquest of Gaul*, VII.29.
2. Hirtius, in Caesar, *The Conquest of Gaul*, VIII.23.
3. "Ver" means "over" or "higher", "cinget" means "warrior" and "rix" means king.
4. Fuller wrote that Caesar kept 400 German horsemen in his service after his defeat of Ariovistus (Fuller, *Julius Caesar, Man, Soldier, and Tyrant*, p. 134), implying that the majority of them were Suebi.
5. Condensed by the author from Caesar, *The Conquest of Gaul*, VII. 14.
6. Richard Stillwell, William L. MacDonald, Marian Holland McAllister, Ed. *AVARICUM (Bourges) Cher, France*, The Princeton Encyclopedia of Classical Sites, perseus.tufts.edu.
7. Caesar, *The Conquest of Gaul*, VII.25.
8. Ibid. VII.29.
9. According to Caesar there were many archers in Gaul (Caesar, *The Conquest of Gaul*, VII.31), although he rarely mentions the bow being used in battle. Fuller speculates that the Gauls used the bow primarily for hunting (Fuller, *Julius Caesar, Man, Soldier, and Tyrant*, p. 138).
10. Ibid. VII.38.
11. Handford suggests that Caesar's real objective was to capture the town by a surprise attack (Caesar, *The Conquest of Gaul*, p. 234).

Chapter 15

1. Caesar, *The Conquest of Gaul*, VII. 86.
2. The presence of the Harii and Aestii is speculative. Caesar never clarifies what tribes his Germanic auxiliaries hailed from, although presumably most came from tribes living close to the Rhine.
3. The scene of the Germanic warriors around the campfires of Caesar's legions is based on descriptions of Germanic tribesmen given by Caesar and Tacitus.
4. Caesar, *The Conquest of Gaul*, VII.71.
5. Plutarch, who lavishes praise upon Caesar throughout his biography, gives an even greater total of 300,000 Gauls for the relief army and 170,000 for the defenders of Alesia.
6. Caesar, *The Conquest of Gaul*, VII.76.
7. Ibid. VII. 86.
8. Ibid. VII. 89.
9. Florus, *Epitome of Roman History*, I.XLVI. The description of Vercingetorix's surrender is a combination of Caesar's, Florus' and Plutarch's narratives, all of which differ slightly.
10. Hirtius in Caesar, *The Conquest of Gaul*, VIII. 36.
11. Plutarch, *Greek and Roman Lives*, p. 335.
12. Suetonius, *The Twelve Caesars*, I. 54.

13. There were minor rebellions in Aquitania in 39 and 30 BC. Another rebellion occurred in 21 AD, as Gaul groaned under the heavy taxation that Rome demanded to finance her campaigns against the German tribes. The Aedui noble, Iulius Sacrovir and the Treveri Iulius Florus, led a weak rebellion easily suppressed by the Romans (Tacitus, *The Annals of Imperial Rome*, translated by Michael Grant, (London: Penguin Books, 1996) p. 139).
14. Suetonius, *The Twelve Caesars*, I. 37.
15. Ibid.I.49
16. Ibid.I.51
17. According to Dio, the affair with Nicomedes vexed Caesar greatly, but whenever he tried to defend himself he only incurred more ridicule.
18. Suetonius, *The Twelve Caesars*, I. 37.
19. Fuller, *Julius Caesar, Man, Soldier, and Tyrant*, p. 285.

Chapter 16
1. Dio, *Roman History*, LV.1.
2. Cary and Scullard estimated from 70 to a 100 million inhabitants of the Roman Empire at the time of Augustus (Cary and Scullard, 1988, p. 339). More recent estimates are lower, Reymer giving a number of 55 million during the first half of the 1st century AD (Reymer, 2012, p. 31) and Kelly 60 million in the 2nd century AD (Kelly, 2006, p. 1).
3. Wells, *The Battle That Stopped Rome*, p. 57.
4. Under Augustus' terms of service, pay and pensions were standardized for both the legions and the auxiliaries. After serving twenty years, the last four on garrison duty in a veteran's corps, the legionaries retired on land grants in the provincial colonies. In 6 AD regular service was extended to the full twenty years. In compensation, money grants for retirement, which increasingly replaced the land grants, were increased and a special fund was set up for them (Cary and Scullard, *A History of Rome*, p 338, Ross Cowan, *Roman Legionary 58 BC–AD 69*, p. 12, 13, Tacitus, *The Annals of Imperial Rome*, I. 36, Suetonius, *The Twelve Caesars*, II. 49).
5. Strabo, *The Geography of Strabo*. VII.1.
6. Jonathan Stock, *Die Stadt Der Stadte*, Geo Epoche Nr. 54 (Hamburg: Gruner + Jahr AG& Co, 2012), p. 121.
7. Pliny the Elder, *The Natural History*, translated by John Bostock and H.T. Riley, Book XVI, Chapter 2, "Wonders connected with Trees in the Northern Regions," Perseus Digital Library.
8. Suetonius, *The Twelve Caesars*, III. 3, V.I.
9. Robert J. Hoeksema, *Designed for Dry Feet, Flood Protection and Land Reclamation in the Netherlands* (Virginia: American Society of Civil Engineers, 2006) p. 7–8 and *Encyclopedia Britannica*, "Zuiderzee", britannica.com.
10. Seneca quoted in *The Germanic Tribes*, DVD. Part I. Chapter 12.
11. Tacitus. *The Agricola and The Germania*, p. 126.
12. Dr. Klaus Grote, "Römer lager bei Hedemünden," grote-archaeologie.de.
13. Dio, *Roman History*, LV.1.
14. Strabo, *Geography*, VII.1.3, Suetonius, *The Twelve Caesars*, III.9.
15. For the identification of Aliso with Haltern see Jona Lendering's article, "The Battle in the Teutoburg Forest (7)," in Livius, livius.org.

Chapter 17
1. Velleius Paterculus quoted in Delbrück, *The Barbarian Invasions* p. 94.
2. All that is known for sure is that prior to the Teutoburg battle, Arminius, like his brother, served as an auxiliary with the Romans and was rewarded for his service. Since the Romans needed troops to deal with the Pannonian and Illyrian uprising, it is reasonable to assume

that this is where Arminius and Flavus served (assuming Flavus was born within a decade of Arminius' birthdate).

3. Stephan Dando-Collins, *Legions of Rome*, p. 237.
4. Velleius Paterculus quoted in Delbrück, *The Barbarian Invasions* p. 93.
5. Ibid. p. 93.
6. Other than Germania, only the freshly subdued Illyricum contained a garrison of five legions (Michael McNally, *Teutoburg Forest AD 9*. Oxford: Osprey Publishing, 2011. p. 18).
7. Florus quoted in Delbrück, *The Barbarian Invasions* p. 95.
8. Ibid. p. 95.
9. March was fittingly named after Mars.
10. The name "Teutoburger Forest" is indicated to us solely by Tacitus, in a single passage ("saltus Teutoburgienses", Tacitus, *The Annals of Imperial Rome*, p. 67). In all probability, "Teutoburg" means "people's castle" (Volksburg)" wrote Hans Delbrück (*The Barbarian Invasions*, p. 79). However, Theodor Mommsen (1817–1903) suggested that "forest" might mean "gap", as in the narrow gap between the forest and the marshlands near Kalkriese where the battle occurred (Michael McNally, *Teutoburg Forest AD 9* (Oxford: Osprey Publishing, 2011), p. 5, 6)
11. The exact location of Varus summer camp remains unknown; possibly it lies under the streets of Minden (McNally, *Teutoburg Forest 9 AD*, p. 29).
12. The estimated strength of 12,000 soldiers for all three legions is based on reduced legion strength due to past attrition and due to garrison duties back in Germania Inferior and in outposts along the route to Varus' summer camp. McNally provides a detailed analysis of the strength and deployment of the Roman army in Germania (McNally, *Teutoburger Forest 9 AD*, p. 18–22).
13. Until 197 AD, when Emperor Septimius Severus lifted the restriction, legionaries were not allowed to marry and marriages prior to enrollment were made void. Despite this there were many unofficial marriages and relationships with camp followers (Dando-Collins Stephen, *Legions of Rome*, p. 21, Wells, *The Battle that Stopped Rome*, p. 94).
14. Velleius Paterculus, *History of Rome*, II, 119.
15. Velleius Paterculus quoted in Delbrück, *The Barbarian Invasions* p. 94
16. Ibid. p. 93.
17. Tacitus, *The Annals of Imperial Rome*, 64.
18. Depending on the density of surrounding settlements, Wells estimates anywhere from 17,000 to 100,000 potential German warriors (Wells, *The Battle That Stopped Rome*, p. 123, 124). McNally adds that the recent Roman campaigns would have taken a toll on the German manpower available which, unlike the Romans, the Germans could only make up through natural population growth (McNally, *Teutoburg Forest 9 AD*, p. 23).
19. Boiocalus later regained his freedom and became king of the Ampsivarii (Tacitus, *Annals*, XIII, 55).
20. To increase their mobility during skirmishes and lacking any body armor, many tribesmen would have stripped the cumbersome woolen clothing they would have normally worn.
21. The site of Varus last camp remains unknown but may have been the Felsenfeld, literally meaning field of rocks or cliffs, near Schwagstorf (McNally, *Teutoburg 9 AD*, p. 66).
22. British army officer Tony Clunn's 1987–8 remarkable discoveries of Roman catapult slingshot in the Kalkriese area, sparked further research by Dr. Wolfgang Schlüter of the Osnabrück Department for Preservation of Archaeological Monuments. Ten years later, there was no doubt that the location of the Teutoburg battle had been found (Tony Clunn, *Quest for the Lost Legions, Discovering the Varus Battlefield* (New York: Savas Beatie LLC, 2009) p. xvi, 1).

Heretofore, the location had been merely hypothetical, with the most common view being held that the battle occurred near Detmold, as championed by Delbrück (1848–1929) in his exhaustive third volume of the History of the Art of War, "The Barbarian

Invasions." It was Theodor Mommsen (1817–1903), however, who correctly theorized that the battle occurred father north and west, near Osnabrück (T. Mommsen, *A History of Rome under the Emperors* (London: Routledge, 1992, p. 99–100)).

23. The loss of 13,000 dead over the 20–30 km is an estimate taken from Clunn, "Give me back my Legions," *Osprey Military Journal*, p. 34.

24. The primary sources make no direct mention of two of Varus' legion commanders, the legates. The senior officers that are mentioned commanding the legions near the end of the multi-day battle are the two camp prefects, Caeonius and Eggius, and Vala Numonius who near the end of the battle commanded the Roman cavalry. Varus' third camp prefect was left commanding a fort east of the Rhine (Velleius, II, 119), almost certainly Aliso. The absence of the legates and broad-strip tribunes (second in command of a legion) may mean that by the time Ceonius and Eggius are mentioned, most of the legion's senior commanders were already killed. Alternatively, based on the Alfred John Church and William Jackson Brodribb translation, the legions may have been unofficered in the first place (Tacitus, *Annals*, II, 46), though the actual Latin text, "vagas legiones," is usually meant to mean "straggling legions," which makes more sense (Tacitus, translated by Michael Grant, p. 100). The rank of Vala Numonius has seen various interpretations, McNally considering him to be the commander of all three legions of Germania Inferior (McNally, *Teutoburg 9 AD*, p. 18) while Dando-Collins considers him a mere prefect of one of Varus' three cavalry wings (Dando-Collins, *The Legions*, p. 239), for example. The Latin text says, "Vala Numonius, legatus Vari," (Perseus Digital Library), meaning that Vala was one of Varus' legates, or legion commanders, which was Delbrück's opinion as well (Delbrück, *The Barbarian Invasions*, p. 95).

25. The attack on the camp of Varus is based on Tacitus' description of the discovery of the battle site and the recounting of events by survivors of the massacre (Tacitus, *Annals*, I, 61). Tacitus actually wrote that the attack happened on Varus' first camp, something that is difficult to reconcile with Dio's account of a multiday running battle (Dio, *Roman History*, Book LVI, 21) and the well over 40 miles trek through adverse terrain and weather until the final, archeologically attested, battle ground at Kalkriese could be reached.

26. Eggius "set a noble example," according to Paterculus (*History of Rome*, II, cxix) as quoted in Delbrück, *The Barbarian Invasions*, p. 94.

27. The Kalkriese finds clarified the location of the Teutoburg battle but also raised new questions. Many of the events of the battle and the campaign remain ambiguous. The scattered Roman military and civilian artifacts at Kalkriese match the ambush at the end of Dio's multiday battle and the forests and swamps of Paterculus. However, none of the literary sources mention the barbarian rampart and the large concentration of Roman objects, discovered at what was apparently the final ambush on Varus' marching column. Conversely, if Varus met his end along the rampart then what of Tacitus' account of Varus meeting his end during a final barbarian assault on the Roman camp? The discovery of the grass muffled mule bells presented yet another mystery.

 With many aspects of the Teutoburg battle open to speculation, historians recreating the battle arrive at different conclusions. Most accounts, from Delbrück to Clunn (Clunn, "Give me back my Legions," *Osprey Military Journal*, p. 31–40) follow Dio's narrative in that the battle was a multiday ambush climaxing in a final doomed stand by the worn down legions. Wells' narrative, on the other hand, limits the entire battle to an hour-long ambush and massacre. He considers Dio's descriptions embellishments to dramatize the story (Wells, *The Battle That Stopped Rome*, p. 176, 228). Modern accounts, like Wells, McNally and Dando-Collins, include the barbarian rampart in their version, but even the nature of the rampart has been disputed. Dando-Collins intriguingly considers the barrier to have been part of Varus' last camp (Dando-Collins, *Legions of Rome* p. 248). With much of the battlefield remaining buried, future discoveries will no doubt add to the knowledge and discussion of the battle.

28. Dio Cassius quoted in Delbrück, *The Barbarian Invasions*, p. 93.

29. Caelius' name and career was preserved into modern times on a tombstone erected by his brother (McNally, Teutoburg 9 AD, p. 40).
30. As opposed to the broad-strip tribunes of the Imperial army, who were the second in command of a legion and usually earned their rank after years of military service, the thin-striped tribunes were teenage officer cadets who served on the legate's staff and had no military authority. This differed from the Republican legion, where all six tribunes of a legion rotated military command over two cohorts each (Stephan Dando Collins, *Legions of Rome*, p. 42–43).
31. Florus quoted in Delbrück, *The Barbarian Invasions*, p. 95.
32. Delbrück, *The Barbarian Invasions*, p. 96.
33. Peter Wells estimates 500 killed and another 1,500 wounded (Wells, *The Battle That Stopped Rome*, p. 182).
34. Archaeology shows that the Roman bases on the River Lippe at Anreppen, Oberaden and Holsterhausen, not mentioned in the classical sources, were abandoned in 9 AD (Wells, *The Battle That Stopped Rome*, p. 103, 104).
35. Suetonius, *The Twelve Caesars*, II.23.

Chapter 18
1. Tacitus, "The Annals," translated by Alfred John Church and William Jackson Brodribb, The Internet Classics Archive, classics.mit.edu., Book II.88.
2. Ibid. Book. I.23.
3. Ibid. Book. I.28.
4. Ibid. Book. I.31.
5. Tacitus. *The Annals of Imperial Rome*, translated by Michael Grant, (London: Penguin Books, 1996), p. 51.
6. Tacitus, "The Annals," translated by Church and Brodribb, Book II. 88.
7. Ibid.
8. Tacitus. *The Annals of Imperial Rome*, translated by Michael Grant, p. 58.
9. Tacitus, "The Annals," translated by Church and Brodribb, I. 49.
10. Tacitus, *The Annals of Imperial Rome*, translated by Michael Grant p. 60.
11. Ibid. I. 49, p. 61.
12. Tacitus, "The Annals," translated by Church and Brodribb, Book I. 51.
13. Ibid. I.51.
14. Ibid. I.58.
15. Ibid. I.58.
16. Ibid. I.57.
17. Ibid. I.59.
18. Tacitus, *The Annals of Imperial Rome*, translated by Michael Grant, p. 69.
19. Germanicus' debarking at or near the mouth of the Ems is based on Tacitus' narrative (Tacitus, *Annals*, II. 8). Since his ultimate destination was the Cherusci lands east of the Weser, the question remains why Germanicus disembarked on the Ems and then proceeded to undertake the long overland march east to the Weser. Instead he could have just sailed up the Weser; after all the whole point of building the fleet was to facilitate a faster approach. To compound the confusion, Tacitus seems to indicate that the Angrivarii revolted to the rear of Germanicus' camp on the Ems, even though the Angrivarii lived on both sides of the lower Weser. More however, in the next section, Germanicus suddenly appears on the Weser (Tacitus, *Annals*, II. 9) without a single word about the journey between the two rivers. Delbrück pointed out that Tacitus was prone to errors in geography and tribal names (Delbrück, *The Barbarian Invasions*, p. 97–98). According to Delbrück, Germanicus in his AD 16 campaign sailed up the Weser and not Ems (Delbrück p. 112).
20. Tacitus, "The Annals," translated by Church and Brodribb, Book II. 9.

21. Ibid. II.12.
22. Ibid. II.13.
23. Ibid.
24. For Roman auspices before battle see Livy 6.41, 10.40., and Jörg Rüpke, "Legitimizing Men," in *A Companion to the Roman Republic*, edited by Nathan Rosenstein (Robert Morstein-Marx. West Sussex: Blackwell Publishing Ltd. 2010) p. 229.
25. Tacitus, op. cit. II.15.
26. Tony Clunn speculates that the Idistaviso was the plain to the south of Minden and the Weser's passage through the Westfalica Gate (Tony Clunn, *Quest for the Lost Legions*, p. XXXVIII). Akin to Tacitus' description, the river bends outward to the west, enclosing a plain with forested hills rising to the east.
27. The color of legionary tunics remains a matter of speculation. Red was cheap to die, and partially because of this is favored by many historians (Stephan Dando-Collins, *Legions of Rome*, p. 30).
28. Due to different and contradictory primary sources, the size of the Imperial legion "continues to be the subject of confusion and disagreement," (*The Size and Organization of the Roman Imperial Legion*, Jonathan Roth, Historia: Zeitschrift fur Alte Geschichte Volume. 43, Issure 3 (3rd Qtr., 1994) published by Franz Steiner Verlag, p. 346–362). "From 30 BC, Augustus took the 6,000 man republican legion, with its ten cohorts of 600 men, and turned it into a unit with nine cohorts of 480 men, and a so-called 'double strength' 1st cohort of 800 men … to this Augustus added a legionary cavalry squadron of 128 men, making a legion, on paper, amount to 5,248 men." (Stephen Dando-Collins, *Legions of Rome* (New York: Thomas Dunne Books, 2010, p. 17). Goldsworthy comes to a similar conclusion, of ten cohorts of 480 men each with an oversized first cohort of 800 men "for at least some of our period," (Goldsworthy, *The Roman Army at War 100 BC-200 AD*, p. 14) and a cavalry contingent of 120 men from the early empire onward (Goldsworthy, p. 13–16), as did Salway: "A legion had a nominal strength of something over 5000 men, and was divided into ten cohorts, each of 480 men, except the first, which probably had 800" (Salway, *A History of Roman Britain*, p. 59). McNally added that each cohort was attended by 120 servants, 20 for each *centuriae* of 80 legionaries (McNally, *Teutoburg Forest 9 AD*, p. 18), so that each legion was supported by 1,200 servants. Legions, however, were rarely at full strength, accounting for losses in battle, due to disease or due to having detachments on garrison duty, hence the range of 3,000 to over 5,000 men in the legions of Germanicus' army.
29. Tacitus, *The Agricola and the Germania*, p. 103.
30. Tacitus, *Ther Annals of Imperial Rome*, translated by Michael Grant, pp. 84–5.
30. Tacitus, "The Annals," translated by Church and Brodribb, Book II.18.
31. Ibid. II.19.
32. The location of the Angrivarii barrier remains unknown, other than that it was along the tribal boundary of the Angrivarii and Cherusci.
33. Ibid. II.22.
34. Ibid. II.24.
35. Ibid. II.26.
36. Tacitus, *The Annals of Imperial Rome*, translated by Michael Grant, p. 238.
37. Ibid. p. 239.
38. Tacitus, "The Annals," translated by Church and Brodribb, Book II. 45.
39. Tacitus, *The Agricola and the Germania*, p. 132.
40. Tacitus, "The Annals," translated by Church and Brodribb, Book II. 46.
41. Ibid.
42. Tacitus. *The Annals of Imperial Rome*, translated by Michael Grant. p. 119. Not surprisingly, Arminius, traditionally known as Hermann in Germany, became a symbol of German nationalism. After the Franco-Prussian War (1870–1871), the famous Hermannsdenkmal,

begun 30 years earlier, was completed. Designed by sculptor Ernst von Bandel, the Hermannsdenkmal looms high above the wooden slopes of the Teutoberg Mountain in North Rhine Westphalia. The 170-foot tall monument is topped by a gigantic Arminius. The statue depicts Arminius with long hair flowing from beneath a winged helmet. A regal beard adorns his noble face. Arminius rests one arm on his shield, while with the other arm he victoriously raises his sword to the sky. Today the Hermannsdenkmal is a major tourist destination (Michael McNally, *Teutoburg Forest AD 9*, p. 5 and *Encyclopeidia Britannica, Detmold*, britannica.com). Another impressive Hermann monument stands in New Ulm Minnesota (newulm.com).

43. Suetonius, *The Twelve Caesars*, p. 140.

Sources

Chapter 1
The natural environment of the Mediterranean lands: Cary and Scullard, *A History of Rome,* p. 4, 5.

Life in early Latium: Cary and Scullard, *A History of Rome,* p. 15, 31, 32.

Etruscan civilization: Cary and Scullard, *A History of Rome,* p. 19, 21, 25, 26, 34, 35, G. Barker and T. Rasmussen, *The Etruscans* (Oxford: Blackwell Publishers LTD, 1998) p. 80–84, S. Moscati Tarquinia, "An Etruscan city-state" in *Vanished Civilizations* (Sydney: Readers Digest, 1983), p. 126, 129, 131, 133.

Legend and myths of the founding of Rome: Cary and Scullard, *A History of Rome,* p. 29, 35, 40, Trip Edward, *The Meridian Handbook of Classical Mythology* (New York: New American Library, 1988), p. 513–517.

Rome under the Etruscans : Cary and Scullard, *A History of Rome* p. 32, 33, 39, 41, 42, 45, 56, S. Moscati, Tarquinia, "An Etruscan city-state" in *Vanished Civilizations,* p. 129, 130, 132, 133, H. Delbrück *Warfare in Antiquity* (Lincoln: University of Nebraska Press, 1990) p. 259, 260.

Etruscan and early Roman wars in Italy: Cary and Scullard, *A History of Rome* p. 26, 55, 70–72, M. Bunson *A Dictionary of the Roman Empire* (New York: Oxford University, 1991), p. 264, P. Wilcox and T. Rafael *Barbarians against Rome* (Oxford: Osprey Publishing, 2000), p. 8.

Chapter 2
Primary Sources:
Plutarch, "The Life of Camillus." *Plutarch's Lives,* translated by Bernadotte Perrin (London: William Heinemann Ltd, 1959), XIV 2, XVII 1–6, XVIII, XIX, XXII.1,2,5,6, XXIII, XXVII, XXVIII, XXIX 4, 5., Dio, *Roman History,* translated by Earnest Cary (London: William Heinemann LTD., 1914), XIV113.4, 113.5, 114.1–4, 115.3–7, 116.7, Livy, *The History of Rome,* Volume V, translated by Roberts Canon, XXXV- XLIX., Polybius, *The Histories,* translated by W.R. Paton (London: William Heinemann LTD., 1967), Book I.

Secondary Sources:
On the origins of the Celts and their arrival into Europe: Cary M. and H. H. Scullard, *A History of Rome,* p. 13, 14, 72, 73, Kimmig W. "The Heuneburg" in *Vanished Civilizations,* p. 134–136, J. Campbell *The Masks of God: Occidental Mythology* (New York: Penguin Books. 1982), p. 293, P. Wilcox and T. Rafael, *Barbarians Against Rome,* p. 53, 54, 56, Norman J.G. Pounds, *An historical geography of Europe* (London: Cambridge University Press), p. 48, Barry Cunliffe, "Iron Age Societies in Western Europe and Beyond, 800–140 BC, in *Prehistoric Europe,* ed. B. Cunliffe (Oxford: Oxford University Press, 1993) p. 358, 361, M. Bunson, *A Dictionary of the Roman Empire* (New York: Oxford University Press, 1991), p. 140, J. Strayer and others. *The Mainstreams of Civilization* (New York: Harcourt, Brace & World, 1969), p. 12, 13.

Early Roman and Gallic armies: Wilcox and Rafael, *Barbarians Against Rome* p. 25, 28, 58, 59, 61, 64–72, N Sekunda and others, *Caesar's Legions. The Roman Soldier 753 BC to 117 AD* (Oxford: Osprey Publishing, 2000), p. 48, 49, Cary and Scullard, *A History of Rome* p. 52, 53, 73, notes

p. 590, Fuller J.F.C., *The Decisive Battles of the Western World*. Volume I. (London: Paladin Grafton Books, 1988), p. 117, 118.

The political and military consequences of the Roman losses to the Gauls: Cary and Scullard, *A History of Rome* p. 72, 84, 85, Sekunda and others, *Caesar's Legions, the Roman Soldier 753 BC to 117 AD*, p. 37, Cunliffe, "Iron Age Societies in Western Europe and Beyond, 800–140 BC," in *Prehistoric Europe*, p. 365–367.

The battle of the Allia and the sack of Rome: Cary and Scullard, *A History of Rome*, p. 73, 74, 590 Note 17, Ellis, *Celt and Roman: The Celts In Italy*, p10.

The Celts in Greece and Asia Minor: T. Taylor, Thracians, "Scythians and Dacians, 800 BC–AD 300" in *Prehistoric Europe*, p. 399, 401, also T. Newark *Celtic Warrior* (Poole: Blandford Press, 1986) and H. Bengston *History of Greece* (Ottawa: The University of Ottawa Press, 1988)

The continuing struggle between Celts, Romans and Etruscans for north Italy: Cary and Scullard, *A History of Rome*, p. 72, 85, 87, 93 and S. Moscati "Tarquinia, An Etruscan city-state" in *Vanished Civilizations*, p. 133, The Celtic Dollberg Fortress: Gemeinde Nonnweiler, Terrex gGmbH, Projekt Ringwall von Otzenhausen. "Virtueller Rundweg." *Keltischer Ringwall Otzenhausen*, keltenring-otzenhausen.de.

Chapter 3
Primary Sources:
Polybius, *The Histories*, Book II. 14–34, Livy, *The History of Rome*, XXXV, XXXVI.

Secondary Sources:
The Samnite, Etruscan, Pyrrhus and Gallic wars: Cary and Scullard, *A History of Rome*, p. 84, 87–96, 121–123, Moscati, Sabatino, "Tarquinia, An Etruscan city-state", in *Vanished Civilizations*, p. 133, Paul McDonnell, The Battle of Telamon (part 2) 225 BC, *Ancient Warfare Magazine*, karwansaraypublishers.com, 2013.

Vulnerability of Roman armor: Adrian K.Goldsworthy, *The Roman Army at War 1 00 BC–200 AD* (Oxford: Claredon Press. 1998), p. 220.

The Celtic Warrior: Wilcox and Trevino, *Barbarians Against Rome*, p. 54, 58–61, 68, 70–74, 95.

Legion symbols: Sekunda and others, Caesar's Legions. *The Roman Soldier 753 BC to 117 AD*, p. 27.

Roman colonies: Cary and Scullard, *A History of Rome*, p. 102.

First and Second Punic War: Cary and Scullard, *A History of Rome*, p. 116, 125, 136, 137, John King, *Kingdoms of the Celts* (London: Blandford, 2000) p. 77.

Roman conquest of Cisalpine Gaul: Cary and Scullard, *A History of Rome*, p. 139, 140, Peter Berresford Ellis, *The Celtic Empire* (London: Constable, 1990), p. 38–43.

Macedonian Wars: Cary and Scullard, *A History of Rome*, p. 151, 154, 155.

Early Celtic culture: Cunliffe, "Iron Age Societies in Western Europe and Beyond, 800–140 BC, in *Prehistoric Europe*, p. 361, King, *Kingdoms of the Celts*, p. 15, 18, 61, 62.

Germanic Celtic interactions: Ellis, *The Celtic Empire*, p. 41, Gemeinde Nonnweiler, Terrex gGmbH, Projekt Ringwall von Otzenhausen, "Gaius Julius Caesar - de bello gallico," *Keltischer Ringwall Otzenhausen*, keltenring-otzenhausen.de.

Chapter 4
Primary Sources:
Appian, *Appian's Roman History*, translated by Horace White (London: William Heinemann, 1912), Book VI (the Spanish Wars).X.58–62, 65, XI.63–66, XII.67–75, Dio. *Roman History*, XXII.73, 78 and Polybius, *The Histories*, XXXIV.5, XXXV.1.

Secondary Sources:
Cultures of Spain: Wilcox and Trevino, *Barbarians Against Rome*, p. 99–102, 104, Cary and Scullard, *A History of Rome*, p. 124.
Rome in Spain and the Viriathus wars: Wilcox and Trevino, *Barbarians Against Rome*, p. 108–115, Cary and Scullard, *A History of Rome*, p. 141–143, Cunliffe, Iron Age Societies in Western Europe and Beyond, 800–140 BC, in *Prehistoric Europe*, p. 370, Simon. J. Keay, *Roman Spain* (University of California Press, 1988) p. 26, 33.
Spanish Armor and Weapons: Wilcox and Trevino, *Barbarians Against Rome*, p. 131–138.
The Gladius: Sekunda and others, *Caesar's Legions. The Roman Soldier 753 BC to 117 AD*, p. 60.

Chapter 5
Primary Sources:
Appian, *Appian's Roman History*, Book VI:IX 48, 49, XIII 80–83, XIV 84–89, XV 90, Dio, *Roman History*, XXIII.79, Livy, *The History of Rome*, translated by Canon Roberts, 1927, Books XXXII.1,7, 28, Plutarch, *Greek and Roman Lives*, translated by John Dryden (Minola: Dover Publications, 2005), p 194, Plutarch, *Plutarch's Lives*, Volume IV, translated by John Langhorne and William Langhorne (New York: Harper and Brothers, 1871), p. 39, Polybius, *The Histories*, Book XXXV.4.

Secondary Sources:
Hispanic tribes: Wilcox and Trevino, *Barbarians Against Rome*, p. 99, 100.
Numantine Wars: Wilcox and Trevino, *Barbarians Against Rome*, p. 115–119, 129–131, Cary and Scullard, *A History of Rome*, p. 145, 146.
The Spanish wars in general: Cunliffe, Iron Age Societies in Western Europe and Beyond, 800–140 BC, in *Prehistoric Europe*, p. 370, Cary and Scullard, *A History of Rome*, p. 141, 143.
Scipio and Carthage: Cary and Scullard, *A History of Rome*, p. 149.
The natural history of Spain: Nick Lloyd, "Iberia Nature, A guide to the environment, climate, wildlife, geography and nature of Spain," iberianature.com.

Chapter 6
Primary Sources:
Livy, *The History of Rome*, Volume 3, XXII.33, Volume 4, XXXI.10, XXXII.31, Volume 5, XXXIII.37, XXXIV.48, XXXV.3–5, 11, XXXVI. 38–40.

Secondary Sources:
Cary and Scullard, *A History of Rome*, p. 13, 140, 210, 211, Cunliffe, Iron Age Societies in Western Europe and Beyond, 800–140 BC, in *Prehistoric Europe*, p. 370, Cunliffe, "The Impact of Rome on Barbarian Society, 140 BC–AD 300," in *Prehistoric Europe*, p. 415, Bunson, A *Dictionary of the Roman Empire*, p. 265.

Chapter 7
Primary sources:
Plutarch, "The Life of Marius," *Plutarch's Lives*, XI.2–8, XIV 1–2, XV 4–5, XVI-XIX 2–7, XX 1–6, XXI 1–4, XXII 1–3, XXIII 1–6, XXIV 2–4, XXV 4–5, 7, XXVI 1–5, XXVII 1–6, Plutarch, *Greek and Roman Lives*, p. 194, Tacitus, *The Agricola and Germania*, translated by H. Mattingly and S.A. Handford (Ontario: Penguin Books, 1987), p. 131,132, Annaeus Florus, *Epitome of Roman History*, Book I., translated by E.S. Forster (London: William Heinemann Ltd., 1925), XXXVIII. 3,7–11,14,16–21, Appian, *Appian's Roman History*, XIII, Livy LXIII, LXV, LXVII, Dio, *Roman History*, XVII, Strabo, *The Geography of Strabo*, translated by Jones L. Horace (London: William Heinemann Ltd., 1923), 4.4.3, Frontinus, *The Stratagems and the Aqueducts of Rome* (London: William Heinemann, 1925), II. II.8, II.IV.6, Orosius, *The Seven Books of History against the Pagans*, translated by Roy J. Deferrari (Washington: The Catholic

University of America Press, 1961) p. 234–237, Caesar, *The Conquest of Gaul*, translated by S.A. Handford (London: Penguin Books, 1982), VII.77, Sallust, *Catiline's Conspiracy, the Jugurthine War, Histories*, translated by William W. Batstone (Oxford: University Press, 2010) 63. p. 94.

Secondary Sources:
The Cimbri and Teutones, Celts or Germans: Theodor Mommsen, *The History of Rome*, Volume III (London: Macmillan and Co., 1901) p. 431, Wilcox and Trevino, *Barbarians Against Rome*, p. 50–51, 86, Malcolm Todd, *Everyday Life of the Barbarians* (New York: Dorset Press, 1988), p. 3–4, Tacitus, *The Agricola and Germania*, Introduction X, King, *Kingdoms of the Celts*, p. 66, Ellis, *The Celtic Empire*, p. 121, J.N.G. and W.F. Ritchie, "Warriors and Warfare," in *The Celtic World*, edited by Miranda J. Green, (London: Routledge, 1995), p. 606, 607, Jurgen Malitz, *Die Historien des Poseidonius* (Munich: C.H. Beck'sche Verlagsbuchhandlung, 1983), p. 204–205.
Cimbri and Teutones migration and battles: P.A. Kildahl, *Caius Marius* (New York: Twayne Publishers Inc., 1968) p. 100, Wilcox and Trevino, *Barbarians Against Rome*, p. 83–86, Cunliffe, "The Impact of Rome on Barbarian Society, 140 BC–AD 300," in *Prehistoric Europe*, p. 416, 425, Duruy, *The History of Rome and the Roman People*, p. 490–492, Cary and Scullard, *A History of Rome*, p. 217–219, W.E. Heitland, *The Roman Republic* (Cambridge: Cambridge University Press, 1909), p. 364, 375, Mommsen, *The History of Rome*, Volume III, p. 433–437, 445, 448, 450, 451.
Barbarian Equipment: Wilcox and Trevino, *Barbarians Against Rome*, p. 16, Todd, *Everyday Life of the Barbarians*, p. 99.
Barbarian fighting tactics: Goldsworthy, *The Roman Army at War*. 100 BC–AD 200, p. 50, Mommsen, *The History of Rome*, Volume III, p. 432.
Cimbri war dogs: Stanley Coren, *Die Intelligenz der Hunde* (Reinbeck: Rowohlt Verlag GmbH., 1997), p. 185.
Career of Marius and legion reforms: Cary and Scullard, *A History of Rome*, p. 213, Kildahl, *Caius Marius*, p. 102–108, H.H. Scullard, *From Gracchi to Nero* (London: Methuen & Co. Ltd., 1976) p. 59, Peter Salway, *A History of Roman Britain* (Oxford: Oxford University Press, 1993), p. 21, Stephan Dando-Collins, *Legions of Rome* (New York: Thomas Dunne Books, 2010) p. 28, 73.
Legions on the march: Peter S.Wells, *The Battle that Stopped Rome*, (New York: W.W. Norton & Company, 2003), p. 131, 137, 138.

Chapter 8
Primary Sources:
Caesar, *The Conquest of Gaul*, I.1–31, 35, 40, Plutarch, The Life of Julius Caesar, *Plutarch's Lives*, XVIII, Appian, *Appian's History of Rome*, Book IV.XV.

Secondary Sources:
On Caesar : J.F.C. Fuller, *Julius Caesar, Man, Soldier, and Tyrant* (New Jersey: Da Capo Press, 1965), p. 49–50, 53, 56, 70–71,102, Bunson, *A Dictionary of the Roman Empire*, p. 66–67, Cary and Scullard p. 248–249, Allan Langguth, *A Noise of War* (New York: Simon and Schuster, 1994), p. 140–141, J. Strayer and others, *The Mainstreams of Civilizations* (New York: Harcourt, Brace & World. 1969), p. 70–71.
The Helvetii and Gaul at the time of Caesar : Cary and Scullard, *A History of Rome*, p. 259, Fuller, *Julius Caesar, Man, Soldier, and Tyrant*, p. 98, 100, Cunliffe, "The Impact of Rome on Barbarian Societies, 140 BC–AD 300, in *Prehistoric Europe*, p. 420, 421, Andres Furger-Gunti, *Die Helvetier: Kulturgeschichte eines Keltenvolkes* p. 118ff, *Encyclopedia Britannica*, *Geneva History*, britannica.com.
The Boii : Cary and Scullard, *A History of Rome*, p. 93, 139, Cunliffe, "Iron Age Societies in Western Europe and Beyond, 800–140 BC", in *Prehistoric Europe*, p. 364–365, 425.

Roman Society: Cary and Scullard, *A History of Rome*, p. 299–310, Salway, *A History of Roman Britain*, p. 20–21.

The Helvetii campaign: Langguth, *A Noise of War*, p. 162–163, Hans Delbrück, *Warfare in Antiquity*, translated by Walter J. Renfroe, Jr. (Lincoln: University of Nebraska Press, 1975) p. 470–478, Fuller, *Julius Caesar, Man, Soldier, and Tyrant*, p. 102–103, 106.

Caesar's Army: Kildahl, *Caius Marius*, p. 102, 105–106, Langguth, *A Noise of War*, p. 161.

The Celts in combat: Fuller, *Julius Caesar, Man, Soldier, and Tyrant*, p. 99, J.N.G. and Ritchie, *Warriors and Warfare in the Celtic World*, ed. Miranda J. Green (London: Routledge, 1995), p. 55.

Chapter 9

Primary Sources:

Caesar, *The Conquest of Gaul*, translated by S.A. Handford (London: Penguin Books, 1982), I.31–37, 39, 40–43, 45–54, IV. 2, 3, VI.10, 28, 29 Tacitus, *The Agricola and Germania*, *Germania*, 4–6, 10, 17, 38, Suetonius, *The Twelve Caesars*, translated by Robert Graves (London: Penguin Books, 1989), I. 43, Plutarch, *Greek and Roman Lives*, translated by John Dryden (Minola: Dover Publications, 2005) p. 337, 338, Orosius, *The Seven Books of History against the Pagans*, VI., Cicero, *De Divinatione*, translated by David Wardle (Oxford: Claredon Press, 2006), 1.41.

Secondary Sources:

Population of Germania and Gaul: Pounds, *A Historical Geography of Europe*, p. 115, Fuller, *Julius Caesar, Man, Soldier, and Tyrant*, p. 97.

Germania in Caesar's time: Todd, *Everyday Life of the Barbarians*, p. 34.

German legends: Eugen Hollerbach, *Father Rhine tells his Sagas*, (Köln: Rahmel-Verla GmbH, 1985) p. 7.

German tribal culture, weapons and equipment: Todd, *Everyday Life of the Barbarians*, p. 85, 101–103, Bunson, *A Dictionary of the Roman Empire*, p. 397.

Germans in Gaul and Caesar's campaign versus Ariovistus : Cary and Scullard, *A History of Rome*, p. 259, Bunson, *A Dictionary of the Roman Empire*, p. 28, 397, T. Rice Holmes, *The Roman Republic and the Founder of the Empire* (Oxford: Clarendon Press, 1923), p. 34, 35, Delbrück, *Warfare in Antiquity*, p. 481, Caesar, *The Conquest of Gaul*, Introduction p. 16, 24, 25, Tacitus, *The Agricola and Germania*, Introduction p. 31.

Romans on campaign: Sekunda and others, *Caesar's Legions. The Roman Soldier 753 BC to 117 AD*, p. 106, 109.

Chapter 10

Primary Sources:

Caesar, *The Conquest of Gaul*, I.1, 38, 54, II.1–35, III.1, 7, IV.21, Suetonius, *The Twelve Caesars*, p. 42, Plutarch, *Greek and Roman Lives*, p. 338, 339, Orosius, *The Seven Books of History against the Pagans*, p. 245.

Secondary Sources:

The Belgae and Celtic culture: Bunson, *A Dictionary of the Roman Empire*, p. 55, Caesar, *The Conquest of Gaul*, Introduction by Handford, p. 15, Goldsworthy, *The Roman Army at War. 100 BC–AD 200*, p. 55, Cary and Scullard, *A History of Rome*, p. 258.

The Belgae Campaign: Fuller, *Julius Caesar, Man, Soldier, and Tyrant*, p. 109–114, Caesar, *The Conquest of Gaul*, Notes, p. 229, Bunson, *A Dictionary of the Roman Empire*, p. 49, Delbrück, *Warfare in Antiquity*, p. 490–492.

Belgae and Celtic Weapons and Armor: Wilcox and Trevino, *Barbarians against Rome*, p. 65–72.

Caesar's Army: Caesar, *The Conquest of Gaul*, Appendix II. p. 242, Fuller, *Julius Caesar, Man, Soldier, and Tyrant*, p. 92–95, 134, Judson p. 19–21, Delbrück, *Warfare in Antiquity*, p. 488, Goldsworthy, *The Roman Army at War. 100 BC–AD 200*, p. 197–198, 201–202, 216, 218–221.

226 The Roman Barbarian Wars

The marching camp and a legionary's equipment: Sekunda and others, *Caesar's Legions. The Roman Soldier 753 BC to 117 AD*, p. 107–108, Stephen Dando-Collins, *Legions of Rome*, p. 69.

On Caesar : Fuller, *Julius Caesar, Man, Soldier, and Tyrant*, p. 53–54, Bunson, *A Dictionary of the Roman Empire*, p. 67, 429.

Crassus and the Maritime tribes: Fuller, *Julius Caesar, Man, Soldier, and Tyrant*, p. 115.

The metalwork of the Treveri : Gemeinde Nonnweiler, Terrex gGmbH, Projekt Ringwall von Otzenhausen, "Ironworking," *Keltischer Ringwall Otzenhausen*, keltenring-otzenhausen.de.

Chapter 11
Primary Sources:
Caesar, *The Conquest of Gaul*, III. 8–29, IV 1–19. Plutarch, *Greek and Roman Lives*, p. 340, Suetonius, *The Twelve Caesars*, p. 23, 24.

Secondary Sources:
On the Campaign against the Maritime tribes: Fuller, *Julius Caesar, Man, Soldier, and Tyrant*, p. 115–118, Jimenez, Ramon L., *Caesar against the Celts*. New York: Sarpedon, 1996, p. 81.

The Usipetes and Tencteri : Caesar, *The Conquest of Gaul*, Notes 23.

Chapter 12
Primary Sources:
Caesar, *The Conquest of Gaul*, IV.20, 22–38, V. 1–5, 8, 9–23., Plutarch, *Greek and Roman Lives*, p. 340, 341, Suetonius, *The Twelve Caesars*, p. 24.

Secondary Sources:
Caesar in Britain: Cary and Scullard, *A History of Rome*, p. 262, Fuller, *Julius Caesar, Man, Soldier, and Tyrant*, p. 121–124, Lloyd Laing, *Celtic Britain* (New York: Biblo and Tannen. 1961), p. 37, Salway, *A History of Roman Britain*, p. 93.

Roman Warships: Bunson, *A Dictionary of the Roman Empire*, p. 387.

Chapter 13
Primary Sources:
Caesar, *The Conquest of Gaul*, V.24, 26–58, VI. 1–10, 29–43, VII.1–8, 13–62. Plutarch, *Greek and Roman Lives*, p. 341, Suetonius, *The Twelve Caesars*, p. 24.

Secondary Sources:
On the Gallic revolt: Fuller, *Julius Caesar, Man, Soldier, and Tyrant*, p. 127–146.

The Treveri Dollberg stronghold: Gemeinde Nonnweiler, Terrex gGmbH, Projekt Ringwall von Otzenhausen, "Virtueller Rundweg," Keltischer Ringwall Otzenhausen, keltenring-otzenhausen.de.

Chapter 14
Primary Sources:
Caesar, *The Conquest of Gaul*, V.24, 26–58, VI. 1–10, 29–43, VII.1–8, 13–62, Plutarch, *Greek and Roman Lives*, p. 342, Suetonius, *The Twelve Caesars*, p. 24.

Secondary Sources:
On the Gallic revolt: Fuller, *Julius Caesar, Man, Soldier, Tyrant*, p. 127–146.

On Vercingetorix : King, *The Kingdoms of the Celts*, p. 122–131.

Chapter 15
Primary Sources:
Caesar, *The Conquest of Gaul*, I. 36, 47, IV.2, 13, 15, VI.13, 21, 26, VII. 62, 63, 65–89, VIII.1–49, Dio, *Roman History*, XLIII., Florus, *Epitome of Roman History*, I.XLV, Plutarch, *Greek and Roman Lives*, p. 343, Suetonius, *The Twelve Caesars*. I. 25, 39, 49, 51, Tacitus, *The Agricola and Germania*, G. 4, 6, 43, 45.

Secondary Sources:
Gallic and German Swords: Wilcox and Trevino, *Barbarians Against Rome*, p. 71.
German retainers and bodyguards: Goldsworthy, *The Roman Army at War. 100 BC–AD 200*, p. 70, 71, Fuller, *Julius Caesar, Man, Soldier, and Tyrant*, p. 134.
German cavalry and weapons: Todd, *Everyday Life of the Barbarians*, p. 98, 99, 101.
Caesar's cavalry and army: Jeremiah McCall, *The Cavalry of the Roman Republic*, (New York: Routledge, 2002) p. 100, 101, Caesar, *The Conquest of Gaul*, Appendix p. 242.
Caesar vs. Vercingetorix : Delbrück, *Warfare in Antiquity*, p. 498, 499, 503, 504, Fuller, *Julius Caesar, Man, Soldier, and Tyrant*, p. 146–158.
End of the revolt: Fuller, *Julius Caesar, Man, Soldier, and Tyrant*, p. 164.
The aftermath: Bunson, *A Dictionary of the Roman Empire*, p. 44–46, 66, 67, 104, 429.

Chapter 16
Primary Sources:
Dio, *Roman History*, LIV 21, 32–34, 36, LV 1,2, 6–8, Suetonius, *The Twelve Caesars*, p. 65, 66, 82, 98, 115, 118 (Tiberius, 9), 186, 215 (Nero, 4), 185 (Claudius, 1), Tacitus, *The Annals of Imperial Rome*, I. 63, Tacitus, *The Agricola and Germania*, G.31, 35, 36, Strabo, *The Geography of Strabo*, VII.1.

Secondary Sources:
Augustus and his Imperial policies: Cary and Scullard, *A History of Rome*, p. 317, 320, 324, 331–336, 338, 347, Bunson, *A Dictionary of the Roman Empire*, p. 8, 100, 169.
Roman Society in the first Century: Cary and Scullard, *A History of Rome*, p. 300–306, 339, Christopher Kelly, *The Roman Empire, A Very Short Introduction* (Oxford: Oxford University Press, 2006) p. 1, Kluver Reymer, *Im Zentrum Der Macht*, Geo Epoche Nr. 54 (Hamburg: Gruner + Jahr AG & Co, 2012), p. 31, Peter S.Wells, *The Battle that Stopped Rome*, (New York: W.W. Norton & Company, 2003), p. 57, 58.
The Legions: Bunson, *A Dictionary of the Roman Empire*, p. 229, Cary and Scullard, *A History of Rome*, p. 338, 339, Stephen Dando-Collins, *Legions of Rome*, p. 18–22, Ross Cowan, *Roman Legionary 58 BC–AD 69* (Oxford: Osprey Publishing, 2003) p. 12, 13.
Augustus' Germany policy: Fuller, *The Decisive Battles of the Western World*, Volume I, p. 171, G. P. Baker, *Tiberius Caesar*, (New York: Dodd, Mead & Company, 1928), p. 52, 53, T. Mommsen, *A History of Rome under the Emperors* (London: Routledge, 1992), p. 108, 109.
Rhaetia and Pannonian campaigns: Bunson, *A Dictionary of the Roman Empire*, p. 310, 356, E.S. Shuckburgh, *Augustus* (London: T.Fisher Unwin,1905) p. 181–183, Wells, *The Battle That Stopped Rome*, p. 154.
Drusus in Germania: Fuller, *The Decisive Battles of the Western World*, p. 172, Baker, *Tiberius Caesar*, p. 57–61, 92, Wells, *The Battle that Stopped Rome*, p. 89, 90. Bunson, *A Dictionary of the Roman Empire*, p. 263.
Tiberius in Germania: Bunson, *A Dictionary of the Roman Empire*, p. 416, 417, Todd, *Everyday Life of the Barbarians*, p. 17, Baker, *Tiberius Caesar*, p. 95, 96, Wells, *The Battle That Stopped Rome*, p. 158–160.
The nature of the Roman conquests in Germania: Delbrück, *Barbarian Invasions*, p. 52, 58–60, 61, 91, Cary and Scullard, *A History of Rome*, p. 335.

Maroboduus: Bunson, *A Dictionary of the Roman Empire*, p. 263, Baker, *Tiberius Caesar*, p. 94, 97, 98.

Pannonian insurrection: Bunson, *A Dictionary of the Roman Empire*, p. 310, Fuller, *The Decisive Battles of the Western World*, Volume I, p. 173, 174, Baker, *Tiberius Caesar*, p. 99–107, Cary and Scullard, *A History of Rome*, p. 337.

Germanic lifestyles: *The Germanic Tribes*, DVD directed by Alexander Hogh (West Long Branch: Kultur, 2009) Part I. Chapter 5, 6, 7, 9 Part II. Chapter 5, Bury, *The Invasion of Europe by the Barbarians* p. 6, 7.

Roman Settlements in Germania: Jona Lendering, "Oberaden", "Haltern", Livius, Articles on Ancient History, livius.org.

Deforestation in the Roman Empire: K.J.W. Oosthoek, "The Role of Wood in World History", Environmental History Resources, eh-resources.org.

Chapter 17
Primary Sources:
The main primary sources for the Teutoburger battle are Dio, *Roman History*, Book LVI Chapters 18–24, Velleius C. Paterculus, *Compendium of Roman History*, translated by Frederick W. Shipley (Cambridge: Harvard University Press, 1924) Book II, Chapters, 72, 117–120, and Florus, *Epitome of Roman History*, II.XXX., Tacitus, *The Annals of Imperial Rome*, Books I, II, XIII, Tacitus, *The Agricola and the Germania*, G.7, 11, 18, 25, Suetonius, *The Twelve Caesars*, II.23, 25, III.17–20, Strabo; *The Geography of Strabo*, Book VII., Frontinus, *The Stratagems and the Aqueducts of Rome*, II.IX.4.

Secondary Sources
Arminius' background: Fuller, The *Decisive Battles of the Western World*, Volume I, p. 175, Baker, *Tiberius Caesar*, p. 105, *The Germanic Tribes*, DVD, Part I, Chapter 2.

Varus' background: Bunson, *A Dictionary of the Roman Empire*, p. 112, 113, 238, 400, 439, Fuller, The *Decisive Battles of the Western World*, Volume I, p. 174, Wells, *The Battle That Stopped Rome*, p. 33, 80–83.

The Teutoburg Forest campaign: Tony Clunn, Major, "Give me back my Legions," *Osprey Military Journal*, Volume 3, Issue 4, p. 31–40, Delbrück, *The Barbarian Invasions*, p. 69–90, Wells, *The Battle That Stopped Rome*, p. 26, 27, 99, 111, 123, 124, 138, 139, 142, 143, 165, 166, 183–185, 189–193, McNally, *Teutoburg Forest 9 AD*, p. 32, 33, 37–39, 50, 66, 70, 72, 82, 84, Stephan Dando-Collins, *Legions of Rome*, p. 235, 239

The Roman Army: Sekunda and others, *Caesar's Legions. The Roman Soldier 753 BC to 117 AD*, p. 104–109, Mommsen, *A History of Rome under the Emperors* p. 113, Wells, *The Battle That Stopped Rome*, p. 20, 21, 25, 102, Bunson, *A Dictionary of the Roman Empire*, p. 230, Goldsworthy, *The Roman Army at War. 100 BC–AD 200*, p. 291, McNally, *Teutoburg Forest 9 AD*, p. 18–19, Stephen Dando-Collins, *Legions of Rome*, p. 22, 40–43, 66–68, 177, Ross Cowan, *Roman Legionary 58 BC–AD 69*, p. 13.

Trade between Germans and Romans: Todd, *Everyday Life of the Barbarians*, p. 15–17.

Settlements and lifestyle in Germania: Todd, *Everyday Life of the Barbarians*, p. 38–52, 65, 66, *Germanic Tribes*, DVD, Part I. Chapters 5, 6.

German weapons and armor: Todd, *Everyday Life of the Barbarians*, p. 99, McNally, *Teutoburg Forest 9 AD*, p. 23–25.

Consequences of the battle and comparison of the Republican versus the Imperial Army recruits: Mommsen, *A History of Rome under the Emperors*, p. 113–115, Sekunda and others, *Caesar's Legions. The Roman Soldier 753 BC to 117 AD*, p. 61, 62.

Chapter 18
Primary Sources:
Tacitus, *The Annals of Imperial Rome*, I, II, Tacitus, *The Agricola and The Germania*, p. 103, 132, Strabo, *The Geography of Strabo*, VII. 1, Suetonius, *The Lives of the Twelve Caesars*, II, III.

Secondary Sources:
Germanicus' career: Bunson, *A Dictionary of the Roman Empire*, p. 180.
Germanicus and Arminius : Delbrück, *The Barbarian Invasions*, p. 97–130, Wells, *The Battle That Stopped Rome*, p. 204–209, Stephen Dando-Collins, *Legions of Rome*, p. 265.
The battle of Long Bridges: Stephen Dando-Collins, *Legions of Rome*, p. 261–165.
The origin of the Twenty-first and Twenty-second legions: Mommsen, *A History of Rome under the Emperors*, p. 114.
Deployment of Roman legions in the Empire: Cary and Scullard, *A History of Rome*, p. 339.
The Roman army and the Praetorian Guard: Boris Rankov, *The Praetorian Guard*, (London: Osprey 1997), p. 30–32, 49, Goldsworthy, *The Roman Army at War. 100 BC–AD 200*, p. 15–18, Stephen Dando-Collins, *Legions of Rome*, p. 75, 265.
Roman Triumphal Marches: Stephen Dando-Collins, *Legions of Rome*, p. 81–81.

Bibliography

Primary Sources

Appian, Appian's *Roman History*. Translated by Horace White. London: William Heinemann, 1912.

Caesar, *The Conquest of Gaul*. Translated by S.A. Handford. London: Penguin Books, 1982.

Caesar, *The Gallic War*. Translated by H.J. Edwards. London: Harvard University Press, 1970.

Cicero, *De Divinatione*. Translated by David Wardle. Oxford: Clarendon Press, 2006.

Dio, *Roman History*. Translated by Earnest Cary. London: William Heinemann Ltd, 1914.

Dionysius, *The Roman Antiquities of Dionysius of Halicarnassus*. Translated by Earnest Cary. London: William Heinemann Ltd, 1960.

Florus Lucius Annaeus, *Epitome of Roman History*. Translated by E.S. Forster. London: William Heinemann Ltd, 1947.

Frontinus, *The Stratagems and the Aqueducts of Rome*. London: William Heinemann. 1925.

Herodotus, *Herodotus*. Translated by William Beloe. London: Henry Colburn and Richard Bentley. 1830.

Livius, *The History of Rome*. Translated by William A. M'Devitte. London: George Bell & Sons, 1903.

Livy, *The History of Rome*. Translated by Canon Roberts. London: New York: Dutto & Co. Inc, 1927.

Maximus Valerius, *Memorable Doings and Sayings*. London: Harvard University Press, 2000.

Orosius Paulus, *The Seven Books of History against the Pagans*. Translated by Deferrari Roy. J. Washington: The Catholic University of America Press, 1961.

Paterculus, Velleius C., *Compendium of Roman History*. Translated by Frederick W. Shipley. Cambridge: Harvard University Press, 1924.

Pliny the Elder, *The Natural History*. Translated by John Bostock and H.T. Riley. London: Taylor and Francis, 1855. Perseus Digital Library.

Plutarch, *Greek and Roman Lives*. Translated by John Dryden. Minola: Dover Publications, 2005.

Plutarch, *Caesar*. Translated and commentary by Christopher Pelling. Oxfort: Oxfort University Press, 2011.

Plutarch, *Plutarch's Lives*. Translated by Bernadotte Perrin. London: William Heinemann LTD, 1959.

Plutarch, *Plutarch's Lives*, Volume IV. Translated by John Langhorne and William Langhorne. New York: Harper and Brothers, 1871.

Polybius, *The Histories*. Translated by W.R. Paton London: William Heinemann LTD, 1967.

Sallust, *Catiline's Conspiracy, the Jugurthine War, Histories*, translated by William W. Batstone (Oxford: University Press, 2010).

Strabo, *The Geography of Strabo*. Translated by Horace L. Jones. London: William Heinemann Ltd, 1923.

Suetonius, *The Twelve Caesars*. Translated by Graves Robert. London: Penguin Books, 1989.

Tacitus, *The Agricola and the Germania*. Translated by H. Mattingly and S.A. Handford. Ontario: Penguin Books, 1987.

Tacitus, "The Annals." Translated by Alfred John Church and William Jackson Brodribb. *The Internet Classic Archive*. <http://classics.mit.edu/Tacitus/annals.html>
Tacitus, *The Annals of Imperial Rome*. Translated by Michael Grant. London: Penguin Books, 1996.

Secondary Sources
Baker G.P., *Tiberius Caesar*. New York: Dodd, Mead & Company, 1928.
Barker and Rasmussen, *The Etruscans*. Oxford: Blackwell Publishers Ltd, 1998.
Bengston Herman, *History of Greece*. Ottawa: The University of Ottawa Press, 1988.
Boardman J., J.Griffin and O. Murray Editors, *The Roman World*. Oxford: Oxford University Press, 1993.
Bunson Matthew, *A Dictionary of the Roman Empire*. New York: Oxford University, 1991.
——, *Encyclopedia of the Roman Empire*. New York: Facts on File Inc., 2002.
Bury J.B., *The Invasion of Europe by the Barbarians*. New York: The Norton Library, 1967.
Bury J.B. and Meiggs Russell, *A History of Greece*. London: Macmillan, 1987.
Campbell Joseph, *The Masks of God: Occidental Mythology*. New York: Penguin Books, 1982.
Cary M. and H.H Scullard, *A History of Rome*. London: Macmillan Education, 1988.
Clunn, Major Tony, "Give me back my Legions," *Osprey Military Journal*. July 2001, 31–40.
Clunn Tony, *Quest for the Lost Legions, Discovering the Varus Battlefield*. New York: Savas Beatie LLC, 2009.
Coren Stanley, *Die Intelligenz der Hunde*. Reinbeck: Rowohlt Verlag GmbH, 1997.
Cowan Ross, *Roman Legionary 58 BC–AD 69*. Oxford: Osprey Publishing, 2003.
Cunliffe Barry, "Iron Age Societies in Western Europe and Beyond, 800–140 BC." In *Prehistoric Europe*, edited by B. Cunliffe. 336–372. Oxford: Oxford University Press, 1993.
Cunliffe Barry, "The Impact of Rome on Barbarian Society, 140 BC–AD 300." In *Prehistoric Europe*, edited by B. Cunliffe. 411–446. Oxford: Oxford University Press, 1993.
Dando-Collins Stephen, *Legions of Rome*. New York: Thomas Dune Books, 2010.
Davies John, *The Celts*. London: Cassel & Co, 2000.
Degrassi A., *Fasti Capitolini*. Torino: G.B. Paravia, 1954.
Delbrück Hans, *The Barbarian Invasions*. Translated by Walter J. Renfroe, Jr. Lincoln: University of Nebraska Press, 1990.
Delbrück Hans, *Warfare in Antiquity*. Translated by Walter J. Renfroe, Jr. Lincoln: University of Nebraska Press, 1990.
Dupuy R. Ernest and N. Trevor, *The Encyclopedia of Military History*. London: Harper & Row, 1977.
Duruy Victor, *History of Rome*, Volume II. London: Kegan Paul, Trench & Co, 1884.
Ellis, Peter Beresford, *Celt and Roman: The Celts In Italy*. London: Constable, 1998.
Ellis, Peter Beresford, *The Celtic Empire*. London: Constable, 1990.
Fuller J.F.C., *Julius Caesar, Man, Soldier, and Tyrant*. New Jersey: Da Capo Press, 1965.
Fuller J.F.C., *The Decisive Battles of the Western World*. London: Paladin Grafton Books, 1988.
Furger-Gunti, Andres, *Die Helvetier: Kulturgeschichte eines Keltenvolkes*. Zürich: Neue Züricher Zeitung, 1984.
Gabriel Richard, *The Roman Navy, Masters of the Mediterranean*, Military History Magazine. Herndon: December, 2007.
Goldsworthy, Adrian Keith. *The Roman Army at War. 100 BC–AD 200*. Oxford: Clarendon Press, 1998.
Grote Klaus, "Römer lager bei Hedemünden", grote-archaeologie.de.
Harris Marvin, *Culture, People, Nature*. New York: Harper & Row, 1988.
Heitland W.E., *The Roman Republic*. Cambridge: Cambridge University Press, 1909.
Hessische Rundfunk. Hr online.de, *Julius Caesar an der Autobahn*. 2.05.2013.

Hoeksema Robert J., *Designed for Dry Feet, Flood Protection and Land Reclamation in the Netherlands*. Virginia: American Society of Civil Engineers, 2006.

Hollerbach Eugen, *Father Rhine tells his Sagas*. Köln: Rahmel-Verlag GMBH, 1985.

Holmes T. Rice, *The Roman Republic and the Founder of the Empire*. Oxford: Clarendon Press, 1923.

Hornung Sabine, Johannes Gutenberg-Universität Mainz, *Römisches Militärlager aus der Zeit der Eroberung Galliens erhellt ein Stück Weltgeschichte*, 28.08.2012, unimainz.de.

Jimenez, Ramon. L., *Caesar against the Celts*. New York: Sarpedon, 1996, p. 81.

J.N.G. and W.F. Ritchie, "Warriors and Warfare." *The Celtic World*. Edited by Miranda J. Green. London: Routledge, 1995.

Judson Harry P., *Caesar's Army*. New York: Biblo and Tannen, 1961.

Kagan Kimberly, *The Eye of Command*. Michigan: University of Michigan Press, 2006.

Keay Simon J., *Roman Spain*. University of California Press, 1988.

Kelly Christopher, *The Roman Empire, A Very Short Introduction*. Oxford: Oxford University Press, 2006.

Kildahl P.A., *Caius Marius*. New York: Twayne Publishers Inc, 1968.

Kimmig Wolfgang, "The Heuneburg". In *Vanished Civilizations*. Sydney: Readers Digest, 1983.

King John, *Kingdoms of the Celts*. London: Blandford, 2000.

Koch John T., *Celtic Culture a Historical Encyclopedia*. Santa Barbara: ABC-CLIO, 2006.

Laing Lloyd, *Celtic Britain*. New York: Charles Scribner's Sons, 1979.

Langguth Allan, *A Noise of War*. New York: Simon & Schuster., 1994.

Lendering Jona, "Caesar and the Aduatuci", "Haltern", "Oberaden", "The Battle in the Teutoburg Forest (7)", Livius, Articles on Ancient History, livius.org.

Lloyd Nick, "Iberia Nature, A guide to the environment, climate, wildlife, geography and nature of Spain", iberianature.com.

Malitz Jurgen, *Die Historien des Poseidonius*. Munich: C.H. Beck'sche Verlagsbuchhandlung, 1983.

McCall Jeremiah, *The Cavalry of the Roman Republic*. New York: Routledge, 2002.

McDonnell Paul, *The Battle of Telamon (part 2) 225 BC*, Ancient Warfare Magazine, karwansaraypublishers.com, 2013.

McNally Michael, *Teutoburg Forest AD 9*. Oxford: Osprey Publishing, 2011.

Mommsen Theodor, *The History of Rome*. London: Richard Bentley and Son, 1894.

Mommsen T., *The History of Rome*. Volume III. London: Macmillan and Co., 1901.

Mommsen T., *A History of Rome under the Emperors*. London: Routledge, 1992.

Mountain, Harry, *Celtic Encyclopedia*. Universal Publishers, 1998.

Moscati Sabatino, "Tarquinia, An Etruscan city-state." In *Vanished Civilizations*. Sydney: Reader's Digest, 1983.

Newark Tim, *Celtic Warriors*. Poole: Blandford Press, 1986.

Oosthoek K.J.W., "The Role of Wood in World History." Environmental History Resources, eh-recsources.org.

Pounds Norman J.G., *A historical geography of Europe. 450 BC–AD 1130*. London: Cambridge University Press, 1973.

Rankov Boris, *The Praetorian Guard*. London: Osprey, 1997.

Reymer Kluver, *Im Zentrum Der Macht* in Geo Epoche Nr. 54. Hamburg: Gruner + Jahr AG& Co, 2012, p. 31.

Richard Stillwell, William L. MacDonald, Marian Holland McAllister, Stillwell, Richard, MacDonald, William L., McAlister, Marian Holland, Ed. Avaricum (Bourges) Cher, France. The Princeton Encyclopedia of Classical Sites, perseus.tufts.edu.

Roth Jonathan, *The Size and Organization of the Roman Imperial Legion*, Historia: Zeitschrift fur Alte Geschichte Volume. 43, Issue 3 (3rd Qtr., 1994), published by Franz Steiner Verlag.

Rüpke Jörg, "Legitimizing Men," in *A Companion to the Roman Republic*, edited by Nathan Rosenstein, Robert Morstein-Marx. West Sussex: Blackwell Publishing Ltd. 2010.

Salway Peter, *A History of Roman Britain*. Oxford: Oxford University Press, 1993.

Sekunda N., S. Northwood, and M. Simkins, *Caesar's Legions. The Roman Soldier 753 BC to 117 AD*. Oxford: Osprey Publishing, 2000.

Scullard H.H., *From Gracchi to Nero*. London: Methuen & Co Ltd, 1976.

Sherratt Andrew, "The Emergence of Elites: Earlier Bronze Age Europe, 2500–1300 BC", in *Prehistoric Europe*, edited by B. Cunliffe. Oxford: Oxford University Press, 1993.

Shuckburgh E.S., *Augustus*. London: T. Fisher Unwin, 1905. Stadt Trier, "History", redaktion. trier.de.

Strayer J., H. Gatzke, E. Harbison, and E. Dunbaugh, *The Mainstreams of Civilization*. New York: Harcourt, Brace & World, 1969.

The Germanic Tribes. DVD. Directed by Alexander Hogh. West Long Branch: Kultur, 2009.

Taylor T., Thracians, "Scythians and Dacians, 800 BC–AD 300." In *Prehistoric Europe*, edited by B. Cunliffe. 373–410. Oxford: Oxford University Press, 1993.

Todd Malcolm, *Everyday Life of the Barbarians*. New York: Dorset Press, 1988.

Trip Edward, *The Meridian Handbook of Classical Mythology*. New York: New American Library, 1974.

Waldman, Carl and Catherine Mason, *Encyclopedia of European Peoples*. New York: Inforbase Publishing, 2006.

Wells Peter S., *The Battle that stopped Rome*. New York: W.W. Norton & Company, 2003.

Wilcox Peter and Rafael Trevino, *Barbarians Against Rome*. Oxford: Osprey Publishing, 2000.

Index

Aduatuci, Belgic tribe descended from Cimbri and Teutones, 93, 98–9, 119, 122, 125, 128, 130

Aedui, Gallic tribe, 50–1, 71–3, 76, 79–84, 90, 93, 127, 136–7, 139–43, 145, 147, 150, 208, 215

Aemilianus, Fabius Maximus, consul, 34

Aemilianus, P. Cornelius Scipio, consul, 42–6, 58, 210

Aemilius, Roman cavalry commander, 194

Agrippa, Marcus Vipsanius, Roman general, 155, 157–9, 168

Agrippina, wife of Germanicus, 192

Ahenobarbus, Gnaeus Domitius, proconsul 121 BC, 50–1

Ahenobarbus, Lucius Domitius, Roman commander in Germania 3 BC 163, 192

Aisne River (the Axona), Battle of, 57 BC, 90–3, 120

Alesia, Gallic stronghold, 144,
  Siege of, 146–50, 215
  numbers of defenders and size of relief army, 146–7, 215

Aliso (Haltern), Roman military camp, 163, 170, 182, 184, 189, 193, 216, 218

Allia, River, 9, 12
  Battle of, 390 BC, 9–11, 15
  size of armies, 9–10, 208

Allobroges, Gallic tribe, 50, 69, 70–2, 75, 99, 145

Ambiani, Belgic tribe, 93, 125

Ambigatus, Bituriges king, 208

Ambiorix, Eburones chief, 119, 121–3, 128–30, 133, 215

Ambrones, Celtic tribe, 56–7, 59–62

Ampsivarii, Germanic tribe, 171, 175, 217

Andes, Gallic Aremorican tribe, 135, 150

Aneroestes, Gaesatae king, 18, 21, 24

Angrivarii-Cherusci barrier, Battle of, 16 AD, 198–9, 221

Angrivarii, Germanic tribe, 173, 175, 193, 198–200, 220–1

Anreppen, Roman military camp at, 164, 170, 172–3, 175, 219

Aquae Sextiae (Aix), Roman veterans' settlement, 50
  Battle of, 102 BC, 60–3, 65

Arausio, Battle of, 105 BC, xvii, 55–7, 207

Arevaci, Celtiberii tribe, 35, 39–40, 135

Ariovistus, Suebi King, 76–7, 80–8, 99, 212, 215

Arminius, Cherusci noble, Germanic resistance leader, xvii, 167–9, 171–5, 177–82, 185, 189–97, 199, 202, 204–206, 221
  battles, Maroboduus, 204
  childhood, early years, 167–8, 216, 217
  Death of, 205
  Tacitus' tribute to, 205

Arpus, Chatti chief, 193

Arverni, Gallic tribe, 50–1, 79–80, 135–6, 139–40, 147, 150, 152, 208

Asprenas, Lucius Nonius, Roman army commander, 170, 182

Atrebates, Belgic tribe, 93, 95–6, 98

Atuatuca, Roman military camp, 119–20, 122, 130–2, 214

Augustus, First Emperor of Rome, 154–5, 158, 162–5, 168–9, 182–5, 188, 190, 201, 203, 209, 216, 220
  appearance, 155
  abandons Germania conquest, 183, 184
  justification for Germania conquest, 159
  personality, 155
  statesmanship, 156–7

Aulerci, Gallic Aremorican tribe, 135, 208

Avaricum, Bituriges stronghold, 137, 142
  Siege of, 52 BC, 138–9, 143

Bacenis forest, 129, 214

Baculus, Publius Sextius, chief centurion, 97, 131–2

Baetorix, Sugambri chief, 157, 202

Basilus, Lucius Minucius, Roman officer, 130

Bastarnae, Germanic-Celtic tribe, 157

Batavi, Germanic tribe, 193–4

Belgae, 59, 66, 87–99, 101, 104, 108–109, 113, 118, 120, 122–6, 133–6, 147, 211, 214
  Caesar's admiration of, 89
  guerrilla warfare, 130
  weapons and armor, 91

Belli, Celtiberii tribe, 32, 34, 39–41, 43, 210

Bellovaci, Belgic tribe, 90, 93, 125, 150

Bellovesus, Bituriges noble, 208

Bibracte, Battle of 58 BC, 73–5

Bituitus, Arverni king, 50

Bituriges, Gallic tribe, 136–7, 150, 208

Boduognatus, Nervii leader, 96

Boii, Celtic tribe, 8, 17–20, 22, 25–7, 47, 49, 53, 69, 73–6, 136–7, 165
Boiocalus, Ampsivarii noble, 171, 175, 217
Boiorix, Cimbri king, 55–6, 59, 62–5
Brennus, Senonian chief, 8, 11–12, 14, 208
Bructeri, Germanic tribe, 164, 175, 184, 188, 191, 201
Brutus, Decimus Junius, Roman commander, cousin of Caesar, 101–102, 136
Brutus, Sextus Junius, Roman general, 37–8

Cadurci, Gallic tribe, 135, 151
Caecina, Aulus Severus, Roman army commander, 186–7, 189, 191–2
Caedicius, Lucius, camp prefect, 170, 182
Caelius, Marcus, first-rank centurion, 174, 176–7, 181, 219
Caeonius, Lucius, camp prefect, 179–80, 218
Caepio, Q. Servilius, consul (106 BC), 55–6, 58, 203
Caepio, Q. Servilius, consul (140 BC), 36
Caesar, Gaius Julius, conqueror of Gaul, 68–95, 97–116, 118–20, 122–3, 125–57, 159, 161, 164, 171, 201, 203, 212–15
    Death of, 154
    early career, 68
    Gallic triumphal march, 153–4
    Games held by, 154
    martial accomplishments in Gallic war, 152
    Nicomedes, affair with, 153, 216
    physical description, 83, 89
    rewards given to soldiers, 154
    Soldiers' songs of, 153
Caligula, Gaius Caesar, son of Germanicus, 187
Camillus, Marcus Furius, Roman dictator, 1, 4, 13–5, 20, 58
Cantabrians, tribe of north Spain, 158
Carbo, Papirus, consul 53–4, 57, 203
Carnutes, Gallic tribe, 127–8, 133, 135–6, 150–1, 208
Carrahae, Battle of, 53 BC, 152
Carthage, xv, xvii, 19–20, 25, 28, 42, 46, 47
Cassivellaunus, Catuvellauni king, 114–16, 213
Cato, Marcus Porcius "the Younger", Roman statesman, 100, 104, 107
Cato, Porcius, consul, 39–40, 43
Catualda, Gotones noble, 205
Catulus, Quintus Lutatius, proconsul, 63–5
Catuvolcus, Eburones chief, 119, 130
Celt-Iberians, 26, 28–9, 39–40, 44, 59, 210
    horses, 31
    military renown, 41–2
    weapons and armor, 32
Celts:
    Atrocities carried out by, 12
    culture, 6–8, 108–109
    migrations, 6–8, 15–16, 208
    ships, 102

strongholds and fortifications, 6, 8, 68, 82, 98, 101, 103, 116, 118, 138
trade, 6–7, 51, 68, 101, 109, 116
weapons and tactics, 9–10, 23, 74, 112, 114–15, 124, 215
women in battle, 75, 142
Cenomani, Celtic tribe, 19–20, 26–7
Ceutrones, Celtic tribe, 26, 71, 122
Chariovalda, Batavi chief, 193–4
Charudes, Germanic tribe, 164
Chatti, Germanic tribe, 161–2, 175, 182, 189, 193, 200–202, 205
Chauci, Germanic tribe, 160, 164, 175, 200–201
Cherusci, Germanic tribe, 160–2, 164, 167–8, 171, 173–5, 178, 181, 189–99, 201–205, 214, 220–1
Cicero, Marcus Tullius, Roman philosopher, orator and statesmen, 81, 100, 104, 117, 122
Cicero, Quintus Tullius, Roman legate, 122–7, 130–1, 214
Cimberius, Suebi noble, 82–3
Cimbri, Germanic-Celtic tribe, 52–7, 59, 62–7, 77–8, 83, 89, 93, 147, 164, 183,
    depredations in Gaul, 54
    Disputed origin of, 52
    size of tribal coalition, 53, 207, 211
Cingetorix, Treveri chief, 118–19, 127, 129
Clastidium, Battle of, 222 BC, 25, 209
Clusium, Etruscan town, 8–9, 20
Commius, Atrebates king, 98, 109, 111–12, 116, 128, 134–5, 147–8, 150–2
Concolitanus, Gaesatae king, 18, 24
Correus, Bellovaci chief, 150
Cotta, Lucius Aurunculeius, Roman legate, 119–21, 123, 127, 130–1, 214
Crassus, Marcus Licinius, Roman general and politician, 68, 86, 99–100, 104, 152, 203
Crassus, Marcus Licinius, Roman questor, elder son of Crassus, M. L., 125, 128
Crassus, Publius, Roman commander, younger son of Crassus, M. L., 86, 99–101, 103–104, 106, 152
Curiosolites, Celtic Aremorican tribe, 101

Dacians, 157, 206
Diviciacus, Aedui chief and druid, 72, 76, 80–1, 90, 93
Divico, Tigurini-Helvetii chief, 54–5, 71–2
Dollberg, Celtic fortress on, 6–7, 25, 89, 118, 127, 152, 213
Drappes, Gallic rebel, 150–1
Drusus, Nero Claudius, son of Empress Livia, 158–65, 171, 184–5, 189, 193, 203
    Mysterious death of, 162–3
Drusus II, Julius Caesar, son of Emperor Tiberius, 186, 201, 204
Dumnorix, Aedui noble, 72

Eburones, Belgic tribe, 119–23, 125, 128, 130–3, 150, 214

Eggius, Lucius, Roman camp prefect, 179–81, 218

Eporedorix, Aedui leader, 140, 143, 147

Etruscans, 2–6, 8, 13, 15, 17–18, 207

Eudusii, Germanic tribe, 86

Fabius, Gaius, Roman general, 125–6, 128, 140–1, 150–1

Faesulae, Battle of, 225 BC, 20–1

Flavus, Cherusci noble, brother of Arminius, 167–8, 171, 194, 202, 217

Florus, Iulius, Treveri rebel, 216

Frisii, Germanic tribe, 160, 171, 178

Gaesatae, Celtic tribe, 18–19, 21–4

Galba, Servius, legate, 99, 109

Galba, Servius Sulpicius, governor of Hispania Ulterior, 29–31

Galba, Suessiones king, 90–3, 120, 125

Gallic, adjective for Gauls see also Celts and Gauls

Gaul:
    Population of, 79
    deprivations suffered in war with Caesar, 152
    rebellions after Caesar's conquest, 157, 215

Gauls, Roman name for Celts from Gaul, 7
    see also Celts

Gergovia, Arverni stronghold, 135, 139
    Battle of, 52 BC, 140–3

Germanicus, Julius Caesar, son of Drusus, 165, 184–204, 206, 220
    accomplishments in the east, 206
    Death of, 206
    Popularity of, 206
    suppresses legion mutiny, 186–7
    triumphal march, 201–202

Germans:
    battle tactics, 84–6, 106, 197, 204
    culture, 78–9, 144
    First appearance of, 25, 222
    human sacrifice and torture, 57, 181
    military renown, 82–3, 132, 203
    population of Germania, 79, 211
    religious customs, 57, 78, 85, 161, 181–2
    Roman conquest, prospect of, 202–203
    settlements, 160–1, 171, 178–9
    trade, 160, 164, 169
    weapons and armor, 53, 64, 79, 172, 177
    women,
        in battle, 61, 65, 86
        roles in society, 57, 85, 160, 175, 178

Gorgobina, Boii stronghold, 136–7

Gotones, Germanic tribe, 205

Gracchus, Tiberius Sempronius, 29, 39–40, 210

Hamilcar, Carthaginian general, 26, 47

Hannibal Barca, Carthaginian general, xvii, 25–6, 47, 183

Harudes, Germanic tribe, 81–2, 86

Helvetii, Celtic tribe, 67–77, 80, 83, 88, 136, 211–12

Helvii, Gallic tribe, 145

Hermunduri, Suebi tribe, 205

Idistaviso plain, Battle of, 16 AD, 196–7, 220

Indutiomarus, Treveri chief, 118–19, 125–9, 133

Inguiomerus, Cherusci noble, 171, 175, 191–2, 195, 197, 199, 202, 204

Insubres, Celtic tribe, 8, 18–19, 22, 25–7, 209

Italicus, the son of Flavus, 202

Jugurtha, Numidian king, 43, 58

Labienus, Titus, legate, 71–3, 89–90, 93, 95, 97, 101, 113, 122, 125–30, 134, 139, 141, 143, 145, 149, 151, 212

Laenas Popillius, Roman general, 36–7

Langobardi, Suebi tribe, 164, 204

Latium, 1–2, 4, 6, 13

Latobrigi, Celtic tribe, 69, 73, 75

Lemovices, Gallic tribe, 135, 149

Lexovii, Gallic Aremorican tribe, 101

Ligurians, Neolithic tribe, 26, 47–50, 56, 61, 69

Lingones, Gallic tribe, 75, 133, 145, 150

Litaviccus, Aedui leader, 140–1, 143

Liva, Drusilla, Roman Empress, wife of Augustus, 158

Lollius, Marcus, Roman general, 157

Long Bridges, Battle of, 15 AD, 192

Longinus, L. Cassius, consul, 54–5, 57, 203

Lucterius the Cadrucan, 136, 150–1

Lucullus Licinius, Roman general, 29, 41

Lusitani, Celt-Iberian tribe, 28–41

Magetobria, Battle of 61 BC, 80

Mancinus, Hostilius, Roman general, 41

Mandubracius, Trinobantes noble, 115–16

Marcellus, M. Claudius, Roman general 102 BC, 61–2

Marcellus, Metellus Claudius, Roman general 152 BC, 40–1

Marcellus, M. Claudius, Roman general 222 BC, 25, 209

Marcomanni, Suebi tribe, 86, 162, 164–5, 204–206

Marius, Gaius, Roman soldier, consul, 42, 45–6, 57–65, 67–8, 83, 203

Maroboduus, Marcomanni king, 162, 165, 181–2, 204–205

Marsi, Germanic tribe, 175, 181, 188–9, 200–201

Marsi, Italian mountain tribe, 20, 209

Maximus, Gnaeus Mallius, consul, 55–6, 203

Maximus, Q. Fabius, consul, 50

Melo, Sugambri chief, 157, 202

Menapii, Belgic coastal tribe, 101, 104–105, 107, 120, 128, 130, 214

Metellus, Q. Caecilius, consul, 41

Meuse River (the Mosa), Battle of, 55 BC, 106–107
Minucius, Quintus, consul, 48–9
Moguntiacum (Mainz), Roman military camp, 159, 162–3, 170
Morbihan Bay, Battle of, 56 BC, 102
Morini, Belgic coastal tribe, 101, 104, 109, 112, 125–6, 157

Narbo, Roman veterans' colony, 51, 136
Nasua, Suebi chief, 82–3
Nemetes, Germanic tribe, 86
Nervii, Belgic tribe, 90, 93–8, 122–3, 125–8, 133, 214
Nitiobroges, Gallic Aquitani tribe, 139
Nobilior, Fulvius, consul, 40–1
Numantia, Celtiberii stronghold, 29, 34, 38–41, 43–6, 57, 210
    size and defenses, 43
Numidians, 20, 48–9, 89, 92
Numonius, Vala, Roman legate, 179–80, 218

Oberaden, Roman camp at, 161, 163, 170, 219
Octavian, Gaius, see Augustus
Oppidum Ubiorum, Ubii capital, 157, 164, 171, 182, 187
Orgetorix, Helvetii chief, 68–9

Pannonia, 158–9, 165–7, 172, 185
Papus, Lucius Aemilius, consul, 21–5
Parisii, Gallic tribe, 135, 139, 143
Pictones, Gallic Aremorican tribe, 135, 150
Piso, Aquitani nobleman, 106
Plautius, Gaius, Roman general, 33
Pompey, Gnaeus Pompeius Magnus, Roman general and politician, 68, 99–100, 104, 128, 152–3
Pullo, Titus, Roman centurion, 124, 214

Rauraci, Celtic tribe, 69, 73
Rebilus Gaius Caninius, Roman general, 150–1
Regulus, Gaius Atilius, consul, 22–3
Remi, Belgic tribe, 90–2, 125, 127, 133, 145, 150
Retogenes, Numantian warrior, 45
Rhaeti, Illyrian Alpine tribe, 158, 162, 197
Roman army:
    Atrocities carried out by, 4, 29–30, 38, 45, 106–107, 130, 132–3, 139, 150, 152, 188–9
    Augustus' reorganization of, 156, 216
    auxiliaries, 89–90, 92, 94, 96, 188, 196–7, 199–200
    Gallic cavalry, 72, 83, 89, 96, 106, 129, 131–2, 137, 139, 141, 143, 145–6, 153
    German cavalry, 137, 143–6, 148, 151, 153, 193–4, 215
    Numidian cavalry, 48–9
    Spanish cavalry, 119, 143, 145–6

fortifications and siege works, 44, 91, 98, 114, 123, 138, 140, 146, 210
individual legions:
    Eighteenth Legion, 170–1, 174, 183
    Eighth Legion, 96–7, 142
    Eleventh Legion, 96–7, 122, 126, 214
    Fifteenth Legion, 128
    Fifth "Alauda" Legion, 104, 157, 170, 186–7
    First Legion, 170, 186–7, 192
    Fourteenth Legion, 89, 91, 94, 97, 119–20, 122, 125, 128–30, 133
    Nineteenth Legion, 163, 170–1, 183, 191
    Ninth Legion, 95–7
    Seventeenth Legion, 170–1, 183
    Seventh Legion, 96–7, 109, 112, 114
    Sixth Legion, 128
    Tenth Legion, 70–1, 83, 95–7, 109–10, 142
    Thirteenth Legion, 89, 91, 94, 97, 127
    Twelfth Legion, 96–7, 99
    Twentieth Legion, 186–7, 189
    Twenty-first Legion, 183, 186–7
    Twenty-second Legion, 183
legions:
    equipment, 60, 94, 177–8, 220
    hoplite legion, 10
    manipular legion, 15, 21, 58, 209
    Marian reforms, 58–9, 211
    marriage, 171, 217
    mutiny, 185–7
    structure and size, 10, 73, 220–1
    weapons and armor, 10, 24, 32, 58, 73, 96
Praetorian Guard, 156, 185–6, 196, 198–9, 206
    ships and navy, 102, 109–11, 113, 193, 200, 213
    siege engines and artillery, 44–5, 91, 110, 139, 148, 199
Rome, city, 3, 12, 15
    description, 67, 155–6
    foundation, 3
    population of city, 67, 155
    population of empire, 155, 216
    religion, 2, 4, 13, 163
    sack of, 12–14
Ruteni, Gallic tribe, 136

Sabinus, Quintus Titurius, Roman legate, 91–2, 101, 103, 119–21, 123, 127, 130–1, 213–14
Sabis, Battle of, 57 BC, 94–8, 213
Sacrovir, Iulius, Aedui noble, 215
Samarobriva (Amiens), Ambiani town, 125–6
Samnites, Italian mountain tribe, 15–16, 19–20, 48, 203
Santones, Gallic tribe, 69–70
Scarus, Marcus Aurelius, legate, 55, 203
Scordisci, Celtic tribe, 16, 53
Sedullus, Lemovices king, 149
Segestes, Cherusci noble, 171, 173–4, 182, 189–90, 202

Segimer, Cherusci chief, father of Arminius and Flavus, 167, 171–2, 202
Segimundus, Cherusci noble, son of Segestes, 171, 182, 189–90, 202
Segovesus, Bituriges noble, 208
Semnones, Suebi tribe, 79, 204
Senones, Gallic tribe of north Italy and of central Gaul, 7, 16–18, 127–8, 133, 135–6, 139, 143, 208
Sequani, Gallic tribe, 69–71, 79–82, 84, 88
Servilianus, Fabius Maximus, consul, 34–6
Silanus, M. Iunius, consul, 54, 57
Silius Caius, Roman army commander, 186, 193, 200
Sotiates, Aquitani tribe, 103
Stertinius, Lucius, Roman commander, 191, 193–4, 197, 199
Suebi, Germanic tribal confederation, 77–82, 86–8, 93, 99, 105, 107, 113, 129, 144, 157, 162, 164–5, 204–205, 214–15
Suessiones, Belgic tribe, 90, 93
Sugambri, Germanic-Celtic tribe, 107, 131–3, 157, 160–3, 170, 175, 202, 213

Tarquinius, Priscus, Etruscan king of Rome, 208
Tarusates, Aquitani tribe, 103
Taurisci, Celtic tribe, 19, 22, 209
Telamon, Battle of, 225 BC, 22–5
    army sizes, 19–20, 209
Tencteri, Germanic tribe, 105–108, 129
Teutobod, Teutones king, 59–60, 62, 212
Teutoburg Forest, 170, 173, 191, 217
    Battle in, 9 AD, xvii, 176–81, 202, 203, 206, 217–19
        army sizes, 171, 175, 217
        Consequences of, 183, 203–204
        Location of, 179, 191, 217–18
Teutomatus, King of the Nitiobroges, 139, 142
Teutones, Germanic-Celtic tribe, 52–7, 59–63, 66–7, 77–8, 83, 89, 93, 147, 183, 210–11
    Disputed origin of, 52
    size of tribal coalition, 53, 207, 211
Thumelicus, son of Arminius, 202
Thusnelda, Cherusci noble, daughter of Segestes, 173–4, 190, 202
Tiberius, Claudius Nero, Roman Emperor, son of Empress Livia, 158–9, 163–8, 171, 183–6, 194, 197, 199, 201, 203–204, 206
Tigurini, Celtic tribe, 54–5, 59, 65, 71, 211–12
Titii, Celtiberii tribe, 32, 34, 39–41, 43, 210
Trebonius, Gaius, Roman general, 115, 125–6, 130
Trebonius, Gaius, Roman knight, 132
Treveri, Celtic tribe, 25, 82, 89–90, 96, 101, 113, 118–19, 125–9, 133, 145, 151–2, 187, 213, 215
Triboces, Germanic tribe, 86

Trinobantes, Briton tribe, 115
Tubantes, Germanic tribe, 188
Tubero Lucius Seius, Roman cavalry commander, 198
Tulingi, Celtic tribe, 69, 73–5
Turoni, Gallic tribe, 135

Ubii, Germanic tribe, 105, 107, 129, 157, 170–1, 187, 189
Unimanus, Claudius, Roman commander, 33
Usipetes, Germanic tribe, 105–108, 129, 160, 188, 201
Uxellodunum, Cadurci town, 151

Vaccaei, Celt-Iberian tribe, 29, 41, 43, 45
Vangiones, Germanic tribe, 86
Varus, Publius Quinctilius, Roman governor, 166, 168–84, 189, 192, 195, 201, 203, 217–19
    Career and personality of, 168–9
    death, 180
Veii, Etruscan City, 1, 4, 11, 13–14, 208
Venelli, Celtic Aremorican tribe, 101, 103, 120
Veneti, Celtic Aremorican tribe, 100–103, 109
Veneti, Pre-Celtic people of north-eastern Italy, 14–15, 19–20
Verbigene, canton of Helvetii, 75
Vercassivellaunus the Arvernian, 147, 149
Vercellae, Battle of, 101 BC, 63–5
Vercingetorix, King of the Gauls, 134–43, 145–51, 153–4, 215
    death, 154
    Surrender of, 149–50
Vesontio (Besançon), Sequani town, 82–3, 88–9
Vetera (Xanten), Roman military camp, 159, 168, 170, 173–4, 186–7, 191
Vetilius, Gaius, legate, 30–2
Vettones, Celt-Iberian tribe, 36
Virdomarus, Insubres chieftain, 25
Viriathus, Lusitani chief, 28–38, 41–2, 46
    death, 37
    personality, 33
Viridomarus, Aedui leader, 140, 143, 147
Viridovix, Venelli chief, 103
Viromandui, Belgic tribe, 93, 95–6
Vocates, Aquitani tribe, 103
Voccio, King of the Celtic Noricum, 80
Volcae Arecomici, Gallic tribe, 145
Volcae Tectosages, Gallic tribe, 54
Volusenus, Gaius, Roman officer, 109–10, 134, 151
Vorenus, Lucius, Roman centurion, 124, 214
Vosges, Battle of, 58 BC (Ariovistus vs. Caesar), 84–7
    army size and casualties, 85, 212

Waldgermis, Roman town at, 164, 182